Sue Lees is ~~Pro~~ ... versity of
North London ... air of the
Women's Studies Network (UK), and is an international consultant
for the journal *Gender and Education* and the book series *Gender and*

ONE WEE~~K~~ ...

... including

... ~~Radio~~ (1997);

... won a ... ~~A~~ward
... in 1994: ... With

Also by Sue Lees:

Policing Sexual Assault (1999)
Ruling Passions (1997)
Sugar and Spice (1993)
Losing Out (1986)

SUE LEES

CARNAL KNOWLEDGE
Rape on Trial

First published in the UK by Hamish Hamilton, 1996

A paperback edition of this book was published by
Penguin Books, 1997

This revised edition published in Great Britain by
The Women's Press Ltd, 2002
A member of the Namara Group
34 Great Sutton Street, London EClV 0LQ
www.the-womens-press.com

British Library Cataloguing-in-Publication Data
A catalogue record for this book is available from the
British Library.

ISBN 0 7043 4753 9

Typeset by FiSH Books, London WC1
Printed and bound in Great Britain by Cox & Wyman,
Reading, Berkshire

This book is dedicated to the many strong women who have shared the most painful experiences of their lives, some for the first time. Their voices of courage and endurance call out for the reform of the judicial system.

Contents

Acknowledgements

This has been a hard book to write and I have many to thank for their contributions. Most of all I would like to thank Lynn Ferguson, a freelance television producer, whose vibrancy, questioning of hallowed principles, and friendship have made this book possible. Lynn first contacted me in 1989 in response to my published research on rape, which formed the basis of the Channel 4 *Dispatches* documentary 'Getting Away with Rape'. Again in 2000 we went on to make a follow up documentary 'Still Getting Away with Rape'. I am grateful to David Lloyd, commissioning editor of *Dispatches* in 1993 for sponsoring a year's research for the first programme and to Dorothy Byrne, commissioning editor of *Dispatches* in 2000 for sponsoring the second programme.

Thanks too to Jeanne Gregory, Jill Radford, the University of North London Woman and Child Abuse Studies Unit, Sandra McNeill of the Campaign to End Rape and to Tony Edwards for comments on the legal chapters. Thanks to Dot Moss for her help with final editing. I would also like to thank Joanna Lovett for her invaluable help in collating background information on the judiciary. John Lea for his helpful criticism and John, Dan and Josie, without whose love and support during the past year when I have been undergoing treatment for cancer, this book would not have been completed.

New introduction

With the exception of murder, rape is considered to be the most serious crime prosecuted by the criminal justice system in the UK and the reporting of such crimes is becoming more prevalent. There has been a steady rise in the number of reported sexual offences since 1995 (see Home Office Criminal Statistics 1995–2001). Yet criminal justice systems all over the world actively perpetuate a world in which rape goes unpunished. In the UK, where the conviction rate for reported rapes in 1999 was a meagre 8 per cent (Harris and Grace 1999), and where most rapes go unreported, the true rate of conviction is clearly appallingly low.

The extremely low prosecution and conviction rate causes great distress to women. Those who give evidence in court describe rape trials as being as traumatic as the rape itself and say it is they who feel they are on trial. Women continue to be cross-examined by defence barristers about their past sexual history and details of their lifestyle. This extends to the clothing worn at court. One English barrister spoke of a case in which 'the girl was basically just cross-examined because she had a miniskirt with a zip in it' (Temkin 2000b). This is almost as ridiculous as the Italian Court of Appeal who in 1999 overturned the conviction of a 45-year-old driving instructor found guilty of raping an 18-year-old pupil on the grounds that she could not be raped because she was wearing jeans (see Lees 1999a). Some of the questions posed are subtle. For example, in one English trial the complainant was asked about red shoes she was wearing at the time of the alleged rape. The defence asked: 'You would admit these shoes are not leather. They are at the cheaper end of the market.' If her shoes were cheap, the implication was that she must be cheap too. Defence barristers should not misportray the complainant's character in this way.

Between 1985 and 1997 in England and Wales there was an almost threefold increase in the number of rapes of females reported to the police, but much less increase in the number of men convicted. (In 1985 450 men were convicted of rape of females out of 1,842 reported rapes compared with 599 out of 6,281 in 1997.)

Since the first edition of *Carnal Knowledge* was published in 1996 rape has rarely been out of the news and has received unprecedented attention and for the first time there seems to be some commitment on behalf of the government to improving the way the criminal justice system treats women who are raped. Yet little concrete improvement has resulted. On the contrary, the proportion of reported rapes resulting in conviction has continued to slide. Between 1996 and 2000 it fell from 10 per cent to a mere 7 per cent (see Appendix 1).

In Scotland, the way the law deals with rape hit an all-time low in March 2001 when Lord Abernethy, a senior judge in the Scottish High Court, ruled that a woman could not be raped unless the accused used force or threat of force. He said 'to have sexual intercourse with a woman without her consent in itself is not rape. There seems to be a common perception that lack of consent is enough for a charge of rape.' Lord Abernethy cleared Edward Watt, 23, a law student at Aberdeen University, of a charge of raping a 21-year-old fellow student who had alleged she had withheld consent. The woman, a virgin before the attack, claimed Watt had locked the door before raping her twice despite her saying 'no, stop. I don't want this' (Tweedie 2001). Lord Abernethy's interpretation of the law was debated on 26 April 2001 in the Scottish Parliament, with a motion brought by Ms Johann Lamont MSP. Describing herself as 'speechless' when she first heard the case, she said: 'When I first heard this, I felt as if we were stepping back generations in our attitudes to rape and what is even more amazing were the people in the legal professions who said Lord Abernethy was right...We need to look at how judges can have such powers in our legal system.' The Lord Advocate agreed to refer the controversial ruling to the Scottish High Court to decide whether or not sex without a woman's consent is or is not rape!

The main focus of this new introduction is to summarize legal developments since 1996 (specifically in the curtailing of sexual history evidence and the extension of similar fact evidence). I shall also outline an important small reform involving the abolition of the right for defendants to defend themselves and cross-examine the complainant. Before this, I shall consider what changes have occurred in the nature of rape cases (such as the elevation of rape as a war crime and the new phenomenon of drug-assisted rape), and provide some background to the stimulus for change in the government concern about rape. I shall draw on more recent research undertaken for the Channel 4 documentary *Still Getting Away with Rape*, shown in April 2000.

The main body of this book has not been largely altered as it was based on research undertaken in the early 1990s that is still as accurate today. It shows how the British criminal justice system is systematically allowing rapists to go free, and how more and more rapists are getting away with it. It documents the way women are encouraged to report rape, and are often intimidated by their assailants, only to be stereotyped as sexually provocative and blamed by the judiciary and press. First it examines some of the prevalent myths about rape, and looks at how rape is defined. It shows how most cases are channelled out of the legal system to reduce the numbers actually going to trial through such practices as 'no-criming' reports, downgrading the rape charges to a lesser offence of indecent assault, or actual bodily harm (ABH), by what is called 'plea-bargaining'. The complainant is, however, rarely involved in such bargaining, which is carried out by the prosecution counsel, whom she is not even allowed to meet, and some convictions are reversed or sentences reduced by the appeal court.

The last chapter, however, has been updated and expanded to include an analysis of the failure of the Labour government to reform the judiciary. This major shortcoming, as we shall also see in this introduction, means that even when reforms such as the restriction of sexual history evidence are introduced into legislation in Parliament, it does not necessarily mean that they will be effectively implemented in practice. Additionally, I put forward proposals to reform the rules of evidence.

Recent Changes in the Nature of Rape Cases

From Stranger to Acquaintance

A great deal of confusion surrounds the question of rape. Most feminists emphasize the gravity of rape describing it as a serious and often life-shattering experience. This should not be taken to imply that all rapes are equally traumatic to the victim. Nor should it be taken to imply that rapes can be easily categorized into those types that are more or less serious depending on the relationship between the defendant and the complainant.

One explanation for the drop in the conviction rate seems to lie in the fact that a steadily increasing proportion of reported rapes do not conform to the stereotypical rape scenario of the psychopathological stranger rapist, seizing women in dark streets. A far higher proportion of the women reporting nowadays are, by contrast, raped by men they know, often in their own homes, and these are precisely the cases where it is most difficult to secure a conviction. This is reflected in the Home Office studies which showed that reported stranger rapes decreased from 39 per cent of the total reported in 1985 (Lloyd and Walmsley 1989) to 12 per cent in 1996 (Harris and Grace 1999). Such acquaintance rapes have increasingly been termed 'date rape' by the media. Such a term carries the implication that such rapes are not as serious as 'stranger rapes', but there is no evidence to support this. There is, however, evidence that acquaintance rapes can be just as traumatic as stranger rape for the victim. Some women we interviewed argued that being raped by someone you know is even more traumatic as it involves a breach of trust (see Chapter 1).

Another misconception is that so-called 'date rapes' are often conceptualized as occurring as a result of men misreading the woman's signals or not realizing that she was not consenting, or that women have sex consensually and then regret it the night after and cry rape. We know that some men claim to misread signals even when the woman has said 'no', or in clearly premeditated cases where the rapist has locked the door. Some rapists have a distorted belief system – and even following conviction are in denial, continuing to maintain that the woman wanted it, just in the way that some paedophiles believe children wanted it.

As well as a higher proportion of reported acquaintance rapes in the past ten years, there has been a marked increase in the proportion of what the Home Office term 'intimate' rapes, between those such as relatives, friends and work colleagues. These increased from 30 per cent to 50 per cent between 1985 and 1996 (Harris and Grace 1999). This category includes rape in marriage which only became a criminal offence in 1991 and only in 1997 did the House of Lords in R. v. R. uphold the Court of Appeal's decision that rape can be committed in marriage (see R. v. R. (1997) 4 All ER 481 HI). Such cases tend to be seen as less serious than stranger rapes and are less likely to be prosecuted. Professor Jennifer Temkin (1997a), for example, found that the Crown Prosecution Service (CPS) are more inclined to drop cases where there is a marital relationship. She describes a case where the defendant had admitted the assault to the police, but the CPS decided not to bring a prosecution, arguing that there was 'very little likelihood' of the man reoffending and that charges would not be in the public interest. There is also evidence that overall sentencing levels are lower in cases where the victim and the offender were known to each other before the rape, and in some cases, at least, the courts appear to have explicitly treated such a relationship as a mitigating factor (Sentencing Advisory Panel, 2001b). However, some rapes by ex-partners or ex-boyfriends, contrary to common belief, are among the most physically violent and dangerous.

Treating rapes by strangers as more serious is based on the myth that these rapists are a significantly more dangerous group. However, there is no evidence that rapists can be divided into distinct groups on the basis of whether or not they rape strangers, acquaintances or wives. Homicidal rapists sometimes rape and kill both their wives and those they know less intimately. Frederick West was charged in 1994 with killing 13 women, many of whom were tortured and raped including his own wife and daughter. John Duffy, a homicidal rapist, was convicted in 1988 of killing two women and raping three others. Richard Baker, a serial rapist, who worked as a nightclub DJ, raped three women whom he dated and leapt on from behind in the classic 'stranger rape' scenario (*Guardian*, 21 May 1999). We do not know how many stranger or acquaintance rapists have previously raped their wives but it certainly seems likely that many have. In 1993 it was reported that a man convicted of raping two women in Scotland had viciously raped his wife some time before (*Sun*, 28 April 1993). It is a myth that different types of men rape girlfriends or wives than rape strangers.

Feminists have long argued that women are most at risk from men they know and that rape is culturally dictated rather than deviant behaviour. Studies of convicted rapists have indicated that such men are not pathological (see Scully 1990). In a recent discussion of the motivational basis of rape, Katherine Baker quotes evidence that macrosociological research strongly suggests that the prevalence of rape is positively correlated with a variety of social phenomena, including the acceptance of gender inequality, the prevalence of pornography, and the degree of social disorganization in a community. She argues that youths are bombarded by a culture which sexualizes commodities and commodifies women's sexuality. Baker (1997: 603) argues that what motivates male rapists may not be substantively different from that which motivates men who go to prostitutes or peep shows. None of these acts requires mutual enjoyment or emotional intimacy. Both are more about power and dominance than sexual intimacy.

This view of rape as normal rather than pathological is supported by studies of rape in war. An important motivation for rape, documented for the first time by Susan Brownmiller in her 1978 book *Against Our Will*, is that rape has been used in all known wars as a weapon to destroy the enemy's morale through power and dominance over their women. She noted the connection between rape and killing reflected in the slogan 'double veterans' – soldiers who raped and killed women in the Vietnam war.

Brownmiller's study indicated that gang rape is a normal aspect of war and the men involved are not psychopaths, but 'ordinary Joes' made unordinary by entry into the most exclusive male-only club in the world. She argued that victory in arms brings group power undreamed of in civilian life. It is for this reason that depicting rape as a war crime is vital.

Rape Elevated to the Status of a War Crime

A significant advance was made in 1998 when rape was declared a war crime by the Geneva Convention following reports of forcible impregnation of thousands of women, mostly Muslims, by Serbian soldiers, as a form of ethnic cleansing in the war in former Yugoslavia. A European Commission report has estimated that 20,000 women were victims of 'organized' rape in Bosnia, while Muslim and Croat sources claimed the numbers were far greater. In January 1993, the Commission investigated the rapes. Hundreds of women were held like animals, receiving daily humiliation and deliberate impregnation, and facing death if they resisted. The International Criminal Tribunal for the former Yugoslavia made a landmark decision. In

November 1998, on the 50th anniversary of the United Nations Declaration of Human Rights, rape was elevated to the status of a war crime alongside other kinds of torture and violence waged against civilian populations. The recognition of rape as a 'war crime', and not simply a sexual crime, is a major step forward and will hopefully act as a deterrent to a violent practice that has long gone unrecognized and unpunished by the international community.

Marital Rape and Murder Linked

It is not always recognized that rape is a common form of domestic violence and is linked with other forms of physical and psychological violence. Stark and Flitcraft (1996: 130) in their review of research on violence against women confirmed Lachman's 1978 conclusion that 'almost a third of all homicides take place within the immediate family, another 21 per cent in romantic triangles or lover's quarrels and 27 per cent among less intimate relatives and friends.' A similar picture emerges from the criminal statistics for England and Wales for 1999. Out of 213 adult women homicides, 119 were killed by their current or former cohabitant spouse or lover. In Scotland too, Soothill *et al.* (1999) found that females were at considerably more risk than males in a partnership while males were at greater risk in other situations. In sum, at least half of all homicides of women are directly or indirectly domestic.

In spite of this finding, judges appear to fail to take into account the connection between marital rape and murder. In one trial I witnessed a husband was charged with raping his estranged wife where she had been rendered unconscious due to being strangled by him. Yet the husband was not charged with attempted murder, although she could easily have died.

Marital rape and murder are linked in a number of ways. Both tend to occur when a relationship is breaking up or shortly after the couple have separated. Ending a relationship with a violent man places a woman at particular risk for her life. Marital rape can be the final straw that leads a woman to leave a violent relationship or it can be an act of revenge on the woman for leaving. Both marital rape and murder are forms of extreme coercion fuelled by revenge at the woman daring to leave or planning to leave preceded by extreme possessiveness. Wilson *et al.* (1993) computed uxoricide (murder of wife) rates for co-residing and estranged wives and found an increased risk immediately after separation. They found that a remarkable proportion of uxoricide victims are estranged from their killers. They draw on a number of Australian historical studies: Allen (1990), for example, reported that almost half of all wives who were killed in New South Wales in the late nineteenth century were separated from their husband-killers at the time of the murder and the proportion was even higher in the 1930s. As well as judges, some barristers, as Temkin (1997a) showed, continue to regard marital rape as less serious. One barrister she interviewed said: 'I feel very strongly that it's a great waste of public money to prosecute the ex-husband rape or the ex-boyfriend rape.' Yet such rapes are among the rapes where women's lives are most at risk, and giving evidence against a present or past partner is also likely to place the woman's life at risk.

This view of sexual violence as taking place predominantly in the home is at odds with the key messages of the Labour government which, as Kelly and Humphreys (2000:20–1) argue, include the following: that violence is widespread, but danger is located away from the home; the two-parent heterosexual family is to be defended as a safe and protected institution; it is the erosion of the nuclear family which is at the heart of the breakdown of community; and that men are increasingly alienated, their masculinity undermined by the changing position of women.

Drug-assisted Rape

A frightening development in the past five years is the appearance of cases where women have been raped when drugged. In such cases the victim does not remember what happened immediately afterwards and, if she does, the drug is only identifiable in the blood for a comparatively short period. The police have had little experience with treating such cases and there is evidence that they often lack the expertise to deal with them. In August 1999, for example, Judge Pearson threw out Britain's first case involving the 'date' rape drug Rohypnol, after describing the investigation as 'grossly incompetent'. The officers had failed to interview staff at the nightclub where the drug was allegedly administered and failed to secure vital video taped footage from the club's security cameras.

This is an area that needs far more attention. In June 2000 Peter Sturman, a Metropolitan police officer, conducted the first Home

Office study into drug rape and set up a Drug Rape Trust. His report *Drug Assisted Sexual Assault* (Sturman 2000) is based on his investigation of this frightening phenomenon. He surveyed 123 victims of drug-assisted rape, finding that 70 per cent of victims knew their attacker, with 27 per cent citing them as a friend, 15 per cent as a fellow student and 15 per cent as a work colleague. Nearly half were drugged in pubs or clubs, but 12 per cent were given rape drugs in their own home and 10 per cent on university campus. The main drugs used – sedatives, which can induce amnesia – were administered via alcohol in over half the cases and slipped into a cup of tea, coffee or hot chocolate in 11 per cent of cases.

One in five could not remember the attack, and around 70 per cent felt physically unable to resist due to the effects of the drugs. Many of the rapists took photographs or videos of their victims during the attack to use for pornographic purposes, to display on the internet, or as a trophy. Many of the rapists acted in pairs. Sturman made numerous recommendations including the setting up of 24-hour rape treatment centres at hospitals (Hall 2000).

According to a press report in August 2001 the Sexual Offences Section of Scotland Yard's Special Investigations Unit recorded 108 possible drug rape offences in London since November 2000, when it first began monitoring cases. Against this background Westminster Council has launched a publicity campaign warning drinkers in West End bars and clubs of the risks attached to accepting drinks from strangers (*Evening Standard*, 10 August 2001: 5).

Very few cases of this sort have led to criminal convictions. Kevin Cobb, a nurse who raped women after drugging them with a powerful sedative used in minor surgery, was found guilty of killing a nursing sister after spiking her drink and of raping two women patients after drugging them. Richard Baker, the DJ who received four life sentences for a string of attacks in 1999, was found to have his pockets stuffed with packets of Rohypnol, one of the drugs associated with drug-assisted rape.

The training of detective inspectors needs to be reviewed in the light of developments in technology and evidence analysis and requires consistency. The present system of 'learning on the job' is outmoded and is far too dependent on the supervision of an individual inspector. As Sturman (2000) suggests in his report, dedicated investigators should be appointed to specialize in this crime.

Background to Government's Concern over Rape Trials

The first publication of *Carnal Knowledge* was influential in bringing about the government's move to restrict sexual history evidence resulting in Section 41 of the Youth Justice and Criminal Evidence Act 2000. The book was widely reviewed in the quality press (*Guardian*, *The Times*, *Counsel of the Bar* and the *Times Literary Supplement*), television and radio. This led to questions being asked in the House of Commons about the falling conviction rate (see Hansard, 12 June 1996: 355–68) and resulted in the setting up of a Home Office investigation by Jessica Harris and Sharon Grace, published in 1999, which confirmed that the attrition rate in rape cases was far too high (Harris and Grace 1999). It was this latter piece of research which was influential in the setting up of the House of Commons Standing Committees and the ensuing legislation.

In June 1996 I had a meeting at the House of Lords with Lord Ashley who had drafted the original Sexual Offences (Amendment) Act 1976 (see Appendix 3). He was very perturbed to hear that it had not been effective. The Act aimed to limit the cross-examination of the complainant about her past sexual history and sexual character, but it was left up to judges' discretion to deem whether or not such evidence was relevant. Judges, however, as my monitoring of trials showed, had often used their discretion to allow such questions to be asked, so the Act had had little effect. Judges frequently regarded such evidence as relevant even when it was unconnected to the offence.

Court of Appeal judgements had also not supported the spirit of the Sexual Offences (Amendment) Act 1976. For example, in the Court of Appeal judgement in Viola in 1982, it was ruled that the complainant's promiscuity was relevant to consent (R. v. Viola (1982) 75 Cr. App. R (125)) and the defendant was acquitted. In another judgement in 1992 (Brown) it was ruled that the judge had to decide in each case whether 'the complainant's attitude to sexual relations could be material upon which in these days a jury could reasonably rely to conclude that the complainant may indeed have consented to the sexual intercourse on the material occasion'. In other words, if the woman had, in the opinion of the judge 'a certain attitude' it was deemed right to cross-examine her about her sexual relationships (House of Commons Standing Committee E 2000).

In 1996 I had several meetings with the Labour Party Policy Officer for Home Affairs and informed him of developments in Australia. This led to the Shadow Home Secretary, Jack Straw, and Tessa Jowell, Shadow Minister for Women, presenting three amendments to the Criminal Procedure and Investigation Bill in 1996. I advised on the drafting of these amendments (one which related to the law on 'similar fact' evidence – (see below) and had lengthy conversations with Tessa Jowell who presented the amendments to Parliament. The amendments called for changes based on the 'tried and tested formula' of the Crimes (Sexual Assault) Amendment Act and Cognate Act of 1981 in New South Wales which had led to a far fairer system in this Australian state. This strictly limits the discretion of judges in allowing sexual history evidence, introduces trial judges' warnings to ignore delays in reporting sexual offences and strengthens the 'similar fact' law (as well as the broadening of the law on 'similar fact' evidence) whereby defendants could be tried for more than one offence at the same time (if they had been accused by different women and there was a sufficient similarity in the attacks). In New South Wales these changes resulted in a higher level of convictions and more defendants pleading guilty.

The suggested amendments to the law in England and Wales failed, but formed the basis of reforms introduced when Labour came to power in 1997. Following the election of a Labour government in May 1997, the Home Secretary, Jack Straw, set up a consultative body to draw up recommendations for law reform. This led to *Speaking Up for Justice* (Home Office 1998), a report of the Interdepartmental Working Group on the treatment of Vulnerable and Intimidated Witnesses in the Criminal Justice System which was published in June 1998.

Transcripts of trials collected for the Channel 4 *Dispatches* programme *Getting Away with Rape* (1994) provided crucial evidence that judges were routinely allowing sexual history evidence to be introduced. The standing committee set up to examine amendments to the Youth Justice and Criminal Evidence Bill 1999, was directed to this evidence published in *Carnal Knowledge* by the Home Secretary and Paul Boateng, the Home Office Minister, in the committee readings of the Act.

The new legislation enshrined in the Youth Justice and Criminal

Evidence Act (see Appendix 3) requires judges to state explicitly their reasons for allowing such sexual history evidence. In cases where consent is the issue, evidence of previous sexual behaviour is only allowed if the evidence or questions rebut evidence led by the prosecution, or the behaviour to which they relate is either alleged to have taken place at or about the same time as the alleged offence; or is so similar to the complainant's alleged behaviour at that time that it cannot reasonably be explained as a coincidence. Paul Boateng, Minister of State at the Home Office said:

In Sue Lees' *Carnal Knowledge* in 1996 she reported that, in trials that she had seen, defence barristers made sweeping statements about complainants apparently on no grounds at all. They suggested that one complainant was 'looking for physical satisfaction'. In one case a judge intervened to ask the defendant 'Did you regard this young woman as respectable... You did not regard her as a tart?' (House of Commons Standing Committee E November 9, 2000).

Subsection (4) will ensure that juries are not invited to pass judgements on the complainant's general character in that way. Only specific allegations of behaviour that can be shown to be relevant to an issue will be admissible, and barristers and juries alike will be forced to concentrate on the issue at trial. Boateng added:

I shall give some examples from Sue Lees' research. Consent was the issue at the trial of a defendant charged with several offences of rape. One complainant was asked about an abortion that she had had three years before the event and when she had last had sex. Of what possible relevance could that be to the issues at trial?

A complainant who had been raped by a taxi driver was asked about her relationship with her boyfriend, including how often she had sex with him and how long she had been going out with him. That was irrelevant to the issues at trial, and will no longer be permitted under clause 40.

Under the provision, the following case reported by Sue Lees would not be allowed. At a trial at the Old Bailey in August 1993, the white complainant was asked whether she 'often slept with ethnics' and what colour the father of her baby was, for no reason other than the rapist happened to be black. We must never again allow offensive and wholly irrelevant questions of that nature in our courts.

A judge, quoted in Sue Lees' research, directed the jury that a complainant was not a promiscuous person but a 'sober, sensitive and religious young lady'. Such a comment, suggesting that if she were not sober, sensitive or religious, she would just take her chances as to how much belief she could inspire demonstrates the problem that we need to tackle (House of Commons Standing Committee E November 20, 2000).

The attempt to restrict the discretion of judges is unprecedented. Lord Carlyle, when interviewed on Radio 5 on 10 December 2000, condemned the change and called on the public to 'trust the judges'. But can the judges as a whole be relied upon or might they in part be responsible for the dramatic drop in the conviction rate for rape? Judges argue that sexual history evidence has only been introduced when it is relevant but my monitoring of trials indicates that this is not so. Despite a clear statement by government since 1997 that judges should not routinely allow sexual history evidence, our monitoring of trials in the year 2000 indicated that this practice has continued unabated. Whether we can trust the judges is an issue that I shall discuss further in the final chapter.

In January 2000 Channel 4 *Dispatches* approached me to undertake the consultancy on a follow-up programme entitled *Still Getting Away with Rape* which was shown in March 2000. This time we monitored all the trials occurring over a two-week period throughout the UK (30 trials in total) and analysed the transcripts of the cross-examination and the summing up of the judge in 15 trials to see why the conviction rate was so low. Additionally, a survey of 120 women who said they had been raped in the last five years was carried out. A quarter of these cases went to trial, from which the court monitoring was confirmed – women were routinely made out to be promiscuous in court, with the implication that their testimony was therefore unreliable.

In a third of the court transcripts, the defendant and complainant had only met on the night in question, in another third they knew each other, usually slightly, as a neighbour or 'friend', and the remaining third were or had been cohabiting. No cases could be identified as 'date rape' in the strict sense of having had a romantic relationship beforehand. In four cases, however, women had gone back home with the defendant or taken the defendant, whom they had only just met, to their home on the night in question, although in two of the four such cases they had been accompanied by friends.

Two of these four cases resulted in convictions so the conviction rate in this group was relatively high. In one of these cases the complainant was a virgin and the defendant had run off, and the other case involved a serial rapist. This latter case, which involved two complainants, only reached court because a woman was found unconscious after falling or being pushed out of a window and was hospitalized. This led to two women coming forward following the police advertising details of the case.

The overall conviction rate was only 30 per cent of all the trials monitored. Taking into account that only the strongest cases reach trial, 80 per cent of reported cases do not reach court at all, this is a very low proportion. My analysis of the outcomes of rape trials monitored in 2000 revealed that only the most extreme cases resulted in convictions. Such cases included serial rapists, where victims were virgins with injuries (but not virgins without injuries), cases where there was a wide age difference between the defendant and complainant, or complaints with life-threatening injuries such as knife wounds to the abdomen.

In the trials monitored the length of relationship did not appear to differentiate the 'guilty' from the 'not guilty' cases. However, the introduction of sexual history and sexual character evidence was a crucial factor. The criteria on which juries are instructed to judge the reliability of the complainant included: whether she had suffered from depression, taken Prozac, been in care, been abused, had an abortion, allegedly had more than one relationship, or invited someone whom she had just met home. The mere introduction of questions about sexual character or behaviour could be very damaging.

One defence tactic we observed was to imply that the live-in child minder had a lesbian relationship with the complainant.

She was asked:

DEFENCE: You told us that Sally was then living with you?
WOMAN: Yes that's right.
DEFENCE: Were you sharing a bed?
WOMAN: No.

Another example of such cross-examination in a case of domestic violence monitored by the programme is given below. The complainant claimed she had been raped by her husband from whom she had been separated for some years.

DEFENCE: Is it fair to say that it would be rare that you would make a sound during sexual intercourse?

WOMAN: I don't know.

JUDGE: Sexual intercourse with whom?

DEFENCE: Thank you, your Honour, I am going to put to her with Mr X and with Mr Y.

In this case, the judge directly elicited information about the complainant's sexual history with other men, even though whether or not a woman is normally silent during sexual intercourse is clearly irrelevant to whether or not a woman has been raped on any particular occasion.

The court monitoring showed that irrelevant sexual history and sexual character evidence is being admitted in a wide range of cases. The result is that a defence barrister has an expectation that a judge will allow him to go on a 'fishing expedition' around the victim's sexual past, which is, ironically, the very thing that the 1976 Sexual Offences (Amendment) Act was supposed to prevent.

Part of the problem is the imbalance between the defence and prosecution. The jury does not know that the prosecution barrister is not allowed to meet with the complainant prior to the day of the hearing to discuss the case, unlike the defendant who can meet with his barrister and can consult him during the trial. Juries do not know that defence barristers are paid much more than the prosecution and are likely to be more experienced. This can mean, as Judge Rafferty when interviewed for *Dispatches* 2000 programme commented, 'The prosecution is going to be outgunned and outclassed by the more seasoned performer.' In not one single transcript did the prosecution intervene to protest at the questions fired at the witness.

When Professor Jennifer Temkin (2000) interviewed 10 experienced barristers who defended and prosecuted in rape cases, a number of QCs (Queen's Councillors) said that they were shocked at the inexperience of some of the counsel prosecuting rape cases. One QC described them as an 'open target' for the defence. Another considered that the low conviction rate in rape cases was directly attributable to the level and quality of some of the people prosecuting.

Complainants interviewed for the 2000 *Dispatches* programme were unanimous in their condemnation of a system where two thirds had not even been introduced to the prosecution barrister. As one complainant commented, 'You need to know your barrister. You need to know that he's going to go in there and he's going to fight for you, because I don't care what anybody says, you are on trial.' The report *Speaking Up for Justice* makes a recommendation (Home Office 1998: Recommendation 27) for meetings between the prosecution and certain vulnerable and intimidated witnesses, which would presumably cover all rape complaints.

In March 2000 *Dispatches* interviewed Linda Fairstein, Assistant District Attorney, and chief of the Sex Crimes Unit in Manhattan. She recounted how in New York, when a woman reports rape, she immediately meets with a specialist advocate – a lawyer who only handles rape cases and who will work with her right through to the time she walks into court to testify. She strongly refuted that meeting with the witness involved coaching; 'Absolutely not. My role as prosecutor is to do justice. And I'm an officer of the court. I am not the victim's advocate and I am clearly aware of that.' She said the use of special advocates has pushed up conviction rates above 50 per cent in Washington and New York.

So beyond the Home Office report, what needs to be done? More accountability to the Bar Code of Conduct, which lays down that certain questions are inadmissible, would certainly help. Special prosecutors should deal with rape cases, meet the complainant beforehand and be properly trained to challenge robustly irrelevant attacks on her credibility, and be paid equivalent fees to the defence. The establishment of the Serious Fraud Office in 1985 establishes that the complexity of particular types of offences requires specialist investigators and prosecutors.

Campaigns around Rape

By the late 1980s, many rape crisis groups were meeting with each other to provide help and assistance in keeping services afloat. This informal structure culminated in a conference in the early 1990s, organized in the Midlands by local rape crisis centres, on the issue of federating. As a result of this work, the Rape Crisis Federation of Wales and England (RCF) was formally launched in October 1996. Although the organization has grown over the years, the work is diverse and demanding for what remains a small group of core workers.

A key aspect of the work is in speaking out about sexual violence. RCF has come to represent the 'victim's voice' on issues of rape and sexual assault. RCF has provided a range of consultative services to various departments of the government and during 1999–2000 participated on the Home Office Sex Offences Review as a member of the external reference group. Good news came in April 2001, when RCF became the first feminist voluntary sector agency to be funded by the Home Office. The bad news is that there is still no statutory responsibility to fund local rape crisis services. All rape crisis services are under-funded and many operate on an annual income of less than £20,000. RCF campaigning work therefore includes a continuing fight for survival as well as fighting for justice for women.

In response to the falling conviction rate, in 1996 a Campaign to End Rape was launched bringing together organizations such as Justice for Women, the Rape Crisis Federation (Wales and England), Action Against Child Sexual Abuse and a number of individuals. The aims of the campaign were to increase the conviction rate, ensure better treatment and representation of victims in court and change the law on consent. The campaign starts from the belief that consent must be negotiated, never presumed and points to Australia where, in the state of Victoria, it is the man who carries the burden of proving consent and evidence relating to the woman's sexual history is also outlawed. The campaign has been influential in lobbying MPs. A joint written intervention was submitted to the House of Lords from the Rape Crisis Federation, the Campaign to End Rape, Justice for Women and the YWCA in relation to the appeal against clause 41 of the Youth and Criminal Evidence Act discussed below. Women Against Rape have also campaigned to improve the law.

In the first edition of this book, I pointed to the need for three major reforms: for the curtailing of sexual history evidence, for changes in the rules of evidence and for the reform of the judiciary. In this new introduction I shall now summarize what developments have occurred since 1996 in the first two of these areas with particular reference to the Human Rights Act which came into force in 2001 (also see Appendix 3). In the last chapter I will discuss the limitations of reforms to the police and the judiciary.

The restriction of sexual history evidence

A major advance to the restriction of sexual history evidence appeared with the introduction of section 41 of the Youth Justice and Criminal Evidence Act, which came into force in December 2000, but was then narrowed by a Law Lords decision in June 2001. Section 41 of the act repeals the Sexual Offences (Amendment) Act 1976 and greatly curtails questioning a complainant in a sex case about her previous sexual history and behaviour. Known as the *rape shield law*, the judge can only allow such questioning in consent cases in very limited circumstances. Evidence of previous sexual intercourse with the accused could only be allowed if they took place *at or about the time* of the alleged offence, or were so similar that it might be said to be part of a pattern of sexual behaviour, or to refute evidence about sexual history that the prosecution has introduced – such as, for example, that the complainant was a virgin.

There was however a loophole. When the Youth Justice and Criminal Evidence Bill was being debated, an important exemption to the ban on sexual history evidence was introduced. It was ruled that if a man honestly believes the woman is consenting, no matter how unreasonable that belief, then it is not rape. Although clause 41 laid down that sexual history was not relevant to consent, the lawyers for the defendants argued that it was relevant to 'belief in consent'. But surely it is quite absurd to say that on the one hand, a jury must bear in mind her previous sexual history when considering his belief in consent, but forget it when they consider whether or not she consented.

The idea that sexual history evidence is not relevant and should be disallowed led to a storm of vociferous opposition by lawyers in both houses. As Dyer (2001a) pointed out opponents, including the former Lord Chief Justice, Lord Bingham, now the senior Law

Lord, argued that the law, in trying to protect women, went too far and stripped defendants of the right to a fair trial. Lord Bingham stated: 'I would not want to see any great weakening of what the prosecution has to establish'.[1] He is by no means alone in continuing to regard sexual history evidence as relevant, overlooking the significance of the distinction been consensual sex and rape. A woman barrister interviewed by Temkin (2000) who regularly prosecutes and defends in rape trials at the Old Bailey holds the view that 'there are lots of women who make complaints of rape who would sleep with the local donkey' and states 'the defendant says "Well, how can she possibly say I raped her when she goes with everybody in sight? I want that brought up".' Such views are not unusual.

The European Convention on Human Rights was incorporated into British law in 2000, which added another dimension to the way rape trials were conducted.

The day after the new act came into force, the new law was challenged at the Central Criminal Court, the Old Bailey, in a case where the defendant claimed to have a past sexual relationship with the complainant. Judge Simon Goldstein discharged the jury and gave leave to appeal 'with enthusiasm' on the grounds that the defendant was being denied a fair trial on the grounds that the new act breached article 6 of the European Convention of Human Rights. The Act forbade the defence from introducing evidence that the complainant had previously had sexual intercourse with the defendant.

The details of the case were as follows: the defendant denied attacking a teacher, who claimed she had been raped by him on a Thames towpath on 14 June 2000. He insisted they had been having a sexual relationship and that she consented to sex in the bushes. His lawyer claimed that this evidence was relevant to the issue of consent and that the new act breached article 6 of the European Convention of Human Rights, which gives him the right to a fair trial. Judge Goldstein said the problem was likely to arise in many cases being heard before crown courts and those involved – judges, lawyers, accused men and alleged victims – had to know where they stood. He revealingly commented that 'the sexual activity of a prostitute or

1. Dyer, C. (2000) 'Top judge against rape law reform,' *Guardian*, 5 November

someone as "chaste as a nun" will never be known because it cannot be explored in court by lawyers'. Such comments by judges show how the polarisation of women into the chaste and the depraved, the virgin and the whore, still operates today.

The Crown Prosecutor asked for the case to be fast-tracked at the Court of Appeal where the grounds for appeal were upheld on 15 January 2001. The Court of Appeal ruled that the defendant was not precluded from adducing evidence if such was the case that he and the complainant had recently taken part in consensual sexual activity (*The Times*, 15 February 2001). Giving leave to appeal to the Law Lords, Lord Justice Rose stated that it was commonsense that it is more likely the woman would have consented if she had previously had sex with him. However, I would argue that this is by no means the case where relationships have broken up. In such cases it might well be less likely that a woman would have sex particularly when there is a history of violence and separation. The case was then referred to the Lords of Appeal.

The Fawcett Society, a society that has a long history of fighting for women's rights, challenged the ability of a panel of male-only judges to rule on whether a woman's previous sexual history should be admissible. All 12 of the Lords of Appeal are white men and have an average age of 67. There has never been a female Law Lord. The intervention claimed that allowing an all-male panel to rule on the case would undermine faith in the justice system and breach Britain's international obligations on ensuring equal representation of women in decision-making. The Director of the Fawcett Society, Mary-Ann Stephenson, called for female Lords of Appeal to be appointed and argued that it was unfair to allow an all-male panel to decide whether to overturn a law which had already been discussed by both genders in Parliament (Stephenson 2001).

Vera Baird QC, Vice Chair of the Fawcett Society, and supporter of the campaigning organisation Justice for Women, said that the reason the rape shield law was passed in the first place was predominantly because 'there was consistently an unconscious bias towards a male point of view'. She argued that to have this decision challenged by a panel of men, who come from the same judicial culture as those who exercised it wrongly in the first place, is wrong (see McVeigh 2001).

At the start of the two day hearing in the House of Lords, David

Perry, Prosecuting Counsel, argued that one of the problems that the new act sought to address was that 'insufficiently relevant' evidence of a complainant's sexual history tended to 'overwhelm' the main issues in a sex trial. In modern society, he argued, it was generally accepted that a woman's sexual experience with partners of her choosing did not indicate a general willingness to consent or any lack of credibility in her evidence. Such evidence 'introduces prejudicial material which invites the jury to condemn the complainant by reason of his or her morality prior to the event'. He supported the view of the home secretary, separately represented at the hearing by David Pannick QC, that the act was workable and would not lead to unfairness because it allowed exceptions (see Special Report: Human Rights in the UK, *Guardian*, 27 March, 2001).

It might appear common sense that where there has been a sexual relationship between the defendant and complainant beforehand, as is alleged in the above case, or in cases where they are married, that the jury should be allowed to know this. The problem is that in practice when such information is allowed, defence barristers ask endless questions about the nature of the sexual relationship which is in no way relevant. In domestic violence or marital rape cases, the defendant and complainant are usually separated and in some cases have been living apart for some years. Yet details of their sex life are dredged up and judges still suggest that such men are trying to 'save their marriages' in some kind of romantic way to which the woman is consenting. The jury are not told that rape is often used by men whose relationships have broken down to take revenge on the woman or that marital rape and murder are also associated. If the jury were given details of the context of the violence, irrelevant information about their past sexual relationship would not be so damaging, but this is rarely the case.

One solution suggested by Vera Baird would be to allow such evidence as background information if a judge rules (under section 43) that it would be unfair distortion of the trial process not to mention it, but for the judge to direct the jury that it was not relevant to consent (see MacNeill 2001).

In their judgement, the Law Lords held that the Youth Justice and Criminal Evidence Act had gone too far and stated that if someone claims to be a victim of rape or sexual assault, their previous sexual relationship with the defendant can be called in evidence if the judge thinks that this relationship is so relevant to the case that to exclude it would create the risk of an unfair trial. This contradicts the Youth Justice and Criminal Evidence Act which laid down that evidence of a previous relationship could not generally be called in a trial. Where consent is the issue, therefore, past sexual history with the defendant *can* be allowed.

'Mistaken Belief' in Consent Defence

The Law Lords also confirmed another ground on which sexual history evidence could be allowed – although they confirmed that the original section 41 had barred evidence of previous sexual encounters between the woman and the man where the issue was whether she consented or not, they ruled that under the act it was admissible where the man's defence was not that the woman consented, but that he believed she was consenting. In other words sexual history evidence could be allowed on the grounds of what is called 'mistaken belief in consent'. According to Section 1 (1) of the Sexual Offences Act 1956 a defendant can only be guilty of rape if he knows that the other person was not consenting to sexual intercourse with him or else he was reckless as to whether that person was consenting or not. The term 'reckless' has been interpreted in cases to mean that he could not care less whether the person was consenting or not. More controversial is the issue of whether a defendant who mistakenly believes that the other person is consenting when he has no reasonable grounds for this belief should be criminally liable. The law answers this in the negative following DPP v. Morgan (1975) where the House of Lords ruled that a man was not guilty if he honestly believed a woman consented to sex; and his view did not have to be reasonable. This explicitly denied a woman's 'no' if a man reads it as consent. Even active resistance could be dismissed as token. The appeal judges said the result of the legislation was that the trial judge would have to direct the jury to take account of the evidence that the couple had a previous sexual relationship in assessing the defendant's state of mind, but to disregard it in assessing the woman's (see Dyer 2001b).

In Australia, New Zealand and America this law has been rejected and requires the belief in consent to be reasonable, but in the UK it has not been revoked and can be used as a way of permitting sexual history evidence to be introduced. There is a significant danger that these restrictions on sexual history evidence will simply lead to strategic adjustments in defence tactics which will relate sexual history more closely to the question of belief in consent.

The iniquitous 'mistaken belief in consent' defence appeals are analysed in an article by Jamieson (1994). She explains that this defence is not used more often because defence counsels find it easier to attack the credibility of the complainant than to argue that the defendant believed that the victim was consenting which might open him up to cross-examination as to the grounds for his mistaken belief. Since the Morgan ruling there have only been two cases of a mistaken belief defence referred to the Court of Appeal.

It is somewhat unclear whether the judgement (see 2001 June House of Lords, Appendix 3) relates only to where there has been a previous sexual relationship between the defendant and the complainant or whether judges also have the discretion to allow sexual history evidence of other men besides the defendant. In regard to mistaken belief in consent, it appears that judges could allow evidence of relationships with other men besides the complainant if they regarded it as relevant to the defendant's belief in consent. This means that all the defendant need do to ensure that the complainant's sexual history is allowed is to argue in his defence that he honestly believed that she consented. This would completely undermine the spirit of the legislation to restrict sexual history evidence.

Compatibility with Human Rights Law

To complicate the issue further, although the Law Lords decided that the rape shield law enshrined in the Youth Justice and Criminal Evidence Act was potentially unfair to the defendant and the interpretation should be revised along the lines suggested above, they argued that it was still compatible with the Human Rights Act (which enshrines the right to a fair trial). To quote from Lord Slynn's ruling:

It seems to me that your Lordships cannot say it is not possible to read section 41(3)(9c) together with Article 6 of the Convention rights in a way which will result in a fair hearing. In my view section 41(3)(9c) is to be read as permitting the admission of evidence or questioning which relates to a relevant issue in the case and which the trial judge considers is necessary to make the trial a fair one.

This is an extraordinary decision. As Melanie Phillips (*Sunday Times* 20 May 2001) pointed out for judges to rewrite what government have decided and parliament has passed is profoundly undemocratic. She went on to comment 'It is also underhand, since the judges are too cowardly to make transparent their challenge to these democratically created laws'. The contradiction is that on the one hand the Law Lords overruled clause 41 to allow sexual history evidence (although the whole point of the clause was to disallow it) and at the same time said the original clause was compatible with the Human Rights Act when of course, excluding sexual history evidence was in their view incompatible with the Human Rights Act (i.e. unfair to the defendant).

The ruling relating to 'belief in consent' appears to allow sexual history evidence at the discretion of the judge in cases both where there has been a sexual relationship between the complainant and the defendant beforehand and with other men. It therefore restores much of the discretion taken away from trial judges by the rape shield law. In future, it will be for the judge to decide if the evidence the man wants to put forward is relevant to the issue of whether or not the woman consented to sex on the occasion in question. If so, the evidence is likely to be allowed. Lord Steyn ruled that:

Due regard always being paid to the importance of seeking to protect the complainant from indignity and from humiliating questions, the test of admissibility is whether the evidence (and questioning in relation to it) is nevertheless so relevant to the issue of consent that to exclude it would endanger the fairness of the trial. If this test is satisfied, the evidence should not be excluded.

Or as Vera Baird pointed out 'We're back to the discretion of a lot of male judges' (quoted in Dyer 2001).

The Law Lords appear to have rewritten the law or produced an interpretation of the Act which managed to override its intentions. So why did they not declare the 1999 Youth Justice and Criminal Evidence Act incompatible with the Human Rights Act? As Melanie Phillips argued 'the answer is that the judges are playing politics. They are bending over backwards not to issue declarations of incompatibility and so put the government on the spot. It is a "Humpty Dumpty" Act which allows them to make the law mean whatever they want it to mean' (*Sunday Times*, 20 May 2001). As Lord Hope, whose reasoning differed from the other Law Lords said in his speech, the role of the judges is to interpret the law not make it themselves. In his view the way his fellow judges had interpreted the rape law to be compatible with the Human Rights Act was simply wrong. Yet again the judges appear to have been able to reassert their right to use their discretion. Failure to limit the judges' discretion led to the failure of the Sexual Offences (Amendment) Act (1976). It looks as though the Youth Justice and Criminal Evidence Act (1999) will face similar problems. Let us hope their discretion is limited to allowing evidence relating to relationships between the defendant and the complainant and is not used to evidence of past sexual history with other men too. However, given the past propensity of judges to consider sexual history evidence relevant – as evidenced by my court monitoring – it is sadly unlikely that the new act will result in a significant reduction in the use of this type of evidence, whether relating to the defendant or other men. However, the legislation should make the judges more alert to the need for a proper basis for the admittance of sexual history evidence. It is here that training is crucial so that judges are consistent and clear about what sexual history evidence is relevant.

Change in the Rules of Evidence in Order to Convict Serial Rapists – Extension of 'Similar Fact' Evidence

During the last decade or so much more extensive DNA testing and more sophisticated computer systems have allowed rapes of different women in different locations and at different times by the same man to be more easily linked.

Dr Zsuzsanna Adler (1987), who analysed 80 trials heard at the Old Bailey, found that men accused of raping more than one woman almost invariably pleaded guilty. Over a third of those who admitted the offence had raped more than one woman, usually on different occasions (Adler 1987: 45). The most likely explanation is that the sheer weight of evidence in cases involving several women considerably increases the likelihood of conviction. Where a man is charged with raping three or four women unknown to one another on separate occasions, the chances of discrediting all of them at the trial are fairly remote and it becomes much more difficult for him to produce a credible account alleging consent on all occasions.

In the 1990s a National Home Office Large Major Enquiry System (HOLMES) was set up whereby DNA information can be downloaded so that offences such as rapes, murders or other crimes can be matched. DNA undermines the defence of mistaken identity where the defendant argues that he was not the assailant.

One would think that this development would lead to an increase in the conviction rate so it is puzzling to discover that over the past decade it has declined even further. It is usually argued that this is entirely due to the fall in the proportion of rapes by strangers (down to 12 per cent of reported rapes in Harris and Grace's 1999 study) and the increase in rapes by acquaintances. What is not recognized is that rapists who attack strangers may well be changing their tactics so as to avoid conviction. These men realize that by chatting up their victims first they can then use the 'consent' defence – i.e. that the woman consented – rather than the defence of identification, which with DNA is no longer a viable defence.

Court monitoring reveals that in the majority – around two thirds – of cases that go to trial, the defendant is acquitted when the defence is consent. It is to overcome the problem of serial rapists being acquitted that the 'similar fact' evidence is so crucial. According to the rules of evidence, judges have discretion to allow juries to hear evidence involving different complainants where the accused has behaved in a similar way if the details of the offence show a strikingly similar pattern of behaviour. In other words, cases involving separate complainants can be heard together if there is a similarity in the tactics used by the defendant. The judge has to decide whether the value of such evidence is so strong as to outweigh the prejudice to the accused. If so, it can be allowed.

Significantly, the application of such evidence has become less stringent than in 1993 when we identified three cases where women had independently reported rape by the same man, but the judge had not allowed the cases to be heard together. It appears that the Channel 4 *Dispatches* programme, *Getting Away with Rape*, and the first edition of *Carnal Knowledge*, drew attention to two important myths that needed to be dispelled. First, serial rapists were not necessarily 'stranger' rapists. Indeed many serial rapists rape both strangers and women they are either married to or already acquainted with. Secondly, what the media insist on depicting as 'date' rapists are often men who are serious serial rapists who had progressed from raping 'strangers' to raping women they had picked up with that intention. (See Chapter 6 for background discussion of 'similar fact' evidence.)

The *Dispatches* programme was unique, as we had the resources and the prestige to contact police forces and search newspaper records to find out about past convictions and in some cases about past acquittals of defendants. One of the basic tenets of British justice is that defendants are innocent until proved guilty, which precludes a national database of acquittals. Until recently there has not been a database for past convictions.

What is curious is that whereas in other trials, where the reputation of the witness is attacked, this is said to 'lower the shield' of the defendant whose past convictions can then be revealed by the prosecution, this does not apply to rape trials where the past history of the defendant is only allowed at the discretion of the judge. This anomaly is not widely known.

The men we identified in the 1993 *Dispatches* programme had all had contact with their victims before the attacks. It seemed they had planned their attacks with care, bearing in mind the possibility that the woman might report the rape and that they would need to present evidence that she had consented. All had extensive experience of the way that courts operated and could be described by what the media like to call 'date rapists'.

One defendant had stood trial four times and been acquitted, before absconding without trace before a fifth trial. Another man, Nicholas Edwards, came to court yet again in the spring and autumn of 2000. He had originally been convicted as a stereotypical 'stranger' rapist and had progressed to adopting the more subtle 'chatting up' tactic before isolating his victim and raping her. This trial was his eighth on rape charges over a 19-year-period, but what was unusual was that this time the jury knew something of his long history.

This breakthrough followed a legal battle by the Crown Prosecution Service to get the evidence of previous acquittals in front of the jury. This was probably due to their frustration at seeing some defendants being acquitted again and again and possibly in response to the *Dispatches* programmes, which had shown so graphically that serial rapists were getting away with rape.

As previously mentioned, judges have a discretion to allow juries to hear evidence that the accused has behaved in a similar way in other cases – so called 'similar fact' evidence – if the details show a strikingly similar pattern of behaviour. The judge has to decide whether the value of the evidence in proving the charges is so strong that it outweighs the prejudice to the accused. If so, and if admitting the evidence will not make the trial unfair, it can be allowed in.

But there is a stumbling block. In a 1950 case the Privy Council had ruled that a jury verdict was binding and conclusive in all subsequent proceedings. For the past 50 years that has been interpreted to mean that once an accused is acquitted, no evidence to show that he actually committed the offence can be brought forward at a later trial. To do so, it was thought, would breach the 'double jeopardy' rule by which no one can be tried twice for the same crime, a cornerstone of the British justice system.

For this reason, in the Edwards Case the trial judge disallowed the evidence. The CPS then took the matter to the appeal court, which dismissed it, ruling that a prior acquittal not only precluded a second prosecution for the same offence but also barred the crown from citing evidence in a later prosecution that showed that the defendant was actually guilty of the charge of which he had been acquitted. However, the court reached this decision 'with regret' and gave permission for an appeal to the Lords.

In September 2000 the Law Lords must be given credit for allowing the prosecution's appeal, overruling the 1950 judgement and setting a new precedent (R. v. Z. *The Times*, 23 June 2000). The five judges said that allowing the women to give their evidence would not breach the double jeopardy rule because Edwards was not now at risk of conviction on the earlier rape charges, but only on the charge for which he was standing trial. The evidence was relevant and came within the ambit of the 'similar fact' rule, and was not inadmissible just because it tended to show that the defendant might in fact be guilty of offences of which he had earlier been acquitted. Four of the women who had accused Edwards and had their accusations dismissed by previous juries were allowed to testify. They were joined by another woman whose story had led to one of his two previous convictions. All alleged being raped by him in strikingly similar circumstances. As a result Edwards was found guilty and sentenced to life imprisonment.[2]

2. An appeal has been lodged.

In each case, it was alleged that he first went up to the woman in a public place. He adopted a low-key approach to gain her confidence, making a date for another meeting. At the second meeting, he continued to chat her up and then isolated her, in most cases by driving her to a secluded spot – in two cases to the same churchyard. Then he changed from Jekyll to Hyde. His mood, previously calm, became angry and he became a domineering, terrifying bully, forcing his victims to give in to his demands. He refused to use a condom and intercourse was accompanied in each case by comments and instructions from him, telling the girl what to do. Afterwards he reverted to friendliness, often denying that anything untoward had occurred.

Like many serial rapists, Edwards had adopted sophisticated tactics and become adept at avoiding conviction. In the latest case he managed to persuade the woman to go to his south London flat. As he would know, juries rarely convict where a woman is raped after accepting an invitation to the man's home. This case would probably not even have come to trial if the other women had not been allowed to give evidence. In this latest trial he claimed to have had sex with 2,000 women. But how many of his conquests consented? After the trial started, two more women came forward to allege Edwards had raped them too.

It is a controversial change to the law and not all lawyers agree with it. The Law Lords' ruling was in line with a recent Law Commission report on double jeopardy, but Andrew Trollope QC, who chaired the Criminal Bar Association group that responded to the Law Commission paper, believes the change breaches the principle that underlies the rule of double jeopardy. 'You may easily draw the conclusion that because a man's been accused of rape eight times over, he must be guilty. That's a very dangerous road to go down. You have to remember that in those instances, or a number of those instances, the facts have been closely examined by previous courts and that there has been a doubt in each case.' Bruce Houlder QC, vice-chairman of the Criminal Bar Association, argues on the other hand that it 'defies common sense' to exclude such evidence.[3]

Implications of the Change

The change in the law can be seen as an acknowledgement that some multiple rapists are going free and that something needed to be done about the high acquittal rate. The acquittal of serial rapists is far more common than often imagined, and most such rapists, contrary to common belief, have contact with their victims beforehand. Edwards was not the mythical unknown rapist who leaps on his victims in the dark. He planned the rapes for which he was convicted carefully and they appear to fall into a common pattern. His victims were not long-standing girlfriends but vulnerable women he had previously met socially and apparently targeted.

Yet we know that serial rapists are still getting away with rape but only when such rapists are finally convicted. Richard Baker, a disc jockey, for example, was convicted of four rapes, but after his trial was accused by many more women who had met him at the holiday resort where he preyed on victims. Adam Carruthers, the policeman found guilty of raping a woman in May 2001, had faced complaints by 20 other women over the years, ranging from indecent exposure to rape. It was alleged that one woman was raped by him several times and attempted suicide after ongoing abuse from him. There was an enquiry undertaken by Dumfries and Galloway police, for whom Carruthers had worked. At the time of writing Carruthers had recieved an extension of time in which to appeal, but grounds for appeal had not yet been lodged.

The implication often drawn is that 'date rapes' are due to men misreading signals and being confused. In an article by Alan Travis[4] the Home Office was reported to have suggested that the decline in the conviction rate could be due to the fact that 'half of all rapes are being reported as "date rapes" – committed by boyfriends, former partners or close friends – compared to 35 per cent a decade ago'.

The term 'date-rape' is misleading and should be abandoned. Attacks by ex-boyfriends frequently occur when the relationship has ended and the man will not let go. They often involve serious injuries and on a significant number of occasions result in murder. It would also be far more accurate to categorize attackers who have met their victims on the same day as strangers.

Attrition rates of some 93 per cent mean that almost all cases in which there is a prior acquaintance between the suspect and the complainant are not prosecuted because the CPS do not believe there is a realistic prospect of a conviction, even when the

3. Lees, S. 2001. 'Found out at last', *Law Report, Guardian*, 25 Sept.
4. Travis, A. 1998. 'Alarm over "Date Rapes"', *Guardian*, 16 June.

acquaintance has been initiated within the past 24 hours. In addition, many women are unwilling to give evidence in court when they are told that the prospects of a conviction are remote. In effect the criminal justice system is condoning such crimes and creating a climate for serial rapists to get away with it.

Abolition of Defendant's Right to Cross-examine Witnesses

A good example of how change is possible although protracted is the process which led up to the abolition of the right of defendants to cross-examine witnesses which resulted from the implementation of sections 34 and 35 of the Youth Justice and Criminal Evidence Act (1999) on 4 September 2000. This appeared to be a relatively minor change, but it took a good five years to be put into effect.

Since 1995 the press had given widespread publicity to several cases where defendants had sacked their counsels and undertaken the cross-examination of their victims themselves. In one of these, Julia Mason gave up her anonymity to protest at the way she had been cross-examined by her assailant, Ralston Edwards, for six days. She fled from the courtroom at one stage, complaining that she felt sick, after being told to give a precise description of the sexual humiliation she alleged she had endured. Edwards wore the same faded jumper and jeans as when he had repeatedly raped her (*The Times*, 23 August 1996). He already had a previous conviction for rape and had been acquitted on another rape charge. He also had a long history of violent offences against women.

Shortly afterwards, in November 1996, Michael Howard, then Conservative Home Secretary, announced that he intended to abolish the defendant's right to undertake his own defence in rape cases.

A year later, following the election of a Labour government, still no change had been made in spite of three further cases where defendants had taken over their own defence. In the first case a 'very dangerous rapist', who had attacked two women at knifepoint, had appeared in court on rape charges on four previous occasions and repeatedly forced his victims to relive their torment and frequently accused them of lying on oath. The following year Floyd Bailey left his victim in tears after making her describe his genitals in graphic detail. She later described her ordeal as 'being violated a second time' (*Press Association Newsfile*, 16 January 1998).

After the third case where the defendant, Milton Brown, who had been acquitted on four previous occasions, was allowed to cross-examine his victims for five days in the witness box, Jack Straw, the new Labour Home Secretary, promised a 'swift change in the law' to take forward the previous government's proposal (*Guardian*, 13 January 1998: 7). Straw declared: 'Women who have been raped should not be victims twice over. I set up an urgent review to identify ways to improve the treatment of vulnerable witnesses at every stage of the criminal justice process.' He said that he planned to put 'the interests of victims, not criminals, first'.

Finally, in October 2000, just before the abolition of the right of defendants to cross-examine witnesses was brought into effect, the defendant Patrick Simms was allowed to put a woman through such a courtroom ordeal for the last time. At the Old Bailey he was found guilty of raping a 23-year-old Japanese student at his flat in July 1999. The victim described how a man she once regarded as Mr Wonderful beat her, tortured her and kept her prisoner, forcing her to submit to sex, abusing her and becoming obsessively jealous about her relationships with other men. She suffered six broken ribs, a fracture of the jaw, chipped teeth and serious bruising when he punched and kicked her. 'I thought I was going to die', she told the jury. During the relationship Simms withdrew thousands of pounds from her bank, buying two cars, a music system and clothes.

Simms had been acquitted of rape on three separate occasions, and had been jailed for eight years in 1993 for raping and causing grievous bodily harm to a previous girlfriend. Sentencing him to life imprisonment, Judge Paul Collins said, 'I hope you will not be released until you are no longer a threat to women.'[5]

Setting the Boundaries – Sexual Offences Review

In June 1998 a Home Office minister announced a review of the sex offences law and said, 'There are many anomalies in the existing legislation which in many respects reflect attitudes and views that are no longer acceptable in modern society. The review of this area of legislation is long overdue.' In February 1999 another Home Office minister said: 'We shall consider the outcome of the review. That in turn will be subject to a proper consultation process and in due

5. Appeal currently pending.

course legislation will be introduced.' The proposal, set out in their review *Setting the Boundaries* (Home Office Communications Directorate 2000), attempts to provide a comprehensive reform of the law on sex offences, to enable abusers to be appropriately punished. It was, however, limited in so far as the rules of evidence were excluded.

The steering group's terms of reference were to provide recommendations on coherent and clear legislation on sex offences which will protect individuals, especially the more vulnerable, from abuse and exploitation; enable abusers to be appropriately punished; and be fair and non-discriminatory in accordance with the European Convention on Human Rights and the Human Rights Act. The review covered child abuse and sexual harassment, and proposed a new law against trafficking, but I shall only discuss the section on sexual assault of adults.

The steering committee proposals widen the definition of rape to include penetration of the mouth by the penis. A further offence of sexual assault by penetration is proposed to cover all other forms of sexual penetration of the anus and genitalia, and should also carry a maximum life sentence. A lesser offence of sexual assault, defined as non-consensual touching which a reasonable bystander would recognize as sexual, is proposed to replace the existing offence of indecent assault, attracting a 10-year maximum sentence. It was proposed that this group of offences should be reinforced by the enactment of new offences of assault with intent to commit a serious sex offence and of abduction with intent to commit a serious sex offence, each with a maximum penalty of seven years, while the existing offence of burglary and intent to rape should be replaced with an offence to trespass to commit a serious sex offence.

The committee soundly rejected the call to make 'date rape' or 'acquaintance rape' a separate, less serious offence with a lower maximum sentence, on the grounds that the available evidence did not support any 'downgrading'. It questioned whether rape by an acquaintance or intimate genuinely is a less serious offence than rape by a stranger:

Some research indicates that the level of violence in partner/ex-partner rape is second only to stranger rape. We were told by those who counsel victim survivors that those raped by friends or family often find it much harder to recover and may take longer to do so. In addition to these powerful arguments, it is hard to see how degrees of rape could be defined – when does a stranger become an acquaintance or a friend? The crime of rape is so serious that it needs to be considered in its totality rather than being constrained by any relationship between the parties (Home Office Communications Directorate 2000).

Instead the committee made the following recommendations concerning the need to define what is meant by 'consent'.

Defining 'Consent'

The most significant change proposed in the recommendations is to define for the first time what is meant by consent and to shift the evidence from physical evidence to evidence of autonomous choice. The steering group recognized the difficulty that has arisen in relation to the interpretation of consent and proposed to overcome this by recommending that consent be defined as 'free agreement'. Under these proposals a defendant would need to show that a complainant's consent had been 'freely agreed'. This would at least put some pressure on the defendant to explain what led him to consider that the woman freely agreed, without altering the burden of proof. They also recommended that there should be a non-exhaustive list of circumstances where consent is not present. Lacey (2001) suggests this is somewhat in line with the Theft Act's treatment of dishonesty, illustrating circumstances in which consent in this sense is not present. This might include model judges' directions; for example, 'In deciding whether the complainant did freely agree to sexual intercourse . . . you should not assume that the complainant did freely agree just because they did not say or do anything . . . or just because they did not protest or physically resist.' These offences would require proof of intent or recklessness, which would be defined subjectively but which would include an attitude of indifference to consent. These include:

- where a person submits or is unable to resist because of force, or fear of force;
- where a person submits or is unable to resist because of threats or fear of serious harm or serious detriment of any type to themselves or another person;

- where a person was asleep, unconscious, or too affected by alcohol or drugs to give free agreement;
- where a person did not understand the nature of the act, whether because they lacked the capacity to understand, or were deceived as to the purpose of the act;
- where a person was mistaken or deceived as to the identity of the person or the nature of the act;
- where agreement is expressed by a third party (Home Office Communications Directorate 2000:19).

Regrettably, the committee rejected proposals to use the benchmark of what the reasonable man would consider to be free agreement. Since a defendant can surely argue that he 'honestly believed' free agreement was given, the proposed change does not advance us much further than the Morgan ruling. For example, a man who honestly believes that a woman is consenting even when she says 'No' would have a valid defence in law. Great emphasis is placed at present by the defence in rape trials on the failure of victims to resist physically or scream and juries are rarely warned that the response of 'freezing' is not uncommon where victims are often terrified for their lives and, therefore, do not show resistance. Silence, ambiguous behaviour and the absence of clearly expressed unwillingness like physical resistance will continue to be treated as evidence that affirmative agreement was present. The significance of equivocal behaviour could be reversed. Indeed, it is possible that the defence will place greater emphasis on victim behaviour like not fighting back, or making no attempt to escape but if the model judges' directions suggested in the Sexual Offences Review were adopted that might help.

No announcement has however been made in the past year and a half about the timing of the new legislation to implement the suggested changes of the Sexual Offences Review Committee. It is clearly not a priority for the government. Martin Bowley QC wrote to the *Guardian* in July 2001 complaining about the delay (Bowley 2001). Beverley Hughes, on behalf of the government, replied a few days later pointing out that consultation on the review's 62 recommendations finished on 1 March 2001 and officials were analysing over 650 responses and would be submitting firm recommendations over the summer. However, at the time of writing (February 2002) no further announcement has been made.

Limitations of the Proposals

If such recommendations are introduced will they lead to more convictions? Perhaps, but defendants will, of course, argue that the complainant did freely agree, and that force or confinement was absent. Rape is rarely corroborated since it usually occurs in private. Other imbalances in the trial procedure not covered by the Sexual Offences Review Committee's remit also need to be addressed. Juries have to decide who is speaking the truth, so the criteria on which they are instructed to judge credibility is crucial. At present, in line with the directions regarding rules of evidence, judges can imply in their summing up that the woman's credibility, unlike the defendant's, rests on evidence regarding her past sexual history and sexual character.

Professor Nicola Lacey (2001) points to two serious limitations of the proposals: the exclusion from its official remit of rules of evidence and of the norms which shape the judiciary – and indeed the whole judicial process. She gives the example of Jennifer Temkin's research on the attitudes of lawyers prosecuting and defending rape cases:

In a system in which a prosecuting lawyer can unabashedly claim that 'I think it's just common sense that if a woman looks like a scrubber she's going to get less sympathy from a jury than someone who looks respectable' and moreover is probably justified in so claiming – and in which a defence lawyer can assert that 'If you've got a sort of tarty woman then you're going to get the softly softly (approach). I mean if you've got a tarty little number with a mini-skirt round her neck who's brassy and will give as good as she gets then you'll be firm with her...' one has to ask how much can be achieved by even radical changes to the adjustment of the definition of rape in substantive criminal law (Lacey 2001: 12).

Lacey argues that a troubling question is whether in the prevailing sexual culture the unmodified adversarial trial process can deliver justice in sexual cases. She concludes that the establishment of a comprehensive review of sexual offences which excluded evidence and procedure was fundamentally misconceived.

Conclusion

Little will be achieved without major reform of the whole process of the law on sexual assault as any piecemeal reforms will be undermined. Other strategies are needed to change the prevailing sexual culture, such as professional education designed to shift cultural attitudes of codes of practice specifying the nature of an advocate's professional responsibility not merely to her or his client but also to the court in such cases; and guidelines for judges specifying their positive responsibility to ensure that the trial – and in particular cross-examination – is conducted in a way which shows adequate respect to victims.

In marked contrast to the situation abroad, in England and Wales any attempt to introduce reforms has been met at times, even when enacted in legislation, with apparent resistance from the judiciary. There are difficulties with gaining rape convictions in all jurisdictions where sexuality is still defined by lawyers as appropriation and possession of the woman, where women's active sexuality is denied and where negotiated consent is not considered necessary (see Naffine 1994). This difficulty is reflected in the length of time it has taken to abolish the marital rape exemption, which in 1991 finally removed support for a husband's demand for the right to non-reciprocal sexual domination. The implication of the marital rape exemption was that the husband had the right to sexual intercourse with his wife whenever he wanted. It was an extension of the historic domination and control of husbands over wives. When laws giving women substantial rights to the joint property on divorce had long been in force, the rape immunity law proved very difficult to abolish precisely because its abolition challenged the view of women as the possessions and passive objects of their husbands' desires. Its abolition, integrated into statute in June 1994, carries the clear implication that a woman does have a right to self-determination or to take an active rather than a passive sexual role, and that acceptable forms of sexuality require the presence of mutual desire and consent.

Apart from the thorny question of how exactly to define consent, there have been significant and comprehensive reforms in other countries that are long overdue in Britain. Legislation removing the discretion from judges regarding sexual character and sexual history evidence occurred fifteen years ago in Australia. The Crimes (Sexual Assault) Amendment Act and Cognate Act of 1981 in New South Wales, Australia, outlawed questioning about the sexual assault victim's past sexual history which was seen as irrelevant to her credibility, and all evidence produced as to the victim's sexual reputation of any kind was defined as 'inadmissible'. In the same way, complainants were prohibited from giving evidence of their own virginity at the time of the offence (Allen 1990). Additionally, the corroboration ruling was abolished. Judges are also required to warn against being prejudiced against women not reporting rape immediately. This has led to a greater willingness on the part of juries to convict. Since these reforms the conviction rate has risen to 82 per cent and the level of arrests has increased. It is still, however, estimated that many cases do not get to trial (Allen 1990: 230–1).

In Michigan a package of reforms were also introduced in the 1980s including the abolition of judicial discretion regarding sexual history evidence (except on two specified grounds), and the abolition of the need for corroboration or for proof of physical force. A major evaluation was conducted involving interviews with court officials, the police and rape crisis centre staff both before and after the new law was enacted. The effect was an increase in the rate of convictions as charged with a corresponding reduction in convictions for lesser offences. Trials are less of an ordeal for women (see Adler 1987: 146). In Canada too a package of reforms were introduced in the 1980s, including the controversial replacement of the crime of rape with three degrees of sexual assault. In regard to sexual history evidence, in 1993 an Act to Amend the Criminal Code (Sexual Assault) was passed which left its introduction up to the discretion of judges, but which requires the defence to submit a written application containing details which will be heard in the absence of the jury and where witnesses may be called if they wish to introduce it. Where the judge allows such evidence he must explain its relevance in writing (Temkin 1993: 18).

Overall, Britain lags far behind other common law jurisdictions where far more sweeping, wide-ranging reforms have been introduced. Effective reform of the system will require resources, in training and retraining, in the provision of adequate support services and in ensuring that the perpetrators of violence are brought to justice. But only a major shake-up of the culture of the Bar, with its engrained complacency which is analysed in the final chapter, can lead to victims gaining the fair trials they deserve.

Chapter 1

Women Speak Out

and when we speak we are afraid
our words will not be heard
nor welcomed
but when we are silent
we are still afraid
so it is better to speak
(Audre Lorde, 'Sister Outsider')

Rape is a notoriously difficult subject to find out about. The guilt, shame and trauma lead many to keep silent. Some do not want to be seen as victims of rape in view of the stigma and others fear they will be blamed. Research is not easy. Even using the word 'victim' presents problems. I shall use it here to describe someone who has had the experience of being raped, not to imply a permanent 'victim' status. I shall also use 'survivor' to avoid the perils of permanently labelling a woman as a victim and to imply that, though a woman is changed by such an experience, she is not powerless to rebuild her life (see Dobash and Dobash 1992: 40).

We know many women tell no one, and some are tragically driven to suicide.[1] Rape is such a stigma in some societies that a woman's reputation is permanently damaged and she is cast out of the community. Rape has come to mean to 'soil' or 'spoil' and is still used in some communities and in war, as we shall see, as a weapon to demoralize or destroy family or community honour. A Muslim woman in Serbia described how before she was raped by twenty men, one of her captors said he wanted to marry her. Then later he

1. See, for example, 'Raped Nurse in Suicide Horror', *The Times*, 30 October 1988, and Barbara McMahon, 'Suicide Probe as Raped Nurse is Found Dead', *Evening Standard* 24 August 1994, which reported that Karen Mokrzycki, a thirty-six-year-old theatre nurse, was found dead three weeks after being raped. Her family said she had been traumatized by the rape. see also reports of two suicides in 1984 (Adler 1987).

said, 'Now I don't want to marry you any more, now that all of them have fucked you down the line' (Stiglmayer 1993: 127). Many women who have been raped feel 'dirty' and cannot stop scrubbing themselves afterwards. Women who have been raped are often seen as polluted. In the ancient fable of the rape of Lucretia, though Lucretia is the victim, it is she who commits suicide. It is for this reason that many women never tell anyone, not even their closest friends or relatives. Many women I interviewed were shocked by the response of some men, and even some women too, if they did tell. It was they, not the rapist, who were often blamed.

Immediate outward adjustment can be deceptive. For many, reaction is delayed and it can be years before their memory returns. Forgetting or shutting the rape out from their mind is one strategy for coping with it and carrying on with life. Many find talking about it painful even when they appreciate how much this can help. Reactivating painful memories can awaken anxiety and lead women to keep silent. Yet women all over the world are beginning to talk about the violence they experience not only from strangers but also from fathers, uncles, brothers, husbands, friends and neighbours. Marital rape, long considered a husband's right since a wife was his 'property' and excluded from the sexual offence laws, became illegal only in 1991. This change is important symbolically in so far as the law is at last beginning to regard women as equal citizens rather than as the chattels of their husbands.

Background to the Research

A number of researchers have interviewed women about their experiences of rape (see Kelly 1988), but few have inquired into their views of the police and the courts. Problems of access and funding are formidable. The most comprehensive study of this kind was carried out by Scottish Office researchers Chambers and Millar (1983). They found that complainants were generally dissatisfied with their treatment by the police and the courts. Regarding the incidence of rape, Ruth Hall conducted a 'women's safety' survey of 2,000 women[2] in London with the volunteer help of the campaign group Women Against Rape (Hall 1985). One in five women had

---

2. The 1,236 returned questionnaires meant a response rate of 62 per cent.

survived rape or attempted rape.3 Press coverage of the survey was both inaccurate and highly critical, implicitly denying the content of the findings (see Soothill and Walby 1991:106–13).

Hall reports that the most upsetting work was analysing the aftereffects of rape, physical, emotional and material. Her findings contest the widespread view of rape as just an act of sex caused by a misunderstanding and the idea that, unless there is lasting physical injury, a woman will be able to shrug the experience off. Many women were deeply affected by rape and sexual assault without anyone around them knowing what had happened. Survivors' lives were often severely disrupted. Fifteen per cent suffered loss of earnings, in some cases loss of job, either resulting from the trauma or from physical injury or illness. Ten per cent were forced to move house, as they no longer felt safe in their own homes or neighbourhoods. Even when arrested the assailant was often released on bail or served only a short prison sentence. Five per cent were pregnant. If young women were subjected to sexual abuse or rape when they were still at school or college, this could have long-term effects on their educational achievement and work prospects. If raped at work, this too led women to leave their jobs. Survivors also faced substantial financial costs as a result of precautions they had to take because of fear, ranging from enrolling in self-defence classes to running a, car or using taxis, changing accommodation or paying more rent to live in an area where they felt safer. Existing sexual relationships were often affected and were sometimes shattered. Fifty-seven per cent of the women who described the effects of rape singled out its repercussions for their sexuality afterwards and the difficulty of relating to men. In some cases, men rejected their wives or girlfriends as being 'soiled' or in some way guilty, or for being too fearful or dependent (Hall 1985:146).

Cathy Roberts, a founder member of the London Rape Crisis Centre, followed up thirty women for a year after they had been raped and analysed their reactions as portrayed in the records of the Rape Crisis Centre (Roberts 1989). Half the women had been involved in some kind of a steady relationship at the time of the rape and half of those had split with that partner within a year of the rape. Some men were not able to cope with the idea of rape and

3. Altogether, including marital rape, two women in every five had experienced rape, attempted rape or another kind of sexual assault.

accused the woman of provoking it. Others were initially sympathetic but found the woman's response to rape difficult to handle.

American researchers (Rodkin et al. 1982) observed partners' reactions when running a support group for male relatives of rape victims. Men initially responded like the victims themselves, showing fear reactions, and then often became very protective and spent more time with their partner. They often blamed themselves for not providing adequate protection. At a later stage, they became irritated with the length of time it took women to recover and resented the partner's dependency. Often women could not bear to be touched. This often led the men to withdraw into work, which was often interpreted by the women as rejection. Relatives often felt overwhelmed with helplessness and needed help in coming to terms with rape.

There seem to be differences in the way men and women respond to rape, as our questionnaires showed. 'Anything exciting happened to you?' one woman's father asked her when she returned home from a holiday abroad. 'Been raped, have you?' This is exactly what had happened. It is often not understood how terrifying the experience is and how women fear for their lives. Judy Katz, a rape survivor, described how some men made jokes about wishing a woman would rape them or asked why women 'cannot lie back and enjoy it'. Others asked questions which she felt put the blame on her, inquiring whether she had left a window open or the attacker was armed. Others wondered why she was so upset. The more 'macho' men offered to kill the rapist or give her protection. She said they never asked her how they could help; rather, they assumed they knew. She concluded that the main concern for them was how to handle their own feelings, not hers (Katz 1984). The ambivalent feelings aroused by rape emerged in the report of one husband who resented the fact that his wife had had anal sex, albeit at knife-point, with her attacker (she had always 'refused him'). This man had clearly internalized the myths of rape so deeply that he associated it with a sexual consent and experience.4

Community reactions to rape are equally mixed. It is not unusual for women who go to court to face threats of retaliation and to be stereotyped as 'sluts'. Some receive death threats. Children also

4. Personal communication with Corinne Sweet, the researcher who interviewed him, April 1995.

often need help if their mother is attacked. Sandra, a woman I interviewed who had been attacked on the way home from collecting her ten-year-old son from school, described his reaction:

He used to see me as this big, strong person who made things happen and then he saw me floored literally. Then there was the time when we had an argument about something I wouldn't let him do and he shoved me and I went right across the kitchen. I don't know whether he was copying the man, but he must have realized that I could be physically overpowered.

The Research: Questionnaire Results

For two years I had been involved in various small projects aimed at contacting women who had not reported rape to the police. I wrote articles in local newspapers leaving a number for women to ring. Many who rang did so when unable to get through to Rape Crisis. In the 1970s the Rape Crisis movement had a major impact on the community and police response to rape. Yet in the 1990s services are underfunded and skeletal and few women receive the help they need (see Lupton and Gillespie 1994). In spite of the resilience and the dedication of women working for Rape Crisis, many who are raped are often left stranded. Rape Crisis is predominantly a telephone help line set up by rape survivors. It is in great need of funds and volunteers and in many areas operates for only a few hours. Another potential source of help is Victim Support, a nationwide service, partly funded by the Home Office, which provides help for all victims of crime. Unlike Rape Crisis, it does not specialize in sexual assault cases and the service does not offer long-term counselling, which some women need, but both provide valuable support for women taking cases to court. Rape Crisis offers long-term help when it can, but rarely has the resources available (see Walklate 1989). Both services rely mainly on volunteers but employ some paid workers, usually partly financed by the local authority and often operating under great pressure. There is rarely money for further training or career progression, vital in posts as stressful as working with survivors. In some areas there are specialized services that offer a twenty-four-hour counselling line, but these are few and far between, as a result of recent cuts in local authority expenditure.

Three of the women who rang said they had never told anyone

about the rape before. One of these, Sylvia, who lived in an isolated farmhouse, had been raped by a man to whom she gave a lift when driving in torrential rain; she allowed him to stay the night and he had then raped her at knife-point. Shortly afterwards, she read in the local newspaper that he had attacked another woman with a knife, but she could not face going to the police. She had caught VD from her assailant and for several years was too ashamed to go for treatment. Another young woman, an Australian on a weekend away from her au pair job, had been horrendously raped and buggered by a stranger in combat gear and had been put on a train without any information about how to get help. She had tried to get through to Rape Crisis without success. She eventually received £10,000 in criminal injuries compensation, but not until a year after her return to Australia. She used the money to come back to Britain to retrace her steps, visiting the police in the Lake District, where she had been assaulted, and the family for whom she had been au pair, in an attempt to come to terms with it. In Sweden women are offered free counselling and legal support from the moment rape is reported. It is time the political parties in Britain addressed this issue and provided funding for Rape Crisis counselling to meet this crying need.

Contacting women who have been raped and are prepared to share their experiences is a major obstacle to undertaking research into such a sensitive topic. In an earlier research project conducted with Jeanne Gregory and funded by the Islington Police Support and Crime Prevention Unit, I interviewed twenty-six women who had reported sexual assault to the police. Later I contacted the women who had suffered rape or attempted rape and asked them to fill in the questionnaire. A snowballing method was used, whereby women who had agreed to fill in questionnaires contacted friends whom they knew had also been raped. Other women - those I knew through work, friends, neighbours, shop workers and ex-students also filled in questionnaires. Like Pauline Bart, who undertook a similar study in the US in the late 1970s (Bart 1978), I was appalled by the amount and degree of hidden violence in women's lives.

The questionnaire was designed and piloted very carefully in view of the sensitive nature of the investigation. We also included a note telling women that it was quite all right to 'opt out' of answering some questions if they caused too much distress. We distributed questionnaires through Victim Support groups, women's centres, counselling services, Rape Crisis centres, student unions and personal contacts throughout the whole of the UK.s A common response to the trauma of rape is to repress the memory totally or at least to 'forget' the details. Often memories re-emerge many years later. One woman interviewed remembered she had been raped three times in adolescence only after her own daughter was born. Three out of four respondents gave their names and offered to supply further information. Many of these offers were subsequently followed up, in some cases with telephone interviews or visits.

Some women found the questionnaire format easier than an interview. Telling an interviewer, however sympathetic, the details of an attack can be embarrassing and sometimes writing things down is easier. One woman I interviewed immediately after she had been horrendously raped filled in a questionnaire over a year later and gave many more details in her written responses than she had face to face. Remembering details of an assault, which may have happened many years ago, is a painful process and the bravery of women who participated in the research should not be underestimated. Another wrote:

This questionnaire has been relieving to fill in – writing it all down has been like a release. I don't think I've ever said this much to any of the people I've told. I have now told a lot of people. At first in an attempt to work it out of my system, but more recently because I've met others like myself. I feel like I've written a lot but it goes round in my head a lot and there are bits that are still very vivid.

The answers all the women gave are a moving testimony to the pain experienced not only as a result of their assaults but also in response to the inadequacy of the criminal justice system to protect them from further assault.

A total of 116 women over the age of sixteen answered the lengthy questionnaire, which took several hours to fill in. Some found it too stressful to fill in at one sitting. Many rang up and shared their feelings. A telephone line was provided once a week

5. Not all Rape crisis centres were prepared to distribute the questionnaires, on the grounds that they would be too upsetting for women to fill in. we considered tnis was a decision the woman herself should take. Many women told us how helpful they had found it, as a way of both 'breaking the silence' and contributing to the assistance of other women who had been through similar experiences.

for five hours to answer queries and refer women to counselling services where they were available. The inadequacy of counselling support throughout the country was not unanticipated, but it was an appalling indictment of the lack of recognition given to the trauma of rape.

Victim Support services are rarely equipped to deal with survivors of rape, particularly since reaction to rape is often delayed. Rape Crisis is underfunded and only operates for a few hours in some areas. Many women failed to get through to their telephone lines, but some women found the help invaluable. Reactions to rape vary but are invariably far more intense than most people imagine. Few understand how devastating rape can be, what a blow it is to feelings of self-worth, how often women blame themselves and are unjustly blamed by others, how easy it is to deny there is a problem, how long it takes even to begin to recover (most women say they never fully recover) and how difficult it is to get help.

For the purposes of the questionnaire, the legal definition of rape was used: 'forced to have sex against your will'; attempted rape was 'attempted to force you to have sex against your will'. For the purposes of the analysis, a completed rape was one where the man had penetrated the woman with his penis – the legal definition of rape does not require ejaculation. Anal and vaginal penetration by anything other than the penis were counted separately, only because the present law does not define these as rape. Eight questionnaires which suggested that the actual offence was indecent assault were excluded, although the lines between attempted rape and indecent assault were not always clear. Rape within marriage was significantly under-represented as the vast majority of respondents were given questionnaires that excluded rapes by husbands and cohabitees residing with the woman. The decision to exclude such rapes was taken at the outset because a recent survey had specifically focused on this kind of assault. This British survey of over 1,000 women (Painter 1991) found that one in seven (14 per cent) of women in their sample had been raped by husbands or cohabitees. It also found that 31 per cent had been raped by other men. Since the extent of marital rape had recently been documented, and our resources were limited, our priority was to find out about the men who are raping women outside the marriage relationship. Some Rape Crisis centres were critical of this and failed to understand our need to limit the scope of our research.

The women were self-selecting, so the survey did not provide a representative sample. Unusually, it had a higher proportion of black and Asian respondents (20 per cent and respondents from other minority ethnic groups such as Turkish and Arab (8 per cent), but this is unlikely to be in any way indicative of the rate of rape in those populations. Seventy per cent of the respondents were white Europeans. The questionnaires revealed 100 rapes (fourteen of which were rapes by more than one assailant) and sixteen attempted rapes (attempted rapes are often where women have repulsed their attacker). Nearly a quarter (24 per cent) of the respondents said they had also been buggered. Almost half (44 per cent) were under twenty-one at the time of the assault. Respondents were drawn from all over England and Scotland, although 8 per cent of the assaults took place abroad. Eighty per cent of the women were single, 9 per cent cohabiting and 11 per cent divorced or separated.

Categories of Assailants

On the basis of the answers given by respondents in the whole questionnaire, rapes were divided into types, according to the respondent's prior relationship with the assailant and the degree of social contact she had had with him prior to the assault. Stranger rapes, or what have been called 'blitz rapes', were defined as an assault by a man who had had no consensual social contact with the woman before the assault: that is, where a man hitherto completely unknown to her suddenly attacked her in the street or broke into her home. Take, for example, this statement by a seventeen-year-old who was raped at a bus stop. The rape was linked forensically with four other rapes of teenagers and police were investigating two other rapes they believed to be connected.

He was holding my shoulder, and he grabbed me tighter and pulled me down. He had me by the neck. I asked what he was trying to do. He said, 'I'll never hurt you.' I said, 'Are you going to kill me?' He said it would not be worth it. I was too scared to run or move.

Strangers were, predictably, more likely to approach the woman in a public place, with 14 per cent breaking into the woman's home or posing as a salesman.

Acquaintance rapes were divided into three groups. The first covered assaults by men who had hitherto been unknown to the woman but with whom she had had some degree of consensual social contact in the twenty-four hours prior to the assault. In this group the woman had usually met the man at a pub, a party, some kind of social gathering or in the street, and was raped within twenty-four hours of meeting him. The second group, characterized as 'general acquaintance', covered assaults by men whom the woman had known for more than twenty-four hours prior to the assault but with whom she had never had consensual sex (such as friends, relatives, colleagues and neighbours). The third group covered assaults by men with whom the woman had previously had a consensual sexual relationship (such as husbands, boyfriends and ex-lovers).[6]

In this study of 100 respondents, only fourteen of the assailants were complete strangers and eighty-six had had some contact with the victim beforehand. This varied from minimal social contact to non-cohabiting boyfriends and ex-cohabitees or husbands, ex-lovers or other relatives. Twenty were raped by men with whom they had had previous consensual sex, forty-six by general acquaintances and twenty by men they had met within the previous twenty-four hours.

Acquaintance within Twenty-four Hours

Alison was a single parent with two children. She had agreed to store some furniture belonging to a friend, so she let the removal man in. It was evening and her children were asleep. She described what happened:

He sat himself down and wouldn't leave. He told me I liked him. He was very cool and unagitated, confident, and condescending. He tripped me up backwards and trapped my hands immediately. He pushed his tongue in my mouth, which caused incredible pain, and wouldn't let go, with his face hard. He let go of my mouth and got himself inside me despite my cries. I begged and begged him not to do it, but he was too strong. He insisted I said I liked him and wanted him. He chatted to himself how you can't rape a woman. It can't be done. It is not possible. He told me I was a nice girl. He was completely unconcerned about my state. He then wanted to rape me again on the bed where my three-year-old was asleep. He found another room and I calmed myself so my kids would not walk in. Afterwards I glared at him. I wanted to

6. The definition of the 'intimate' groups is different from that in Grace's Home Office study (Grace et al. 1992), where the intimate category includes rapes by relatives with whom the woman has not previously had a sexual relationship.

destroy him. My mind was ablaze. I still wanted to be calm. I didn't want to be in prison for murder. Now I hate men. I want them to be castrated or tagged.

Sue met a student when she had visited the student accommodation service on first arriving at university.

I went back to his room for a coffee. I had a kiss but I said I didn't want to go any further. He told me that I'd 'asked for it' by accepting his invitation for coffee and letting him kiss me. He said that I knew exactly what would happen if I went back for coffee. I was scared he was going to kill me and I physically froze. The whole experience lasted four hours. He had hidden my clothes, locked the door and hidden the key. I sat in a corner of the room for some time, naked, until he went to sleep. I found the clothes, got dressed, woke him and he gave me the key to get out.

General Acquaintance Rape

Most of the women were raped by men they knew. Of these, more than half were friends, colleagues, neighbours or casual acquaintances – men with whom they had never had consensual sex. Most assaults appear to have been carefully planned,. Men approached the women in a variety of situations, but most commonly in the social setting of a pub, club or party. Many women were taken unsuspectingly to a place where the rapist would not be disturbed. With regard to the men the victims knew well or fairly well, first contact with the victim was most likely to be made in the man or woman's home (60 per cent), or an inside public place (17 per cent), and least likely to be made on a date (3 per cent). Yet many people believe that a woman who goes to the home or flat of a man on the first date implies she is willing to have sex. Others believe that it is the woman's fault if she gets herself into the situation where she is likely to be raped.

Sandy was only sixteen and a virgin when she was raped by a man introduced to her by a teacher and therefore holding a position of trust. This is what she wrote:

I was sixteen and attending guitar evening classes where the teacher introduced me to this man. He was far older than I and occasionally took me home from the classes and then later for a drink on the way home. The relationship was platonic and I trusted him as an adult who listened to me. I valued his opinions. He took me home as usual, discovered my parents were away, said he'd had too much to drink to drive and felt giddy. I put him in the guest room of our house, then went to bed and to sleep myself. I woke to find a man in my room who raped me. I did not realize until afterwards that it had been him. I thought a stranger had broken in. I woke in the dark. He was kneeling on the bed. As I moved he forced my legs apart, then lay on top of me with his arm across my throat. My hands were underneath me. I spoke just before he put his arm across my throat. I don't know exactly when he penetrated me. He didn't say anything apart from 'that was good' when he got off me after ejaculating. I said, 'What have you done? I'm bleeding.' He smiled and said, 'Oh, good, a virgin.'

I threatened to go to the doctor. He sat very close to me and said no one would believe me. I'd lose everything. I was now his, no other man would want me. It was impossible to force a girl. I must have wanted it because he had been able to do it. It was my upbringing that made me accept that I'd really wanted it. He told me the bleeding was nothing to worry about, to have a bath and he'd ring me later. I was very confused. It all happened so fast. I asked what he was doing, then the pain was so extreme I felt as if I was away from this, looking down on the scene. I was totally incapable of movement. All I seemed to hear was his breathing I remember thinking 'move', but couldn't. I turned on the light, wanting to shout for my friend, then saw that it was in fact him as he was pulling on his trousers. I seemed incapable of independent thought. Everything he said I believed. After he left I had a bath and the bleeding did stop, so he'd been right about that and so I knew he was right about everything. I went to school and remember people asking me if I was all right. Finally a teacher asked, but as I'd been introduced to the man by a teacher I wasn't able to speak to this one. Then a steel door in my mind seemed to go clang and I 'forgot' about it, only felt 'irrational' fear the next time we met.

When her parents had realized Sandy was no longer a virgin, they threw her out.

In several cases the woman was drugged or plied with drinks. Mary, a professional young woman, described how she had gone for a drink with a work colleague whom she had known for five years. She described him as well liked.

I went to his house for a drink – I thought of him as a friend. My drinks were tampered with. I blacked out when I had been drinking. When I woke up, sexual intercourse had taken place. I was sick in the bathroom and then I left. I couldn't tell anyone. I feel it was my fault. I feel physically ill when I see him or think about it. I don't trust men any more.

More typical of an acquaintance rape was Elaine's experience of being raped by her boyfriend's friend, whom she had known slightly for several months.

I was looking for my boyfriend, so when I saw his friend, I thought he'd know where he was. My boyfriend and I often stayed at his house, so I wasn't worried about going there and I had no reason to fear the man. His mood stayed the same; he just kept telling me that I was different. His tone of voice was the same. He was not aggressive in any way. He totally took me by surprise. I suspected nothing until he pounced on me.

We were in his living room. We talked, mainly me wanting to know when my boyfriend might show up. He kept saying that I was different. I didn't eat meat, and I was strong and very opinionated. I presume he was trying to sweet-talk/flatter me. He got me on the carpet so quickly I didn't know what was happening. I mainly wear trousers, but unfortunately this night I had a skirt on. I struggled and fought relentlessly. It was no use. He was a lot older and a lot stronger. I was trapped under what seemed to be an enormous body, suffocated. It seemed like he was totally ignoring me. I was crying and pleading with him as well as fighting. He didn't care. I felt sick.

Mica described how she was attacked by a colleague whom she had worked with for eighteen months who had come round on the pretext of talking about work. She had cooked him a meal and they had listened to classical music. Then, suddenly, he viciously attacked her from behind. She described how he suddenly changed:

His mood had changed in a matter of minutes. He became argumentative, aggressive, almost like a different person. He didn't really speak that much, but when he did it seemed very out of character and not the person I had been talking to earlier. He pushed me to the floor. I made it clear I was not interested. He produced a knife and told me to do exactly what he said.

The effect on her life was devastating. She explained:

I moved house, changed jobs. I felt claustrophobic, which I still do. I was often off sick. I couldn't hold a proper conversation with friends. I burst into tears for no apparent reason. 'Then I went through a phase of a year or so of needing to prove I was attractive. I had a series of one-night stands to prove to myself I could have sex properly.

Over a year later the rapist traced her and broke into her house. She reported it to the police and at court the rape charge was dropped but he was found guilty of breaking and entering

A middle-aged professional woman was raped by a younger colleague she had known for ten years through a professional organization when they were away on a residential course. She had never told anybody before filling in the questionnaire. This is what she wrote:

He had always previously had a pleasant, friendly and slightly deferential attitude towards me – I assumed out of respect for my age, as he had become much more successful than me during the time I knew him. We had been talking about professional and career matters until five minutes before the attack. He never said anything at all from immediately before the attack until a few minutes after. He knocked on my bedroom door. I opened it (having first checked his identity) and the attack started immediately. I was in a hotel room, surrounded by respected and well-known colleagues. He came into the room, kissed me forcibly, felt all over my body and entered me vaginally within two or three minutes. Being overwhelmed with embarrassment, I felt unable to leave the room with no clothes on. He insulted and ridiculed me. Afterwards he said sarcastically that I could tell everyone that he had slept with me – that I could boast about it. He just went after putting his clothes back on. He said no one would believe I did not want him. He totally ignored me throughout. I could not believe what was happening He was tall, handsome and successful. I am an overweight post-menopausal woman. I felt faint, then sick, then my insides seemed to turn to concrete, but above all I could not understand why he was doing this. Eventually I did start to feel angry, but could not express my anger very forcibly.

The aftermath was horrific.

I could write a book about it. It's nine months now since the attack and I am still experiencing changing emotions and effects. I have withdrawn from the professional association and all other commitments which involved staying away from home [she had several professional responsibilities which involved this]. My previous sexual experience has been limited exclusively to my husband. I have had no involvement with any other man apart from him over twenty-two years. To move from this state to a raped one has been very difficult to accept.

Acquaintance Rape Where Previous Sex has Occurred

Some of the most violent cases of rape occurred after the breakup of a sexual relationship. In some cases there had been a history of violence. Sandra and Jane described the way their ex-boyfriends had reacted with extreme violence when they ended the relationship after a few months. Sandra had known the man for eight months and had previously been to court on account of his violence:

The man was very violent towards me before the rape. There was a court order telling him to stay away from me. There was a court case pending. He had broken into my home and was threatening to kill me. He had beaten me up on a number of occasions. I was having a relationship with him before the attacks. The relationship only lasted a few weeks before he started to attack me physically. He said he promised he wouldn't hit me any more.

Jane also had split up because of the man's violence, but later he broke into her house.

He had attempted to kill me before in fits of anger. The choice between dying and being fucked is no choice. He simply walked into my bedroom as I was getting into bed, put his hands round my neck from the back, started talking about his knife (which I knew he had – a Bowie knife). He was unhappy and depressed, angry and aggressive. He tore my pyjamas off and raped me. I had been hurt before by him – he had a dreadful temper – I knew that it would pass, that actual danger would happen only if I angered him excessively. I also knew that he would be upset and depressed by what he did afterwards, would punish himself more than I could have provided I didn't react aggressively by physically opposing him, so I simply let it happen. I decided to make certain he couldn't get in again. He attempted to justify himself.

Annie was also raped by an ex-boyfriend after they had broken up.

He came to my home unexpectedly using a key he'd cut without my knowledge by taking my spare key one day at the beginning of our relationship. He had kept this copy a secret for about six months. I was woken up startled, but he reassured me that he just wanted to talk to me. He proceeded to try to persuade me that everything would be OK and we should go back out together. Once he realized I wasn't going to change my mind, then he sexually assaulted me. He said that I must want it for the last time too.

Jenny, aged thirty-three and separated from her husband,

described a violent assault by her husband and his friend, involving buggery and rape:

I was not willingly in his company. I was shopping alone when suddenly I was knocked unconscious by my husband and another man and dragged into a car. When I became conscious I was in a strange house and was bleeding. My clothes were all muddy. My husband came and just laughed at me, saying it was my fault that he had attacked me. He got his friend to hold me down. He put it in any hole he could find. When he finished his friend had a go.

Women describe rape as a life-threatening event, as sexual coercion aimed to humiliate rather than give pleasure, in which their main concern is to survive. Why juries do not believe such accounts needs some explanation as it seems incredible that any of the cases I heard could have been fabricated. Witness these accounts:

I kept saying, 'Don't hurt me. Please don't hurt me.' He picked me up with a hand round my mouth and one hand round my throat, with my feet off the floor, and carried me into the bedroom. I put a slap here and there and I scratched him. I panicked. I was scared. I'm asthmatic. I couldn't breathe. He was carrying me by the throat so I couldn't scream. He threw me on the bed. I said, 'I have a period at the moment.' He said, 'Don't give me that bullshit.' He ripped my skirt and my blouse. There weren't any injuries. I didn't want a bottle over my head.

He said he had chosen me as a victim because he could control me with violence. At knife-point he ordered me to masturbate him. He was unable to penetrate. He forced me to have oral sex and when he could [when he had an erection] he raped me.

The Aftermath of Rape

I think torture is the only thing you can equate it with. If you've been tortured you come out very shaky and unsure of your personality and you've had something subjected on you against your will and it takes a lot to reconstruct your strength and your confidence.

Rape, like torture, often has after-effects which take time to come to terms with. Rape is an infringement of one's whole being and many women said it had affected every aspect of their life afterwards. The unlucky ones were also faced with venereal diseases or abortion.

Women raped by acquaintances found the experience even more difficult to come to terms with than those raped by strangers. They felt betrayed – not just by the men but by their own judgement. It also made them more fearful of men generally, since they no longer knew whom to trust. The fact that some women also blamed themselves for the rape made it harder for them to recover.

The analysis of the questionnaires indicated that the effects on survivors were often dramatic and long-lasting. As already mentioned, many changed their lifestyle, moved house through fear that the rapist might return, had time off or gave up work, broke up relationships with men and required long-term medication or counselling which was not often available. Many reactions are typical of what American researchers Holmstrom and Burgess (1978) named the 'rape trauma syndrome', which many rape victims suffer from to some degree. The use of such a medical term to describe reactions to rape has been criticized as it reduces the complexity of women's experiences to a set of 'individual symptoms' which, once understood, can be cured by the medical profession (see Foley 1994: 44).

None the less, it does appear that there are common reactions which could provide corroboration for rape; Absence of particular reactions should not, however, be used as evidence for false allegations as some reactions may not appear for some time. Reactions to any stress also vary and some women were more able to cope than others. Crucial to the aftermath is the response of others and the opportunity to talk about the experience. Blocking or failing to talk about it can have disastrous long-term effects. Many considered their lives had been permanently damaged. A staggering one in five (20 per cent) lost their virginity as a result of the rape, nearly a quarter were buggered, seven became pregnant (one with twins)[7] and seven caught a sexually transmitted disease. Some women expressed fear of contracting the HIV virus. Forty per cent of the survivors of the US 1992 National Women's Study 'Rape in America: A Report to the Nation' (conducted by the Crime Victims Research and Treatment Center) said they feared contracting HIV.

The question of HIV and sexual assault is beginning to be addressed in Britain. It raises all sorts of crucial questions, perhaps

7. One of the women decided to go ahead with her pregnancy and at the time of filling in the questionnaire had a daughter of seven.

the most important of which is whether or not survivors should be able to force suspects under some circumstances to be tested. Defendants in the US challenged compulsory HIV testing on a number of constitutional grounds, notably the Fourth Amendment right to be free from unreasonable searches and seizures. However, emerging case law indicates that, with safeguards, a carefully crafted testing programme would be held to be constitutional. The American Foundation for AIDS research has developed guidelines regarding testing (see Gostin et al. 1994) which need to be developed in Britain too, now that 20–25 per cent of HIV carriers are known to be heterosexual.[8] The long delay before trials means that, to be useful, the victim needs to have access to these results quickly. Clearly, in the event of becoming infected, even if this is unlikely, immediate testing is crucial. It is not at present possible to pinpoint the moment or source of infection, but it may soon be possible to match infection with source (see Moran 1994). Some British National Health Service sexual assault counselling agencies are already encountering women who have been found to be HIV-positive after sexual assaults. According to research in the US, some women are carrying condoms as a preventive measure so that in the event of an assault they can try to persuade the assailant to use protection (see Moran 1994). One victim in a trial I attended had not been told that the defendant was HIV-positive although the police had known this for months.

Emotional Reactions

One woman who had tried to resist was eventually forced to have oral sex. She had been counselled by Rape Crisis and a psychiatrist, whom she considered totally unsympathetic; he said the rape was her fault as she had not fought off her assailant. This is how she described the effects:

shock, numbness, humiliation, degradation, disbelief, guilty, self-blame and anger which led to me mutilating myself, embarrassment, loss of control, severe depression (I take anti-depressants), irritability, mood swings, fear of being alone, crying a lot, inability to sleep, nightmares, relationship

8. The 1991 British 'Health of the Nation 2000' study, based on an HIV survey of clinics, found that one in 150 heterosexual women were HIV-positive and one in ninety heterosexual men.

problems with family and friends, no enthusiasm for life, anorexia, loss of concentration, feelings of being dirty, defiled, contaminated (constantly washing), loss of self-trust, safety and independence.

The pain and anguish and isolation experienced by many women are appalling

I felt afraid of men, afraid of sex, of having another boyfriend. I didn't want to look 'nice' in case anyone looked at me. I wanted to hide, run away. I felt very badly about myself.

Several women described feeling suicidal:

I felt suicidal afterwards and felt it was not worth living. There were too many changes. I just couldn't cope and I wished he'd killed me.

I wanted to die. I could not stop crying. I thought everybody was looking at me and could see what I was feeling inside. I felt dirty, bathing all the time as I needed to be clean. I couldn't sleep, couldn't eat, I had nightmares. I was frightened to go out. I was scared of being left alone. I could smell him all the time. I kept scratching myself to get him out of my body. I smashed all the mirrors in my bedroom and cut up the clothes I had been wearing.

Apart from depression, several women described how they had 'blocked out' the experience. Most of the women who did this had not gone to counselling and had a delayed reaction later. Their experiences affected other relationships. Flashbacks, nightmares and sleeplessness were the most common responses. Janet describes how she felt:

I blocked it out for about two years. But even in that time, it made me feel nervous around men. More recently, I sometimes have flashbacks (usually during sex). Partly as a result I rarely have sex. I didn't go for counselling or need medication.

I'm still dealing with the emotional and psychological effects. In fact it's only recently that I've begun to get my head straight about it all and it's hard. I still want to block it out but I have to deal with it because I've only just realized that it affects relationships I have with other men. The degradation and humiliation are something I feel I have stamped on my forehead sometimes – that makes me feel vulnerable.

Some respondents described how the experience had put them completely off sex:

I suffered (still do to a lesser extent) from nightmares, insomnia, a fear of going out. I lost a lot of hair and I find it very difficult to go near anyone now. I was put on sleeping tablets and antibiotics (in case I had picked up any disease) and I had to see a psychologist. I became withdrawn, cautious and less trusting. I didn't want sex. The first time about six months afterwards was horrendous. I have panic attacks and frighten easily and unnecessarily.

I had been violently raped by someone else three years before this particular event but by a different man. I do not trust men particularly and quite often find sex something that is painful. I find it very difficult and uncomfortable to let anyone touch me.

Others were driven to promiscuity in order to try and help them to feel something. Such evidence is often used against the complainant if she goes to court (see Chapter 3, the Kydd case). Anna explained how she felt:

Almost the same week I suddenly wanted love. I craved love and attention so I had as many boyfriends as I could. I found love through sex, which I now know made things worse, and things went downhill from that time. I craved attention even if it was negative and I made my boyfriends hit me. I didn't feel anything for other people and I ended up treating most people like dirt. I feel I was put on ice for five years. I couldn't move forward. The only peace I would have is to make sure he didn't hurt another girl, but I failed to stop that as well.

Laura suffered the most horrific attack when abroad and living in multi-occupied housing. She met an Australian in a bar who said he had nowhere to sleep. She kindly offered to let him stay in the house, where he violently attacked her with a knife. She described the effect it had on her:

I blanked it all out for a while. I began drinking heavily. About four months later I had a routine doctor's appointment. I turned up slightly merry and when quizzed about my drinking it all came out. I was referred to a psychiatrist. I told my mother and she was supportive. I'd also met a really nice guy with whom I wanted a relationship, but I was finding that difficult unless I wasn't sober. I was honest with him and he seemed to understand (our relationship lasted five years). The psychiatrist was the most uncaring, patronizing woman I'd ever met and by the time I left I'd made my mind up not to go back. I decided I could cope. I decided that I wouldn't let the man who assaulted me rule my life. I went to self-defence classes and, even today, if I want to walk home alone I do. I am always very wary and I'm forever telling other girls not to walk home alone but to get taxis. I know that what happened to me is nothing compared to some women's experiences but it still hurts. *What he did to me has made me into the person I am today and he robbed me of the person I used to be. I really want to be that old me again, but I know it's not possible.* I am not a particularly nice person. I'm miserable and very cynical and pessimistic.

One survival strategy was to go on as though nothing had happened. As Annie, raped when she was only fourteen, explained:

I pretended it hadn't happened and, if it had, then it was normal, like shopping or school. I didn't know what it was in my head, so I couldn't understand the reality. I said goodbye and went indoors. I didn't cry. I had a wash and went to bed, then went to school the next day.

Some women got VD or had abortions.

He gave me VD, so I had to have injections. I needed medication to clear the infection. I shake a lot. I couldn't talk about it. I was ashamed, because it had happened before. I was afraid to go out. A friend would escort me everywhere.

One woman tried to kill herself and several women mutilated or cut themselves. Janet said she inflicted injury on herself most days. She was very depressed and scared of relationships with men on any level whatsoever. She had bad nightmares. Others reported being victimized after the offence. As Jacky described:

The worst part was after, when he continually harassed and shadowed me. Silent phone calls each night. He followed me in his van or appeared near my home. I lived in continual fear and intimidation on a regular basis for four years.

All the women felt they had been changed by the experience, but were determined to try to avoid feeling humiliated or degraded. Almost all the women had become far more cautious and were less confident about going out on their own. This can be seen as a positive survival strategy.

I became more aware of the potential for such situations, determined not to allow them to affect my life or my children. I became more conscious of man's moods.

Many became far less trusting of men. Sylvia explained:

I've become much more mistrusting and more sceptical about the motivation in relationships with men. I've become more cautious about the way I dress. I never wear skirts. I just don't feel comfortable in them. I've become a lot more aggressive.

June, who had fought off her attacker, who was married with three children, described the effect:

I do not wear make-up, smart clothes, perfume, swimwear, a blouse unless it is covered with a big jumper. I keep myself and my body from view. I do not go out to a restaurant, as I would feel I would have to wear feminine clothes. To feel that you have no other function other than as an object to be used and thrown away completely destroys your confidence and makes you feel powerless, worthless, ashamed and guilty.

To argue that uncovering the secrecy and agony, yet also the bravery and courage of survivors of rape, encourages a victim mentality is absurd. This is how one survivor described her reaction:

It took me a long time to come to terms with what happened. I still suffer from severe depression. I was taking anti-depressants and tranquillizers for about a year. I moved into a women's safe house, where I became dependent on drink and drugs, as I did not want to live in the real world any more.

But I would like to add that because of this experience I have become a much stronger woman. I wouldn't wish it upon anyone, as the healing process is soul-destroying, but I have to believe some good has come from it all. I am now a volunteer worker for Rape Crisis. I don't depend on drink or drugs any more. I feel very strong and I have met some wonderful women through all this. I am no longer a victim, I am a survivor.

It was the most terrifying experience of my life. It has changed my whole outlook on life. But thanks to Rape Crisis I have come through it a much stronger person. I feel more in control of my life. Without the help and support I got from them, it could have destroyed me.

I think that the problem with most women, including myself, is that somehow we feel it is our fault that this has happened. Because I had nobody to talk to about it, I continued to blame myself. It also did a lot of damage to my self-esteem, as I already had a low opinion of myself. I think that things have to change drastically so that women no longer feel they are to blame and men start feeling responsible for what they have done.

The sad thing is that I felt worthless, so therefore I really became worthless, and I am still working on that now.

Reporting to the Police

The police treatment of rape victims has radically changed in recent years. The catalyst for this was an explosive episode of the BBC television series *Police* in 1982, in which police officers were seen in a live investigation of a woman reporting rape. This brought to the public's attention the harsh interrogation techniques rape complainants were subjected to and provided the impetus for the police to reform their procedures (see Scott and Dickens 1989). As a result of pressure from the Women's National Commission following publication of its report 'Violence against Women' (1985), the Home Office issued a circular[9] calling for improved police training to deal with rape and sexual assault, the appointment of more women police surgeons and the provision of better facilities for the medical examination of women who had been attacked. Police handling of rape complainants, if not perfect,[10] has certainly greatly improved. Most police officers who deal with rape complainants have now had some training (although this is often pretty minim, all. and a chaperonage system, whereby one female officer is assigned to work with a particular complainant throughout the investigation, has been introduced in many stations so the woman feels supported. At the same time, in 1986, in response to. public outrage at lenient sentences imposed by a number of judges in cases of rape and attempted rape,[11] Lord Chief Justice Lane issued new sentencing guidelines (R. v. Billam [1986] 1 All ER 986), aimed at substantially increasing sentences for rape.

The number of women reporting rape and sexual assault to the police has more than trebled over the past two decades in Britain, but the proportion of reported rapes resulting in a conviction has more than halved. The proportion who report rape are, however, only the tip of the iceberg. There are several possible reasons why

9. 69/86 Sexual Offences Investigation Steering Committee, February 1993, Metropolitan Police.

10. According to the London Rape Crisis Centre Annual Report (1989), sometimes a woman is questioned at length and goes away thinking the police have recorded her complaint, only to discover later that the police station has no record of it.

11. In particular, Judge Kichard's fine of £2,000 to an Ipswich businessman in 1982.

more women are reporting rape: confidence that the police will believe them has undoubtedly increased and greater acknowledgement of the prevalence of violence against women within the community could well have had an effect; but there could also have been an actual increase in the prevalence of rape.

Forty per cent of the women who replied to the questionnaire had been assaulted on more than one occasion, usually by different men. It seems that women are more likely to report assaults if they recur. This was reflected in some other research I was involved with in 1993, when we wrote to all the women who had reported rape and sexual assault at two London police stations over a two-year period (Lees and Gregory 1993). Many of these women had been assaulted more than once but had reported the assault to the police only on the second or third occasion. They were asked to supply details of just the most recent assault.

In the analysis of the loo questionnaires, 41 per cent of the respondents reported the rape to the police. This is a much higher proportion than in victimization studies, where the rate of reporting is under 10 per cent. By distributing our questionnaires through Victim Support and Rape Crisis centres, we expected to find that a higher proportion had reported the assault. We asked respondents who had not reported the rape to explain why. The most common reason (57 per cent) was lack of confidence that the police would believe them, or take them seriously, particularly if they knew the man well or fairly well. Other reasons were fear of further attack from the assailant or his friends (18 per cent), fear that the man would return, as he now knew where they lived (14 per cent), fear that if the man was of professional status he would have the advantage over them (in one case the assailant was a high-ranking policeman). Several women did not report because they felt, or were made to feel, that the rape was their fault because they had gone willingly to the man's home or had been sexually involved before. Finally, fifteen women were put off reporting because they did not want to testify in court. Reasons included belief that a conviction was unlikely; belief that she, the victim, would be 'on trial'; fear of reprisals by the man; not wishing to involve relatives; and not wishing other people to find out. The reality of women's fears of retaliation were brought home by the case in 1995 of a husband who was acquitted of raping his wife but then returned days later and beat her to death in front of the children.[12]

In their 1985 report the Women's National Commission recommended that every woman who had been sexually assaulted should be able to insist on having a woman doctor to examine her. Although in theory this is offered, in practice a woman doctor is often not available, and in 50 per cent of the cases where women were interviewed, the medical examination had been undertaken by a man. Almost all the women expressed a preference for a woman doctor. This is how Sylvia, when interviewed, described her experience:

The police medical centre was absolutely beautiful and they were after spending something like £n2 million to do it up, but the female doctor wouldn't come out, and the only one who would was a man doctor. They did say they would report her for not coming out. The doctor was a bit pissed off, having to get out of bed in the middle of the night, and just said, 'They couldn't get a woman.'

You are so exposed, and the reactions and comments of the doctor are going to validate what you've said, and his reactions and comments are actually what's happened to you, or comments on the state of your body or whatever. I would have expected the doctor to say a few kind, personal things. He was very impersonal and very distant. If he could have said, 'You must be really feeling bad', or something. I don't remember him saying anything like that. He did explain what was going on in the medical examination. I just felt he did not have any sympathy or compassion and he had no notion of what state I was in. He was just doing his job so he could get back home back to bed. I didn't get a good feeling from him. Whereas I did from some of the police officers.

Women often felt they were treated like objects or criminals. Two women described their feelings:

I looked down at myself with this sheet wrapped around me and he [the medical officer] turned to the WPC and said, 'Cover her up, will you?' I felt like a piece of something on a slab – cover that up, we should not be looking at that.

12. See John Steele, 'Husband Cleared of Raping Wife Beat Her to Death', *Daily Telegraph*, 9 February 1995.

The one thing I didn't like was the police surgeon. I don't think the police told him I was the victim and he seemed to treat me as if somehow I was a criminal. I ended up in tears. He just seemed so rude to me, all the time, and he wanted me to spit in a pot and I couldn't and every time I tried to spit I wanted to be sick. It was really horrible the way he treated me. Because of being m the medical profession, I notice things like that, as I'm involved in training doctors ... I'm sure no one told him that this is a victim, not a criminal. I'm sure no one said anything to him.

Resisting Violence

If a woman physically resists and is severely hurt, she is told she should have acted more passively; on the other hand, if she decides not to resist, she is seen as accepting the violence. Clearly this is a no-win situation (Kelly 1988: 184)

Women resisted assaults in all sorts of different ways: by screaming, fighting and biting, running away, refusing to cooperate, pretending they were pregnant or had AIDS and by attempting to reason. In one of the acquaintance gang rapes described in the next chapter, resisting did stop the men from raping her. In several cases, if they resisted early and were not in too isolated a position, the women were able to escape.

In most cases, however, the rapist had taken care to isolate the victim and resistance was met with higher levels of violence. The use of violence was similar and substantial in both the stranger and the acquaintance groups (69.6 and 63.9 per cent respectively). A higher proportion of strangers threatened to kill their victims (39 as against 14 per cent) and twice as many of the women raped by strangers believed their lives to be in danger (81.1 as against 42 per cent). Both groups, however, were likely to slap, push or handle their victims roughly, or forcibly hold them down (70–80 per cent), and more of the acquaintance group choked or strangled their victims (23 as against 15 per cent). This puts women in greater danger than is often appreciated as, in England, strangulation is a common method by which men kill women they know. Injuries and physical effects suffered by the women in both groups were remarkably similar. About half of both groups suffered minor bruises, scratches and soreness (55 and 46 per cent), and 27 and 28 per cent of respective groups suffered severe bruising and 2 per cent serious cuts and wounds. Of the total group 7 per cent caught a sexually transmitted disease, or another 6 per cent got pregnant. One woman raped by a stranger had a fractured jaw and two of the women raped by acquaintances had bite marks. More of the stranger group required hospital treatment (48 as against 26 per cent).

The attempted rape cases were all where women had managed to avoid being raped by resisting, although, as we have just said, resistance is not always effective for avoiding rape. It will depend on what chance the woman has of escaping, which varies from situation to situation. In cases where women were raped, resistance had often led to an escalation of violence. Rita described the effect her resistance had after being dragged by a stranger from a bus stop:

> I remember thinking what people say you should do if you are attacked, 'I'd punch, kick them in the balls.' So I punched him there and he grabbed my head and slammed it into the wall and called me a 'fucking bitch'. I started to cry, and he said if I didn't climb over the gate before he counted to ten he would kill me, and then started counting...He put his penis in my mouth and said that if I bit it, I was dead.

Thirty-five per cent of the strangers threatened physical harm or punishment if the woman resisted, and a significant proportion of respondents (47 and 23 per cent) said the man became more violent in response to their resistance. Thirty-eight per cent of the acquaintance group said that their resistance seemed to turn him on (as against only six per cent of the stranger group). This was also the experience of women raped by Serbs in Bosnia, where women suffered severe injuries (see Stiglmayer 1993: 161). Certainly the main reason why women do not resist more strenuously is that they fear they will get seriously injured or even killed. Only two men of both groups became less violent in response to the woman's resistance.

Some of the most serious injuries were inflicted on women who had been or were cohabiting. Val explained how she had had to have hospital treatment for concussion, a fractured cheekbone, black eyes and bruising She explained the assailant's response:

> When it ended he cried. He said sorry – and tried to make up. I felt physical pain, confusion. I didn't realize the severity of the event at the time, because I blocked it out. I looked more at the physical pain than the mental pain. I

thought the mental pain would go away, like the physical pain did, but it didn't. It never goes away.

More than half of the women in both groups resisted physically (61 per cent of strangers and 55 per cent of acquaintances) and roughly half tried to reason with the assailant. Sally had been thrown to the ground and, when the man kissed her, she bit his tongue:

One minute I was pressing the button for the lift and the next thing I was on the floor and he was on top of me. I bit him and he got off me and ran. It was not a conscious decision. I just did it. I was completely shocked as well. I couldn't breathe. I kept thinking I was going to throw up.

This case was classified by the police not as attempted rape but as indecent assault and the defendant was not caught.

Pat, who had gone back for coffee with an Old Etonian she had met in the pub, explained:

I cautioned him by saying, 'This is going to be rape if you continue.' Then I bit him on the chest deeply and screamed incredibly loudly. I was trying to get out of the front door and he was trying again to get my tights down, holding me against the wall. I was screaming and someone appeared at the top of the stairs. This startled him and I escaped.

He was acquitted when the case went to court.

Moira, aged nineteen, was less fortunate. She was raped by a fellow student she had spoken to but never been alone with. She described how he put his arm around her when they were in a group of friends and asked his friends to leave. He then put his hands round her neck and became agitated, angry and knocked her to the ground.

Initially I fought back, but I realized that he was determined and very strong and so I thought the only way to survive was to stop resisting and I lay still. I pleaded with him but he put his hand over my mouth.

After the rape, he threatened that he would kill her if she told anyone and instructed her to 'make sure she never had sex again'. He insulted her and laughed as she ran off.

American research suggests that physical resistance can be a very effective way of avoiding rape. Pauline Bart (in Klein and Steinberg 1989), when comparing rape-avoidance strategies, found that talking by itself was ineffective and pleading was associated with being raped. She found physically resisting by yelling or screaming and/or by fleeing were more successful strategies. Diana Scully (1990) too found that women who resist physically have a better chance of avoiding rape than those who do not. In her research, injuries were similar among women who resisted and those who did not. In addition, she found that the more different strategies the woman used, the more likely she was to avoid rape. Women who avoided rape focused more on not being raped, while those who were raped focused more on not being mutilated or killed. Women who had attended self-defence courses and who exercised regularly were more likely to avoid rape. Mary Koss, an American researcher, also compared the reactions of women raped by strangers and acquaintances, and found few significant differences in their use and strategies of resistance (Koss 1988). Over half used such strategies as turning cold, reasoning or pleading, crying or sobbing, running away and physically struggling.

None of this should detract from the importance of where the rape takes place. Most rapes occur in circumstances where it is very difficult for the woman to resist. In gang rapes it is impossible, yet complainants are still asked why they did not fight back. Women do get killed by rapists – we do not know how many women have been killed resisting It is impossible to make generalizations about when and how to resist (see Kelly 1988). Women's experiences of rape and perceived sexual danger are widespread and consequently women's precautions do not guarantee protection (see Stanko 1990).

In our study the physical pressure used to force the victim to have sex was roughly equivalent in rape by strangers and by acquaintances. Seventy-one per cent of stranger rapists used physical violence, as against 67 per cent of acquaintance rapists. But while extreme physical violence was used in only a small minority of rapes (most women were too terrified to resist), acquaintance rapists were slightly more likely to injure their victims. Twenty-one per cent of acquaintance rapists beat, punched or kicked the woman as against 9 per cent for stranger rapists. Eleven per cent of women raped by acquaintances were harmed with a weapon, as against g per cent for strangers. Eleven per cent had serious cuts and wounds after acquaintance rape, as against 7 per cent for stranger rapists.

The gravity of a rape should not be judged solely by the injuries sustained by the woman. Most men who raped acquaintances did not need to use violence, because the threat was sufficient. Here is one woman's account of a rape by someone she knew:

He got a kettle of boiling water and threatened to throw it over me if I didn't get undressed. He also picked up a knife and threatened to cut me He told me to lie down and put the knife at the opening of my vagina and threatened to put it up if I resisted.

Other men used a more subtle approach. One secured the compliance of his terrified victim by threatening to rape her in front of her children if she resisted. This woman had no physical injuries and her assailant, a casual acquaintance, was later acquitted in court. The same man, reported for rape by seven different women, has never been convicted (see Chapter 6).

Women raped by acquaintances were more likely to suffer violent sexual acts. As well as being raped, 24 per cent of women were buggered by their assailants. Sixty per cent of these were acquaintances. Unreported acquaintance rapes were just as violent as reported cases, but here the class of the assailant was significant. Professional men formed 11 per cent of assailants in the sample. Yet not one of these rapes was reported to the police. Therefore, acquaintance rapes are less likely to be reported. The myth that it is only strangers who rape was expressed by Shareen, who said:

I thought rape was something that strangers did. I thought rape was something that men jumped out at you and they did in secret. I didn't realize they'd do it openly. I didn't realize that a man could be so confident about

Women's Experiences in Court

Of the thirty-nine women who reported to the police, twenty-one (54 per cent) came to trial. Home Office statistics for 1991 give a percentage of 31 per cent of reported rapes which end up in the high court. The higher than average number in our sample may be due to the fact that the women who were prepared to fill in our lengthy questionnaire were both able to talk about their experiences and had the motivation to contribute to, hopefully, changing the system. The other eighteen cases in our sample 'dropped out' of the judicial system for a number of reasons. Some women were not prepared to testify in court and others dropped their charges, but in the majority of cases the police and the CPS decided not to proceed. In two cases, the women withdrew their complaints before the cases came to court. In one case, she could not face standing up in court and going into detail about the rape, and in the other the police decided to give the man, an ex-boyfriend who had broken into her home, a caution.

Fifteen cases did not go to trial, although the women were prepared to testify. The respondents believed there were three main reasons: inability of the police to identify a suspect (three cases of stranger rape); the police not believing the women (two cases of acquaintance rape; in one, where the man was an acquaintance of less than twenty-four hours, the police encouraged the woman to drop the complaint); and – most frequent – the police/CPS having insufficient evidence against the man to prove guilt (three cases of stranger rape and five of acquaintance rape). In two cases, the women had no idea why the cases were not proceeded with. Of the twenty-one cases that did go to trial, four were stranger rapes and seventeen were acquaintance rapes (six of the latter were by men met within twenty-four hours, nine were by general acquaintances and two were by intimates – men with whom the women had had consensual sex at some time in the past). While all the stranger rapists were found guilty, only one in three of the acquaintance rapists was convicted.[13] This conforms with the court research, which will be described in Chapters 4 and 5.

The majority of women found their experiences in court humiliating and distressing A very common complaint by women was that they were not allowed to explain fully what had happened to them, or how they *felt* during the rape. In court, most women were confined to answering questions briefly, and often to simply answering yes or no. The large majority of women (72 per cent) complained of being treated unsympathetically and being asked irrelevant and unfair questions. Despite the existence of the Sexual Offences (Amendment) Act (1976), over half the women raped by acquaintances were asked about previous sex with men other than the defendant. Women were asked what they felt to be

13. Overall 48 per cent of the cases taken to court were found guilty. Of all acquaintances, 35 per cent.were found guilty.

inappropriate and irrelevant questions about their dress, behaviour and lifestyle. Indeed, the vast majority of women (83 per cent) felt as if they were on trial and not the defendant.

The effect of going through all the anxiety of taking the case to trial, being asked unnecessary and demeaning questions in court and then seeing your rapist walk free undoubtedly contributes to the difficulty of coming to terms with the rape. To not be believed by the jury is shattering and many women are too shocked to be able to talk about it. In the Islington project (see Appendix 2), the only women who were prepared to be interviewed after their cases had gone to trial were those who had seen their attacker convicted. Ten women who were not prepared to be interviewed wrote to say they found the situation too painful to speak about. Half of these had taken the case to court and the suspect had been found not guilty. The reasons they gave for not speaking to us are a moving testimony of the pain they had experienced and wanted so desperately to forget. It is significant that none of the defendants in these cases had been convicted and several cases had been 'no-crimed' – in other words, not recorded as offences. The following are typical of the replies:

I just try to forget what happened. (From a woman who had gone to court and the defendant, an acquaintance, had been found not guilty of rape and ABH)

I am just getting over the assault and do not wish to discuss the matter, because it is still painful to do so. (From a woman who was raped by her ex-boyfriend, who was found not guilty at the crown court)

I am finding it hard to cope and do not want to go through any questions that will remind me of what happened. I'm sorry. (From a victim of a case of attempted rape that had been 'no-crimed' on the grounds that the woman was a prostitute the police report reads, 'Prostitute agreed to have sex for £20, apparently changed her mind')

Because I would like to put the past behind me. (From a woman whose case of attempted rape was 'no-crimed')

Thank you for your concern, but I would like it if it was not brought up again. Many thanks again. (From a woman who was indecently assaulted but whose case was not taken to court because of 'insufficient evidence')

I do not want to take part. Bringing back memories, suffering shock, paranoia, nightmares. Although it might help me to get support, I'm surviving. (From a woman whose case went to court but the defendant was also found not guilty)

We can only guess at the pain and anguish and destroyed lives that lie behind the silence of the women who chose not to respond.

Finally, a poignant account is given by Helen, who was raped by one of the men whose cases we monitored at the Old Bailey. He was given bail at the magistrates court, even though he was awaiting trial for another retrial of a rape case (since the jury had been unable to decide). According to Helen, she was subjected to hours of horrifying and humiliating sexual acts. She ran naked into the street in an attempt to escape, but was dragged back into the flat. In an article for a newspaper she wrote:

The man was deranged and it was crucial to my ultimate survival that I engaged in his delusions and played along with the fantasy he had, which was that I was some kind of girlfriend to him and didn't really mind this inhuman domination and display of anger.

Despite her immediate reporting of the rapes and evidence of bruising, the man was again bailed. According to the police, who had opposed bail, he used his previous acquittals as evidence that he was innocent and was being victimized. He also argued that since he had always turned up for his trials before, it was safe to bail him. Helen was totally devastated.

I was chaotic for about a week. I fancied I'd seen him in Euston station. I was consumed by fear. I felt totally unsupported... Who is going to tell me why this man got bail? Why are men such as this allowed bail? Do the people who permit bail care so little about the welfare of women or understand so little about the nature of rape and the damage it wreaks on people's lives?

During the next months she learned that the man had been suspected of eleven similar attacks. The trial was delayed until October, although Helen was not informed why. By this time he had absconded again. Helen was appalled by the judicial process. She wrote:

Why did I go through what I did to enable his capture? Why did the police do all that work? Why did I submit to the indignities and the probing of the system as they photographed my naked and bruised body, combed my pubic hair and invaded my vagina with the tools of their investigation?

What in God's name is wrong with the system? Do you think for a minute that men would tolerate such ritualized dismantling of their sexuality if it was happening to them? How many of us are there? Eleven have reported but how many more, perhaps wiser than us and knowing the futility of the system, have kept their tragedy to themselves, not willing to be publicly judged as, at worst, a complete liar or, at best, a poor bewildered, confused woman. What kind of a legal system is this?"[14]

Conclusion

The survey discussed here represents one of the first accounts of British women's experiences of sexual assault and their descriptions of sexual attack. By distributing the questionnaires through Rape Crisis centres, student unions and counselling services, and by providing a help line, women felt sufficiently confident to contribute to this study. Some had never told anyone of the attack before and the majority had not reported the attacks to the police. It provides an invaluable insight into the trauma of sexual attack and the resilience of women in coping with the effects.

Each woman's testimony, her voice, her experience, her account of what happened, is from the start constricted and curtailed in the court process, as we shall see. In one rape trial I attended where the woman was explaining how she felt, the defence counsel successfully intervened with the words, 'I sympathize, your honour, but I fear this is becoming a speech' (see page 120). Instead of hearing about the assault and the effect it has had on her life, the ground rules are laid by the defence, whose task is to use every means available to discredit the complainant.

The women's voices heard here strongly contest the views that women are exaggerating the effects of sexual assault and that speaking out produces what Katie Roiphe calls a 'victim mentality'. She argued that by so exaggerating the threat of violence, activists have provoked unnecessary terror and have reawakened old stereotypes of bestial male predators and fragile female victims. She goes on to bemoan the fact that

in this era of 'Just Say No' and 'No Means No', we don't have many words for embracing experience. So instead of liberation and libido, the

14. 'Raped and the Real Ordeal Began', *Evening Stadard*, 9 December 1993.

emphasis is on trauma and disease. Now the idea of random encounters, of joyful, loveless sex, raises eyebrows. The possibility of adventure is clouded by the spectre of illness. It's a difficult backdrop for conducting one's youth (1993: 12)

She is right that it is a difficult world, where the threat of HIV has made sex a life-and-death issue. We would all prefer this not to be so and to be able to embrace love with the abandon that romantic fiction dictates. However, the world is just not that simple and we have a responsibility to prepare young women for the world as it regrettably is.

Blaming women for speaking out about male violence is a subtle way the 'backlash' against feminism works. As Faludi (1991) points out, women are blamed for the very problems that they face. Roiphe blames feminists not only for male violence but also for the problems of AIDS, which has indeed made the threat of disease an all too present risk of unprotected sex with 'random encounters'. Katie Roiphe needs a better grasp of history. She is right that the AIDS outbreak has made it a difficult backdrop for conducting one's youth, but blaming feminists is more than absurd; it is obscene. Her joyful world of loveless sex carries risks for men as well as for women, as the homosexual community has had to recognize and adapt to. But Katie Roiphe prefers to blame feminists, the very women who have given women the limited freedom they have today.

Women often blame themselves when raped and 'absorb within themselves the pain of violent, degrading and undermining assaults' (Hall 1985: 25). The survey results here contest the assumption often made that the high acquittal rate for acquaintance rape is because they are less serious, violent or traumatic than stranger rapes. Nor are unreported rapes necessarily less serious or violent than those reported, and acquaintance rapes are just as serious as stranger rapes. It is of grave concern that the vast majority of acquaintance rapists go free, and most are likely to go on to rape time and time again if left unpunished. Over half (55 per cent) of women who responded to the questionnaire believed that the man who raped them had previously raped other women. Thirty-two per cent of those actually knew of other women the man had raped. If women are to be protected from dangerous rapists, society and the law must recognize that most of the men who commit these horrifically violent crimes do not jump out from behind bushes or break into women's homes. While the present myths and stereotypes about rapists are perpetuated, the vast majority of men who rape will continue to go free to rape again and again.

The women who are brave enough to speak out about violence should perhaps not be named 'victims' but rather rebels who are unprepared to remain silent. By reporting assaults to the police, they become targets of punishment themselves for the transgression of speaking out. As bell hooks, an American feminist, argues:

Within patriarchal society, women who are victimized by male violence have had to pay a price for breaking the silence and naming the problem. They have had to be seen as fallen women, who have failed in their 'feminine' role to sensitize and civilize the beast in man (hooks 1989: 89).

The 'judicial' rape, where a woman's reputation is put on trial by the court, is, according to many victims, as humiliating as the actual rape. In some respects, it is worse – more deliberate and systematic, more subtle and dishonest, masquerading under the name of justice.

Chapter 2

Gang Rape: The Unreported Crime

A Croatian researcher, Slavenka Drakulic, interviewed a woman gang-raped by four men in Bosnia in 1993, and asked, 'Were they drunk? Did they look abnormal? How did they look?' She said, 'No. No. They were perfectly normal men. If you were to, meet them in the street, you wouldn't say they were rapists' (Bennett 1993).

Men who rape in war are ordinary Joes, made unordinary by entry into the most exclusive male-only club in the world. Victory in arms brings group power undreamed of in civilian life. Power for men alone (Brownmiller 1978: 32).

We think of rape as an individual not a group act. It is difficult to grasp its social dimension. We assume that, like sex, it takes place in private. It is difficult enough to face the idea of rape. To envisage gang rape is even harder. It is easier to ignore the distinction, to class it all as rape. Yet the historical origins of rape rest with the gang The Latin word from which rape derives means 'to seize or carry off'. In ancient times, warring tribes abducted women, who then became the spoils of war. Gang rape and rape in war reflect an extreme form of stereotyped 'macho' behaviour, which is associated with what Bob Connell, an Australian sociologist, has described as 'hegemonic' or the dominant form of masculinity (Connell 1990). By definition it occurs in all-male groups where extreme forms of macho behaviour are encouraged. In this chapter I examine the phenomena of gang and pair rape: their incidence, characteristics and relevance to war.

It is commonly believed that men who gang-rape must be pathological bullies, fiends or maniacs, and that gang rape is far less common than individual rape. The findings of research refute these assumptions. One of the first American researchers to analyse the characteristics of men reported to the police for rape found to his amazement that 43 per cent of the 1,292 men studied in Philadelphia operated in pairs or gangs (Amir 1971). This surprised him, as the psychiatric literature had painted a picture of the solitary psychopathological rapist. Contrary to past belief, his research revealed that 71 per cent of the rapes were planned, rather than being the spontaneous explosion of pent-up emotions. He suggested that the need for coordination meant that all the pair and gang rapes were planned. A victim had to be agreed on, a place where the rape could take place undisturbed located and avoidance of detection calculated. Other studies have supported the finding that gang and pair rapes are common. One American study found that 10 per cent of male students had attempted rape in episodes involving more than one attacker (see Warshaw 1988: 101, which is based on the 1982 survey in *Ms* magazine).

Gang or pair rape, rather than being pathological, appears to be more about an extreme form of normative.masculinity. It is in all male communities such as the army, adolescent gangs, prison, college fraternities in America and competitive team sports that gang rape generally occurs. In war, gang rape takes on an added dimension and can be an integral tactic of warfare. Whether in peace or war, its function is to enhance male solidarity and domination. It appears to involve a process by which men distance themselves from everything denoting femininity. Women, homosexuals or those seen to be un-macho are the targets. The sexual orientation of many men who rape men and the victims who are raped, contrary to common belief, is heterosexual rather than homosexual (see McMullen 1990: 123).

Gang or pair rape may be as common as individual rape. An American review on group rape suggested that approximately one-third of rapes reported to the police were by gangs (Rozee Koker and Polk 1986). It appears to occur particularly in adolescence, when young men are concerned with developing a 'masculine' identity. According to one researcher:

Boys gang-rape for each other, in a kind of frenzied machismo, to prove themselves, to show off, to be part of the gang, or at best out of fear to being ostracized if they don't (Benedict 1985).

In their interviews with convicted rapists in an American prison in Virginia, American researchers concluded that gang rapists were mostly in the late teens or early twenties when convicted and usually carefully planned their rapes. When they asked convicted rapists why they raped, power and domination were frequently mentioned as an explanation.

We felt powerful, we were in control. I wanted sex and there was peer pressure. She wasn't like a person, no personality, just domination on my part. Just to show I do do it – you know, macho (Scully and Marolla 1985).

Humiliating and defiling the woman appear to enhance male cohesion, a point made by Susan Brownmiller (1978), who also argues that male domination is strengthened by denigration and contempt for women. An Australian professor who studied gang rape suggested that the reason the gang defiled the female body in other appalling ways, often excretory, was in order to gain or maintain prestige within the group by over-emphasizing the values of toughness and disregard for femininity other than as a sexual tool (see Brownmiller 1978: 196).

More recent research into gang rape supports the view that gang rapes are characterized by a level of vilification often far greater than in rapes by a single man. The following characteristics have been found to be twice as likely to occur in gang than individual rape: insult, forced fellatio, pulling, biting and burning the breasts, urinating on the victim and putting semen on her body. An American researcher concluded:

As they participate in gang rape, they experience a special bonding with each other, a unity of purpose that comes from the pride they feel in reducing their victim to nothing more than a collective vessel for their masculinity. Through the rape they prove their sexual ability to group members and underscore their status. Often, the group's leader is the first man to rape the woman; his underlings then follow. Sometimes the woman may have had consensual sex with one member of the group and afterwards that man invites the others to take their turns (Warshaw 1988: 101).

The enhancement of male solidarity through such violence does raise the question of what constitutes and enhances male-bonding. A number of studies have indicated that men's friendships are generally less personal than women's (see Rubin 1983). Intimacy, the sharing of innermost thoughts and emotions, the main characteristic of female friendship, is not typical of male groups, where bonding is enhanced by posturing, competitiveness, toughness, jokes and risk-taking (see Rotundo 1989). Since one area of competitiveness is sexual, where to 'score' is a way to impress friends, this inevitably involves exploiting women. Emphasis on 'scoring' and objectifying women are forms of enhancing male power. Through rape, therefore, men can experience power, and avoid tenderness and intimacy, which often involve a conflict for men. Feelings of emotional dependence and vulnerability conflict with the way masculinity is constructed and make it hard for men to integrate sex with intimacy (see Giddens 1992). To be a man is to be hard and tough, with emotional involvement kept at bay.

There may be a particular need at present to enhance 'manhood', with rising male unemployment and women increasingly entering the workforce, albeit in low-paid, low-status jobs. Similarly, the development of all-male societies in the nineteenth century, such as fraternities, male clubs and lodges, could be seen as 'a defence against threatened manhood at a time when manhood was under assault due to industrial capitalism, the rise of female values and the cultural critique of masculinity' (Nardi 1992: 41). One of the main characteristics of such groups was to valorize 'all that was not female', which served to enhance male power.

Peggy Reeves Sanday, an American anthropologist who studied the cross-cultural incidence of rape in tribal societies, argues that rape is part of a cultural configuration that includes interpersonal violence, male dominance and sexual separation (Sanday 1981). She found great differences in the prevalence of male dominance in different tribal societies: roughly half tribal societies were rape-free, 18 per cent rape-prone and the others somewhere in between. In societies where food was scarce, migration and other factors contributed to feelings that the natural environment was out of control and humans were dependent on male efforts 'to control and harness destructive natural forces'. In other societies where nature was held to be sacred, male sexual aggression was very rare. Capitalist society, where the relations between men and women have undergone such a major transformation, male 'rights of ownership' are being gradually undermined and other sources of male identity, such as manual work, superseded, may have similar characteristics to Sanday's 'rape-prone' societies.

Brownmiller (1978: 90–91) also found that the prevalence of rape varied from one society to another and that rape-proneness is associated with the status of women. She found marked differences between the levels of rape among the Vietcong and American GIs in the Vietnam war. Her evidence suggests that rape was considered a serious crime among the Vietcong soldiers and it was seen as a serious political blunder to rape and loot. Women who were raped were considered to be heroines, examples of enemy atrocity. The taboo on rape among the Vietcong appeared to be associated with the high status of women, who were seen as equals in military operations. The presence of women in the military acted as a check on male violence.

Contradicting the assumption that gang rape is predominantly a lower-class phenomenon or part of the 'subculture of violence', in her study of fraternity gang rape Sanday (1990) describes how 'pulling train', the activity where a group of men line up like train cars to take turns having sex with the same woman, who is usually unconscious, is defined as normal and natural by some middle-class men on American university campuses. She explains this as a form of male-bonding which enhances male identity and dominance. She argues that in such gang rapes, the sexual act is not concerned with sexual gratification but with the deployment of the penis as a concrete symbol of masculine social power and dominance. Seduction means plying women with alcohol or giving them drugs in order to 'break down resistance'. A drunken woman is not defined as being in need of protection but as 'asking for it'. The brothers watch each other perform sexual acts and then brag about 'getting laid'. Female participants are degraded to the status of what the boys call 'red meat' or 'fish'. The woman whose body facilitates all of this is sloughed off at the end like a used condom. It is assumed that male sexuality is more natural and more explosive than female sexuality, and men are expected to find an outlet with male friends or with prostitutes. Men who do not join in or object to such behaviour run the risk of being labelled wimps or, worse still in their eyes, 'gays' or 'faggots'.

Sanday argues that participation in such behaviour is a way of legitimizing homosexual feelings otherwise outlawed by hetero-sexuality. Likewise, Enloe (1988) argues that in all-male institutions such as the army, gang rape can be seen as a form of control over homosexual feelings, which may be important for the cohesion of all-male groups but dangerous in terms of heterosexual identity. For men in the army to have close relationships with women weakens their loyalty and ties to the other men. Yet to develop too strong relationships with other men endangers their sexual identity. By participating in gang rape they enhance their solidarity with each other, but still confirm their heterosexual identity.

The men vent their interest in one another through the body of a woman. The fact that the woman is often unconscious highlights her status as a surrogate victim in a drama where the main agents are the males interacting with each other.

The victim embodies the sexual urges of the brothers; she is defined as 'wanting it' – even though she may be unconscious during the event – so that the men can satisfy their urges for one another at her expense. By defining the victim as 'wanting it' the men convince themselves of their heterosexual prowess and delude themselves as to the real object of their lust. If they were to admit the real object, they would give up their position in the male status hierarchy as superior, heterosexual males. The expulsion and degradation of the victim both brings a momentary end to urges that would divide the men and presents a social statement of phallic heterosexuality (Sanday 1990:13).

Another study of fraternities portrayed the vocabulary of this sexually aggressive culture. Recently arrived women are referred to as 'new meat' and invited to hogfests or cattle drives (both names for parties).

While fraternity brothers score, the women they score against, often called ho's (slang for 'whores') by the members are said to have gotten boned. At one Maine school, fraternity members participate in ledging: that's where, in the words of one woman graduate, 'a fraternity member invites all his brothers to watch his conquest of a naive freshman woman, and then she hears about it for months afterwards'. The name 'ledging' for this practice refers to the woman's being driven to the point of suicide by the harassment (Warshaw 1988:108 9).

Sanday (1990:14) argues that the most important social conditions promoting the act of 'pulling train' is the university's tendency to ignore or cover up reports of specific incidents. The lack of sanctions against abusive party sex helps to explain the high rate of sexual harassment reported on American campuses (Koss et al. 1987). Sanday (1990:126) also outlines how speaking out against date and gang rape leads to abuse, obscene telephone calls and death threats, which she argues 'are frightening because they demonstrate how far some men will go, at least in fantasy, to defend male privilege and power.

In another study of fraternity gang rape, O'Sullivan looked at group sexual assaults on American campuses and argues that male friendship involves competition and camaraderie. Since one area of competitiveness is sexual, where to 'score' is the way to impress your friends, this inevitably involves exploiting women. To be masculine in American society, she argues, involves independence from relationships, lack of sentimentality, sexual success (which can mean both having access to many women and making women engage in acts against their will), physical toughness and worldly success, measured in terms of dollars. She concludes:

Each of these elements of constructed masculinity has implications for a male's relationship with women. The requirement that a man be physically tough means tuning out his own pain, which weakens his capacity for empathy. Attachment to a woman can threaten his independence and produce accusations that a man is 'dominated' or 'pussy-whipped' by his mother, girlfriend or wife. A man's need to 'score' and to push women into sexual acts that earn masculinity credits objectifies women (O'Sullivan 1993: 27).

Taking Gang Rape to Trial

The very low rate of reporting such gang attacks makes it very hard to estimate their incidence. Occasionally women are courageous enough to report such horrendous ordeals to the police and give evidence in court. Even here gaining a conviction is by no means assured. In 1985 thirty men were arrested and thirteen paratroopers charged with raping a woman member of the Royal Army Corps (see Soothill and Walby 1991: 71). The twenty-two-year-old woman stated she had been stripped naked, held down, raped several times, abused and assaulted with a broom. The paratroopers claimed she had consented. She had been smuggled into the barracks and had spent the day drinking twelve pints of lager and cider. All the men were cleared of rape and it was the victim who was blamed for laying herself open to the attack and was pilloried in the press.'

A case heard in March 1994 at the Old Bailey did lead to convictions – but only after over five hours' deliberation by the jury, despite substantial corroborative evidence. To make matters worse,

1. For example, the headline in the *Daily Mirror*, 16 November 1985, was 'The Big Un's Sex Sessions'.

the woman's attackers demanded that she give evidence without the protection of a screen to shield her from them in court. The Recorder of London did not regard the case as being 'exceptional' the only circumstance in which a screen is allowed – in spite of evidence that she had been handcuffed, blindfolded and forced to have sex six times at knife-point by the three assailants. Her life was threatened as the men laughed and joked, ignoring her pretence to have AIDS. Her ordeal had lasted over two hours. The handcuffs had been found in the flat, the police had tape-recorded the young woman's immediate distress call to the police, which was played in court, and the youngest of the men had made a statement implying that he had forced her to have sex with him, yet even here the jury deliberated for five hours. They were clearly having difficulty reaching a decision when one of the jurors requested that they should hear the recording of the victim reporting the case to the police, which had been played at the start of the trial. The jury were brought back into court and, after listening to her distraught voice, immediately reached a majority decision and the men were convicted. This illustrates how easy it is for jurors to forget the impact of evidence heard early in the trial. Another,important factor which may well have influenced the jury's decision was that the woman showed great bravery in sitting on her own in court throughout the whole trial after she had given her evidence.2

Survey Accounts and Press Reports of Gang Rape

In Britain, gang rape has not previously been investigated. The significant proportion of gang or pair rapes was one extraordinary finding of the questionnaire research. Fourteen of the women who replied to the questionnaire had been raped by more than one assailant and in addition one had suffered a gang/pair rape attempt. On the basis of an analysis of these fifteen cases of gang rape, four categories emerged: the blitz planned stranger pair/gang rape; the abduction gang rape; the date gang rape; and the opportunist gang rape. These categories overlap: for example, an abduction rape could be said to be opportunistic, although very often such rapes are, I would argue, likely to be planned.

2. The rapists were all given between six and eight years' imprisonment.

Stranger Gang Rape

A nineteen-year-old young woman from Scotland had never told anyone before about her experience of being raped by strangers two years previously. 'Nobody knows,' she wrote, I do not know how or where she obtained the questionnaire. She gave no name or address. She wrote:

I was walking home past an old railway building. As I got past the entrance I felt a sudden hand grab my arm and pull me into the building. He pinned me against the wall and another man grabbed a plank of wood and wedged it between my feet so my legs were apart. The third man then put a rag over my mouth. One man smiled at me and stroked my hair. Then as he held a knife at my cheek, he said in a very nonchalant tone, 'A young lass like you should not go out alone at night. It's dangerous.'

He then laughed very creepily. The men held her down and removed her clothes. One man sucked her breasts, while another had intercourse with her. They then swapped round and the other two had intercourse. They rubbed their penises against her and then pushed her out of the door. She described the devastating effect it had had on her, how isolated she feels and how she has not been able to tell anyone:

I couldn't stop crying but no tears came. I didn't feel angry but guilty, but I didn't know why. I got straight into the bath and scrubbed myself, and I was sick a couple of times.

She was too frightened to report it, as the rapists said the police would say she was asking for it.

I haven't told anyone before now. I still have nightmares over it and I won't go out at night alone now. Sometimes I can't bear to be touched and I feel all dirty, so I get a scrub and shower. I feel very isolated.

What an indictment of our society that this young woman should feel that she is to blame after such an appalling attack.

A woman who did report her rape to the police had been raped by two men, one of them John Duffy, who in January 1988 was charged at the Old Bailey with murdering three women and raping seven others. This attack was a stereotypical violent attack at knifepoint. The woman was robbed first and her life threatened. One of the men alternated between using obscene language and saying affectionate things such as 'I love you.' Fortunately, they left when interrupted. She described what happened:

I was pushed down an alley at knife-point. I was robbed first. The contact was basic, 'Give us your money, give us your jewellery. Right, get your knickers off.' One said to his friend, 'She's enjoying it', because I gasped when being entered. He seemed to have trouble coming and excited himself by talking about my beautiful bum. He didn't know whether to come in my face or my bum. His friend was anxious and hurried him up. We stood at the alley entrance and he lit a cigarette for him and me and then said, 'You go that way'. I ran off and they headed in the opposite direction.

The two men were very different. One was cold, anxious and indifferent. The other (the one I have described) was almost embarrassed. He was the one who went on to murder three women. It was clear to me he was the one capable of it.

She described the effect it had had on her life:

I have gone through years of emotional changes. My lifestyle was changed in that I didn't speak to people or go out on my own. I am careful with myself. Emotionally I was terrified and quite unstable. I thought people might kill me.

Her description illustrates three typical characteristics of gang rape: they have usually been carefully planned or at least premeditated; the men's behaviour suddenly changes and they start to treat the woman as an object; and finally the men seem to regard rape as a perfectly natural way to behave. It is common for gang members to legitimize rape by painting the victim as a nymphomaniac or 'really wanting it'. The rapists may refer to the rape as 'a gang bang' and boast about it later to their friends.

Contrary to the typical stereotype of the gang or pair rape, eleven of the fifteen already knew or had had contact with the men prior to the assault. The typical gang or pair rape is therefore committed by acquaintances or men known to the victim rather than by strangers. A recent Home Office stud, in comparing gang and single offenders convicted of rape, found that most of the gang or pair rapes (63 per cent) that reached court were by men known to the victim (Lloyd and Walmsley 1989). Just over a third were gang-raped by strangers (37 per cent), and two-thirds by acquaintances or intimates. Eighteen per cent of the men had gang-

or pair-raped women with whom they had previously had a sexual relationship. Taking into consideration that stranger gang rapes are far more likely to be reported, it would seem that acquaintance gang rapes are even more common than those figures reflect.

In December 1993, while my research was progressing, *The Times* reported that a crowd of youths cheered while two schoolgirls were gang-raped in an alley in south-east London. The girls, aged fourteen and fifteen, were surrounded by a gang of about twenty-five youths and raped or indecently assaulted by about six of them. Detective Inspector Philip Kent, who headed the inquiry, said that some of the youths were as young as fifteen. The girls did not know their attackers, but recognized them as local. *The Times* reported:

The girls' fifteen-minute ordeal began after they were approached by about four young men as they entered a McDonald's restaurant at Catford on Wednesday and were frogmarched to an alley at the back of a nearby pub. It is an absolutely dreadful attack. The sheer numbers involved are extraordinary. It seems there were about 25 involved in the actual attack. I think most of them were there as spectators or keeping watch. It happened in a busy road and there must have been people who saw the girls approached by the youths.

In the US two gang rapes obtained worldwide publicity in the 1980S and illustrate the ambivalence with which gang rape is regarded. In 1983 six men from the Portuguese community were charged with aggravated gang rape. They had taken turns sexually assaulting a young woman on a pool table in Big Dan's Tavern, New Bedford, Massachusetts. No one had come to her help. A candlelit vigil attended by more than 2,500 was held and money was donated to set up a Rape Crisis centre. Yet after the conviction of four of the defendants, the tide of sympathy turned from the victim to the perpetrators and a much larger demonstration of between 10,000 and 15,000 marched in solidarity with the accused to protest at their convictions. Many of these argued that the woman was 'no victim but an active and culpable participant' (Koss and Harvey 1991: 90). This became the basis for the film The Accused, starring Jodie Foster, which became a box-office success both in the US and in Britain. The moral outrage this case caused led to a change in the law in Massachusetts, making it possible now to charge bystanders who encourage participants with criminal behaviour.

The other case in 1989 where a gang of teenagers also went 'wilding', the name given to violent revelry, and raped a middle-class jogger in New York's Central Park in broad daylight served as what The Times referred to as 'a symbol of American moral failure' (see Bremner 1989). The 'wolfpack' of boys, all under the age of seventeen, brutalized the jogger, aged twenty-eight, leaving her in a coma with permanent brain damage caused by multiple and severe injuries and then joked to the police about the 'fun' they had had. Contrary to expectation, the young boys were not drug-taking thugs but came from relatively well-off, stable homes. The indifference displayed by parents was another puzzling feature. The police said that none inquired about the state of the victim and one asked if her son could go home because 'he only held the girl's legs'. To add insult to injury, after the horrendous ordeal of giving evidence in court, the victim was faced with spectator calls of 'The boyfriend did it; the boyfriend did it' as she left the court (Koss and Harvey 1991: 91).

Such assaults are rarely reported. Jean, one of the respondents, described how she had been raped when she was nineteen, ten years previously, by two men whom she knew by sight. They had clearly planned the assault. She was terrified they would return.

The two men followed me and then walked by and said, 'Hello.' They went past, then stopped and as I went past, one man grabbed my arm. He said to his friend, 'You hold her – I'll fuck her.' He raped me, then put his penis in my mouth while his friend buggered me. Then he said, 'I'll make you enjoy this', and he raped me with a knife. They didn't talk much. After he used the knife on me, he urinated on me and then told me to fuck off and if I told anyone he would kill me. I ran and locked myself in.

The effects of Gang Rape

The effects of group rape have been found to be even more traumatic than individual rape. Group sexual-assault victims are more likely to have contemplated suicide and to have sought therapy (see Gidycz and Koss 1990). Jean describes how the after-effects had lasted for many years after the assault.

I have no confidence. I am still [aged twenty-nine] in counselling. I have never worked since. I can't sit next to a man on a bus. I have anorexia. I have tried to kill myself at least fifteen times. I now have black-outs and am always depressed. This has ruined my life. I will never marry. I do not trust men. I had a good job before this happened. I have no confidence. It has also ruined my mum's life.

Different tactics are used to isolate women. Sometimes the victim is abducted in a car and driven off and raped at a different location. She may be kept in captivity (that is, kidnapped). She could be hitchhiking, or could be offered a lift or persuaded to get into the car on some pretext. Or one of the men could pick up the woman and take her to a prearranged place, where he would be joined by others. One young man revealed that this was so common that a friend of his had rented a house for the purpose. The rape was seen as justified because 'usually the girl had a bad reputation, or we knew it was what she liked' (Scully 1990). Lastly, there is the opportunistic gang rape, where a woman just turns up at the wrong time, when rapists have planned to rape any woman they can isolate, or where, though the men may not have premeditated the rape, a situation arises which they can exploit – say, for example, burglars coming across a woman in the course of breaking into a house.

Gang rapes can also be differentiated according to the relationship between the assailants and the victim, whether they are strangers, acquaintances or past or present lovers (intimates). The stereotypical rape is, of course, the stranger gang rape, but this is unlikely to be the most common, although it may well be the most often reported. Out of the fifteen cases in my research, only four were gang rapes by strangers, three of which were reported. In addition to making use of three categories of gang or pair rapes similar to those used by Scully and Marolla (1985), I have also differentiated a group of gang rapes perpetrated by relatives or lovers, although these could be categorized under the opportunistic category. Clearly the opportunities are endless in the privacy of the home.

Gang Rapes by Acquaintances and Intimates

It is important to be clear that in talking about 'gang date rape', this refers to the way the woman is abducted from a date, not that she agrees to have a date with more than one man at a time. A typical date gang rape was described by Sandra, aged nineteen, who went to her local pub and started chatting to two men. She accepted a drink from one of them and arranged to see him again.

We met a second tune, for a date, in a pub. We got on well and he seemed

OK. He offered to take me home. Then in the car, he took me to his home for coffee. When inside I met his two friends and the attack took place ten to fifteen minutes later.

He became aggressive and didn't listen to me. I can't remember words, only the feelings and the tension in the room. He said, 'Do what I say or else.' I tried to reason with him by saying I had a period and VD. He didn't believe me. I stopped struggling when it became obvious that I would be hurt if I didn't. Then I let them do what they wanted. When it was happening I don't remember what was said. I became very passive. It went on for some while, but I can't remember how long.

They laughed and joked with each other. They told me that no one would believe I didn't want to have sex. I can't remember what else was said. I left when they got tired of what they were doing, and let me get dressed. I walked home, five miles away. I didn't talk to anyone and tried to stop thinking about it. I was too young to realize exactly what had happened. I felt very guilty for getting myself into that situation. I became quiet, withdrawn, over-emotional, distrustful.

Several women pointed to the way the men had laughed and joked with each other, treating them as objects to be denigrated and defiled. They had the impression that this bound the men together, enhancing their solidarity with each other.

Marion, who now works as an administrator, explained how when she was seventeen her boyfriend of the time, with whom she had previously had a sexual relationship, had arranged to take her out for the day to a country pub. She was surprised when he had arrived with his stepbrother, whose wife was pregnant, in tow. She thought it strange that he had not invited his wife, but did not say anything and relaxed when everything was as usual, joking and laughing. Then suddenly the car stopped in the middle of nowhere and the men both began to behave oddly. They ordered her to lie on the grass and take her clothes off. She was too scared to struggle. She felt she had brought it on herself by being too trusting. Her 'boyfriend' had obviously planned it all. She felt the worst aspect was that the man she had previously had sex with had obviously planned the attack. She was horrified at being raped by his brother-in-law and shouted at them that they were disgusting. She accused them of rape, but this did not stop them. Nor did threatening to tell his wife and her boyfriend's mother stop them. They drove home without a word. She described the effect it had on her:

I never got over it completely, but I only really let myself think about it about a year ago when the trial of that boxer [Mike Tyson] raping the beauty queen came up. It was only then that I realized that there were two incidents in my life that I'd more or less blacked out which were in fact rapes. I have problems relating sexually to men that I trust (i.e. my husband). I'm only now examining my feelings about these incidents and feel very conscious of a change in myself. I'm beginning to feel stronger but know that I can't maintain a regular relationship, although I seem to be able to handle the idea of sexual encounters where I don't have to trust or give emotionally to the man.

She attributed the irretrievable breakdown of her later marriage to another man to the rape.

Joanna, another respondent, described what had happened when she went out with a group of four 'friends', two girls and two boys, when she was seventeen:

We were walking home as a group of four, then my friend left as we got to her house. The two boys I was with suggested taking a short cut, so I agreed, because it was cold. We just talked about the film and the boy I was with was being quite friendly. Then in some way something changed about him, the look on his face and the way he looked at me. He pushed me on to a wall in the stairwell of a block of flats. Then they dragged me into some nearby flats and assaulted me.

I couldn't move and he began to undo my trousers while the other one was telling me to shut up and stay still and then nothing would happen to me. He pulled my trousers and underwear off and took my top off. Then he took his trousers off and forced me to have sex. Then the other one did the same. I couldn't move and couldn't stop them. I can remember hearing footsteps, then I think they panicked and he said, 'Let's get out of here', and they both ran off and left me.

She did not report it as 'it was my word against two others" and she was also threatened by the boy and his friends. The level of intimidation is very underestimated in such cases. As Brownmiller (1978) states:

When men rape in pairs or gangs, the sheer physical advantage of their position is clear-cut and unquestionable. No simple conquest of man over woman, group rape is the conquest of men over 'Woman'.

Joanna described the effect it had had on her:

I blotted it out for a while, then seven months later I lost my voice. I didn't think this was connected, but I realize that it was now.

Abduction / Kidnap Gang Rape

Abduction gang rape can occur when the woman is hitchhiking, but also when men are driving around and snatch a woman from the street. When travelling through the Alps hitchhiking with a friend in my late teens, we were stranded in the mountains and accepted a lift from two men, which under normal circumstances we avoided doing. My Italian was good enough to understand their conversation, which was taking an ugly turn, so my friend, a drama student at the time, put on an excellent performance of being sick, causing them to stop and let us out on the main road. Carol, who filled in one of our questionnaires, was not so lucky.

I was hitchhiking with another friend of mine. It was almost dark; the car with two men stopped. We talked in the car. They seemed very nice. They invited us for a drink for a short time. They were very kind, very normal, not aggressive, not ugly, polite, about thirty years old. Then they took another road, wrong direction. After five-ten minutes we were in the forest or park. It was dark, no light nowhere. I started to talk with them. They didn't want to talk any more. They stopped talking in English. They gave me Spanish answers as though they didn't understand what I wanted to tell them. Then they raped me. I had to get into the car again. They drove me back to the road, left me in the middle of nowhere, friendly, saying goodbye, wanting to shake hands. The men took rape as something normal. We should be friends. Before I didn't believe that this could happen to me. I experienced a complete split between my body and mind.

In two of the gang rapes the assailants were friends of the woman's boyfriend. In the following case Myra, a young woman aged seventeen, had been going out with a young man whose friends had forced her back to their fiat and raped her. Her boyfriend was not involved. Myra was sure the gang had done it before, possibly frequently. They appeared to be highly confident and experienced. She explained what had happened:

I was at the sports club. The man said that my boyfriend of the time was outside and wanted to talk to me. Once I was outside the building I was surrounded by all four men and physically abducted. This was when I realized that I was going to be raped. They tried to persuade me that there was nothing wrong with the situation. I struggled quite hard and hit the bloke who raped me first. Their tone and attitude were persuasive, authoritative and patronizing. At first I couldn't quite believe it was happening. Then I struggled to avoid it, reasoned with the first man, went numb and stopped resisting. The worst shock was when I realized they all intended to rape me. I felt stunned. I was in a state of shock.

The first man removed my shoes and trousers. He attempted to arouse me by licking my breasts and then he raped me. All four men raped me in turn – one of them spied through the door while his friend was raping me. He said that if I resisted he might have to hurt me. I was released. They took me out of the flat. In the lift one of them told me not to go to the police or tell anyone else. They then let me go.

Later I quickly went home and had a bath because I had to go and pick up a friend's child from nursery. I simply couldn't take it in.

Myra, in looking back on gang rape, thought she had been very naïve, but she could hardly have anticipated what would happen. It is difficult for women to appreciate that they are at risk of such horrific attacks, and it is all too common for women to blame themselves when they do occur.

Opportunistic Gang Rape

Even the protection of a decent boyfriend does not always prevent pair rape. One young woman, Barbara, was raped while on holiday with her boyfriend in Majorca. She described what happened:

I was lying with my boyfriend on a sunbed on a beach after the disco. One man came up to us. My boyfriend got up and the man pointed at me. I realized something was wrong and ran – straight into another man, who was waiting. He put his hand around my throat, squeezed till I blacked out. They threw me on the sand. He was very strong. He pinned me to the ground with one hand around my throat, the other poised, with his fist as if going to punch me in the face. When I started shouting he said, 'Shut up or I will kill you.' He was very strong. Once I realized their intention I became very calm, almost detached from myself I kept very still in the hope that they would do what they wanted and leave me alive.

One man had sex with me. The other man watched and then had oral sex with me. I used my teeth and he stopped. Then the other man buggered me. Then one man had intercourse until he came. Then the other man did.

I just lay there, but the second man couldn't come, so I moved my hips just to get rid of him. They laughed and joked.

Once the man had come I hoped he wouldn't kill me, so I lay there still with my T-shirt over my face so I wouldn't recognize them. He said, 'Don't move', and soon after I realized I was on my own. I sat up and saw him running away. I pulled my clothes on and went back to my hotel. After I felt relieved. I looked for my boyfriend but he had gone. I pulled my clothes on and walked, ran back to my hotel to my room-mate, and cried and cried. We went down to the foyer and saw the manager. I was hysterical and kept asking, 'Why?'

She identified the men and found out that they were married with children. The trial did not come up until a year later and she could not face going through with it. The rape had an appalling effect on her:

I lived on my own but had to have my brother sleep over for four months afterwards. I was more concerned with other people's feelings than mine. I cracked after six weeks and saw a psychiatrist. I also rang a Rape Crisis line. I suffered guilt because I didn't put up more of a fight but there were two of them and they were extremely strong, as they were roustabouts at a circus.

In only one case was the victim drunk when raped. Aged fifteen, she was on holiday from boarding school and got drunk with some friends, whom she did not know well. She was sure one of them had planned it.

I don't know if he planned it because there were a few of my friends there. I got very drunk and had a spliff and passed out. I annoyed him. I remember coming round and him having sex with me in a shed.

As I was very drunk and out of it, I don't recall too much. It was violent rough sex as I passed out and was on my back while he was laying on top of me penetrating me. I passed out only to find a second man on me penetrating me and then he moved down and had oral sex. I passed out again. I came round alone in the shed. I pulled my clothes on. The men were in the garden and showed no sign anything took place. It was all very nightmarish. I know I was raped.

Probably the least reported are where the woman has previously had sex with the assailant or where they are relatives. Diana, a woman in her thirties, had been raped on three occasions by her brother-in-law, a high-ranking policeman. She described how she was visiting her sister at the time and had stayed overnight. She was sleeping in the guest room, next door to her sister and brother-in-law. She explained what happened:

I was asleep and was awoken with the sheets off. He was raping me. I was shocked. After ejaculating, he tried to force his penis into my mouth. He made no comment. I remained in bed some minutes, not believing what had happened. I went to the bathroom and vomited. I felt guilty, dirty, ashamed and scared.

Then some time later, her brother-in-law turned up at her house with a colleague. They had both been drinking and appeared to be conspiring. Both raped and buggered her. Her brother-in-law had thrust money into her bag but she had thrown it back at him. She had not reported it to the police because 'they were the police'.

I am afraid other people will find out. The man knows me and I'm afraid he'll come back. The police will not take me seriously. They will not believe me. I am not prepared to testify against a relative.

She was afraid of hurting her sister and her parents. However, on the third occasion, nine months later, her brother-in-law again brought the same colleague home and they both raped and buggered her. This time they had left her bleeding After this, Diana had driven to a police station out of the area and had reported the rape, although she had made it clear that she did not want to take it to court. She said this same man, a high-ranking police officer, had set up courses about how to treat sexual assault complainants. Hypocrisy has no bounds.

Only four out of fifteen gang/pair rape cases were reported to the police. In only one case was the defendant convicted and even then the conviction was not for the rape reported here. This was the case of Duffy, who was also charged with killing three women and numerous rapes. His companion was never brought to trial. In one of the four reported cases no suspect was identified. The two other cases did reach court. One took place in Majorca but was delayed for thirteen months, by which time the woman could not face going ahead with the trial. In the second case the assailants were acquitted.

Reporting Gang Rape

A shocking finding of my analysis of gang/pair rapes was how few were reported. The women did not think they would be believed. Only four of the gang or pair rapes were reported. Of those reported three out of the four were raped by stranger gangs or pairs. Only one of the ten women who had been raped by more than one man with whom they had had some prior acquaintance had reported the rapes to the police. In this case the defendants were acquitted.

No wonder many women do not think it is worth challenging the threat of intimidation to report such attacks. We do not know whether the rate of reporting is lower than for single rapes but there are three reasons why women may be even more reluctant to report gangs. First, the appalling degradation which women suffer as a result of such attacks makes it hard for them to tell anyone. Reporting to the police and being subjected to a medical examination may be out of the question. The feelings of degradation result not only from the appalling callousness of the way they have been treated but also from the implication that a woman who has been raped is 'defiled' or a 'bad woman'. She is so. often blamed for failing to take precautions against rape that she ends up blaming herself. Second, in view of the sheer numbers involved, fear of further attacks or reprisals must be a paramount consideration when so many of the assailants are acquaintances. These men often know all about the woman – her name, where she lives and where she works. This implies that the incidence is far higher than commonly imagined. Third, the idea of testifying in court against two or more men who are likely to corroborate each other's stories may appear too daunting. The gang will stick to the story that the woman wanted it and support each other should the case reach court.

An American researcher who interviewed convicted rapists found that gang rapes in her study were particularly brutal and violent, frequently leading to serious physical injury, or even death of the victims. She concluded:

It is frightening to imagine the number of high-school age hitchhike-abduction and 'gang date' rapes that are never reported or, if reported, are not processed because of the tendency to disbelieve the victims of such rapes unless extensive injury accompanies them. The male 'recreational' attack on girls and women is chilling indeed (Scully 1990: 157).

One young man she interviewed confessed to participating in twenty to thirty gang 'date' rapes: that is, where one man had originally made 'the date'.

Even when women do report gang rape there is no certainty that the rapists will be prosecuted, as occurred in the infamous 1982 Glasgow rape case, where a woman was appallingly razor-slashed within an inch of her life and yet the police did not prosecute and the case came to trial only due to the perseverance of two journalists.[3]

Witnesses usually need persuasion to testify. In October 1993, Jill Cook, aged twenty-four, from Dunfermline in Fife, said she was extremely bitter about the way she had been let down by the judicial system. The three men accused of raping her walked free after the prosecution decided not to proceed with the case on a technicality after one of the participants to the gang rape, who had agreed to testify, failed to appear.[4] She said only a criminal trial would justify the humiliation of a thorough medical examination in front of three strangers and the investigation of her life by an assortment of professionals.[5] Since the alleged rape, she had moved home and has seen a doctor to combat depression.

There is a narrow line between actual engagement in gang rape and collusion with rape by egging others on to sexual exploits, disregarding or dispensing with female consent. An example of this is the case of Constable Waters, a twenty-year-old policewoman of four years' standing, who wrote a harrowing account of how she had been raped by a colleague.[6] She later discovered he had accepted a bet over a bottle of Scotch from other policemen working in the same station that he could not 'have' her. Her assailant had then come to her police quarters saying he had

3. The prosecution argued mistakenly that the victim was too traumatized. This case led to the resignation of Nicholas Fairbairn as Scotland's Solicitor-General. The successful prosecution that followed made legal history, and Joseph Sweeney was eventually jailed for twelve years for the crime.

4. The trial was held on the second to last day before the time limit for the case ran out, Lord Clyde refused to grant an extension and the case was abandoned. In Scotland, criminal proceedings must be brought within 365 days from the date of an accused person's release on bail, unless there are exceptional circumstances that justify an extension.

5. *Scotsman*, 1 October 1993.

6. 'A Cry of Rape within the Ranks', *Guardian*, 6 February 1993.

forgotten his key. The connivance of the whole force in silencing her complaint laid bare the hypocrisy of the police force. When she reported the assault to her superiors, she was met with blanket disbelief and it was she who faced a disciplinary allegation against her as a result of her complaint. She was given a career check and transferred to another station. She insisted on an industrial tribunal (in August 1992), where a technicality of the alleged assailant not being on duty that day led to the dismissal of her complaint.

Alison Halford, the Merseyside Assistant Chief Constable, who complained of sex discrimination and retired from the police after serving for thirty years, commented:

Do we have to wait for the murder of a woman officer; a macho, late-night drinking session that turns into a controlled, legless orgy when the gangbangers leave a female officer dead among the debris and the drunks? How would the Complaints Investigation Bureau sort out that little mess, I wonder? The stakes would be higher than the bottle of Scotch on offer for the Waters challengers.[7]

She lamented the collective failure of the Met's senior officers to ensure that Waters was supported in even the smallest measure, which 'had brought still lower what used to be the greatest force in the world'.[8]

Rape and War

Rape and war have much in common. Both involve the fight for domination – in rape of a woman and in war of an 'enemy'. If successful, both involve the humiliation of the object of 'conquest'. This sometimes involves male gang rape. Invading armies traditionally raped the conquered army, denuding them of power (see Seabrook 1990). Boasting about military conquests and daring deeds has much in common with the way some men, particularly adolescent boys, boast about how many girls they have 'laid'. Boys 'mouth' or make up stories of sexual conquests; they boast about

7. Alison Halford, 'The Met That Dare Not Speak Its Shame', *Guardian*, 9 February 1993.

8. Women make up under 14 per cent of the British police force. In February 1993, a report published the findings of a study of sex discrimination in the police based on the views of 1,800 policewomen. Six per cent reported sexual attack and 30 per cent had been punched or touched.

their prowess, their bravery, in a similar way to soldiers boasting about their military exploits – boys with their toys, toys that can be lethal. A young, unemployed British teenager on his way to become a mercenary in the war in Serbia, for a pittance, when interviewed on TV, said he wanted to find out what it was like to kill as many people as the Yorkshire Ripper, only legitimately.[9] Films and videos encourage this macho form of masculinity. The language of sex reflects the language of war. We draw analogies between the conquering of land and of women, of the rape of the countryside and of women.

Rape in war occurs most frequently when victorious armies march through conquered territories. It is one of the 'spoils' of war. Women who are raped also have their reputations 'spoiled'. Rape is used as a weapon to demoralize or destroy family or community honour. Men who had raped and killed women in the Vietnam war were called 'double veterans'.[10] Soldiers abused women's bodies as a way of humiliating the enemy and dealing with their own frustrations. Enloe (1988: 35) outlines the horror of rape atrocities, where pubescent girls were ruthlessly gang-raped at gunpoint, and attributes their common occurrence in war to the exclusiveness of all-male communities, where men are expected to conform to standards of male behaviour twenty-four hours a day, where the world outside is viewed as chaotic and in need of control. The need to maintain solidarity is crucial during war and gang rape can be a tool to reinforce this. The perpetrators hardly perceive their victims as concrete people and are unable to describe them afterwards unless they knew them beforehand (see Seifert 1993).

Susan Brownmiller (1978) charts the appalling history of rape in war, in pogroms and in slavery throughout history, arguing that rape is a violent rather than a sexual act and is 'nothing more nor less than a conscious process of intimidation by which all men keep women in a state of fear'. She indicates that gang rape is a normal rather than an abnormal aspect of war, yet until recently it has been almost completely hidden (see Introduction on rape in war).In Australia ample evidence exists of gang rape of convicts and aboriginal women in the early days of colonial settlement

---

9. See Channel 4 *Inside Story*, 'Dogs Of War', 20 May 1992.
10. US veteran, quoted in Mark Baker, Nam, London, Sphere, 1982, pp. 208–9.

(Carmody 1992) and in America the same was true for women slaves on the plantations. A recent study of rape in the Australian aboriginal community (Arkinson 1990) found that about 20 per cent had been 'pack-raped'. In a very similar way slave owners impregnated women in order to increase their labour force in the Southern states of America, as so movingly described by Toni Morrison in her 1987 Nobel Prize-winning book *Beloved*. The only way to understand the mass scale of such atrocities is as a reflection of sexual inequality and misogyny. Men have licence to rape when they have the licence to kill. Angela Davis described how gang rape was a weapon of the Ku Klux Klan after the American Civil War (Davis 1981: 176).

The Bosnia-Herzegovina War

This silence regarding rape in war was broken in the 1990S by the presence of an active women's movement which publicized the mass rapes of Muslim and Serb women in the Bosnia-Herzegovina war. An international movement developed to have rape declared a war crime by the Geneva Convention. Reports of forcible impregnation of thousands of women, mostly Muslims by Serbian soldiers as a form of ethnic cleansing, aroused outrage in the West.[11] A European Commission report estimated that 20,000 women had been victims of 'organized rape' in Bosnia, while Muslim and Croat sources claim the numbers are far greater.

Alexandra Stiglmayer went and interviewed women who had been held at gunpoint in rape camps and forced brothels in Bosnia, and her moving account of the atrocities makes agonizing reading. She proposes (Stiglmayer 1993) that in war men rape for various motives and each war provides its own specific motivations. In Vietnam Americans raped out of frustration at being in a foreign country. In Bosnia rape was used as a weapon to drive women out of their homes, as part of Serbian plans to create a purely Serbian community. The European Community mission that investigated the rapes concluded that 'rape cannot be seen as incidental to the main purpose of the aggression but as serving a strategic purpose in itself' (European Community Commission 1993: 5).

11. Julie Wainwright, 'War's Hidden Horror', *Guardian*, 13 February 1991.

When Stiglmayer first arrived, she was told that she would find very few women willing to speak about the atrocities; they were so ashamed. She was told by a doctor, 'If you ask them what happened to them, if they want to return to their homes, they say, "Oh, no, absolutely not." But they don't say why. They won't talk with us, let alone with you.' She eventually found some women who were prepared to talk. She heard how in the rape camps women faced daily humiliation and deliberate impregnation. Many were gangraped in front of their children. They reported the men saying that they would show them 'what real Serbian men were like' (1993: 109). The United Nations Commission of experts that investigated the rapes found 119 cases of pregnancy resulting from rapes in the larger women's clinics of Zagreb. They concluded that rape was used as an instrument of ethnic cleansing (Amnesty International 1991).

Bosnian women were not the only ones raped. The UN investigators found victims from 'all ethnic groups involved in the conflict'. Stiglmayer attributes the greater silence of Serbian women to lack of interest by journalists in investigating atrocities to women who were wives, daughters and sisters of the aggressors. It is also likely that Serbian women were raped for other reasons than to drive them out. She suggests they were probably raped primarily for revenge or to celebrate male supremacy (1993: 138). The most pessimistic conclusion regarding the perpetrators is:

Everyone participates in the rapes: regular soldiers as well as members of paramilitary groups; simple foot soldiers as well as high officers and commandants, policemen as well as friends, co-workers and acquaintances of the raped women – 'ordinary Joes' (1993:147).

War and Prostitution

The link between gang rape, prostitution and war is only beginning to be recognized. The Japanese military government in the 1930s and 1940s used prostitution of Korean women as an integral tool of military expansionism. Tens of thousands of women were forced to work in a vast network of government-run brothels to provide sex for the Japanese soldiers (see Enloe 1988; Vickers 1993). In every area the Japanese conquered during the Second World War, prostitution was restored. In fact, in 1941 the Japanese authorities actually conscripted Korean women into a corps of 'entertainers' to 'comfort' the Japanese troops in Manchuria. With the beginning of the Pacific War, between 50,000 and 70,000 Korean girls and women were drafted and sent to the front to 'entertain' the Japanese troops (see Hane 1982).

The unspoken military theory in Vietnam was that women's bodies were not only a reward of war but a necessary provision, 'like soda pop and ice cream to keep our boys healthy and happy'. At the height of the Vietnam war there were 600,000 soldiers and 500,000 prostitutes, almost one for every GI (see Brownmiller 1978: 98). During the Gulf war, prostitutes were transported to the desert to service the troops, where they queued up in line. If such practices, where women are treated as commodities for the servicing of male sexual needs, are institutionalized, it is hardly surprising that gang rape occurs in war. Prostitutes are supposed to enhance soldiers' morale by fulfilling their presumed sexual needs.[12]

The language of war is laced with sexual imagery. Carol Cohn (1987) describes how, when working for the American nuclear establishment, she became aware that the scientists talked in a technical language which was loaded with sexist meaning Joan Smith (1989), in her analysis of American Air Force pilots songs at a British air base, found they reflected the links between their two main concerns, sex and war. She suggested their magazines' advertisements for new weapons rivalled *Playboy* as a catalogue of men's sexual anxieties and fantasies. The Russians were referred to as 'those fuckers' who would be 'assholed', male rape being the final humiliation. Being 'ready' can equally apply to preparedness for war and for sex, and the 'big mushroom cloud' to the after-effects of detonation or metaphorically to orgasm. Women's bodies are described in terms of overwhelming contempt and disgust, where the real enemy appears to be women or 'not real' men. If warfare is an extreme means of gaining and enhancing masculinity, then everything associated with femininity is to be defiled. Disgust with the female body is a way of distancing oneself from femininity, and repressing desire.

12. Aids is changing the militarized policies of bases, as Enloe (1988) points out in drawing analogies with the Contagious Diseases Acts of the late nineteenth century, designed to protect the military from syphilis.

From this standpoint, we can see gang rape is a normal, inevitable part of warfare rather than a rare pathological event. A Vietnam veteran in 1971 told a conference on war crimes how he saw seven friends from his company, all 'basically nice people', rape a young Vietnamese girl.

I just couldn't figure out what was going on to make people like this do it. It was just part of the everyday routine. [An American soldier explained how in Vietnam] Let's face it. Nature is nature. There are women available. Those women are of another culture, another colour, another society. You don't want a prostitute. You've got an M-16. What do you need to pay for a lady for? You go down to the village and you take what you want. I saw guys who I believe had never had any kind of sex with a woman before in that kind of scene (quoted in Enloe 1988).

Rape as a Counter-insurgency Tool

Another distasteful development outlined by Enloe is the use of rape as a tool in counter-insurgency strategy, used to protect Third World governments from poor and landless peasants. It is designed to allow the local regime to carry out counter-insurgency operations without depending on foreign military. It relies on irregular militarized vigilantes and, according to Third World feminists, is not merely one more offence in a litany of atrocities.

Rape is being used as a tool of this kind of warfare. As part of village 'sweeps' or as a systematic part of torture while under arrest, rape may be integral to the very strategy of sustaining the existing social order in the face of women's growing 'subversiveness' (Enloe 1988: xxxiii).

Increasing numbers of rapes by policemen have been reported in India on landless labourers and poor tribal women. Government agents use rape and sexual abuse as deliberate policies to coerce, humiliate, punish and intimidate women all over the world (Amnesty International 1991).

So why do men gang-rape in war? One reason often put forward is that their superiors force them to do so at gunpoint. Brownmiller (1978) refutes this and argues:

My point has always been that you don't need orchestration or commands from on high when you have a young soldier with a gun. You don't need any order to rape. The penis can be used as a weapon; in warfare it becomes another weapon.

None the less, there is evidence that in war situations soldiers are given orders to rape and that rape can be used as a military strategy. In Bosnia perpetrators and victims described the use of rape as a military strategy to 'build up solidarity' by promoting 'hatred' of the enemy, by teaching who is 'good' and who is 'contemptible'. Forcing soldiers to rape women is a very effective way of destroying any bonds between people who have hitherto been neighbours, as with the Serbs, Croats and Muslims. According to Stiglmayer (1993), propaganda about the 'fundamentalist Muslims' and 'fascist Croats' who must be driven out and annihilated, itself an incitement to rape, came from the highest level. This certainly would go some way towards explaining how 'ordinary' men could behave in such an unimaginably sadistic way, mass-raping young women, many no more than fifteen or sixteen, and then bayoneting them. Reading reports of such abominations does suggest that killing and rape are connected – both are forms of ultimate domination.

Special camps were constructed for the express purpose of rape and sexual torture (see Seifert 1993). Teaching men to rape appears to be synonymous with teaching them to kill, as suggested in a galling account by a Serb of how he was forced to do both much against his will. Rape was used as a tactic of war and of ethnic cleansing However, this does not account for victims' accounts of many men appearing to enjoy rape, to take pleasure in humiliating women and in celebrating their 'manhood' afterwards. Tragically, there is evidence that some UN troops participated in raping Muslim and Croat women taken from Serb-run rape death camps (see MacKinnon 1993). Misogyny is certainly encouraged and celebrated more overtly in war than in peacetime. Rape both demoralizes and humiliates the enemy, defiles his property and deters him from propagating his own people through the bodies of violated females, and hence assists in crushing a people (see Bennett 1993). In peacetime women are raped because they are objectified; in wartime they are doubly objectified, as women and as the enemy.

Conclusion

Our survey suggests that gang rape is far more common than people think, as it is so rarely reported. It functions to enhance male cohesion and dominance. It appears to be a facet of all-male communities – adolescent gangs and other all-male groups – where less serious forms of sexual harassment are also rife. There is evidence that in wartime it is used as a military tactic to demoralize the enemy and enhance solidarity between the soldiers. Crucial to the prevalence of gang rape is the response (or lack of response) of institutions, the community and the judicial system. Gang rape does not occur in a vacuum. Its incidence is likely to vary from one culture to another and to be encouraged or discouraged by the sanctions placed on the occurrence of such appalling group denigration and humiliation of women. The incidence of gang rape appears to be particularly associated with the status of women within a given society (see Brownmiller 1978).

The ideology that promotes 'gang rape' is reflected in all kinds of misogynous group practices: calling girls 'slags' and 'sluts', treating women as sexual commodities, depicting women who are drunk not as vulnerable but as 'asking for it'. Jurors are still loath to believe women who report pair or gang rape. I have shown the way in which rape can be a weapon of war, used with cruel effect to demoralize an enemy by inflicting permanent physical and psychological wounds on the female members of the 'enemy' community. The sphere of sexuality is in this way linked to issues of war and militarism. Yet in non-war situations the typical rape trial is conducted on the basis of apportioning blame, and the character and behaviour of the woman not the man are denounced.

Chapter 3

Rape Masquerading as Seduction

When the media discovers a feminist concern, it gets less than five minutes of serious consideration, then comes the five-year attack (Faludi 1991).

As we will see 'Date rape' became a household term in the UK in the autumn of 1993 with the cases of the students Donnellan and Kydd, who were both acquitted, and the lawyer, Diggle, who was convicted. An outcry in the national press followed, raising the spectre of naive or calculating women crying rape when dissatisfied with sex or vengefully making false allegations. Diggle's conviction seemed to be more to do with the fact that the victim was a lawyer who was not asked any questions regarding her character or past sexual history, which, as we shall see in the 'cases examined later in this book, can be so prejudicial. This case can therefore be seen as a model for how rape trials should be conducted. I shall show how the reporting of these cases presented a totally false picture of the operation of the judicial system, where under 10 per cent of men reported for rape are convicted, and where 'date rape' is increasingly being used to describe rapes where there has been some contact between the defendant and victim beforehand but not a prearranged 'date'.[1] By extending the term 'date rape' to cover other rapes, the implication is presumably that such rapes are not as serious as 'real' rapes.

In this chapter, I shall critically examine three ways in which the press distort rape trials. First, they give great prominence to high-profile cases, recently described as 'date rapes', minimizing reports on rapes by intimates (friends, fathers and partners), which is the category of rapes which has shown the greatest increase in reported cases in recent years. Second, they give much less prominence to the complainant's version of what happened than to arguments

---

1. In my monitoring period, only two out of the thirty-eight cases which came up could be classified as 'date rapes' and the Diggle case was the only one which resulted in a conviction.

presented by the defence that the alleged rape was sedu
than a violent attack, or took place because the ass
'misreading signals'. The violence of the assault is left c
mentioned, is interpreted as what the victim wanted. Third. ney
stereotype complainants as hysterical, promiscuous ('sluts') or
manipulative (or all three), presenting aU kinds or reasons why they
might make false allegations or naively 'precipitate' rape. As a
woman police officer who brought a case against a colleague
explained, 'For the first day I was the poor weeping WPC, then I
became this drunken temptress, covered in love bites, causing
trouble.'[2] This includes a tendency to present men rather than
women as the true victims. As a result, the press have been known
to go so far as to report acquittals as 'victories' and rape convictions
as 'miscarriages of justice'.

According to one American researcher, the portrayals of sex,
crime and rape both in myth and in the news media serve to
reinforce negative images of women and of social justice (Barak
1994). A study of four well-publicized rape cases in the US[3] sums
up the print media's portrayal of victims of rape as follows:

Pushed into subordinate roles of sex objects, wives, mothers or crime victims,
they have little opportunity to be portrayed as self-determining individuals.
When a reporter sits down to write a story about any woman, therefore, let
alone a woman who has been victimized in a sex crime, he or she has an
enormous burden of assumptions, habits and cliches to carry to the story. Not
only are conventional images of women limited, but our very language
promotes those images. It is not surprising, therefore, that the public and the
press tend to combine the bias in our language, the images of women and rape
myths into a shared narrative about sex crimes that goes like this:

The 'Vamp' version: the woman, by her looks, behaviour or generally
loose morality, drove the man to such extremes of lust that he was
compelled to commit the crime. The 'Virgin' version: the man, a depraved
and perverted monster, sullied the innocent victim, who is now a martyr to
the flaws of society (Benedict 1992: 23).

2. 'WPC Tells of Ordeal by Rape Trial and Media', *Observer*, 26 February 1995.
3. The 1979 Greta and John Rideour marital rape case in Oregon; the 1983 pool-
table gang rape of a woman in Massachusetts; the 1986 sex-related killing of Jennifer
Levin by Robert Chambers in New York; and the 1989 gang rape and beating of the
Central Park jogger.

Sex crime victims tend to be squeezed into one or other of these images, as either a wanton female who provoked the assailant with her sexuality or a pure and innocent victim attacked by monsters.

Both of these narratives are destructive to the victims of rape and to public understanding of the subject. The vamp version is destructive because it blames the victim of the crime instead of the perpetrator. The virgin version is destructive because it perpetuates the idea that women can only be Madonnas or whores, paints women dishonestly and relies on portraying the suspects as inhuman monsters (Benedict 1992: 24).

Such media representations are also reflected in the British press, and serve to shape public perceptions of rape, having a marked effect on the way that jurors reach decisions. We have seen how the proportion of reported rapes resulting in a conviction has dramatically fallen in recent years. Cases that do reach court, described in the next chapters, show that 'dates' are not always what they seem and can be used by rapists to camouflage their intentions. 'Date rape' is also used loosely to refer to chance meetings rather than prearranged dates. Recent press reports of rape, where disputes have surfaced as never before in both the US and Britain, reflect a very different reality and instead give a misleading impression that men are increasingly under threat from women making false allegations.

The Context of Date Rape Cases

In 1991 in the US, William Kennedy Smith, nephew of the former president, was charged with date rape. The case was widely publicized and was the first rape trial to be televised in full on American TV, avidly watched by millions.[4] The complainant was pilloried by the press, who broke anonymity by revealing her name.[5] The defendant's acquittal led to a marked decrease in the number of women reporting rape in the state.[6] This case was swiftly followed by

4. In Britain cameras are not allowed in courtrooms during trials.
5. *New York Times*, 17 April 1991; pointed out by E. McAuliffe.
6. According to J. White and S. sorensen, 'A Sociocultural View of Sexual Assault: From Discrepancy to Diversity, *Journal of Social Issues*, 48(1) 1992, pp. 187–95.

the conviction of Mike Tyson, a working-class black hero from the ghetto who had risen to become world heavyweight boxing champion. The reason why Tyson was convicted could well have been due to the impressiveness of the complainant, Desiree Washington, a beauty queen who 'radiated truthfulness and tangible distress' (Kennedy 1992: 128), and to Tyson's known record of personal violence. This did not, however, prevent many ordinary Americans from clamouring for his release on the grounds that he was an innocent man who had merely misread the signals of a predatory female. The race issue, with all its connotations of lynching, renders it a particularly difficult and emotive issue (see Jordan 1992).

The Mike Tyson and William Kennedy Smith trials in the States, occurring at a time when more women students were demanding that universities develop sexual harassment policies in response to assaults on university campuses, had led to an outburst of controversy in the US. The publication in 1993 of Katie Roiphe's book *The Morning After*, in which she disputed the prevalence of rape in America and attacked feminists for exaggerating its incidence and thus heightening fears of violence, coincided with the reporting of the three British cases discussed here and received much publicity in Britain. She poured scorn on the findings of recent American victimization studies that one in four women reported being raped, suggesting this figure had come out of the 'addled brains of first-year students' and accused anti-rape activists of manipulating statistics to frighten students with a non-existent epidemic of rape and of encouraging them to view unsatisfactory or bad sex as rape and 'everyday experience' – sexist jokes, professorial leers, men's everyday straying hands and other body parts – as intolerable insults and assaults. Ignoring the evidence that most women fear to speak out about male violence, Roiphe argued that feminists, by encouraging women to 'break the silence', had led them to view men as predators and to exaggerate fear of violence. This, she argued, was fuelling women's fear of rape, which militated against women's freedom, leading to a 'victim' mentality.[7]

Three issues are raised here: whether the incidence of rape has

7. This is a classic example of how feminists are sometimes blamed for women's subordination (see Faludi 1991).

been exaggerated, whether women do confuse bad sex with rape, and whether the 'everyday experience' of sexual harassment is a matter of concern or just nothing to be worried about. Assessing the true incidence of rape is difficult, as we know that many women are too ashamed, traumatized or frightened to tell anyone. Others do not necessarily define coercive sex (or sex without consent) as rape. It is difficult enough to assess the prevalence of campus rape in the US (where most student accommodation is provided on campus sites, away from city centres, providing a relatively segregated population to study) and where well-funded research projects have been carried out, let alone in Britain, where campus universities are the exception and little research has been funded. None the less, with reference to numerous American and British victimization studies that have been carried out, we can confidently conclude that the extent of rape has been underestimated, and that rape by intimates – fathers, husbands, boyfriends, uncles and ex-boyfriends – is far more common than the reported numbers reflect. The 1992 US National Women's Study 'Rape in America: A Report to the Nation' (conducted by the Crime Victims Research and Treatment Centre) found that only 16 per cent of rapes (approximately one in six) were reported to the police (Buchwald et al. 1993).

Mary Koss and her colleagues (1987), who carried out the most extensive survey of rape, among 6,159 US college students, found that over a quarter (27.5 per cent) had been subjected to what the legal system would define as rape or attempted rape.[8] This statistic does not mean, as Roiphe implies, that Koss was suggesting they had been raped at university. Half of the estimated rapes or attempted rapes had occurred before the age of fourteen. Appalling as this finding is, it does lower the estimated incidence of campus rapes, on which Roiphe poured such scorn. Koss's actual estimate of the annual incidence of campus rape was 111 college women out of 1,000, some assaulted more than once.[9] Roiphe blamed feminists for encouraging women to view men as predators

8. Included in her definition were oral and anal sex, in line with most US state laws.

9. A more recent random survey of 3,500 Americans confirmed that 22 per cent reported being forced to perform a sexual act: see Linda Grant, 'Some Bleak Facts about Sex', *Independent on Sunday*, 16 October 1994, discussing the book *Sex in America* just published by Little, Brown.

by speaking out about male violence and thus restricting women's experience of freedom. She added that women were being encouraged to make false allegations, quoting one case of a woman who had apparently spoken out about rape and then retracted later. She failed to mention that at Princeton University, with its 2,600 students, where she taught, not one case of rape was reported to the police.

Confusion over Rape

What evidence is there that women confuse rape with bad sex, or that disappointment in bed is what leads women to 'cry rape' (if this were so, the rape of one in four might well be a gross underestimate!)? It is important to differentiate between two different issues here: first, do women confuse bad sex with sex under coercion; and, second, are these cases likely to be reported to the police?

Victimization studies have found that if women are asked whether they have ever had sex when they have been coerced, a far higher proportion say they have than would reply 'Yes' if asked whether they had been raped. In a British study of rape in marriage (Painter 1991), one in seven married women said they had been 'coerced' into sex and that this had had a very detrimental effect on their marriages. Studies such as these have concluded that it is far more common for women not to recognize 'being coerced into sex' as rape than to 'cry rape' when dissatisfied with sex. There was not the slightest evidence that women confused the experience of bad sex with rape. Great care was taken to differentiate between the times when women did not really feel like sex and those when they clearly refused consent and were raped, and where violence was threatened or used. Women distinguished quite clearly between those times when they had sex when disinclined (when tired, uninterested and unwell) and those times when they had been coerced. Rather than being eager to classify themselves as having been raped, the opposite appeared to be the case. In other words, when they were raped, they were often disinclined to see it as rape. Painter concluded firmly that women are not prone to 'cry rape'. It is important to be clear that consenting to sex, however reluctantly, is different from being raped. Additionally, not resisting in response to threats or coercion is also distinct from reluctantly consenting. There is, however, evidence that most women do not report rape, as we shall see, for good reasons.

The third issue is equally contentious. Roiphe's dismissal of the effects of sexual harassment as just part of 'everyday experience' overlooks mounting evidence that harassment undermines women's self-esteem and limits their autonomy. To accept such behaviour as unimportant is to deny its impact on women and its connection to more serious violence. It is easy to dismiss sexual harassment as irrelevant or emanating from an over-obsessive concern with political correctness. My own British research on adolescent girls made me aware of the importance of verbal sexual abuse in constricting their lives. I found that calling young women slag, bitch, cow, cunt or slut (all used as synonyms for whore) was rampant, and that defence of sexual reputation was a constant concern (see Lees 1993). To accept such terms as unimportant is to misunderstand their effect on girls' lives, where 'reputation' was a constant preoccupation and where such verbal abuse undermined many girls' confidence. The recent introduction of legal sanctions against sexual harassment is a welcome development (see Ashiagbor 1995). There is also evidence that sexual harassment does not exist in a vacuum, that everyday sexual harassment and aberrant sexual abuse shade into each other (see Kelly 1988). Resisting harassment is therefore a necessary first step to counteracting more serious violence. It is not uncommon for women who have been raped to be sexually harassed both before and after. Such harassment, occurring after the rape, if it is referred to in court at all, is frequently used by the defence as proof that the attack did not happen and that the defendant is 'in love'.

Does Speaking out about Sexual Violence Increase Fear?

For all its shortcomings, Roiphe's book highlights one crucial contradiction which is hard to resolve. speaking out about male violence can lead to a heightened fear of violence. Roiphe argues that by exaggerating the dangers awaiting women, feminists have taken away the sexual freedom that her mother's generation fought so hard to win. By implying that women are victims, they have made women feel weak and afraid. Fear of violence is, therefore, far greater than its actual incidence.

This argument fails to appreciate the fact that since, as we have seen, women are loath to report violence from men known to them, it is difficult to assess how exaggerated women's fear of violence actually is. But unfortunately only naivety can lead to the dismissal of the real threat of violence and the way it cOnstricts women's lives. Naïvety also puts women at risk, as studies have found that young women who are aware of the hazards and are not over-trusting are overall less likely to be assaulted. This does not mean, I emphasize, that many assaults are possible to avoid. All men do not rape, but it is difficult to tell those that do from the others. As we have seen, rapists appear to be perfectly nice men until they rape.

When undertaking this research into rape, I became increasingly concerned about the welfare of my teenage daughter, particularly after a young girl was raped and murdered at the train station she used on a daily basis. When I was pressing her to take care and to be home in good time, she turned on me and said, 'I thought you were in favour of women's independence.' There is a real conflict here, but surely its resolution involves speaking out about violence and campaigning for changes to what are now regarded as acceptable levels of male violence. Until such changes occur, however, we have no alternative but to prepare our daughters for the world as it is, and regrettably that requires warning them of the dangers. We should perhaps warn them to trust only men who have proved themselves trustworthy. It also means changing society's attitudes to women entering the public sphere, and working to provide a safe environment and to have sexual violence taken seriously. A balance must be struck between empowering women to be independent, taking precautions, in so far as is possible, and campaigning for a change in the status quo. Roiphe avoids facing such contradictions.

Roiphe's book undoubtedly hit a raw nerve in the US. It was greeted with jubilation by the press in general and was well reviewed in the *New York Times*. Roiphe was fêted, with interviews and meetings on both sides of the Atlantic. However, her book did not do well in Britain. This could be partly due to a more critical view of her highly controversial stance and also to the inapplicability of her views to the British context, where campus universities are, as we have seen, the exception and the whole issue of sexual harassment and rape at universities has not reached the same pitch of controversy. This may well change, as, for example, the 1990 study conducted by the Oxford

University Student Union suggests that sexual harassment and rape are not uncommon, and university administrations are being pressured to develop policies to address the issue.

Changes in Media Reporting of Sex Crimes

In the past twenty years there has been a big increase in the reporting of sex crimes in the media. In their analysis of the British press, Soothill and Walby (1991) found reports to be 'typically sensational and titillating, rather than serious accounts of these crimes'. Until recently, press reports of rape concentrated on the stereotype of the stranger rapist, or evil psychopathic fiend. Soothill (1991: 391) examined the media representation of rape in the context of the changing profile of reported rapes analysed by Home Office researchers Lloyd and Walmsley (1989: 42), who compared the number of rape cases leading to a conviction in 1973 and 1985. They divided rapes into three groups dependent on the previous contact with the victim: strangers had had no contact; acquaintances had had some contact; and intimates were well known, such as relatives, friends and partners. They found there had been a decrease in the number of gang rapes and of stranger (from 47 per cent in 1973 to 39 per cent in 1985) and acquaintance offences but a significant increase in offences by intimates. There had been a slow but steady rise in the proportion reported where offender and victim were known to each other prior to the rape (from 53 per cent in 1973 to 61 per cent in 1985). This was not reflected in media representation. Contrary to the statistical profile, rapes by intimates were largely absent from press reports. Instead, the media depicted rape as primarily about sexual attacks in public places by strangers'[10] and gangs – quite the opposite of Lloyd and Walmsley's findings. This limited view of rape was exactly what the women's movement had campaigned against.

In the last decade media reporting of rape shifted from an emphasis on stranger rapes to the coverage of a few high-profile cases of acquaintance rape. As Soothill (1991: 385) concludes:

10. For example, the *Islington Gazette*'s headline of 14 January 1993 was 'Sex Beast's Reign of Terror', and began; 'A sex-crazed maniac tried to rape three Islington women three times in a day'.

There have been some trials (usually those involving murder, sexual peccadilloes or a celebrity, and preferably all three) which attract so much publicity that they become like a national soap opera.

The 1993 Donnellan date rape case had just such ingredients: student sex at a prestigious university, 'false' allegations, drunkenness and a celebrity Lord Russell). Again, this recent trend of concentrating on date rapes gives a distorted picture of the overall profile.

The scapegoating and blaming of the victim are marked trends that have been noted (see Soothill 1991; Soothill and Soothill 1993); their past and their behaviour at the time of the attack are scrutinized, thereby subtly shifting the responsibility on to them. Both the prosecution and defence counsel submissions are used to provide damaging material in the way they present the case, as though the victim was partly culpable for the rape. For example, in the 1985 Brixton gang rape, where two teenage girls were raped forty-five times at knife-point by six youths in a deserted garage after trying to return home by bus from a pop concert, the prosecution counsel was reported to have commented, 'It would have been much better if those girls had been tucked up in bed.' The detective inspector in charge of the case added, 'It was not wise for these two young girls to be out so late' (Soothill and Walby 1991: 70). Journalist Anne Robinson commented in the *Daily Mirror* on 6 November 1985:

I find these comments worrying. Because, whether intentional or not, both these men come close to implying the girls were partly to blame. And we are coming dangerously near to admitting total defeat if we lamely accept the solution to street violence is for women to forgo their liberty and put themselves under virtual night-time house arrest.

Robinson puts her finger on another feature of both court trials and their depiction in the press, which is to draw a line for legitimate behaviour by women. One function of rape trials is to act as a form of control over autonomous female behaviour, particularly if it impinges on what is regarded as male territory. A classic example of this is the 1985 paratroopers case we have already looked at (see page 43). A woman who ventures into the public sphere – the male sphere – whether it is the street, a public house or a male-dominated workplace such as an army barracks, is in danger of being seen as 'fair game' (Soothill and Walby 1991: 70).

A third trend in rape reporting is the tendency to present men rather than women as the true victims. This involves presenting the defendant as the kind of man who could not possibly be a rapist. Donnellan, the student whose case is discussed below, was presented as 'the perfect gentleman' and in far more sympathetic a light than the complainant. Diggle, who was convicted, was described as 'not good at picking up social signals from women', and was depicted as sexually naive rather than coercive, which contrasted with his behaviour as revealed in the transcripts of the trial. It was reported that Judge David Williams, sentencing him, had said that his naïvety in sexual matters had contributed considerably to the offence. He was reported to be living with his widowed mother.

When date rape hit the news-stands in 1993 this provided the perfect opportunity for the press to argue that the pendulum had swung too far in favour of women's rights and claim that women were crying rape on all sorts of pretexts. Scorn was poured on reports that male American undergraduates had to attend sexual awareness and date rape training courses and that universities were required to provide counselling for students who had been assaulted. Antioch College, it was reported, had gone further still. Under pressure from the federal law, the college had not only introduced written policies on date rape and sexual harassment but also become the first to define its general prohibition against 'sexual offences' in terms of specific student behaviour. The press ridiculed the idea that verbal consent should be obtained with each new level of physical and/or sexual contact in any given interaction, regardless of who initiates it. The Antioch policy states that asking, 'Do you want to have sex with me?' is not enough. 'Willing and verbal consent' must be received at each stage of sexual progress – from holding hands in the cinema to undoing each clasp down a dress. 'Are you comfortable?' must be asked before each advance.[11]

To ridicule Antioch's sexual harassment policies in this way is all too easy, but to dismiss the whole idea of verbally negotiated consent is a mistake. The Antioch policy represents a first attempt by women students to define what exactly is meant by consent and to attempt to draw up a policy that will have an effect on limiting the sexual violence on American campuses. No mention was made in press reports of why such policies are necessary or of the very low conviction rate for rape.

11. See *Daily Mail*, 19 October 1993.

The basic idea behind the rules (that men should take care that they have sex only with willing partners) was ignored. Instructions like these obviously raise problems about how to implement the policing of such 'private' behaviour, and are easy to pour scorn on, but the press reports did' not recognize that men get away with rape which masquerades as seduction and that some 'dates' are premeditated rape. The idea that verbal consent should be negotiated when having sex with someone for the first time, along with birth control and AIDS avoidance, may interfere with the 'flow', but wonderful as good sex is, some way of avoiding men masquerading rape as seduction is required. It would also avoid defendants' arguments that they had 'misread signals' and at least mean they had to confirm that they had verbally negotiated to have sex.

The British Date Rape Controversy

Rape is becoming less of a taboo subject and more women are reporting rape to the police. In response to this development, the focus of press reporting has shifted in the past decade from an emphasis on the 'psychopathological rapist' to the detailed reporting of a few high-profile cases (see Soothill and Walby 1991; Soothill 1991). The emphasis on the psychopathological rapist or 'sex beast' is usually based on the selective reporting of specific facts and masks the reality of most sex crimes, which are committed by men who do not appear to be abnormal or psychologically disturbed. Often the sex beast of the media is linked to earlier fiends, such as Jack the Ripper or Dracula.

The recent date rape phenomenon can be seen as another form of distortion, linking the term 'date', which should be pleasurable, with rape to imply that the assault was not really rape (see Estrich 1987). Yet, paradoxically, we know that some women have been murdered on 'dates'. The increased coverage given to such cases is probably a reflection of the increased number of cases of rape that are reported to the police where there is some degree of acquaintance between the suspect and the complainant.

'Date rape' is used by the press in a misleading way to refer to rape by any acquaintance, whether it be someone the woman knows by sight (but may not know by name) or someone she knows well or very well. 'Date rape', according to Mary Koss, the American psychologist who coined the term, refers rather to a special form of acquaintance rape, where the victim and perpetrator had some level of mutual romantic interest between them in which consensual sexual intercourse would be seen as entirely appropriate within the relationship (Koss 1988). Increasingly in the media, the term is used not only in situations where the couple have made a date to go out together but also synonymously with acquaintance rapes of all kinds. It is applied to situations where a woman chats to a man in a pub or accepts a lift from a party or is asked in for a coffee after a brief social encounter. It is misleading and dangerous to use the term this way. If all acquaintance rapes are referred to as date rapes, the implication is that they are not only less serious but not real rapes at all. Applying 'date' to the situation where a woman asks someone in for coffee or is escorted home carries the message that she is inviting sexual intercourse, and is misleading and distorting. For these reasons, 'date rape' should be abandoned, as it carries connotations of casual consensual sex.

At the very least the term should be confined to situations where the couple had made a date or some prior commitment to meet socially or romantically. This would exclude the use, of 'date rape' with reference to the student Donnellan, who had met the complainant at a party but had not arranged to go out with her beforehand. Date rape, therefore, would not refer to situations where the woman was offered a lift in a car or was invited to go somewhere under false pretences, or where she invited into her home someone who had accompanied her there. Such rapes are acquaintance rapes. Date rape should be used only in cases where there is a more defined relationship between the parties, from a first date to a more established romantic relationship. This is the way the term will be used here.

The significance of the widespread reporting of date rape as not real rape is that it contributes to the myth that false allegations are the rule rather than the exception. The outburst of publicity in autumn 1993, bordering on the hysterical, contrasted with the normal muted approach taken to rape trials. As the Daily Express (20 October 1993) argued, 'The word "rape" should not be used to describe these student couplings, often if not always lubricated with alcohol.' The women complainants in both cases were mercilessly portrayed as false accusers and the defendants were presented as the true victims of their accusations, so that rape acquittals were celebrated as victories for justice.

The Donnellan Case

The quality and gutter press unanimously celebrated the acquittal of Austen Donnellan, a history graduate from King's College, London, with headlines and prominent pictures over several days. Half-page pictures of Donnellan kissing his supportive mother on his acquittal appeared on the front pages of the national newspapers on 20 October 1993. 'Told You So, Mummy: Joy as the "Cry Rape" Student is Freed' with a half-page picture of Donnellan kissing his mother filled most of the front page of the *Daily Mirror*, while the *Daily Express*, after announcing, 'A Model Student Forced to Fight for His Reputation', followed up on the day of Donnellan's acquittal with, 'I Knew He was Innocent. My Brilliant Boy's Been So Strong: Mother's Joy as Student is Cleared of Rape'. The *Daily Star* headed the story, 'The Gamble of the Perfect Gent: Brave Student Took Big Risk to Fight Rape Slur'. The *Evening Standard* declared, 'Hugs and Shrieks as Jury Clears Date Rape Case Student', and the *Daily Mirror* capped it by filling the whole front page with a 'World Exclusive' on Donnellan's new relationship, entitled 'Rape Trial Student's Own Story', headed 'Love That Saved My Life'. – '"We make love passionately," Donnellan declared, "but I always ask, 'Is this okay?'"' *The Times* (19 October) confirmed this picture by heading their story, 'Rape Trial Student Perfect Gentleman, Say Women Friends'. The trial sparked a national debate about what the *Daily Mail* (20 October) referred to as the rules of the mating game:

We continue to excoriate the insensitivity that the male-dominated judiciary not infrequently still displays towards women who have suffered the outrage of rape, but in this date-rape age when common sense and the accepted decencies are being hijacked by the zealots of Political Correctness, is not the pendulum in danger of swinging too far?

The case sparked widespread calls for restoring the law, abolished in 1988, under which rape defendants were unnamed unless convicted. The *Sunday Mirror* declared (24 October), 'We agree with Austen that men cleared of rape are victims too. They should be anonymous until found guilty.' In an article hysterically headed, 'Head-Butting a Moving Train was an Easy Option...In Prison They would have Murdered Me Anyway', with the subheading, 'Raped by the Law', Donnellan spoke of his anguish and his dread of being killed in prison. Other calls were made for the abolition of anonymity for the complainant. With a photograph of the victim with only a strip across her eyes (a clear breach of her anonymity), the *Daily Mail* (20 October) hypocritically proclaimed, 'Shouldn't she now be named?' (Rape complainants were given anonymity in 1976 Sexual Offences [Amendment] Act.) *The Times* (21 October) carried an article arguing that definitions of rape had become so contentious that all concerned should remain anonymous.

The Mail (20 October) also carried two further articles, one an interview with the complainant and below a profile of Donnellan. No comment was made about the complainant, but Donnellan was described as a sexual innocent:

an awkward Catholic boy in a hedonist hotbed [who] had no qualifications to prepare him for life in this sexual hunting ground, socially inadequate and romantically inexperienced he must have gawped at the hedonism that he saw all around him.

Donnellan's mother was quoted as saying 'his idea of a good time was to help her do the weekly shopping at Sainsbury'. The complainant's Catholic background, on the other hand, as an 'ex-Convent schoolgirl' was given very different connotations, quite unreasonably since she was reported to have been a virgin on arrival at university, unlike Donnellan, who had lost his virginity in the back of a Fiat at sixteen and had a previous sexual history. This was very similar to the description given in the *New York Times* (11 May 1991) of Kennedy Smith, who was described as 'quiet, different and somewhat aloof', the implication being that he was not the kind of man who would rape. The same paper (17 April 1991), on the other hand, had depicted the complainant as someone who liked 'to drive fast cars, go to parties and skip class', who, according to someone who claimed to have known her, 'had a wild streak'. The *New York Times* broke anonymity by not only naming the rape victim but also printing details of her sexual past. Similarly, the complainant in the Donnellan case was referred to by the *Daily Mirror* (20 October), as a 'campus wild child'. As Lisa Longstaff of Women Against Rape commented in the *Sunday Telegraph* (24 October), 'She had been painted as the venomous character seeking retribution. He had been called the perfect gentleman.'

The medical evidence presented in the trial went well beyond professional judgement and joined in condemning the complainant. Dr Robin Moffat, a senior police forensic expert, giving evidence was widely reported (for example, *Daily Mail*, 19 October) to say that from the amount the alleged rape victim had drunk – three pints of cider, a vodka and two Drambuies – although her alcohol level would not be enough to induce a coma, drink was an aphrodisiac and she would have been 'very very drunk and very very sexy'. This is hardly a detached professional opinion but was widely reported.

Had the pendulum swung too far in taking women's allegations of rape seriously? Are men routinely being falsely accused, charged or, even worse, unjustly convicted like the Guildford Four and Birmingham Six? As the *Daily Mail* leader (20 October) put it:

In recent decades, women have won many rights – deservedly so. They now unequivocally have the right to say 'No'. But in return, they also have the duty to behave responsibly. If they swill alcohol and lurch around with naked abandon . . . if they indulge in passionate and provocative foreplay... they may still think the morning after that they had the right to say 'No'. What they should not have is the right to besmirch a man's reputation by dragging him through the courts and then themselves remain anonymous, even after such a man has been found innocent.

The bare facts of the case were as follows. The couple, both twenty-one years old, had not had a previous sexual relationship but had been seen kissing at a Christmas party, where they were both very drunk. According to Donnellan's evidence, the complainant had taken him back to her room and had consented to sex. Donnellan claimed that their on-off non-sexual relationship (as she had refused to sleep with him) had fizzled out after five months. The alleged rape happened after this. The complainant, on the other hand, could not remember what exactly had happened as she had passed out, but the next day had accused Donnellan of rape. She had first complained to the college authorities, who had apparently asked for Donnellan to apologize. According to informal sources, the reason why she reported it was that Donnellan had continued to harass her at lectures, which she shared with him as they were on the same course. She had gone to her tutor and asked to be excused from lectures. The college did not have any parallel courses for her to attend, and the tutor said this could be arranged only if she made a formal complaint.

In January 1993 Donnellan had been asked to appear before an internal disciplinary tribunal. His tutor, Lord Conrad Russell, the philosopher Bertrand Russell's nephew, and a professor of history, had agreed to represent him and reported to *The Times* that it was Donnellan who had 'insisted that the police were brought in'. Both the complainant and the college authorities had wanted the matter dealt with by the disciplinary committee of the university. The college appear to have been confused as to how to respond to a serious charge of sex without consent and to have inadequate procedures for dealing with such an allegation. According to the *Sunday Mirror* (24 October), 'They were used to dealing with problems like broken windows or stolen library books – not one of the most serious criminal offences imaginable.'

The hearing was set for three months on. Four academics, two young women from the Students' Union and an independent legal consultant would be deciding Austen's fate. It was at this point that Donnellan, on the apparent advice of Lord Russell, contacted the police himself and demanded that he stand trial, instead of going to the college disciplinary hearing. According to the *Guardian* (16 October), Donnellan suspected college authorities of attempting to expel him. Whether or not he was actually at risk of being forced to leave college has never been clarified by the college authorities. Most sexual harassment procedures are in their infancy in educational institutions. At King's, their powers ranged from a reprimand to dismissal, but since they had asked Donnellan to apologize for a lesser charge than rape, it is questionable whether he would have been dismissed. (After the court case, a judicial review of what had happened ensued under Judge Marcus Edwards, who ruled that college disciplinary tribunals should not deal with criminal matters. This led to new rules being devised in 1994, which were circulated to all colleges. However, it is possible that college authorities, if they receive rape allegations where the complainant does not wish to take legal action, could be faced with dilemmas similar to those raised by this case.)[12]

It is most unusual, if not unique, for an accused to demand a criminal trial. No woman complainant has such a right and, as we have seen, the proportion of cases not recommended by the CPS for trial has trebled since 1985. According to the *Daily Telegraph* (20 October), in the Donnellan case neither the alleged victim nor the

12. See the 1994 'Zellick Report on Student Disciplinary Procedures', where universities are now instructed to exclude serious offences, including rape, from their internal codes.

university wished it to reach court. As reported in the *Sunday Mirror* (24 October), Donnellan explained: 'I wasn't charged until 20 March. The main problem was that Miss X was desperate to avoid a court hearing. We later learned that she had been to the police station three times before agreeing to give a statement.'

It is not at all clear why the CPS, who decide whether to take cases to court, agreed to do so. Crown Prosecutors are required to consider four main criteria in deciding whether a case should go to trial: whether there is sufficient evidence; whether there is a realistic prospect of a conviction; the credibility of the witness or victim; and the public interest. Only about one in four of reported rape cases reaches court and informally it is said that the CPS take rape cases only if they consider there is 50 per cent chance of a conviction. In this case, the reasons for taking the case to court can hardly have been based on the expectation of a conviction. Of all the cases I investigated, not one had reached court where the delay between the event and reporting was anything approaching three months – the time which had elapsed before this case came to the notice of the police. A level of corroboration (evidence from an independent source) is usually needed in rape cases, yet the three-month delay in reporting to the police meant there was only the report to the college authorities. The absence of corroboration and the inebriated state of the complainant can hardly have provided any chance of a criminal conviction where the standard of proof must be 'beyond any reasonable doubt'. Her evidence can hardly have led the CPS to regard her as a 'good' witness. Her failure to be able to remember what happened on the night in question raised a major problem. When drunk, people behave in ways that they would not behave when sober and do not always remember exactly what happened. Anyone could see that there was no way Donnellan could be convicted in our present judicial system.

So why did the case go to trial? Public interest, with the encouragement of Lord Russell, may well have been the main reason why the CPS took the case forward to trial with a reluctant witness, insufficient evidence and no realistic possibility of conviction. According to the *Daily Telegraph* (20 October), Donnellan's solicitor, Michael Fisher, said that Lord Russell's status in the House of Lords gave him access to 'the finest legal brains in the land'. The public interest criterion is very vague. In this case it was presumably aimed at clearing Donnellan from malicious attacks on his reputation. But he could have taken out civil proceedings for libel to clear his name. The effect of publicly humiliating the victim may well have served to discourage women from coming forward when assaulted or raped. The CPS is a national service with a code of practice that aims to achieve universality and consistency, but cases of this kind give one little confidence that these aims are being achieved.

Paradoxically, in response to Donnellan's trial, which is quite atypical for the reasons I have cited, some newspapers drew the totally false conclusion that too many rape cases were proceeding to trial, although in fact, as we have seen, the proportion has in recent years decreased. The *Sunday Mirror* (24 October), for example, argued, 'The Crown Prosecution Service MUST look again at how it brings cases to trial. The victims of rape are not served by cases which are brought to court which should never come before a jury.'

The *Sun* was one of the only newspapers which asked the relevant question. In its leader of 21 October it said:

One question has yet to be answered in the rape charges against student Austen Donnellan. Why was the case brought in the first place? The evidence against Donnellan was thin to the point of near invisibility. Yet the Crown Prosecution Service insisted on mounting a lengthy and expensive trial which it must have known stood little chance of securing a conviction. Usually it's the other way round. The CPS is notorious for DROPPING cases unless the evidence is absolutely overwhelming. Maybe the real criminals are too tough a nut to crack. So the CPS goes after innocent students instead.

Journalists on the whole, however, rallied to support Donnellan in protecting his reputation from the girl's allegation. The girl was labelled by sections of the press as his 'false accuser', although in terms of the criminal proceedings she was actually an unwilling witness, as she did not even want the case to go to court. A correspondent to the *Guardian* (25 October) wrote:

The triumphalism among particular men I have hitherto believed to be gentle, intelligent and rational beings has all but taken away my breath. It is as if they had been biding their time waiting for the day when they could claim righteousness on their side by exposing women as irresponsible vindictive liars who are driven by a need to lodge false allegations against them.

Lord Russell, on the other hand, commented that his confidence in British justice had been renewed. A more enlightened press response was made by Matthew Parris in *The Times* (26 October), when he pointed out that, reading the papers, you could have been forgiven for thinking that rape had been shown to be a female plot against men. The case played into the hands of reactionaries. The press gave it enormous coverage and failed to question the sense of criminal trials, which are not to clear male 'reputations' but to bring guilty men to trial.

The Kydd Case

'Student cleared of raping "slut of the year"' claimed the headline in the *Guardian* (2 November 1993) at the acquittal of Matthew Kydd, a student at the University of East Anglia. The report went on:

the court heard that the girl was rumoured to have slept with every boy in the residences. Mr Kydd told police he did not want to have sex with the girl because she *smelled* and because he was *scared he could catch Aids*. He said she agreed to all the sex acts that took place and had initiated some. Mr Kydd's solicitor said, 'My client is just glad it is all over. He does not think it should ever have come this far' [*my italics*].

In this report, an eighteen-year-old undergraduate is blatantly stigmatized as a 'slut' and, by implication, a 'false accuser'. Additionally, she is presented as potentially polluted, contaminated, unclean, the source of germs, dirt and finally the possible carrier of disease and death in the form of AIDS. The Guardian, a quality liberal newspaper which prides itself on its high standards of investigatory journalism, provides a totally one-sided report of the trial. No mention is made of the young woman's anger at the way she had been portrayed, or that another student had come forward alleging an assault at Kydd's hands.[13] The victim's description of the attack she had suffered is absent from the press coverage. 'What kind of women?' (abnormal, dirty, unfeminine) rather than 'What kind of man?' permeates the press reports on rape and the same question is the focus of court hearings. The result is that the positions of victim and assailant are subtly reversed – the suspect

13. She was interviewed on ITV's *Twenty-Twenty* documentary.

becomes the victim and the complainant, who has spoken out about male violence, becomes the culprit.

Absent from this *Guardian* report is any mention of the woman's testimony; similarly, in court the woman's testimony was severely curtailed. There are parallels in the press ad the judicial accounts of rape (see LaFree 1989). The woman's voice – her standpoint, her story – is allowed only within very defined boundaries. The pain and anguish she experienced are rarely considered relevant. Instead, the defence focuses on the intricacies of the actual assault in terms of body positioning, all centred round the penis. Kydd, we are told, said that 'the woman consented to all the acts and initiated some' and that he 'did not think it should have gone this far'. The report implies that the woman is making a mountain out of a molehill, or is perhaps one of the band of evil or hysterical women who make false allegations. According to her account, absent from most press reports, she accepted an invitation for coffee and, once in his room, Kydd forced her to perform several sexual acts and then assaulted her with a truncheon. She stated he held her round her neck, throttling her, and raped her. In her evidence, she said he told her that she 'liked pain as much as he did' and, that she should return the next night 'in schoolgirl outfit'. When she was eventually allowed to leave, she said he threatened that if she told anyone he would kill her. Reporting such as this makes a mockery of the 'objectivity' of the press. What is presented as objective, rational and factual is in fact objective, rational and factual only from the male standpoint; from the woman's point of view, Kydd's statement is subjective and distorted.

The press concentrated on scapegoating the victim and vilifying her. It was alleged by Kydd that she had been named 'slut of the year' by students at a university ball. The complainant claimed this reputation was entirely false. This is an indication of the rampant double standards to which even female university undergraduates are still subjected. Some years ago, after giving a paper at St John's College, Oxford, I was shown a college rag where on the front page was displayed a league table with girls' names and the number of assumed affairs they had had. The girl at the top of the league was humiliated. In my research into adolescent girls, I found that a girl's reputation often bore no relation to her actual sexual activity (Lees 1993). Moreover, all sorts of perfectly normal behaviour can open girls up to the 'slag' categorization, such as favouring particular fashions, liking to be independent or going around with a number of boys.

The question which should have been asked is why the judge considered such allegations relevant to whether or not the complainant had been raped. If she had slept around so much, why should she make a false allegation and why should it have any bearing on her complaint of being kept a prisoner and forced to perform sexual acts for four hours? And why did the press report the assumed reputation of the young woman with such glee? Press reports of the case were even more loaded than in the Donnellan case. The *Independent* headed their article 'Rape Case Woman had Sex Two Days Later', and made the misleading claim that 'Student Admits She was Nominated as "Slut" of the Year at College', adding that she was said to have 'slept with everyone in her hall'. In fact, she had strongly objected to the label (*The Times*, 27 October 1993). The tendency of newspapers to use defence allegations as statements of fact has been pointed out by other research (see Soothill and Soothill 1993).

Also allowed was evidence that the complainant had taken part in a college rag dressed as a slavegirl to raise, money for charity, and had once appeared in a 'stripogram' (although the complainant said it was in fact a kissogram and she had been respectably dressed and had raised more money than any other student for rag week). The defendant did not enter the witness box but claimed his 'right to silence'. No evidence about his character, attitudes to women or past sexual history was therefore allowed. In his summing up, Judge Michael Hyam said:

Experience has shown that complainants make up such allegations for various reasons and sometimes for no reason at all. The girl was quite disturbed and craved affection and was quite able on occasions when it suited her to tell untruths and deceive herself. It could well be said that the young woman . . . had convinced herself that she had been raped. It seemed that her notion of developing a friendship was the reverse of what is normally done. With her it was a sexual relationship first in order to become friendly.

To argue that experience has shown that women make false allegations is an embroidering of the corroboration warning by Judge Hyam. It should consist of no more than a warning to juries that they should be careful about convicting where there is no evidence from another source (corroboration). To suggest that the woman is incapable of 'making friends' before jumping into bed and of knowing the difference between sex and rape is absurd and deeply offensive. The jury took thirty-five minutes to return a verdict of 'not guilty'. The girl did not feel able to return to finish her degree and must have been as appalled by the press reports as by the court hearing'4. Unlike the defendant, the complainant has no right to appeal against an unfair trial.

The 'Big Story', an ITV *Twenty-Twenty* programme shown shortly afterwards, based on interviews with other students at the University of East Anglia, contained other allegations against Kydd. It transpired that Ann Brown (not her real name), a fellow student, had given evidence to the police that she also had suffered a similar assault. She swore an affidavit for the 'Big Story', detailing her treatment at Kydd's hands. She said he pulled her hair and moved her head around and used her as a rag doll, exactly as the complainant said he had. He had spoken about his past, saying he had been involved in a lot of violent acts, but that if she told anyone he would 'rearrange her face'. He had ordered her about and pushed her inside a wardrobe. A third student said that she had felt very threatened by him and found him very unnerving. Norfolk police had given Ann Brown's evidence to the CPS, but their lawyers had considered that the evidence was 'not of a sufficiently similar nature' (see Introduction and Chapter 7 for similar fact evidence) for the three cases to be dealt with together. This was in sharp contrast to the way the complainant's character was considered to be relevant and the judge gave his discretion for her past sexual history to be paraded before the court.

The Diggle Case

The case of Angus Diggle, a thirty-five-year-old solicitor, was heard in January 1993, during my monitoring of trials at the Old Bailey, and we were able to examine an official transcript of the trial. The couple, who lived in different areas of Britain, had met before but had not gone out together. THe jury heard that they arranged to go to a solicitors' ball in London. At the ball they both drank a great deal and, after what was described as 'eight hours of revelry', returned to the flat belonging to the woman's friends to change before they both

---

14. I received a tragic letter from a relative outlining the trauma she had suffered as a result of the trial and ensuing publicity.

caught early trains home. The woman's friends were asleep in the only bedroom.

According to the prosecution, the woman took off her ballgown and went straight to sleep on the couch. Later Diggle got on to the couch with her while she was asleep, put a condom on, climbed on top of her and tried to have sex. The woman managed to fight him off and, by screaming loudly, woke the owners of the flat, who came in to find Diggle wearing only the lace cuffs of his Highland dress. In his defence, Diggle described a different scenario. He argued that he believed the complainant had wanted sex, as she had taken off her dress and sat facing him, naked, with her legs open on the couch. He claimed he had 'misread' the signals.

Press reports suggested that the case was simply a question of judging one person's word against another, but the complainant had a bruise which provided corroborative medical evidence of a struggle and witnesses to her distress. It is also inconceivable that the complainant would have reported the attack if Diggle had not refused to leave and antagonized the couple who owned the flat, who then called the police when he refused to leave. According to his statement to the police, he did not help his case by saying, 'I spent £200 on her. Why can't I do what I did to her?' Even so, it is unlikely that the case would have resulted in a conviction if the complainant had not been a professional woman with legal knowledge.

This was one of the few court transcripts I examined where no questions whatsoever were asked about the complainant's past sexual history or her sexual character, in spite of the fact that she had had a very considerable amount to drink. Additionally, in spite of her evidence that she had probably taken off her dress in Diggle's presence (although with her back to him), in order to have a sleep on the sofa, her clothes were not passed around, her intentions were not mocked and reasons were not suggested for why she might be making false allegations. She was also given the opportunity to describe the effect the attempted rape had had on her, and the judge, in his summing-up, pointed out that although not corroboration, her conduct after the alleged incident could confirm her other evidence. It was one of the few cases where the prosecution was excellent. To sum up, it was a case where it was clear that the defendant not the complainant was on trial. The importance of this case lies in the impeccable way that it was conducted, due, no doubt, to the fact that the complainant was herself not only a respectable professional woman but also a lawyer who may well therefore have been aware of the pitfalls of rape trials. If trials were conducted appropriately, which, according to Temkin (1993) is not the case, if the 1976 Sexual Offences (Amendment) Act was implemented and the past sexual history and sexual character of the complainant were not dredged up, if the defendant was cross-examined regarding his attitudes and about what led him to believe the woman consented, if his credibility was the focus, then many more trials would result in convictions. This case can be seen as a model of how trials should be conducted, where instead of focusing on the credibility of the complainant, the prosecution was adept at cross-examining the defendant.

It was Diggle, the defendant, who was cross-examined about his sexual history by his own defence counsel. The defence counsel's aim was presumably to imply that his lack of sexual experience rendered him less likely to have attempted rape. Diggle was questioned about when he had bought the condoms he had on him the night of the ball and about the comment he had made to the arresting PO. This was the only trial I monitored in which the defendant's sexual attitudes were questioned, and, paradoxically, by the defence counsel not the prosecution. The following questioning ensued:

DEFENCE COUNSEL: The jury may be concerned about the comment about spending money. Does the idea of taking a woman out and spending money on her give you the right to sex? Is that an attitude that prevails with you?

DIGGLE: No, not at all.

DC: You say not at all. What is your attitude towards ladies in general?

D: Take that evening, the only reason – the only reason to go to the flat was to change – the only purpose of the ball was to dance the night away. I was very surprised when Ms J took off all her clothes. She could have done a number of other things, put on a nightgown, a jumper made some coffee, could have made some coffee in the kitchen together.

The prosecution counsel took up the same theme and asked Diggle what kind of signals the complainant gave him to suggest that she wanted a sexual relationship. His reply to this was to say, 'I would say she never rebuffed any of my advances.' Finally, the defence counsel tried once more to encourage Diggle to give the impression that he was the last person to press his affections on anyone.

DEFENCE COUNSEL: Are you a person that had had a lot of experience in sexual intercourse?

DIGGLE: I would not say so, no.

DC: Would you tell the court the last time you had sexual intercourse?

D: I am not prepared to.

DC: Was it shortly before the event or some time ago?

D: Some time ago.

Diggle was in a 'double bind' here and was at a loss as to how to reply; to admit to rarely having sex would be a slight on his manhood, even if it would have helped his case. He was found guilty of attempted rape by a majority verdict (two jurors dissenting) and was sentenced to three years' imprisonment. Some months later, this was reduced to two years.'[15] After the case it emerged that, some months before, Diggle had been dismissed from his job with a health authority after he was fined by Manchester City magistrates for harassing a woman on a train in August 1992. He pleaded guilty to 'interfering with the comfort of passengers' and was fined. It is not unusual for the CPS to support a case where the defendant is known to have previous convictions, as this indicates that he may have attacked other women.

Perhaps even more significant in accounting for Diggle's conviction was the reticence of the defence counsel to make their usual insinuations when faced with a complainant who was not only middle-class but also a lawyer. The judge also seemed to take a more active interest in the complainant's version of events than is the case in most trials. In his summing up, he drew the attention of the jury to what he considered a relevant point: 'If she was willing, why was there no foreplay of any kind? On his account he got straight on top of her without any foreplay or talking.' Very rarely in other trials was 'foreplay' investigated or mentioned.

Some of the press, despite Diggle's conviction, persisted in seeing him as the true victim, but they were forced to be muted in their depiction of the complainant. The assault was presented as a question of misreading sexual signals, and no mention was made of the complainant's evidence that she had been asleep when assaulted. The headline in *The Times* (20 August 1993) on the third day they

15. Lord Justice Evans, delivering judgement, said that Diggle regards himself as a victim.

reported the case was 'Lawyer mistook "sex invitation"' and the report presented only the case for the defence, which gave the impression not that the woman had been fast asleep when attacked, but that she 'quickly took off her clothes…then went to sit on the bed with her legs slightly apart in my [Diggle's] direction'. The *Daily Telegraph* (1 October 1993) was predictably incensed by Diggle's conviction and announced, 'Victim's Shock as Lawyer Diggle Gets Three Years', reporting that the victim had said, 'I'm not saying it's too harsh, but from my own experience of similar cases I did not expect it would be so long. I am quite shocked actually.' The defence counsel was reported to have said, 'The consequences of this conviction are catastrophic. They amount to a complete ruination of his character', adding, 'It was inevitable. I expect he will be struck off from the roll of solicitors and the loss of all he holds in high esteem.' In fact in January 1995 he was suspended for just a year. Such language is never used to refer to the effects of rape on a woman's reputation.

Another equally specious conclusion drawn from the case was that it represented a significant change in the implementation of the law on rape. The *Sunday Telegraph* (12 June 1994) devoted a whole page to how the decision of the appeal court not to reverse the Diggle ruling 'throws light on new attitudes in the law'. The article, entitled 'When Sex is Crime', bemoaned the 'miscarriage of justice' and put down his conviction to general wrong-thinkingness. He might be 'a man whose attitude to women left a lot to be desired, a man who had the arrogance to regard himself as the victim, a man who had failed to express remorse', but he was no rapist. The article continued, 'The conviction only makes sense on the basis that Diggle was being punished not for what he actually thought would be Ms X's attitude to his advances, but for what he ought to have thought.' Since the jury accepted that the complainant was asleep when Diggle assaulted her, he certainly ought to have considered whether she consented. It is difficult to understand what the writer objects to here. He appears to be putting forward a justification for rape.

Conclusion

The argument that the date rape controversy of 1993 was sparked by concerns about increasing numbers of rape convictions, whether founded or unfounded, and women's greater proneness to making 'false allegations' is utterly false and represents highly irresponsible press coverage. We have seen that the real conviction rate for reported rapes fell from 24 per cent in 1985 to 10 per cent in 1993. This appears to be mainly due to a lower proportion of cases going to trial since the CPS was set up. It could, of course, be argued that this is due to an increasing number of spurious allegations of rape being made, but it is more likely the result of constraints on the CPS's allowing cases to go forward to trial. The detective inspector on one of the cases we followed told me that a CPS branch prosecutor had explained his reluctance to take cases forward by saying that his promotion prospects might be damaged if too many cases resulted in acquittals.

I have shown how press reporting of rape is often biased, inaccurate and irresponsible and presents a distorted picture of the victims, the perpetrators and the actual conduct of rape trials. It is deeply partisan, makes no attempt to put trials in context and appears to be directed at discounting women's allegations of rape and justifying the masquerading of rape as seduction. In particular, assaults are described in sexual terms rather Than as violent attacks. This reflects the way the press, like the courts, often present issues only from the male, and therefore the defendant's, standpoint, which is then treated as the only objective, rational position to hold. First, I have shown how there is a misrepresentation of the categories of reported rapes which have recently increased, with an emphasis on acquaintance rapes where there has not previously been a sexual or intimate relationship between the two, with particular focus on socialized 'date rapes'. Second, the complainant is scapegoated as a 'slut' or as unreliable, and her account of what happened is rarely reported, while the defendant's version is often given as incontrovertible fact. Third, men are often represented as the true victims of false allegations. Finally, the true statistical picture, which, as we have seen, shows a drop in the proportion of cases reaching court, is totally absent. Instead, the impression is given that more cases of a flimsy nature are reaching court (or that the pendulum has swung too far in favour of women's rights), implying that innocent men are being dragged unjustly to trial.

What, then, can be learned from the outburst of press hysteria which I have documented? One plausible explanation for the fact that the Donnellan case went to trial is that it was considered to be 'in the public interest' to prevent such allegations. At a time when student unions were, for the first time in Britain, taking sexual harassment seriously, and when women were coming forward to complain of sexism, the press appears to have found it necessary to label women who dare to speak out as 'sluts', fallen women whose word cannot be relied on. Any woman who takes that road risks scapegoating of the most extreme kind. Blaming women for speaking out about male violence is a subtle way the 'backlash' against feminism works. As Faludi (1991) points out, women are blamed for the very problems that they face. It appears that today the press coverage has shifted from a focus on the few stranger rapists who commit such atrocities to attacks on women who make such allegations, depicting men as the true victims. This new development appears to have arisen in response to the fear that women are challenging taken-for-granted sexual practices and becoming too powerful. Contrary to the press outcry, a far lower proportion of rapists are convicted than ten years ago and the courts, far from having been reformed, are just as prejudiced against complainants. The changes that the press are reacting to are not therefore changes occurring in the courts but in society at large, where, for the first time, women, and particularly young women, are' challenging chauvinist behaviour.

The publicity around date rape and political correctness can also be seen as a reaction to the greater recognition of the reality of male violence. Faludi (1991) argues that women's equality in America was more myth than reality, and that campaigns for equality led to a virulent backlash emanating from Conservative New Right's hostility to feminism. In Britain, the moral crusade against single mothers and Social Security, which it was claimed encouraged single parenthood, coincided with an attack on women making allegations of date rape and on political correctness in the early 1990S (see Family Studies Centre 1994). While a backlash might arise because there has been real change, it is also possible that it comes about in response to the fear of change rather than the change itself As the psychologist Jean Baker Miller (1976: 14) observes, it is almost as if the leaders of the backlash use the fear of change as a threat before any major change has had time to take place.

Chapter 4

Justice Imbalanced

> I don't believe it's the clever barrister who tricks the witness that fools the jury into acquitting the defendant. I don't think it's the pompous judge who is so unrealistic that creates such an atmosphere – atmosphere of unreality that the jury say, you know, this is nonsense. I personally, indeed, think that if there's a high acquittal rate in rape it is because it is not, if you like, a crime of a technical criminal nature (David Lederman, QC, interview October 1993).

In the last five years, the conviction rate for rape has drastically fallen in spite of the advances in DNA which have led to the identifying of more rapists. According to the Home Office statistics for 1985 (covering England and Wales), out of 1,842 rapes reported to the police, 450 (24 per cent) resulted in convictions. By 2000, the number of rapes reported had increased to 7,929 but the number convicted had dropped to 594 (only 7 per cent). Some cases do not even enter into the Home Office statistics, as they are discontinued or 'no-crimed'. In effect this means that the conviction rate is even lower than the 7 per cent of reported cases. In America conviction rates are also low. According to the Federal Bureau of Investigation statistics, of every loo reported rapes, only 16 per cent of the accused persons are actually convicted of rape (Steketee and Austen 1989).

I shall first examine the processes by which cases are dropped out of the judicial system, with reference to research undertaken with Jeanne Gregory in Islington, a central police district of London, in the early 1990s (see Lees and Gregory 1993). This research aimed at examining the process of attrition, the term used to describe the process by which cases are lost or dropped as they go through the various stages of the judicial system from reporting to conviction. We identified four major points in the judicial process at which cases are excluded. The first is when a case is 'no-crimed' by the police; the second is when police fail to refer a case to the CPS; the third is when the CPS decides not to proceed or to reduce the charge through plea-bargaining (the process by which the accused pleads guilty to a lesser offence than the one he is originally charged with and this is accepted by the judge in order to make a trial by jury unnecessary and so expedite the proceedings); and the fourth is when the jury finds the defendant 'not guilty'. I shall study these processes with reference to my research into police recording practices (see Appendix 2) and by examining the transcripts of trials I monitored at the Central Criminal Court in London. The names of defendants and survivors have been changed.

The Islington Study of Police Recording Practices: 1988–90

The Islington Police Committee has been at the forefront of a number of crime prevention initiatives, beginning with the Islington Crime Survey, set up to investigate the extent of violence against women (Jones et al. 1986) and the Domestic Violence Project (Mooney 1993) The Police and Crime Prevention Unit reacted positively to our initial proposal to undertake an analysis of the process of attrition and multi-agency approaches to sexual assault, and the Women's Committee, of which I had been a member for some years, were very supportive. A unique combination of an imaginative Police and Crime Prevention Sub-Committee and central government funding for inner city projects enabled this research to go ahead, not to mention our persistence.

After an arduous process of negotiation,[1] we collected and analysed all police record forms for rape, attempted rape, buggery and indecent assault (of all cases where the complainants were over sixteen) for a two-year period at two London police stations, totalling 301 forms. Where cases were ongoing, they often had to be tracked down to different police stations. We were fortunate to have the active cooperation of the police. Discussions were held with representatives from various local professional agencies and volunteer groups concerned with issue of sexual assault, such as Victim Support, Rape Crisis, Social Services and police officers working at all levels of the

---

1. Scotland Yard insisted that we wait a year before embarking on the research and access to the records was withdrawn after an initial agreement, which set the project back eighteen months. I think the chief superintendents hoped we would eventually give up and go away.

police hierarchy, including police surgeons, members of the child protection team and the Serious Sexual Crimes Committee of Scotland Yard. I also interviewed twenty-eight women who reported rape to the police.[2]

Criminal justice professionals have their own concerns and agenda for change. In deciding whether or not to grant access to outside researchers, they have to weigh the possibility that the findings will be critical rather than supportive against the possible adverse consequences of non-cooperation. It may be more desirable from their point of view to grant at least partial access, in the hope of retaining some control over the shape and direction of the research. Not all the gatekeepers of different parts of the criminal justice process necessarily resolve this dilemma in the same way. In our research, there was a marked difference between the reactions of the police, who, after some initial hesitation, cooperated fully with the project, and the CPS, who retained a defensive stance throughout, blocking our access to the 'frontline' lawyers with the most experience of handling rape and sexual assault cases.

The Process of Attrition

The high attrition rate in rape and sexual assault cases was well documented in British studies undertaken in the early and mid1980s by Scottish Office and Home Office researchers (Chambers and Millar 1983; Wright 1984; L. Smith 1989; Grace et al. 1992). These studies found that a high proportion of reported cases were categorized by the police as 'no-crimes' and so were not recorded as offences, and cases were frequently dropped between report and committal (Chambers and Millar 1983). Of those cases that did proceed to court, several resulted in a conviction for a less serious offence and many more resulted in acquittals (Wright 1984; Chambers and Millar 1986; L. Smith 1989; Grace et al. 1992). At each stage in the criminal justice process, cases in which there was some prior acquaintance between the complainant and the suspect were more

2. On 12 October 1993 we had a meeting with the Serious Sexual Crimes Committee of Scotland Yard. Detective inspectors, police superintendents and senior medical officers attended and generally agreed that changes in the judicial system were long overdue.

likely to be dropped or downgraded to a less serious offence than cases of stranger attacks (L. Smith 1989; Grace et al. 1992).

Recording Practices

When women first report an assault to the police, a report form is filled in, and after the initial investigation the case is categorized (broadly speaking as rape, attempted ·rape, indecent assault or buggery or combinations of these charges). What further action will be taken is also decided. It is at this point that some cases, where for various reasons no further action is to be taken, are 'no-crimed', which in effect means that the cases are not included in the statistical returns to the Home Office. The inadequacy of police recording practices has been identified in a number of recent studies. The Home Office circular 69: 1986, subsequently reinforced in a series of Force Orders issued by the Metropolitan Police, advised that only false complainants should be 'no-crimed'; unsubstantiated complainants and cases where the victim withdrew her complaint were to remain recorded as crime. Cases should be 'no-crimed' only when they were proved to be mistaken, frivolous or vindictive – in other words, inherently malicious. Despite these clear Home Office guidelines, the two most recent Home Office studies found this category was widely used; the average 'no-criming' rate was still high, although there was considerable variation between forces (Lloyd and Walmsley 1989; Grace et al. 1992).

Our findings reflect this high rate of attrition; if anything the rate was even higher than reported elsewhere. One reason for this is that with access to police records, we were able to ensure that all cases of rape and sexual assault against women reported over the two-year period were included. This differs from the strategy adopted in the two recent Home Office studies (L. Smith 1989; Grace et al. 1992), which excluded cases which were 'no-crimed' by the police during the first month, as the analysis was based on the monthly police returns sent to the Home Office. In our study 38 per cent of the cases, over a third of all cases, were 'no-crimed', which is in line with overall 'no-criming' figures. Reasons varied, from the woman's decision not to proceed (whether as a result of threats or an unwillingness to go to court) to the police's regarding the cases as lacking sufficient corroboration or viewing the complainant as unreliable. Neither of these reasons adhere to the Force Order instructions on 'no-criming'. 'No-criming' gives the impression that many women were making false allegations, reinforcing the view that women reporting sexual attacks to the police are still not always taken seriously. 'No-criming' does occur in other offences besides physical and sexual assault against women, but the overall 'no-crime' rate is only 3 per cent (Bottomley and Coleman 1981).

Downgrading of Offences and Plea-Bargaining

Another reason for attrition is the downgrading of cases by the police and at a later stage through plea-bargaining (the process by which prosecution lawyers make deals with the defence in return for the suspect's pleading guilty to a lesser charge). It appears that the police sometimes downgrade cases of attempted rape to indecent assault. Nineteen cases were downgraded to reflect a less serious offence; two reports of rape and six reports of attempted rape were reclassified as indecent assault. One case of indecent assault became indecent exposure and in the remaining ten cases the sexual assault dimension of the crime was removed altogether. Clearly, it is in the interests of the victim to reduce the charge if there is insufficient evidence to proceed with the more serious charge; such decisions have to be made on the basis of experience and judgement. However, some of the cases in which the sexual assault classification was removed altogether are rather puzzling. They include a case classified simply as robbery, although the suspect had squeezed the victim's breast and put his hand on her inner thigh, and a charge of grievous bodily harm (GBH) in which the attacker had ripped off the victim's T-shirt and bra and put a finger in her vagina, slashing her breasts while threatening to cut them off. In another case classified as common assault, the victim regained consciousness to find the suspect urinating on her.

In several of these cases where the complainant was interviewed, the description of the attack appeared to indicate attempted rape but it was classified as indecent assault. The distinction was often unclear and it is debatable what should constitute the difference. How exactly is intention to rape to be measured? Is it genital contact and, if so, what kind of contact, or is verbal expression of intent sufficient? Does throwing a woman on the ground or on a bed, trying to remove her knickers and then being fought off constitute intention to rape? Several of the women interviewed described attacks which had been classified as indecent assault but appeared to be as serious as other cases classified as attempted rape. If the woman is knocked off her feet, pinned down and kissed or groped, this should surely be classified as attempted rape. Consider the following case of Lizzie:

I was attacked in the lobby of a block of flats where I used to live as I came home quite late at night. It was about two in the morning. I was just about to get into the lift when suddenly a man appeared wearing just a shirt, nothing else, and he started moving towards me and he actually had an erection and was masturbating. My first instinct was just to kick. I aimed for his groin and I missed and the next thing I knew he'd thrown me around against the wall and I obviously screamed very loudly, but he then covered my mouth and my nose so I couldn't breathe. After a few minutes of struggling we ended up on the floor and I managed to get his hands off my mouth and I decided to talk to him. I told him that I was two months pregnant and that my husband was waiting for me upstairs – and said, 'Please, please, let me go.' He released his grip and I managed to get out and ran into the street. I was looking for a phone and couldn't find one, even though if I'd thought about it I knew where one was. I stopped a taxi and got him to take me round the block and asked the taxi driver to come in with me. I phoned the police as soon as I got in.

It transpired that the suspect lived in the same block of flats and over the next weeks Lizzie kept catching sight of him and was terrified of coming face to face with him. She eventually moved her flat, as she was so frightened of running into him. After seeing him she alerted the police and he was arrested. She spent a day in the police station picking him out of an identification parade. The assailant was already on a suspended sentence for another sexual offence and had since attacked two other women, who had also picked him out of an identification parade. Yet he was not charged with attempted rape but instead the charge was indecent assault. He was found guilty of two counts of indecent assault (both of which appeared to be attempted rapes) and received only an eighteen-month sentence to be served on top of the eighteen months of his suspended sentence. Lizzie had been terrorized and suffered from nightmares and panic attacks. It appears that if a woman fights back and gets away from her assailant, he is unlikely to be charged with attempted rape, even if he is masturbating, has an erect penis, is half naked and is pinning a woman down with his hand over her mouth.

The only case where a woman had reported her separated husband as her assailant shows how indecent assault cases are often difficult to prove even when the charge is combined with ABH. Una described what happened:

I was married for seventeen years. I took a lot over the years for the sake of the children. But you get to the point when you think 'that's it'. You can't explain the kind of pressure I was under when I left, phone calls and hassle. I had an injunction as well to keep him away. But he just flipped. I thought he was going to kill me. I'd never seen him like that. He said, 'Sleep with me and I'll give you some money.' Then he tried to rape me. I fought and he beat me up. My daughter was in the house and she heard everything. The police arrested him for indecent assault. I said I wanted him arrested for attempted rape. He got off for indecent assault but was found guilty for ABH. I would rather he had been found guilty on the indecent assault than the ABH charge.

It is important to consider why the police would wish to downgrade cases. One senior policewoman helped to throw light on the question when she recounted how, on returning to the station from other duties at the end of 1988, she had taken a statement from a rape victim who did not wish to proceed with the case. In accordance with previous practice, she had 'no-crimed' the report and was reprimanded for doing so, since this is now a complicated process. Instead, she was told to downgrade it to indecent assault, in which case it could be 'no-crimed' without any fuss.

The third main point of attrition is the CPS, whose lawyers decide whether cases that the police regard as sound should go to court. According to the CPS Code of Practice, cases should go to trial only if they consider there is a good chance of conviction. Since few reported rapes result in a conviction, the CPS are unwilling to take cases to court which they think will result in an acquittal. A discussion with the Branch Crown Prosecutor of the Northern Branch, Inner London Area, of the CPS served to throw some light on the observations made by the police officers interviewed. He stated that if many cases were being lost in court, the CPS lawyers would have to take this into account in deciding whether or not to prosecute. The Code of Practice requires the prosecutor to take account of two factors: if there is a reasonable prospect of a conviction and if it is in the public interest for the case to go forward. He has to be convinced of the sufficiency of the evidence, including the credibility of any witnesses. Unfortunately, it is all too easy for defence lawyers to destroy the credibility of the chief prosecution witness (that is, the complainant) in rape and sexual assault trials. The police unwittingly assist in this process by anticipating the defence's line of questioning in their own interviews with the complainant. The common practice of taking the complainant's medical history, including whether she has had an abortion, can be particularly damaging. The defence lawyer is supplied with a written record of these interviews which contain precisely the ammunition required. There are strong grounds for insisting on the confidentiality of such information, as is the case in the US (see Gostin et al. 1994). Having assessed the strength of the evidence, the prosecutor also has to weigh the likely penalty with the estimated length and cost of the proceedings, in order to determine whether a prosecution is in the public interest. One method of cutting costs is plea-bargaining, with the defendant pleading guilty to a lesser charge so there is no need for a trial.

It is not much comfort to a victim of attempted rape or sexual assault to have the case expedited and her own role in the trial made less traumatic, merely to see her attacker charged with a minor offence and given a trivial sentence. The interviews conducted with victims in the present study revealed how shocked and insulted many of them were at the lenient sentences frequently meted out to their attackers in the magistrates courts. One seventeen-year-old who had been thrown to the ground and assaulted recounted how her attacker had been called a 'little molester' and was ordered to pay her £20 compensation, which she never collected. She equated this with being paid like a prostitute, by order of the court.

The Court Process

The final point of attrition is due to the imbalances in the trial which make it very difficult to gain a conviction. Of the log cases of rape and attempted rape reported over the two-year period, only thirty reached the crown court and in only ten of these cases was the defendant found guilty of rape or attempted rape. All of these but one led to substantial prison sentences; the exception involved two teenage boys who raped a thirteen-year-old in council care and were given community service orders. In almost all cases the men convicted were involved in more than one offence of rape, or with other offences such as burglary or ABH taken into consideration. In one case I looked at, the suspect had been found guilty of the woman's attempted rape only after being caught and brought to trial as the result of committing another rape.[3] The most relevant factor affecting whether or not cases led to conviction was whether there had been any consensual social contact between the two beforehand. Six of the convicted men were complete strangers.

It is clear that attrition occurs at each stage of the criminal justice process but that it is particularly high at an early stage, when the police decide whether or not to record the complaint as a crime, and at the final hurdle, when the case comes to court but does not result in a conviction. In this research project 38 per cent of the initial complaints were 'no-crimed' by the police and only about half of those going to court resulted in a conviction. We also found that the greater the degree of former intimacy, the more difficult it was for a case to progress. The intimate category experienced the highest rate of 'no-criming' (60 per cent) and secured no convictions at the trial stage at all.[4] Such obstacles are not caused by the difficulty of judging one person's word against another, but by the imbalance in trials which gives all the advantages to the defendant and leaves the complainant stranded. She does not even have legal representation. Although the research is conducted in England, its relevance to the US lies in the similar myths and distortions that are the bread and butter of trials in both countries. We have seen from the analysis of trials reported here that the law allows most rapists to go free. In Australia, where a package of reforms has been implemented, 82 per cent of men tried for rape are found guilty (see Allen 1990). Identifying three serial rapists at two crown courts has serious and far-reaching implications. Rape acquittals are not synonymous with innocence, whatever the Court of Appeal and the press proclaim. In the next two chapters I shall examine the discriminatory court procedures and practices that lead to false acquittals.

3. Compared to the Home Office study (Grace et al. 1992) based on 1985 data, where 51 per cent of cases resulted in a prosecution, only 25 per cent of our sample reached court. Whereas in the Home Office sample two-thirds resulted in a conviction, in our sample only a third did so.

4. The Home Office conviction rate of those cases that do reach trial (of the intimate category) is higher than for acquaintance rape. This appears to be a result of the extensive injuries often suffered (see L. Smith 1989; Grace et al. 1992).

The Monitoring of Trials at the Central Criminal Court

During a four-month period in the summer of 1993 with the help of researchers from *Dispatches* (see Appendix 2), Lynn Ferguson and I monitored all rape trials where the victim was over sixteen years old at the Old Bailey, the Central Criminal Court in London, and eleven at Nottingham Crown Court and a London crown court. Only 32 per cent of cases which came to trial at the Old Bailey where 'consent' (rather than identification) was at issue resulted in a conviction.[5] This does not mean that 32 per cent of men accused of rape are convicted. Most cases are not even reported to the police at all. Of the cases that are reported, under 20 per cent, as we have seen, actually reach court.

Researchers who undertook a thorough study of rape cases in Scotland (Brown et al. 1993) found that 78 per cent of cases going to trial resulted in a 'not proven' or a 'not guilty' verdict. Therefore only 22 per cent were convicted, an even smaller rate than in England and Wales. Stranger rape cases, where identification is the issue, have a higher conviction rate now, owing mainly to advances in DNA analysis.

These advances would suggest that the conviction rate for rape should have increased over recent years rather than decreased. The stranger rapes which came to trial during my monitoring period were puzzling in that the forensic evidence appeared to be clear-cut yet cases where there seemed no doubt at all that the defendant was guilty were given a full trial. All of the cases were stereotypical 'blitz' attacks, where a stranger leaps in the dark or breaks into a house, and resulted in convictions and yet all the defendants had pleaded not guilty. If more incentive in the form of sentence reduction were given, more defendants might plead guilty, which would save court time.

Home Office statistics do not signify what proportion of defendants plead guilty. Zsuzsanna Adler (1987) cites a 1976 study which showed that 60 per cent of rape defendants plead not guilty, a higher proportion than for most other crimes at the crown court. Of

5. This attrition rate is similar to the Home Office statistics for 1991, which found that of over 1,300 rapes, only 42 per cent resulted in a conviction. This included guilty pleas and stranger rapes.

the thirty-eight trials I monitored, fifteen were dropped, postponed or, in the Johnson case, the defendant absconded. In several cases plea-bargaining occurred, and a guilty plea to a lesser charge was accepted before the trial without any consultation with the complainant. In a small number of cases the judge directed the jury to acquit, whether because of insufficient evidence or because the woman was unwilling or did not feel able to testify. Altogether twenty-three adult rape cases were tried before a jury and verdicts reached on the principal charge. Four of the defendants were strangers to the complainant and all of these were found guilty. Three of their defence pleas were based on identification and in all cases DNA evidence was, in my view, incontestable. Ten of the cases were general acquaintances of the women, and only two of these, Diggle and one other case (where the defendant had said, 'I did it, I did it' when arrested) were found guilty. Only two cases could be classified as 'date rapes' and in the one other case besides Diggle (as we saw in Chapter 3) the defendant was acquitted.

Of the seven cases where there had been a sexual relationship between the defendant and the complainant, four were acquitted. The three who were found guilty had all inflicted significant injuries on their victim. The relatively high number of convictions for intimate acquaintances reflects the extremely high level of violence used by assailants in this category. Some of the other acquittals were astonishing In one case, a husband was acquitted of rape although his wife, from whom he was separated, had taken out several court injunctions to stop him molesting her. There was evidence that he had broken her nose and tried to strangle her. His history of previous violent criminal offences was disallowed and the prosecution was ineffective at cross-examining the defendant about his views.

Until recently all rape cases had a preliminary hearing in the magistrates courts. Under the Criminal Justice and Public Order Act (1994), only paper committals are now necessary. All cases that are liable to lead to a sentence of over six months are sent up to the crown court, so serious charges, such as for rape or indecent assault, unless very minor, are referred on. Long delays, usually of over a year, are common practice. Cases are sometimes held up due to the suspect not being apprehended immediately, as in the Mulherne case (not his real name), but there is often an unnecessary delay between the magistrates and crown court hearings. The long delay (where a common survival strategy for the victim is to develop some emotional distance from the trauma, which can suggest to the jury that she is not that upset) puts unnecessary pressure on women who have to relive the experience so long afterwards, and have sometimes been subjected to intimidation in the meantime.

There are several reasons why so few defendants are convicted.

No Counsel for the Complainant

Jurors have no idea about the imbalances in the trial procedure in England and Wales,[6] nor of how disadvantaged the complainant is. They do not know that, unlike the defendant, she has no access to a lawyer either before or during the trial. In the British adversarial system a criminal case involves two parties: the state, represented by the prosecution counsel, whose role should be 'impartial', against the defendant, represented by the defence counsel, whose role is solely to defend. In rape trials the complainant is only the first witness for the prosecution. The prosecution has to prove the case 'beyond any reasonable doubt' and the jury is often given no guidance as to how to interpret this. Yet incredibly the prosecution is not allowed to meet the complainant beforehand or even speak to her on the day of the court hearing (sometimes prosecutors do introduce themselves, but this is not encouraged). When I tell people this, they are incredulous. They cannot believe the system is so unfair. The defendant, from the moment he is arrested, is entitled to legal advice and then has the opportunity of preparing his case with a defence counsel. Not meeting the complainant beforehand must contribute to the prosecution counsel's often appearing disinterested and failing to object to the cross-examination of the claimant's character and past sexual history which was evident in my monitoring of trials. Previous research has found that women feel particularly let down by the prosecution, feeling that they 'could have acted in a more robust way to provide protection from defence questioning'. Women thought they were as much on trial as the accused yet, unlike the accused with his defence counsel, they were unrepresented (see Chambers and Millar 1987: 65).

Jurors are unlikely to realize that the victim is rarely allowed to

6. Scotland has a separate judicial system.

describe the rape or her anguish – one of the aspects of rape trials that complainants find most frustrating. Nor are they allowed to see their police statement, often made over a year before, until just before the court hearing. Some women also complain that their statements have not been recorded in their own words. For example, this account was repeated in the Rape Crisis report (1989).

DEFENCE COUNSEL: You said, 'He had my wrists in his hands, pinning me down...He became crazy. He was sex crazy...He punched me in the face, etc.'

COMPLAINANT: It's not me who printed the statement.

DEFENCE COUNSEL: They printed what you told them.

COMPLAINANT: I don't know because I wasn't there. I wasn't there when they printed it.

Since the defence prepares the case beforehand with the defendant and has access to the woman's statement, he or she is in a far more powerful position to refute the complainant's evidence. He can even employ solicitors or private detectives to spy on the complainant to gain evidence against her. In one case I attended a young woman had not wanted her mother to know about the rape, but the defendant's solicitor had written to her, as well as spying for several days outside her house. The defence counsel had the gall to use the fact that the complainant had shouted at them to 'fuck off' as evidence of her lack of respectability and said that it had interfered with the defence solicitor's questioning of a neighbour who could not speak English:

DEFENCE COUNSEL: You shouted abuse at the solicitors?

COMPLAINANT: That's right...They weren't embarrassed. DC: Half the street could hear.

C: No...I didn't shout as loud as I could.

DC: What did you shout?

C: I told them to fuck off and leave me alone. She doesn't know anything about the case.

The prosecution counsel never criticized the unfairness and harassment that the complainant had been subjected to. On the other hand, the defence counsel used the woman's outrage at being harassed by the solicitors as evidence against her. In another case where the man was acquitted of rape but convicted of the lesser charge of buggery, the defendant was asked:

PROSECUTING COUNSEL: Did you say. She's a liar. She wanted it. She wanted
    it all ways, so I done it up her arse. She's a slag. She needs sorting out.'
DEFENDANT: Yes, I said that.
PC: Did you think she was consenting?
D: Yes.

The prosecution then simply dropped the questioning, even
though the man's statement betrayed not only woman-hating
attitudes but an aggressive and contemptuous attitude towards the
woman herself. In several cases crucial inconsistencies in the
defendant's case were simply not taken up by the prosecution.

Where extremely violent defendants are involved, defence
witnesses may be coerced into giving entirely false evidence under
duress. The whole context of fear and threats which women are
often subject to often affects both their friends and relatives but is
unacknowledged in court proceedings.[7] Failure to report rape
immediately is often used by defence counsels to throw doubt on the
complainant's credibility. There is a real reluctance on the part of
the legal profession to accept that for many women it was not an
obvious reaction to report the incident immediately to the police
(see Chambers and Millar 1987: 69). Many jurors have little idea of
the intimidation many women are under to drop cases. One woman
I interviewed was so terrified of threats from the assailant's friends
that she had moved house and gone into hiding Another woman
was too frightened to give evidence at a retrial after the jury had
been unable to reach a verdict on the first trial so the defendant
went free when she failed to show up. The failure to allow the
complainant in rape trials to meet with the prosecution beforehand,
as is the case in America, as described by Rowland (1986), results in
a highly disinterested representation on the-woman's behalf.

7. Gregory Matoesian, an American sociologist, analysed court transcripts of
trials and illustrated the subtle processes of domination embedded in the linguistic
practices of the cross-examination. He showed how 'a woman's experience of
violation is transformed into routine consensual sex through the organization of
courtroom linguistic practice' (1993: 21).

One Person's Word against Another's?

With developments in DNA there is rarely much problem in deciding whether sexual intercourse took place. The main issue in most rape trials arises over consent. Jurors are told that their task is to judge one person's word against another, but this is not the case. In our adversarial system of justice it is for the prosecution to prove beyond any reasonable doubt that the defendant is guilty. This means that the balance of proof has to be strongly weighted towards the prosecution's case.[8] Additionally, the rules of evidence allow the defence counsel a number of vital advantages over the prosecution. These are intended as a safeguard against wrongful convictions, but in rape trials they serve to deny complainants justice. The jury, in coming to their verdict, are unaware of these advantages which make the trial process so unfair to the complainant and are not in a position to take a critical view of the judge's direction, even if they wanted to. They are often quite overwhelmed by the long-winded inaccessibility of the language and the outmoded practices of the law. On more than one occasion during my court research, jurors were seen to 'nod off' during the proceedings.

Corroboration

The corroboration ruling refers to the common law rules which require a judge to give a warning about the danger of relying on the uncorroborated testimony of two categories of witness, accomplices and complainants in sexual offences. Generally in England and Wales the evidence of a single witness, if believed, is sufficient to prove the case against the accused. There are, however, some exceptions to this rule. With certain sexual offences, such as procuring a woman for the purposes of prostitution, the victim's evidence alone is incapable of securing a conviction. There must be some additional confirmatory evidence which implicates the accused person and tends to confirm his guilt. This is known as the 'corroboration ruling'. For other sexual offences, both homosexual or heterosexual, and whether or not consent is an ingredient of the offence, corroboration is not actually required, but until 1995, when the

---

8. In civil as opposed to criminal proceedings the case is decided 'on the balance of probabilities' rather than 'beyond any reasonable doubt'.

Criminal Justice and Public Order Act (1994) came into force, making the corroboration ruling discretionary, the judge was obliged to warn the jury of the danger of convicting solely on the basis of the evidence of the complainant. The whole issue of corroboration is directly related to the question of reputation: the woman is considered credible, then the idea is that corroboration is not necessary.

Some judges appear to mislead juries rather than clarify the court procedures. In giving the corroboration warning, judges often embroider it with comments about false allegations. Some judges say, for example, that it is easy for a woman to make allegations, when in practice it involves a long, arduous process lasting several days, medical examinations, days of police questioning and often attending identification parades. It is doubtful whether the abolition of the mandatory corroboration ruling introduced by the Criminal Justice and Public Order Act (1994) will prevent the introduction of such comments by some judges.

One of the main barriers to gaining convictions in rape cases is the belief that rape cannot be corroborated: since the act takes place in private and rests on the presence or absence of the woman's consent, it is argued that independent corroboration is impossible. This is not always true, as trials often rest not simply on the question of consent but on two divergent accounts of what happened. There are various ways in which the whole issue of corroboration seems to unfairly prejudice the case against the complainant. Sometimes it is a question of the prosecution not explaining clearly enough for the jury to understand that there is clear corroboration. Evidence to back the man's or the woman's story is given but is often not emphasized as corroborative. For example, in one case Mr Yates (not his real name) said he had never been on the wasteland where the complainant claimed rape had taken place. A can of beer with his fingerprints was found close to where the grass had been flattened as though two people had lain there. Yet the prosecution did not emphasize this as corroborative evidence.

The way corroboration is defined is not fair to the complainant and differs from one jurisdiction to another. In Scotland, for example, the woman's distressed state when she reports the rape is considered to be corroborative. In England and Wales, it is sometimes seen as consistent but not as corroborative. This can be very confusing to juries when they are directed by the judge that it is possible but inadvisable to convict without corroboration and are then told that certain evidence (like a tape-recorded report to the police) is not corroborative. This should surely be up to the jury to decide.

The real issue is how the jury is directed to view corroboration.[9] The compulsory nature of this warning was abolished in the 1994 Criminal Justice Act,[10] but it is likely that some judges will continue to warn the jury in one way or another about the assumed propensity of women to make false allegations. Judges now argue that the ruling is given in a totally neutral way, but I found that they frequently embroider the warning in a most disturbing fashion. Over and over again, judges argue that allegations of sexual misconduct are very easy to make and very difficult to disprove. Unlikely reasons why women might make such allegations are often suggested quite blatantly by judges. The judge pulls this bias against the complainant together in his directions to the jury, often arguing, for example, that people lie more about their sexual behaviour than about any other area of human conduct. For example, one said:

What is the most difficult and the most intimate part of our lives? It is our sexual life. It is not only the most difficult but the most unstable part of our lives. It has become a rule of law that some supporting evidence is needed that is wholly independent.

And here is how Judge Smedley, in a case heard at the Old Bailey on 1 September 1993, gave the corroboration warning:

Experience has shown that people who allege sexual offences, whether women, men, boys or girls, for some reason or no reason at all tell false stories. Some reasons are obvious. More common in the past was unwanted pregnancy. Also wicked jealousy, spite, or revenge, as suggested here, may be a motive. Allegations of that kind are relatively easy to make and are difficult for a man to refute. It is difficult for a man to prove she consented.

9. Only in very few cases is the jury actually forbidden to convict in the absence of corroboration. Until 1988 the unsworn evidence of children was one such category.

10. Besides the compulsory ruling, there are other cases where it is a 'rule of practice' that the jury is warned about the danger of convicting without corroboration (see Wells 1990). Some classes of witness fit the 'rationaie' but not the strict definition of the common law rule, such as people with a motive for giving false evidence, psychiatric patients or those giving evidence of identification. In such cases the judge has to decide whether there is a need for special caution.

In the trial of Simpson on 22 November 1993 Judge Grigson gave the 'special warning', since he could find no reason why the complainant should make a false allegation, by arguing:

Complaints of this nature are easy to make and difficult to refute. It is the experience of the courts that sometimes false complaints are made. Whilst the motives for making such complaints may sometimes be obvious, on other occasions the complainant's motives may be obscure or the real reason for her acting in that way may never come to light.

Here he quite fallaciously states that false allegations are common, which is simply not true. There is no evidence that such cases ever reach court. It is certainly not the experience of the courts that false complaints are made. Some judges are, however, wholeheartedly opposed to the corroboration ruling. Judge Perleman referred to it as an anachronism, an absolute insult, and said, 'I do it because I have to do it, and I take a deep breath, but I don't like to do it.'[11]

Evidence of Resistance

Rape victims alone among all victims of crime are expected to fight back, to prove they did not consent. Men often do not fight back when attacked, yet few wonder whether they were asking for it. Absence of injury is taken as evidence of consent rather than the result of a paralysing and realistic fear of being killed or a feeling that submitting holds the best chance of survival. Women certainly have reason to fear the threats. The defendant usually knows their name and sometimes where they live or work. Sometimes rapists actually return to rape the woman again.[12] Even if they don't, the fear that they will is real enough. In court, however, these threats are trivialized.

Juries are not reminded that some rapists kill their victims and many women (and men) are frozen with fear when confronted by a violent attack. Instead, evidence that they did not fight their

11. In In the BBC 1 *Panorama* documentary 'The Rape of Justice', July 1993.

12. In one case the defendant had broken into a woman's flat, raped and threatened her; he returned some months later to rape her again. In another case (*Daily Mirror*, 5 February 1985) a man who was released from prison returned to murder the woman who had testified against him.

assailant or run away at the first opportunity is frequently held against them. In one case, Sharon was asked why she did not dig her fingernails into her assailant's penis, or 'put a construction in front of the door' when her assailant went to the toilet. Both of these actions are ludicrous for a woman who is in fear of her life to contemplate. Women often use various tactics to survive, such as humouring the rapist or not running away, if frozen in fright and this is often held against them in trials. The prosecution rarely explains adequately why the woman does not have injuries. In one trial heard in August 1993 at the Old Bailey, where the complainant had allegedly been raped in a cab that she had hailed to take her home from a nightclub and the defendant was acquitted, the defence counsel asked why she was not injured. She explained, 'The only way I could have had bruises is if he had physically beaten me.'

Jurors often expect the victim to have suffered injuries, without realizing that genuine fear for their lives prevents many women from resisting physically and sustaining severe injuries. Often without an adequate rebuttal from the prosecution, who, as we have seen, has not had the opportunity to prepare the case with the complainant, forensic defence counsels expertly create red-herring tales around supporting evidence. Their aim is to raise 'reasonable doubt', and often they confuse the jury by raising 'unreasonable doubt', which can make it difficult for a jury to bring in a guilty verdict. The evidence is so confusing and its relevance often so obscure that the jury, though they may well assume that there is some doubt about important evidence, becomes confused.

Normally in trials the prosecution presents its case, witnesses are questioned by the defence counsel and then the defence presents its case. The confusion arises when the defence starts to introduce allegations which contradict evidence from the prosecution witnesses after they have been dismissed and are therefore not available to be cross-examined. We have a 'contest' system of trials where each of the witnesses appears for one side or the other and each lawyer then has a turn at questioning them. The order in which evidence is heard is also unfair to the complainant when she is the object of allegations about her character, as is so often the case, and she is questioned first. After several days of other evidence, the poignancy of her account of the rape may well not be uppermost in jurors' minds. Complainants who are brave enough to sit through the trial after they have given evidence may well further their case by thus 'reminding' jurors of their account of their assault.

Evidence from a witness can be contradicted some hours later when the witness is no longer available to be cross-examined. This is a major problem with the adversarial system of justice and puts considerable strain on the jury to remember exactly what was said (Spencer 1989). The defence also has an advantage in having prior access to the medical reports, which often inadvertently include details of the woman's past sexual history (such as whether she has ever had an abortion or given birth, and details of her menstrual cycle). This can raise particular problems in rape trials, where it gives an advantage to the defence, who can contradict what witnesses have argued without any comeback.

An example of such discrimination arose in the case of Stevens (not his real name), who was charged in two separate trials of raping three women, where an outlandish story was presented by the defence. It was argued that the marks around the complainant's neck had been caused by the boyfriend of another girl living in the house. He had been called as a witness, but had not been asked about this allegation and was not recalled when the defence made the allegation. The prosecuting counsel is on the defensive without knowing exactly what the defence is going to argue. The prosecution does not know in advance the basis of the defence case, so has little chance to prepare evidence to refute false allegations made by defence witnesses.

It appears that forensic evidence is a crucial area of dispute between the prosecution and defence lawyers, where conflicting medical opinion is often used to plant seeds of doubt in the jurors' minds about whether or not the woman consented. Such evidence is based far more on bias and prejudice, and reference is rarely made to evidence based on research. Instead the defence aims to 'blind' the jurors with supposed 'scientific evidence'. The most common tactic is to argue that if raped, the woman should have vaginal injuries. This does not fit with the evidence from the medical examination of rape victims, where vaginal injuries are rare for the simple reason that most women are too terrified to resist. Yet again and again, doctors called by the defence argue that women who have been raped should have vaginal injuries. The prosecution are often inept at countering such claims and fail to emphasize the common response of both men and women to attack when threatened with violence or with their lives. Men who are raped or assaulted behave exactly the same way. There is a strong argument that 'expert witnesses' should be called to explain to the jury just what is known about rape and survivors' reactions. Such witnesses should not be doctors but Rape Crisis workers, who are conversant with survivors' reactions, or academics who are conversant with the extensive research that has now been carried out into rapists as well as their victims.

Forensic doctors play a crucial 'expert' role in analysing women's responses and sometimes give conflicting accounts of the 'typical' bodily signs and symptoms of rape. Clark (1987) argues that the detail women are required to go into to describe the assault has increased with the development of forensic science. The defence counsel can call his/her own doctor to question the evidence of the police doctor. In the Simpson case (discussed in Chapter 6) we shall see how this tactic is used to great effect. Many defendants take advantage of the argument that lack of resistance implies consent and maintain that because the woman did not resist, they did not know that she did not consent. The intelligence of defendants at using such sexist arguments to their advantage is grossly underestimated. Some rapists, according to Ray Wyre, who set up a treatment programme for convicted rapists at the Gracewell Clinic in Birmingham (now sadly closed down), argues that they kid themselves that it was not rape and say, '"Why didn't she stop me? . . . She must have known I didn't want to do it", as if it was her responsibility to save him from himself' (Wyre and Swift 1990: 6). Jurors are not aware of the subtle way the woman's experience of rape is discounted. They are not informed that a common pattern of psychological reactions has been shown to differentiate rape from other experiences, nor are they told how traumatic and long-term the effects are. Judge Nina Lowry, at that time the only woman judge at the Old Bailey who tries rape cases, is aware of the lack of sympathy for victims, commenting in 1990, 'Our male judges have been insensitive to the horror and anguish suffered at the hand of male rapists.'

Evidence of Consent

The main emphasis should not be on why the woman did not resist but on the process of negotiation between the defendant and the complainant that led up to the alleged rape, the attitudes of the defendant towards women and the defendant's past sexual experience.

Sex and rape, it is often argued, are difficult to distinguish between. As a recent *Times* leader (30 April 1994) explained:

The sex act is a normal human function which becomes a crime only when it is carried out against the will of one of the participants. Thus the act of rape – as opposed to any other violence which might accompany it – exists only if it is perceived as such.

But is this really so? It is sometimes not as difficult as imagined to differentiate between consensual and non-consensual sex. It is argued that rape is a difficult crime to prove because it leaves no physical trace, but this is true of other crimes too. The difference between stealing and borrowing and cases of fraud raise the same problem as rape. They depend on the evidence of the complainant. Yet if a woman reports a burglary, or makes an insurance claim, her word is not automatically doubted, her reliability as a witness attacked (see Temkin 1987). Her integrity would not be questioned, her statement would not be picked to pieces and her whole life would not come under investigation, as is the case in rape trials.

In determining consent or non-consent, more weight is given to indirect indicators such as the use of force and signs of resistance than to the credibility of the complainant and her account of what happened. To overcome this, feminists have proposed that a clear distinction needs to be made between 'voluntary agreement' and 'acquiescence' or submission as a result of threat or fear (see Scutt 1977). Discovering whether the woman gave her active consent should be investigated, rather than assuming consent was given unless there is strong evidence to the contrary. Kennedy (1992) suggests that the standard of the reasonable person should be applied, and rather than having to prove that the woman did not consent, as is the case at present, the jury should be asked whether the reasonable person should have known that the woman was not consenting. The criteria would be absence of consent not presence of dissent.

Defence counsels resort to all kinds of argument to suggest that the woman really consented. In one trial I monitored the defence incongruously asked the complainant, 'Did you tell him he turned you on?' When asked why she sarcastically smiled, she replied incredulously, 'I don't say that sort of thing, it's not in my personality.'

Arguments about whether or not women were 'lubricated' are particularly pernicious. Much confused thinking pervades this issue.

A woman police officer I spoke to who had been on the special course on sexual assault at Hendon Police Training College in London told me quite fallaciously that forensic tests could ascertain from the fluids whether or not the complainant had consented. If some police believe this, jurors are often equally confused by the lack of injuries. It is understandable that such an argument can plant a seed of doubt in the jury's mind, particularly if not refuted by the judge.

Myths about women 'really wanting it' appear in different guises. In one trial a woman was asked the following questions:

DEFENCE COUNSEL: Did you unzip his private parts...his fly?

COMPLAINANT: No. We were sitting on different sofas.

DC: You fondled his private parts and then invited him to the bedroom and had sex with him with his full consent?

C: No.

DC: Why didn't you grab his penis?

C: I didn't want to touch him.

DC: Didn't you want to stop him?

C: What could I have done?

DC: You had long fingernails, didn't you? You wanted to have a child with him, didn't you? I put it to you that you have been telling nothing but lies.

Paradoxically, if she had grabbed his penis, it would probably have been used as evidence that she was aroused. Such questions completely overlook what is and is not possible in such situations.

In another case the defendant was asked whether the complainant fondled his penis, whether she put her mouth on his penis, whether she helped him put his penis in her vagina, to which he replied; 'She enjoyed it. I think it got inside by itself. Or, I suppose, she was wet; she definitely wasn't dry. She was enjoying it.'

Evidence of lubrication came up in several trials I attended. This is how a defence counsel cross-examined a complainant:

DEFENCE COUNSEL: As far as your knickers were concerned, you didn't assist him?

COMPLAINANT: No.

DC: How could he get them off without your help?

C: I don't know, but he did.

DC: What happened to them?

c: I threw them away and burnt them.

DC: Why didn't you save them to show to the police?

c: What for?

(*No answer. The DC changes the subject.*)

DC: He touched your vagina and it was lubricated.

c: It was not lubricated.

The defence counsel's suggestion of lubrication is to imply that the woman is enjoying the experience.

A woman I interviewed about her medical examination described how she felt when the doctor commented on the state of her vagina:

At one point the doctor examining me said, 'Well, your vagina feels moist, seems like a normal vagina', and I thought, 'What is he telling me that for? Is he saying I enjoyed it, or there is no trauma there so it did not happen?' I did not really know what his comment was for.

The confusion here is over the meaning of biological or physiological changes. Sexual arousal may cause the vagina to lubricate, but this does not mean that a moist vagina necessarily implies sexual arousal. There is great variability among women as to the changing state of the vagina at different points of the menstrual cycle and lubrication does not necessarily have anything to do with sexual arousal. Fear could affect lubrication, as could alcohol. Additionally, it is quite possible to be sexually aroused by being raped, which does not make the assault any less serious. The assumption in the above example is that a woman could want sex without even knowing herself. It reduces the whole issue of consent to absurdity, in which the woman is denied any subjectivity or knowledge of her own desire. This becomes clear in the following cross-examination of the defendant:

PROSECUTING COUNSEL: You gave her a kiss but there was no response.

DEFENDANT: No.

PC: That is because you frightened her into submitting?

D: No...Women, they're really complicated, you know. I've come across women who play hard to get, but when I make a move they respond. I'm saying she wanted it. Her body wanted it but her mind was somewhere else.

PC: You told us she wasn't a good conversationalist?

The response of the prosecuting counsel is as baffling as the defendant's statement. He does nothing to counter the defendant's assertion that the woman really wanted sex by reference to her own account of the assault, in which she described how she had tried everything to get him to go, making it quite clear that she never wanted to have sex with him. He does not suggest to the jury that the defendant's sexist views – he does not believe that when women say 'No' they mean 'No', and his argument that because she was lubricated, he can assert his right to take the decision for her corroborate her version of events. Her subjectivity is irrelevant.

A physiological reaction to sexual assault therefore means nothing about whether or not the woman consented. Similarly with male rape, victims sometimes have erections and even ejaculate, which can undermine the victim's feelings of self-worth as he feels he is in some way colluding with his assailant (McMullen 1990: 73).[13] This in no way implies consent. These issues are complicated and should be explained to the jury rather than being used as a way of manipulating them into disbelieving the women.

Absence of Distress

Paradoxically, the complainant's distress is not seen as corroborative, but absence of distress can be used against her. Let us look at some of the arguments judges put forward regarding the woman's distress. Judge Williams, in summing up the Diggle case on 20 August 1993, argued that the woman's distress cannot corroborate other evidence but can confirm it:

What is not independent is Ms H's apparent distress when she ran into her friends' bedroom. Nor is it when the policewoman asked her about what had happened, as it is not an independent source, although it is not irrelevant. It may show her conduct after the alleged incident. It may confirm her other evidence.

On 1 September 1993, in another case heard at the Old Bailey, Judge Smedley commented on why evidence of the complainant's distress should not be regarded as relevant at all:

13. Kinsey (1948) pointed out that erections and ejaculations among boys can be caused by fear, anger or being yelled at, and such sexual responses have absolutely no relevance to whether or not the individuals consented or were in any way responsible for what happened to them.

A word of warning. If the account the complainant is giving was completely fabricated, you may think she is clever, then clever enough to act out distress.

The grounds for excluding such evidence as corroborative is that the victim is the source of the distress and corroboration has to be evidence from a different source.[14]

One difficulty jurors experience is that rape often has no visible signs. This is why asking the victim about the aftermath of rape is so vital. In the Vicarage rape case, burglars broke into a vicarage and raped Jill Saward, the vicar's daughter. The men were sentenced more harshly for the burglary than the rape. Michael Saward, the vicar, admitted that he misread his daughter's inward state by her outward demeanour: 'Both the judge and myself made, I suppose you might say, a masculine response.[15] This may well be true, but why then is the complainant not asked about her reaction? 'What are we meant to do?' his daughter asks. 'Wear a sign? Nobody in the court ever asked how I felt, or asked anybody else how I was' (Saward 1990).

A stark example of this was in the trial of Simpson on 17 November 1993 (see page 164), where the complainant, Mary, the woman allegedly raped in the church courtyard, had begun to describe her reaction to being raped: .

Since that night it happened everyone in the house has not known what to say to me and I have been trying to be normal so they don't have to be different to me. [*Pause*] At least so per cent of the time I'm depressed. I can't play with the children any more. Every girl or woman imagines [pause] meeting someone and perhaps even marrying someone, and I can't even imagine going to a club and dancing with someone or getting in a cab.

The defence counsel interrupted at this point and, turning to the judge, said, 'I sympathize, your honour, but I fear this is becoming a speech...' The defendant, who had been acquitted four times, was acquitted again.

14. In Scotland, on the other hand, in order to achieve a standard of proof 'beyond reasonable doubt' the prosecution evidence must be corroborated. However, the woman's distress is regarded as corroboration. There is a requirement that evidence is corroborated by the testimony of at least two witnesses or by other evidence incriminating the accused from two separate sources. A person cannot, unless statute authorizes it, be convicted on the evidence of a single witness. The accused can decide not to give evidence and undergo the ordeal of cross-examination.

15. In the BBC 1 *Everyman* documentary 'No Great Trauma', 16 September 1990.

In several cases evidence was given by witnesses that the complainant had been in a state of shock when, half clad, in the middle of the night, she had rung desperately at a neighbour's door. Not only was this disregarded as irrelevant in a number of trials, but the prosecution rarely even found it necessary to explain why else she should have been in this state. The argument is put forward that she could be faking it and it is not considered necessary to explain why, as the myth lives that women are known to frequently make false allegations.

One of the main findings of research into reactions to rape is that there is no typical reaction. Some women express anxiety immediately; for others the reaction may be delayed, but is every bit as traumatic. A common tactic used by the defence to support the idea that the woman is making a false allegation is to suggest that her reactions are not typical of a rape victim. In one of the Mulherne trials (see page 191), evidence that the complainant had not broken down was used to imply that she had not been raped. In her cross-examination, the defence counsel argued that, according to the doctor, Jessica was 'not at all distressed' and had cried for about twenty seconds while talking but then smiled and carried on talking. Here is her cross-examination by the defence counsel:

DEFENCE COUNSEL: So the doctor has got it wrong?

JESSICA: Well, I was distressed.

JUDGE: Were you showing...the doctor can probably only go on what she can see. Did you show any signs of distress to the doctor beyond the twenty seconds?

J: Well, for a while I did, yeah, but I was calm as well.

DC: What signs, in the light of His Honour's questions, were you showing of distress to this doctor?

J: Well, I did cry and...

DC: Anything else? I mean, is this doctor right or wrong or just mistaken?

J: Well, maybe, I wasn't showing signs of distress at some times, but I was feeling it.

DC: I see. So this doctor it was a woman doctor – failed to see that underneath it you were, in fact, distressed, as you said. She says you were not at all distressed, making the point you cried for about twenty seconds but then smiled and carried on talking What is the picture that we should have?

J: I was distressed, but she was doing her best to try and, you know, be nice and cheer me up.

As Jessica explained:

A lot of people expect you to be in tears because that sort of thing happened, but I'm not that sort of person. I don't show anyone my feelings. What happened to me, I deal with it in my own way. I don't need anyone else's help.

Jessica is perfectly right and the judge should be aware of the research findings in regard to rape trauma syndrome, rather than collude with the defence counsel's position.

On only one occasion did I hear a woman forensic doctor refute the defence counsel's suggestion that anger was an unusual response to rape and that, more typically, victims reacted with tears. Her emphasis that women can respond in different ways, that a moist vagina does not indicate consent and rape does not necessarily leave any visible signs of damage or reddening, was crucial in leading to the conviction of the defendant.

DEFENCE COUNSEL: What state was she in?

DOCTOR: She seemed very annoyed.

DC: Would you expect to see that in a rape victim?

D: You see all sorts of reactions.

DC: You don't usually see annoyance or anger. D: Oh yes, you do.

DC: Her vulva was moist. Do you attach any significance to that?

D: Moisture could be consistent with sucking.

DC: Can you help me with this? If a woman is being subjected to forceful intercourse at a time when she describes herself as rigid, wouldn't you expect to see reddening?

D: No, very often you see nothing.

Lack of injuries can be taken as an indication of consent. In the following case lack of supportive proof in the form of material injuries resulting from the woman's resistance was taken as evidence that she had consented, even though she claimed she did not and had been frozen with fear. Take the following two extracts:

POLICE CONSTABLE: She says she screamed.

DEFENDANT: She was squeaking, not screaming

PC: What did you think that meant?

D: I thought she was enjoying it.

DEFENCE COUNSEL: You're bigger than him. How could he make you do anything?

COMPLAINANT: You probably haven't ever been scared in your life. He said he'd punch me in the face if I didn't do what he wanted...

DC: When he entered, you were lubricated.

C: No.

DC: You weren't responding much to him and he got off.

C: He was raping me.

DC: Was it possible you wanted to have sex with someone else and were making do with him?

C: (*Incredulous*) No!

In rape trials, jurors are instructed that under the influence of sex women lie so convincingly that they will fabricate a story of rape. The judge does not draw the jury's attention to the fact that most women who have been raped cannot face the ordeal they will have to go through if they complain to the police (many, indeed, cannot face telling anyone; and they are often threatened with retaliation if they do go to the police). One woman, when asked why she had not gone at once to the police, replied, 'Because he told me that if I told anyone or went to the police, he'd come back for me and the children.' Only if she is half dead can the jury be sure she is not a malicious schemer.

Another procedural problem I encountered is that jurors are not told that if they fail to reach a verdict, there will be a retrial. However, very often the complainant cannot face giving evidence again. In some cases, no verdict is reached at the retrial, in which case the case is dropped. Juries should be told of the importance of reaching a verdict. In one case, after only three hours the jury were called back into court, where the judge directed them to reach a majority verdict if they were unable to reach a unanimous one. After only another half an hour, they were called back into court, having failed to reach a majority verdict, and were dismissed by the judge. In a murder trial they would have been given far more time and would even have been put up for the night if they could not reach a verdict. This case was not unusual and few of the cases I attended ever went on after 4.30 p.m.

Discounting Rape: The Myth of False Allegations

Myths about women making false allegations override commonsense explanations of why they should run naked into the street, cry compulsively, spend the night in police stations for fear of retribution for taking the case to court, change their name, move house or go into hiding. In one case, several police officers, including a police surgeon, all agreed the complainant was in acute distress and showing every sign that she had been raped. The prosecution counsel (who was presenting her case) failed even to mention her distress in his summing-up. In this case I abandoned my role as observer and followed him out of the court to ask him why. He said it was absurd to regard the woman's state as important as she could be faking distress. This exemplifies the lack of sympathy between the prosecution counsel and the complainant, and the way it can prejudice her case.

The myth of women crying rape, whether after bad sex or for whatever reason, is crucial to the condoning of rape. The problem is not that women falsely report being raped but that most women do not report rape at all, and those who do are subjected to a process of character assassination which leaves them bewildered.

The phrase 'false allegations' needs unpicking. The malicious woman who concocts a false story to take revenge on her past lover would not get very far in the legal system, where a past sexual relationship usually precludes cases even getting to court. It is possible that on rare occasions women who have perhaps been raped or abused in the past may allege that it has happened again, but it is unlikely that a sensitive investigator would not be able to uncover this. Temkin (1987) points out that there is no evidence that fabricating allegations happens more often in rape cases than in other types of crime. In the Home Office study (L. Smith 1989: 12), the police decided that they had evidence of this in only seventeen of the cases reported to them from two London boroughs over a three-year period. There is no evidence such cases reach court. According to a Scottish study of police response published in 1983, although some officers talked about a high rate of false allegations, they found it very difficult to recall particular cases they had dealt with that were unquestionably false. When I asked the director of one of the regional CPS offices who had worked for the CPS since 1985 if he had ever come across a case in which a woman had made a false allegation, he somewhat sheepishly admitted that he could not think of one.

Most commonly, however, false allegations refer to the woman's word pitted against the defendant's protestation that she consented. In most trials, the fact of sexual intercourse is not disputed; the issue is the meaning of consent. Men's exaggerated fear of false allegation is perhaps more about men's fantasies about women. It reflects a society where forced sex is far more common than imagined and where women who are forced into sex often do not name this as rape.

Two Scottish Office researchers found that reasons given by the police for complainant fabrication included the following: to explain a pregnancy; as an excuse for getting home late; spite; because of a hyperactive imagination; and remorse (Chambers and Millar 1987: 61). Similar arguments are presented in court by the defence.

The emotive language used by defence counsels is well illustrated by the summing-up of the case of a musician who had moved in with the complainant for six weeks when he was rendered homeless. He had borrowed money from her and the relationship had ended when he failed to pay her back. Three months after he had moved out, during which time she had made a number of attempts to contact him in order to get back her money, amounting to over £1,000, he came round and, according to her evidence, raped her. The defence counsel painted her as a vindictive woman who had been passionately in love with the defendant and, when rejected, planned his downfall:

This is a case of a woman scorned. Hell hath no fury like a woman scorned. An emotional case, a case of love-hate, passion and ultimate destruction. The heights she went to destroy this man, the utmost to pull the wool over your eyes rape, an emotive word. Don't be fooled by her tears.

This kind of rhetoric is justified in the adversarial system on the grounds that it is the defence counsel's role to produce any kind of argument, however fallacious, which will win the case. But this would be fair only if the prosecution presented the complainant's case with equal deviousness or at the very least a degree of candour. Yet the prosecution often does little to refute such outlandish accusations and, since he or she has not even met the complainant beforehand, is in no position to do so. Imbalances between the defence and prosecution counsel's approach pervade all the trials. This could be due too to the greater motivation of defence counsels to win the case, or it could be that the prosecution sees its role as being to dispassionately present the facts. The defence has no such intention.

So what other reasons, besides revenge, are presented for women making false allegations? The second most common reason put forward is fear of parents or the community. This is the argument used where the young woman is a virgin, like in the Simpson case, involving Mary, a highly respectable young woman of twenty-six. The judge here appears to have found it difficult to think of a reason why the complainant should make a false allegation. This is perhaps why, in his summing-up, he advised the jury:

Now that the offence is a sexual offence and consequently there is a special warning that I must give you. Complaints of this nature are easy to make and difficult to refute. It is the experience of the courts that sometimes false complaints are made. Whilst the motives for making such complaints may sometimes be obvious, on other occasions the complainant's motives may be obscure or the real reason for her acting in that way may never come to light.

In other words, juries are being instructed to be suspicious of a woman's word even if no possible reason can be uncovered for her to have lied. In this case the complainant was cross-examined about whether she had falsely alleged rape in order to explain her late arrival home to her parents. She denied this adamantly and said she would not have got into trouble for being home half an hour later than expected in any case. The defence counsel, in his summing-up, questioned her testimony in the following words:

I'm not suggesting she is barking mad but she may have underlying problems that have brought her to lie in this way. By the time she has got to court she has fully rehearsed in the story she is going to tell. They can act out the lies, they can hold their head for the whole time they are giving evidence, their pulse rate and blood pressure may go through the roof.

In other words, women are prone to be very clever and devious and you should not believe a word they say. He continued:

She may have problems at home. She may have strict parents, more than she would admit. She was more than a few moments overdue. The kebab shop was a twenty-minute walk away so she would have been significantly later than she was expected.

Commonly it is argued that women make false allegations through fear of their boyfriend or husband, who, it is alleged, they are two-timing. Rarely does the question arise of why they do not just keep quiet about it if this were the case. Fear of the defendant's girlfriend was put forward in another case.'Since the complainant had told the girlfriend about the rape, this seemed completely farfetched. Yet the defence counsel asked, 'Did she lead him on, prostitute herself, or consent and then change her mind at the last minute when the man was unable to control himself?' This is based on the commonly accepted idea that male sexuality, once aroused, is uncontrollable.

Results of Analysis of Trials

In the twenty trials of acquaintance rape where we took transcripts, the defendant was found guilty only when he was shown to have blatantly lied in his statement (Mulherne's one conviction) or to have admitted that he raped the woman (another case, in which, when arrested, the defendant said, 'I did it', in the hearing of the complainant and two policemen), or, in the case of the lawyer Diggle, to have said to the police on arrest, 'I spent £200 on her. Why can't I do what I did to her?' In two of the cases involving Mulherne, he was also shown to have lied, but this did not prevent an acquittal. Since the acquittal rate is so high for rape, to assume that men who do not have any previous convictions are innocent is unjustified. Defining recidivism as repeated convictions for the same crime rests on the untenable assumption that most rapes result in convictions.

Conclusion

In this chapter I have shown how from the moment rape is reported to the police various processes are set in motion to channel cases out of the legal system to reduce the numbers that actually go to trial. Such practices include the 'no-criming' of reports, the downgrading of the charge of rape to a lesser offence by the police and plea-bargaining. The Islington research reported here shows that even before cases reach the CPS as many as half the cases of rape or attempted rape originally reported have been dropped. Most of them are not even included in police statistical returns to the Home

Office as they have been 'no-crimed'. There is also a tendency for the police to reclassify cases of attempted rape to indecent assault in order to improve their clear-up figures. Jurors are unaware of how few cases reach court or of the various ways in which the complainant is at a disadvantage in the court procedure.

The reluctance of the CPS to take more cases to court is mainly due to the difficulty in gaining convictions. The research based on the monitoring of trials at the Central Criminal Court indicates that the main purpose of trials appears to be to protect men from false allegations rather than to give victims justice. The failure to provide women with their own legal representation makes a mockery of the idea that rape trials involve judging one person's word against another. The emphasis on corroboration and the exclusion or lack of emphasis on the complainant's version and reaction weight the trial in favour of the defendant. Additionally, as we shall see in the next chapter, the different criteria used to judge the credibility of the defendant and the complainant are deeply distorting and sexist and against the spirit of the improvements suggested by the Sexual Offences (Amendment) Act of 1976 and the Youth Justice and Criminal Evidence Act of 1999.

Chapter 5

Sexual Reputation and Credibility

There is no branch of law, no class of case, where it is so easy for a woman to make an allegation of this kind and to make it against a professional man. It is men too who require protection of their reputations against baseless allegations of rape, which frequently occur (QC quoted in Adler 1987: 84).

Have you ever asked a woman who has been raped whether she enjoyed it? Have you ever asked her whether she asked for it by wearing a short skirt or false eyelashes, going out late at night or inviting someone in for coffee? Have you ever asked her whether her shoes are not 'real' leather but 'cheap', implying she might be too? Have you ever asked her to describe loudly and clearly in a roomful of people exactly what happened in the assault, where and how she was touched, what she felt at each point and why she did not fight back more strenuously? Have you ever asked her whether she has ever had an abortion, or a past lover, or demanded details of her menstrual cycle? Have you ever asked a seventeen-year-old girl whose father has just died of AIDS why she did not go to see her father in hospital when he was dying? Probably not, but this is what is inflicted on the minority of women whose cases are backed by the CPS and taken forward to jury trial. Under 15 per cent of reported cases get this far, including cases where the defendant pleads guilty. The rest are dropped, as we have seen, before ever reaching a jury trial, without any consultation with the complainant.[1] These are the types of question which defence counsels in wigs and gowns are encouraged to put, on the grounds that this is the only way men can be protected from false allegations. Another explanation is that such

1. According to the Home Office studies, one in four reported cases reached jury trial in 1985, but this excluded cases 'no-crimed' by the police during the first month and does not take into consideration the declining number taken forward by the CPS.

questions are asked to destroy the credibility of the complainant. In this chapter, with reference to the trials monitored, I shall show why the conviction rate is so low. The names of the defendants in the trials that we monitored have all been changed.

The image of the law is one of impartiality, objectivity, rationality and neutrality. Traditionally, the law is supposed to treat all who come before the courts equally, regardless of class, race, sex or creed. This is far from the case. Stark examples of how male bias enters into court proceedings in rape trials are given by examining the criteria used to evaluate reputation, which is the basis on which credibility is judged. In this chapter I question the grounds for the rules of evidence, which determine how the woman's and the man's evidence should be judged, and show how these rules are used in a discriminatory way. A close look at the conduct of rape trials and at the failure of reforms to alter the way the complainant's sexual reputation and sexual character are put on trial suggests that the law is being misused and far too many rapists are being wrongly acquitted. This is due to the inbuilt sexism of the law, its procedures and practices, and many judges, at both crown court and court of appeal level, who use their discretion to perpetuate the sexism rather than implement the reforms of the Sexual Offences (Amendment) Act (1976).

In this chapter, two core questions are addressed. First, I show how defence counsels were successful at circumventing the protection the 1976 Act aimed to give complainants. Instead they continue to subject the complainant to a barrage of questions regarding their sexual character or, on some occasions, their past sexual history. Second, I illustrate how judging the man's credibility on the basis of lack of a past criminal record and his occupation is totally misleading and often gives the defendant an unfair advantage. I argue that judges' directions to the jury to weigh up the relative reputations of the complainant and defendant should be eliminated and that sexual history evidence should not be allowed unless it is strictly relevant.

Trial judges in British rape cases have considerable influence on the way in which evidence is presented and judged. They can question witnesses at any stage and cross-examine the accused if he gives evidence, as long as such questions do not indicate that he is guilty. After the prosecution and the defence have summed up the evidence, the judge, in his final comments, directs the jury on how to evaluate it in order to reach a verdict. There is considerable scope here to influence the jury. Judges can direct an acquittal but must not direct a conviction. Fear of excessive judicial influence has led many US states to restrict the summing-up to an explanation of the law, leaving the jury to untangle the facts for themselves. In the UK judges sum up the facts as well as the law, which gives them a great deal more influence (see McEwan 1992).

In their summing-up, judges instruct jurors to judge one person's word against another and then go on to advise them on how to do this. They direct them to base this judgement on the respective reputations of the man and woman, determined by totally different criteria, criteria reflected in social life where reputation has different meanings. In talking of a woman of good repute, the implication is that she is chaste, whereas for a man, good reputation implies that he is professionally sound. In court, therefore, a woman's reputation is judged on the basis of her assumed sexual character and past sexual history. For a man, his occupation and lack of previous criminal record are the two main factors deemed to be relevant. Quite apart from the personal bias of individual judges, then, sexist assumptions are already built into the way the rules of evidence on character and credibility are interpreted and applied in court.

As we have seen in the adversarial system of justice, a defendant is innocent unless the prosecution proves beyond reasonable doubt that he is guilty. The defendant does not have to prove his innocence; the prosecution has to prove guilt. So how the jury are directed to view evidence is crucial, as if they have the slightest doubt about the woman's credibility, then they are directed to acquit.

In order to understand the justification for the disparity, we need to look at the historical basis of the present rules of evidence, which determine how the woman's and the man's statements should be judged. The justification for these rules lies with the ruling made by Lord Chief Justice Matthew Hale in the seventeenth century, where he described rape as a charge 'easily to be made and hard to be proved, and harder to be defended by the party accused, tho' never so innocent'.[2] Hale argued that the one who so easily charges 'rape'

---

2. Sir Matthew Hale, *The History of the Pleas of the Crown*, 1 (London Professional Books, 1971). This statement is the usual basis for, if not the actual wording of, the 'cautionary' instruction given to juries in rape cases.

must first prove her own lack of guilt. In this respect three issues are considered relevant: corroboration of the victim's account; prompt reporting by the woman; and the woman's past sexual history. The first two issues were discussed in the last chapter.

Sexual Character Evidence

The Relevance of Reputation

In their summing-up of the trial judges are required to direct the jury to take into account the defendant's lack of previous convictions, his present occupation and any evidence regarding his standing in the community. In view of the high acquittal rate, which indicates that at least some men without convictions must be guilty, this has little relevance. As we shall see in Chapter 6, the defendants had been acquitted three and five times. Two American researchers pointed out that by defining recidivism as repeated conviction for the same crime involved making untenable assumptions that all rapes are reported and all reports result in conviction (Groth and Mcfadin 1982). They asked two groups of convicted rapists in a confidential questionnaire to record any offences for which they had not been convicted or which had not been detected. Fifty-five per cent of the sample admitted an average of five other offences. They regarded this as an underestimation. Lack of previous convictions has no bearing on whether or not the defendant is guilty.

The judge is not similarly obliged in law to direct the jury to consider the good character of the complainant, or her lack of previous convictions, when reaching their verdict. Instead, by default, the jury are left to assess her character on the basis of the evidence adduced at the trial. Since such evidence rests on her sexual character and, at the discretion of the judge, her past sexual history, the jury are obliged to assess relative credibility on the basis of two completely different sets of criteria. Ironically, the defendant's sexual behaviour is not often questioned, even though he is on trial for a sexual offence. His past sexual history is not allowed to be brought up. It is in relation to character evidence that sexism invades most starkly into the legal process.

As has already been seen, for a woman to speak of her reputation has sexual connotations; her sexual reputation is central to her social identity. In adolescence, a young woman's reputation is based on her *assumed* sexual behaviour – not on whether she really is promiscuous but on whether or not she is assumed to have 'slept around'. For young women, reputation is something to be guarded. It is under threat not merely if she is known to have sex with anyone other than her steady boyfriend but for a whole range of behavioural traits that have little to do with actual sexual experience. The battery of verbal insults they can be subjected to 'slag', 'slut' or 'bitch' – though used as synonymous with 'whore', often bore no relation to the young woman's actual sexual behaviour. The designation 'slag' is liable to be applied on the basis of a variety of factors aside from promiscuity itself: dress, make-up, talking to or about men, or talking about sexuality, premeditating sex by using contraception, going out alone, being seen with more than one man. Appearance is crucial: wearing too much make-up, having your skirt slit too high, or your trousers too tight, or your tops too low. When examining how such insults were used, I found (Lees 1993) that girls who did not have a steady boyfriend or were 'unattached' were the most likely to be so categorized. Getting a steady boyfriend or getting married is therefore the only sure way to protect your reputation. A woman who is seen as 'autonomous', a woman who is not married, or is a single parent, is seen as unrespectable. Exactly the same criteria are deemed to be relevant in rape trials. Being single, divorced or a single mother also carry the implication of promiscuity or lack of respectability.

A man's reputation or virtue is not determined by his sexual status or conquests. Indeed, his reputation is 'at risk' if he is deemed sexually inexperienced, as we saw in the Diggle case. Paradoxically, defence counsels sometimes use a man's sexual history for example, evidence of a girlfriend, wife or regular sex to imply that he is not a rapist. Such evidence (of promiscuity) can act in his favour. Of greater importance, however, is his standing in the world. At school his fighting or sporting prowess, his good looks or his brain may determine his ranking in the group and his 'reputation'. Additionally, being sexist and 'hard' and denigrating women are crucial ingredients of reputation in some male circles.

The Complainant's Sexual Character

In the trial transcripts I examined I found that the perfectly normal behaviour of young women is presented as evidence that they provoked the man's attack or asked for it. Questions addressed to the woman in the trials I monitored included whether she had had previous sex with men other than the defendant; whether she was a single mother; whether the man she was living with was the father of her children; the colour of her present and past boyfriends (where the woman was white); who looked after her children while she was at work; whether she was in the habit of going to nightclubs on her own late at night; whether she smoked cannabis and drank alcohol (when there was no evidence of this); what underwear she had on; whether she wore false eyelashes and red lipstick; whether the defendant 'had used her previously' (rather than raped her); details of her menstrual flow; and on one occasion whether she had a vibrator in her drawer wrapped in a purple sock. It was frequently insinuated that she had told 'nothing but lies'. In the Scottish Office studies (see Chambers and Millar 1986; Brown et al. 1992), attacks on character were also common. In more than half the cases where consent was at issue, questioning included whether the complainant was divorced, was an unmarried mother, had a habit of drinking with strangers or drank to excess.

Irrelevant past sexual history evidence was still brought up again and again in research undertaken in the late 1980s, 1990s and early 2000 for Channel 4 *Dispatches*. One woman in my 1989 research was asked whether she had had an abortion and whether she had had sex with her boyfriend afterwards. Neither of these questions was the least bit relevant to the alleged rape. Witness the following dialogue:

DEFENCE COUNSEL: With regard to your stomach hurting, you said this was because you had had a termination and you weren't supposed to have sex? When had you previously had sex?

COMPLAINANT: I think it was Saturday.

DC: So you were able to have sex?

C: *Having sex with your boyfriend is different to someone raping you.*

In one of Mulherne's trials, Jessica, the complainant, who was nineteen years old, was asked when cross-examined by the defence counsel about an abortion she had had three years previously. He asked, 'When did you have an abortion?' To which she replied, 'When I was sixteen. *That's got nothing to do with it, has it?*' The defence counsel then asked the judge's permission to question her further about her sexual history:

DC: Before this incident on 5 February, when was the last time that you had had sexual intercourse with anyone?

C: That was with my boyfriend.

These questions should not, according to the spirit of the Sexual Offences (Amendment) Act (1976), have been allowed.

Sometimes questions about past sexual history are not direct but are insinuated. On one occasion when the defence counsel did not ask for permission to question the complainant about her past sexual history, it was suggested that when the defendant penetrated her anus, he meant to have vaginal intercourse from behind and the defence counsel slipped in the question, 'You've had intercourse like that before?', with the implication that she was sexually experienced.

Being homeless and on Social Security came up in one case and was used to imply that the complainant had 'asked for it'.

DEFENCE COUNSEL: You didn't have anywhere to live, did you?

COMPLAINANT: I've got friends, that s where I went.

DC: I suggest you asked him if you could stay at his flat.

C: No, I didn't. He suggested it.

Lack of a husband or partner was emphasized in several cases.

DEFENCE COUNSEL: Being a single mother must be hard?

COMPLAINANT: Not really.

DC: Were you keen to have a relationship?

C: Not really.

DC: Were you keen to have a man around?

C: Not really.

Janine, a lesbian aged twenty-five, who said she was raped in a minicab on her way home from a gay club, was asked (where the jury could not reach a verdict) how much she had had to drink, what she was wearing, why she was wearing no pants and whether alcohol made her do things she would not normally do. Finally, the following cross-examination ensued:

DEFENCE COUNSEL: He asked you if you'd had a nice evening and you said, 'Not really. They're all poofters in there, I'm looking for a real man.' He said, 'You've got one here.'

COMPLAINANT: No – and I would never use that phrase about gay men. It's very insulting.

DC: You then said, 'Prove it. Pull over', and you climbed from the back seat into the front seat.

(*And later*)

You felt his sex organ on the outside and inside of his trousers.

(*At this point Janine tried to subvert the cross-examination:*)

C: *You must be joking!*

Even after sitting through a number of trials where the defendant was acquitted, I found Janine's case astonishing. In this case the jury failed to reach a verdict in both the trial and retrial, so the defendant went free. He had apparently laughed and smirked throughout the attack. It made no sense that a woman who was a lesbian would have had sex in these circumstances – with such a man or with a man at all. Nor was there any reason why she should make a false allegation. The main reason the jury were unable to reach a verdict appears to have been the introduction of a 'red herring' concerning whether the alleged rape had taken place in the front or the back of the minicab. Forensic analysts had failed to test the car covers, so the issue could not be resolved. This was presented as important, as there was a discrepancy between their versions and such evidence, if it had been available, would have provided corroboration. This was skilfully used by the defence to plant doubt in the jury's mind. It is also possible that a woman who defines herself as a lesbian is seen as a less reliable witness.

In another case the defence suggested that the complainant was an obsessive hysterical woman, asking such questions as, 'You used to ring him up anywhere that he went, didn't you?', 'You wanted to know where he was all the time', 'You wanted his entire attention on you', 'You tried to get close to him', 'You became obsessive', 'You admired him...because you heard he was a singer going places', 'You hoped he'd start loving you.' She replied 'No' to each of these questions, but finally burst out angrily, 'I've lived on my own for five years. I don't need a man. You're trying to put it across that I tried to trap him, that I wanted him to be the only person in my life, but that's not true.' She was also questioned about going out to work, which carried implications of neglectful mothering:

DEFENCE COUNSEL: Who looked after the baby? Friends or family? No regular pattern?

COMPLAINANT: I left him with friends.

DC: You were giving him money to the extent that you starved your daughter?

C: No, I'd saved food for her and he promised to bring more for her.

In his summing-up the defence counsel in the case argued, based on no evidence whatsoever, 'It's not just men who want sex. It also applies to women, that they're keen for physical contact when they're without a relationship, and she was somebody who was looking for physical satisfaction.' Even if she had wanted a relationship, this does not explain why she would 'cry rape' when he had come round.

In another case lack of contact with her children's fathers was used as evidence to suggest that the complainant was 'embittered towards men' and was promiscuous.

DEFENCE COUNSEL: As far as your two children are concerned, you don't have contact with either of the fathers?

COMPLAINANT: No.

DC: You don't know where they live?

C: I do know. They have got nothing to do with this case.

DC: They don't support you in any way?

C: No.

In several cases heard at the Old Bailey in August 1993, race was a theme to which the prosecution counsel continually returned. One woman who said she had been raped by a West Indian she had gone out with was asked, 'Do you often sleep with "ethnics"?' In another case the complainant (who was white) was asked about the colour of the father of her baby and whether or not he was a Rastafarian. She refused to answer. Racist questions were often quite explicit:

DEFENCE COUNSEL: Your ex-boyfriend, he's a Rastafarian, isn't he?

COMPLAINANT: *Might be.*

DC: Well, he's black anyway, isn't he?

C: *Might be.*

DC: Your boyfriend is known as Tony?

C: Yes.

DC: And Tracy's [her daughter] father?

C: Yes, not the same person.

DC: But Tracy's dad is West Indian?

C: Yes.

In the above case, the defendant, Dick, had been the victim's boyfriend five years previously. Her cohabitee was in prison for drunken driving and was a friend of his. She said Dick came round at 2 a.m. after drinking six pints and raped her. Details of sexual history with the defendant could be seen as relevant, in view of her past sexual relationship with him, albeit some years previously, but there was no reason why she should have been asked about the paternity of her child, about how old she was when she first had sex with the child's father, a different man altogether. On discovering that she had given birth when she was eighteen, the defence counsel commented, 'You began young.' The questioning of white women about the race of their assailants is undoubtedly aimed at undermining their respectability – that is, having a black lover carries this racist implication.

In several cases, it is questionable whether any sexual history evidence was relevant at all. In one, where the complainant alleged she had been raped by a minicab driver on the way back from going to a nightclub, she was asked by the prosecution whether she had a boyfriend, how long she had been going out with him, how long she had lived with him, whether she ever went out alone in the evenings and how often they had sex – all quite irrelevant questions. The defence counsel then asked her whether the relationship had its problems, whether her boyfriend was in court and whether she had discussed the case with him. He then went on to allege that she had cried rape when she discovered she had caught VD from the defendant. The complainant, Michelle, then burst out:

You have been implying this all the time. You have brought up my infection that this man Mr W – gave to me. I don't go around just having sex with any man. *I don't understand the relevance of the questions. You are just trying to embarrass me.*

In rape trials exactly the same criteria for judging a woman's reputation emerge again and again. The young woman who dresses quite normally in today's fashions is put on trial because of it. The purpose of such distortion is to give jurors the impression that the woman is provocative and therefore to blame for the assault. The identification of women as 'prey', liable to be attacked on the basis of how they dress or as a result of all kinds of perfectly normal behaviour, is a reflection of women's subordinate situation in society at large. The misogyny behind such depictions may not be apparent to most jurors, it is so taken for granted.

Some cases where the suspect went free beggar belief Simone, a twenty-year-old A-level student, was allegedly raped twice on her way home from a nightclub by a minicab driver. She managed to get out of the car and run away after the rape, leaving her coat in the car. No contraception was used and the complainant was terrified she might have contracted HIV. She went to a VD clinic and was found to have an infection, but not HIV. In the trial, great emphasis was placed on her clothing, which, by forcing her to discuss her underwear, seemed to be designed implicitly to undermine her credibility. First, she was cross-examined in the following way by the prosecution counsel:

PROSECUTION COUNSEL: Would you agree it's a dressy dress?

SIMONE: Yes.

PC: And the shoes are dressy shoes?

S: Yes.

RC: And would you say you were wearing a jacket which is quite a flimsy jacket?

S: No.

PC: Describe the material.

S: I can't.

PC: It was black.

S: Yes.

PC: Made out of cotton or wool?

S: I don't know.

PC: Were you dressed up or were you dressed in the usual way you dress for the club?

S: Dressed in the usual way.

The defense counsel later continued this line of questioning:

DEFENCE COUNSEL: What kind of material is your underwear made of? S: I don't know.

DC: It is actually transparent?

S: No.

DC: Please take it in your hands.

   (*At this point Simone tried to subvert the cross-examination:*)

S: *You are going to ask me to put it on, are you? It is not transparent.*

DC: Hold it up – so you say it's not transparent material?

S: No, it is opaque.

DC: It is material you can see through sufficiently in the light. S: No. Because I am dark, you can't see through it.

DC: You could see if you were wearing pants that night? S: Yes.

DC: But you weren't wearing any?

S: Yes, I was. I was wearing a G-string.

DC: Are you sure you described having your knickers pulled off you – that is, if you were wearing any, and I suggest you weren't?

S: I was.

DC: You weren't wearing any tights?

S: No.

DC: Stockings?

S: No.

DC: Socks?

S: No.

DC: And did you not have a petticoat on? S: No. I saw people with worse clothes than that.

DC: What do you mean by worse?

S: *It's no one's business what I wear: I wasn't naked.*

Simone is standing her ground but is in too weak a position to counteract the cross-examination successfully. The judge in his summing-up said the jury had to decide whether she was wearing a G-string or pants without explaining why this was relevant. The defendant was acquitted.

On some occasions the defence counsel goes to great pains to try to show the complainant is giving a false impression in court by not appearing as she normally does. This occurred in the Mulherne case:

DEFENCE COUNSEL: Forgive me for asking. I needn't put it to you again. Did you have make-up on in court yesterday?

STEPHANIE: Yes. Yes. Do you want to know why?

JUDGE: Well, I think he's more interested in whether yesterday's make-up would be termed your normal make-up.

S: It's my normal make-up.

DC: Foundation cream?

S: Yeah.

DC: Eyeshadow, bright red lipstick?

S: Did I have bright red lipstick on yesterday?

DC: Bright red lipstick. s: I can't remember what lipstick I had on. DC: Eye pencil?

s: Don't wear eye pencil.

DC: Never?

s: I used to.

DC: At time of this incident?

s: Probably.

DC: Mascara?

s: Yeah.

DC: Hair done prettily?

s: If you could call it pretty. No more than what I normally only do every day.

The implication of the above cross-examination is not simply that Stephanie is a tart, but also that she is a crafty young woman who has not put on make-up to try to deceive the jury. It is also worth noting that when she tries to explain why she is not wearing makeup, she is given no chance to do so. The aim of such cross-examination is to intimidate the witness and prevent her from appearing as credible. Another purpose is to uncover whether she is a 'good' or a 'bad' woman. Sometimes this underlying assumption is expressed quite explicitly. For example, in a trial on 2–4 August 1993 Judge Taylor intervened in the cross-examination of a young man accused of rape by a girl he had taken out to ask:

JUDGE: Did you regard this young woman as being respectable?

DEFENDANT: Yes.

J: You did not regard her as a tart?

Judges should intervene in trials only to clarify issues which they regard as crucial. The purpose of this question is puzzling It is not clear whether regarding her as a whore would have provided an excuse for the defendant to rape her. Indeed, it is not clear what the judge exactly is implying, what 'issue' he is clarifying.

In another trial I attended a seventeen-year-old girl had a row with the man she was cohabiting with and was locked out of her flat. Returning the next day and finding no one in, she met a neighbour, twice her age, whom she knew by sight and accepted his offer to wait in his flat. He raped her and she ran half clothed and hysterical into the street across the road to her flat and immediately rang the police. By the time the police arrived, the suspect had left in the middle of the night. He was not picked up for several days. She was so scared he would come and get her that she insisted on spending one night in a police cell during this time.

In court, according to the defendant, he agreed that he had asked the young woman if she would like to wait for her boyfriend in his flat. He claimed that when she had disappeared, he had gone to look for her and, to his astonishment, had found her naked in his bed. He said she had invited him to join her and claimed she had agreed to intercourse. At this point the judge, who had given the impression that he found the complainant very attractive, intervened with the following preposterous question:

JUDGE: Did you find her attractive as a woman, a girl?
DEFENDANT: She was attractive enough.
J: When you went into the bedroom you must have thought it was Christmas and Easter put together when you found her naked in your bed.

This appeared to be a blatant example of male camaraderie and titillation. The woman's reputation should be irrelevant to whether or not she has been raped. The law makes clear that it is against the law to rape a prostitute. Rendering the woman unrespectable is, however, one way the defence counsel casts doubt on her credibility. The woman's rather than the man's sexual character and credibility are what is on trial. The defendant was acquitted.

Even middle-aged married women are not immune from quite absurd questioning. Nora, aged fifty-two, whose house had been broken into when her husband was dying of cancer and who had woken to find a stranger on top of her with a knife at her throat, also had a gruelling experience in court. The fact that the case came up when her husband's cancer had progressed, just after he had had a brain operation, could not have helped. He was too ill to go to court. Nora said she could understand why people did not go through with the court process when women were treated as she was.

The defence said, 'I'm not saying you're lying but I suggest you were dreaming and you dreamt this.' I said, 'I suggest you're a bloody fool if you think that I would stand here and say all this if it's not true.' I just thought, 'Stand down, you bloody fool.'... It's horrible, because your mouth goes dry and you walk into that court and they've all got wigs on and it's awful really.

I thought I was going to drop. I must have a strong heart not to have had a heart attack from all this. When I get night terrors, I think I'm going to get a heart attack.

Menstruation

Clark (1987) argues that the detail with which women are required to describe assaults has increased with the development of forensic science and that this constitutes a process of disqualification. She compares the way rape was treated in the eighteenth and nineteenth centuries with today and shows how the very act of speaking about rape rendered women unrespectable in the Victorian era. At the most extreme, magistrates were known to dismiss cases on the basis that they could corrupt public morals. Now women are required to describe the assault in the minutest detail. As Carol Smart, a British criminologist, describes:

The woman is required to deny her part in a standard soft-porn fantasy scenario. This account is common currency, not only in pornographic magazines, but in downmarket tabloid newspapers. Accounts of sexy 'housewives' and frustrated nymphettes abound (Smart 1989: 40).

When attending rape trials I was puzzled by the frequent reference to menstruation. I began to understand it had a dual purpose: to publicly humiliate the complainant (as no respectable woman would broach such a subject in public, let alone in the lofty setting of a crown court) and to imply that she was a bit off key, perhaps totally irrational, a little hysterical, certainly an unreliable witness, prone to make false allegations. The frequent reference to menstruation in rape trials also alludes to women as seducers whose powers are overwhelming when menstruating.

The menstrual taboo can be traced back as far as recorded time. In many societies women are seen as polluting either in general or at particular times. A strong taboo against intercourse with a menstruating woman has existed since antiquity. The Old Testament declares a menstruating woman unclean for seven days, and anyone who touches her or anything she has touched or anything touched by someone she has touched is also unclean. Both Jews and Christians saw menstrual blood as unclean and responsible for child deformities (Ranke-Heinemann 1991: 21). In some communities women have been confined to menstrual huts and menstruating women have been seen as contaminated and banned from the worship of God. They are defiled. In the nineteenth century disordered menstruation, gynaecologists argued, could lead to injury to the nervous system and thus to mental illness (Groneman 1994).

Today the menstrual taboo lives on. The sense of shame attached to menstruation is reflected in sanitary advertisements connoting cleanliness and discretion. The defence counsel's disgust with the subject is often quite blatant. Witness this excerpt from Stephanie's cross-examination in the Mulherne trial, heard at a London crown court in August 1993. Even the judge intervenes in this exchange between the defence counsel and the complainant to question its relevance.

DEFENCE COUNSEL: Let me put it to you that in fact you were just coming off, finishing your period at the time of having sexual intercourse with Mr Mulherne. Do you agree with that?

STEPHANIE: I was on for another couple of days. DC: Another what?

S: Two days. I was on for another two days after that.

DC: This is the early hours of Wednesday, so do you mean until the Friday, or when?

   (*At this point Stephanie tried to contest the relevance of the questions but was brusquely told to answer the D C.*)

S: I can't remember. *What has my period got to do with that?*

DC: Just answer the questions please. These questions may not be very tasteful, but I have got to put them to you. In order for him to insert his penis, he has to cope then with the debris of your period and the tampon, is that right? He wouldn't find that easy, would he?

JUDGE: Well, she can't answer what he would or wouldn't find easy.

DC: The point is – I am sorry to have to put it to you – that the channel was obstructed.

J: I think you're making a comment. DC: Am I? All right.

This farcical cross-examination beggars belief. How is it possible for a complainant to be asked whether her tampon and the 'debris' of her period caused the rapist problems? What on earth is the justification for lawyers indulging in such questioning and what possible relevance has it to whether or not Stephanie consented?

In another trial the complainant was also cross-examined in the following terms:

DEFENCE COUNSEL: You began to rub his penis through his jeans.

COMPLAINANT: None of this is true.

DC: You were both on the floor and you helped him put his penis into your vagina and had consensual sex.

C: This is untrue.

DC: You weren't frightened.

C: That is absolute rubbish.

DC: He began to kiss your breasts and your bra may have been pushed up. He began to briefly perform oral sex on you.

C: It was the first day of my period. They are my heaviest days. I would never have sex during my period.

DC: He didn't know you had a period. C: He took the tampon out so he should have known.

DC: You were never unconscious.

C: Yes, I was.

DC: He never put his arm round your throat.

C: He did.

DC: It was lovemaking You told him you loved him and you were glad he was back.

C: I didn't.

DC: When women start menstruating, the first few days are the lightest, don't you agree?

C: No, I don't find that. My first days are heaviest.

Drink and Drugs

Of all the factors used to discredit the complainant, the most common was the consumption of alcohol and drugs. Yet the defendant, even if very drunk, was rarely questioned about his use of alcohol. The use of alcohol and drugs carries different meanings for men and women. For men heavy drinking serves to enhance their male status, it signifies 'real manhood'. For women, on the other hand, alcohol carries the taint of immorality and promiscuity. A sociologist who studied attitudes to women and alcohol, suggests that 'a woman who drinks does not need to be a prostitute to have a promiscuous image. She is promiscuous by the very fact that she is a drinker' (Ettorre 1992: 38). Drinking and drug use were introduced to discredit the complainant in two ways. The first was to suggest that their consumption would lower the woman's inhibitions and unleash her sexuality. Thus she would have been likely to consent to something which she would regret later. The second was to suggest that a woman under the influence of alcohol would be more likely to act irrationally or vindictively and make a false complaint. Often the only evidence for the complainant's use of drugs was the defendant's allegation.

Drink and drugs are seen as dangerous in unleashing a woman's sexuality, which once unleashed is irresistible to men. A man is not held responsible for his sexual desires; all the onus is on the woman to control his sexuality. The view that alcohol lowers inhibitions and gives female sexuality a free rein[3] is a constant theme in the doctor's evidence in the Donnellan trial (see pages 80–81).

Doctors frequently disagree about the effects of alcohol. In one trial I attended, a woman doctor with thirty-six years' experience argued persuasively that alcohol does not necessarily lower inhibition. She said, 'In some people it can. It depends on the person. Some people can become quite stubborn or stroppy.' The defence then called a doctor who argued that it lowered inhibition. In no trial was a doctor called to give evidence that men who are drunk might be more likely to rape.

Evidence that the complainant has taken drugs, even in the past, is usually fatal to obtaining a conviction. In one rape trial I attended, a street trader had chatted up a beautiful young Italian girl visiting London. She had agreed to go back to his flat and they had taken a taxi. In the taxi he had smoked a joint (cannabis) and had persuaded her to take a puff. Once back at his place she alleged he had first raped her, then beaten her with a leather belt and finally buggered her. Photographs of appalling injuries were handed round the court. The jury could not reach a decision on the rape charge but found him guilty of ABH and buggery. A retrial was ordered. At the retrial the woman, who had expressed great fear of the defendant, failed to turn up as she was too frightened. Evidence that she had had a puff of the joint was crucial in leading to the defendant's acquittal. The defence counsel argued, 'They were two people who had used cannabis. As to mischief, the abuse of drugs perhaps puts the case in

3. According to a study of sexual relations in an Andalusian town (Brandes 1981), women are portrayed as seductresses and whores possessed of insatiable lustful appetites while men are seen as suffering the consequences of female whims and passions. When women wield their power, men are forced to relinquish control over their passions.

a different context. It wasn't an unwilling party.' The defendant was set free as he had already served a short sentence for the other charges. At the end of the trial he turned to me and asked if I would like to write his memoirs.

Notions of 'purity' and 'pollution' are intrinsic to sexuality and drug abuse. Mary Douglas, a British anthropologist, defines pollution as 'a type of danger which is unlikely to occur except where the lines of structure, cosmic or social, are clearly defined' (Douglas 1966: 113). With women the social boundaries are more sharply defined in the sense that there are clear lines between what is and is not legitimate or respectable behaviour for women as compared to men. The controls over their social behaviour are more stringent. Transgressing such boundaries (poisoning themselves, being out of control and so on) turns female heroin users into polluted women:

In private they are regarded as potentially sexless, bad mothers, uncaring for their children or irresponsible wives, not considering the needs of their husbands. In public they are viewed as unforgivably out of control in their domestic and/or work situations, fallen angels, evil sluts or loose women who cannot be trusted

As a polluted woman with a spoiled identity the woman heroin user is low on the hierarchy of women generally and women substance users in particular. Being viewed as 'deviant' and a 'whore' she is engaged in using a drug which is seen as low (that is bad, evil) on the hierarchy of drugs. Perhaps it could be argued that for women, the lower the drug on the hierarchy, the closer the connection exists between them and the 'whore image of wo.men' (Ettorre 1992.151).

In another case I attended, Miranda and Jenny, who were friends, both alleged Michael had raped them. Jenny had been an addict in the past but claimed not to have taken drugs for many years. She had been medically examined after reporting the rape and was clean. This is how the defence counsel, drawing on the stereotype of the female heroin addict, summed up with sickening irony:

It's easy to feel enormous sympathy for the two complainants because of the wretched way they live their lives. One might just find oneself going sympathetically along with what they say, but be careful. You're not dealing with a typical witness. You must not look at every witness in the same way. But of course you are considering the credibility of their evidence. It's impossible for a heroin addict to get off the drug If it is possible for someone to be weaned off, it takes a very long time. Money is the one thing that people in her situation want. Drug addicts will fail to behave in a way normal people would.

The conclusion is clear. She must be supporting her alleged habit by prostitution. He ignores the doctor's evidence that the complainant was clean and not under the influence of drugs or drink, but plays on the prejudices of the jurors. He then alleges the complainant is spiteful, 'the sort of person who with five pints of Tennents in her might go to a police station and make up a story'.

Being under medication is sometimes used as an argument that the woman consented. On one occasion the complainant's medication on release from mental hospital was held against her. This was used to suggest that she had sex willingly with a complete stranger in a lift shaft of the underground in the middle of the night and then made a false allegation. In this case, no one had informed the complainant that the defendant was HIV-positive.

HIV is an area which is likely to raise difficult issues in future and needs to be addressed. Complainants who may become infected as a result of rape at the very least require counselling and support if they decide to be tested. A number of crucial legal issues will follow.

For all the apparent 'rationality' of the proceedings, the male participants do not seem to be able to resist a certain vicarious fascination in the detail of the alleged rape. Here is an example of another kind of exchange:

DEFENCE COUNSEL: Do you recognize that garment?

COMPLAINANT: Yes.

DC: Your knickers. Are they clean?

C: I don't know.

(*The usher ostentatiously puts on rubber gloves and picks up the exhibit.*)

DC: I think they are the ones you took off.

JUDGE: (to C) Would you like some plastic gloves? Or I don't suppose you mind handling your own knickers.

Why is it that her intimate garments and not his are used as objects to be pored over, handled with veiled disgust, passed around and made the subject of cross-examination? Why is it that her under-clothes are referred to as knickers rather than pants – why, indeed, is he not questioned about taking off his knickers? For presumably he did take them off, with some intention in mind. Yet in no trial was this an object of investigation. In most trials, evidence of intercourse is not the issue; the dispute is over consent, so who removed whose clothes with what intention is important. But is there really a need for her garments to be handed round and for the details of the assault to be discussed in salacious detail? It is not simply degrading for the woman (who has, remember, no separate legal representation of her own) to have to respond, to describe and name in public intimate parts of her own and the defendant's sexual anatomy which the defendant is not called on to do; the act of describing in exact detail what the man did and how she responded is enough subtly to render her 'unrespectable'. Judge Perleman has remarked that many rape complainants find the handing round of their panties the most appalling part of the trial, even worse than describing the actual assault.[4]

Mandy's ordeal, in the case mentioned above, was not over. The case was adjourned later in order for the jury to return a verdict in another case. Mandy had just broken down in tears while giving evidence about the rape, which was clearly very stressful for her. She was asked to sit on a bench at the back of the tiny court as the judge and jury withdrew. At this point, the defendant, who was on bail and was not therefore taken down to the cells, was shown by the usher to a place next to Mandy, where he hemmed her in. It was an extraordinary moment. She had just described how he had threatened her life and then raped her. Yet the court officials were so oblivious to her distress that they failed to predict that sitting next to him would alarm her. Her distress was unexpected to them. She went berserk, shouting and screaming at her opponent, 'You bloody bastard, they treat you like a king' Her cries could be heard from outside the court for some time during the next case, but the judge and jury never knew what had happened.Mandy was forced to endure another two hours of humiliating cross-examination, where again she was asked demeaning and unnecessary questions which left her incredulous. (How, for example, had the defendant managed to remove her Tampax? Had he had difficulty with the string?) She frequently broke down in tears. The defendant was acquitted.

4. In the BBC 1 *Panorama* documentary 'The Rape of Justice', July 1993.

Sexual History Evidence

The relevance of the complainant's sexual history has been the subject of considerable controversy. The Sexual Offences (Amendment) Act (1976) precluded questioning about the sexual past of the complainant other than with the accused except at the discretion of the judge. This act put into effect some of the recommendations of the Advisory Group on the Law on Rape (the Heilbron Committee[5]), which had been set up to review the rape legislation in 1975 following public concern about the conduct of rape trials, and the fact that women were not coming forward through fear that their entire sexual history would be put on trial. This committee was very critical of the way in which in many trials the woman's private life was cross-examined. They argued:

> In contemporary society sexual relationships outside marriage, both steady and of a more casual character, are fairly widespread, and it seems now to be agreed that a woman's sexual experiences with partners of her own choice are neither indicative of untruthfulness nor of a general willingness to consent.

The committee recommended that legislation should specify the circumstances in which a woman could be cross-examined about her sexual history with other men, and it envisaged that this should only be done very rarely, if, for example, the complainant was a prostitute or had had sexual relations with the defendant previously. It concluded that 'unless there are some restrictions, questioning can take place which does not advance the cause of justice but in effect puts the woman on trial'.[6] Its recommendations regarding the banning of past-history evidence (except where the defendant had had sex with the woman beforehand or where, at the judge's discretion, it was considered to be unfair to the defendant not to allow it) were implemented in the 1976 Sexual Offences (Amendment) Act. The committee also proposed that questions relating to the moral character of the complainant ought not to be admitted unless an application was made by the defence counsel to the judge, in the absence of the jury.

5. The composition of the committee was unusual: psychiatrists, chiidren's officers and lawyers (see Edwards 1981: 158).

6. Its recommendations included the case for more sympathetic treatment of the victim both pre-and post-trial, but these were not implemented.

Parliamentary opinion regarding the recommendations was divided. The most dissension was attached to the question of whether the cross-examination of the complainant should be limited even at the discretion of the judge.[7]

The Heilbron Committee recommended that the judge should use his discretion only where the association with the defendant is relevant, or where an issue arising in the trial 'relates to a previous incident (or incidents) which is or are strikingly similar'. As we have seen, there is evidence that judges are often not impartial observers and use their discretion in different ways. What is particularly unfair is that the prosecution does not know and cannot test out the accuracy of the allegations. In Canada there is now a mechanism whereby this kind of evidence is going to be tried and tested before the judge decides whether or not it is relevant.

In reviewing the failure of this legislation to be properly implemented, Temkin (1993) points to the crux of the problem. Since it was the judges who were responsible for allowing sexual history evidence so freely in rape trials in the past, it scarcely made sense to leave it to them to decide whether and when to exclude it in the future. She reviews the way judges have ignored the legislation. In 1977 at Nottingham Crown Court in the case of Lawrence, the judge ruled that the complainant's sexual history evidence should be allowed where it 'might reasonably lead the jury, properly directed in the summing-up, to take a different view of the complainant's evidence from that which they might take if the question or series of questions was or were not allowed', which is of course precisely the reason why Heilbron considered it should be excluded. Even more prejudicial was the case of Viola in 1982, where the court of appeal approved the Lawrence test and added, 'If the questions are relevant to an issue in the trial in the light of the way the case is being run – for instance, relevant to the issue of consent, as opposed merely to credit – they are likely to be admitted.'

In Scotland research has revealed a similar picture. In January

7. In proposing an amendment to leave out this clause, MP Mr Lee explained, 'We are dealing with situations in which there is a high degree of emotion – situations made for the neurotic, the unbalanced, and indeed the exhibitionist kind of person' (*Parliamentary Debates*, Vol. 911, 5th Series, 1976, c. 1982–4; quoted in Edwards 1981: 162).

1986 new statutory rules of evidence came into force restricting the use of evidence concerning a complainer's sexual character and history in trials for sexual offences. Yet a Scottish Office research report (Brown et al. 1992) found that, contrary to the rules,[8] frequently sexual history evidence was introduced by the defence without prior permission from the judge and was rarely contested. The defence did all they could to circumvent the protection the legislation was supposed to give women. Overall complainants were asked questions concerning their sexual conduct in about half the sexual offence trials. The defence was also permitted to introduce evidence or questioning on the grounds of its relevance to credibility, when the same evidence might not have been admitted as relevant to consent or character, and the acquittal rate remained very high, at 78 per cent. Defence practitioners interviewed by the researchers admitted that they would do their best to create 'a smokescreen of immorality around the girl'. The Edinburgh Rape Crisis Centre (1993: 11) expressed concern that defence advocates were exploiting confusion over the legislation, disregarding and undermining it, and confirmed my findings that the prosecution failed to intervene to prevent unscrupulous attacks or insinuations by the defence.

Sexual history evidence is enormously prejudicial as it plays on all the stereotypes about women 'asking for it'. The assumption is that if a woman has sex with one man, she will automatically have sex with another because she's that sort of woman; if a woman is sexually active, then she's sexually available; if she says 'Yes' to one man, then she is more likely to say 'Yes' to another. Barbara Hewson, QC, had this to say about sexual history evidence:

In the old days, sexual history used to be admitted in two situations – one, if the woman was either a prostitute or known to have sexual relationships with a lot of men; or else if she'd had previous sexual relationships with the defendant. But now sexual history is being admitted in a whole range of cases and the result is that a defence barrister more or less has an expectation that a judge will allow him to go fishing around in the victim's past, which is, ironically, the very thing that the legislation was supposed to prevent.[9]

8. Introduced in Scotland in the Criminal Procedure (Scotland) Act (1975), as inserted by the Law Reform (Miscellaneous Provisions) Scotland Act (1985).

9. Interview in October 1993 for the *Dispatches* programme, shown on Channel 4 in February 1994.

At common law only two categories of case were regarded as relevant to consent: evidence of prostitution or a notorious reputation for lack of chastity; and evidence of a past sexual relationship with the defendant. As Temkin (1993) concludes, the question of what is thought to be relevant to consent on the facts of the case and in the light of the way the case is being run has not become the dominant consideration.

In most of the trials which I monitored the importance of alleged reputation was underlined. Judge Richardson, though absolving this particular complainant of provoking the rape, made clear the criteria he regarded as important in judging the woman's credibility:

She is not a promiscuous person. She is a sober, sensitive and religious young lady who will bear the mental scars for a very long time to come. Did she provoke the incident by the clothes she wore, the amount she had drunk, by dancing provocatively, going to the defendant's flat, being out late at night, asking the defendant back, taking drugs or soliciting?

The defence counsel often argues that any indication of autonomous behaviour or taking an active rather than a passive sexual role implies that the woman could have avoided rape and therefore must have consented. For example, although the complainant said that the man, not she, had insisted on coming back to her flat (in the afternoon), the defence counsel argued:

She is not a young innocent girl straight off the boat from Ireland, the sort of young woman who is not well able to look after herself. She is not delicate and retiring in her appearance. Not a small girl. Why did she invite him back to her flat?

In America evidence of past sexual encounters is also allowed. As the William Kennedy Smith rape trial, televised in December 1991, highlighted so clearly, in the eyes of the law and the press, having a sexual history still makes a woman a bad girl. Naomi Wolf realized she herself was one of these bad girls, 'wild, cheap and probably beyond redemption', when:

In looking back over my 28 years, I have to confess to having committed almost all the acts that would put virtually any woman who may have been sexually assaulted or abused beyond the pale of respectability – at least in the eyes of the press, the courts and those who buy into their sexual double standards (Wolf 1991).

She describes how, like the alleged victim, she had talked to boys. She refers to the way the defence attorney tried to cast doubt on the story of Patricia Bowman, the complainant, by producing a witness who testified that he observed her speaking flirtatiously to a member of the team, engaging in sexual banter and using intimate body language. Her word was suspect because she had drunk several vodka and orange drinks. Kennedy Smith portrayed Patricia Bowman as a sexually aggressive and disturbed woman who turned spiteful in a *Fatal Attraction* way. Her 'lacy satin bra' and 'a pair of flimsy panties' came under scrutiny and she was relentlessly pressed by the defence lawyer on the minutiae of the alleged rape, down to the condition of her sex organs and whether or not she socialized with barmen. As Wolf (1991) commented:

If the 'promiscuity' attributed to the alleged victims means they deserve censure then so do most of us. Young women are no longer expected to go straight from their father's protection to their husband's, their virginity intact. Griswold v. Connecticut signalled society's willingness to make contraception widely available. Roe v. Wade signals our acceptance of women's right to reproductive freedom in the form of legal abortion without the normal marital bond. Universities have gone co-ed and abandoned the double standard for curfew. Current fashion makes it obvious that the fifties sartorial distinction between respectable girls and 'tramps' no longer holds... Why then, when a young woman who acts on those rights, says she's raped or sexually abused, is it all suddenly 1954? How can we ask her what she was wearing and what has become of her virtue, her chaperone and her shame?

In England, the complainant is at an even greater disadvantage, however, as the laws limiting the evidence an American defence can present (called rape shield laws) are more stringent and their implementation is compulsory, not up to the judge's discretion. The defence in the Kennedy Smith trial was not therefore allowed to mention that Patricia Bowman was illegitimate, or refer to her relationships with other men. As one American researcher comments:

Rape shield laws eliminate some of the nightmare aspect of a rape trial for the alleged victim: that of having her prior sex life and any prior 'indiscretions' aired in public for the sole purpose of making her look bad and/or look like the sort of person who would 'cry rape' to cover up alleged indiscretions (Boumil et al. 1992).

The Defendant's Reputation

As we have already seen, when in adulthood we speak of a man's reputation, it is usually to refer to his public and professional standing, his occupation and his ranking in the social hierarchy, not to his private life or sexual conduct. For a woman, on the other hand, reputation almost always refers to her private life, her sexual reputation and her marital status. This difference is crucial in rape trials. Although rape usually occurs in private, it is a man's public, not his private, life that is deemed relevant to his credibility. Yet for men virtue is achieved largely irrespective of sexuality and sexual reputation is largely excluded from the moral evaluation of conduct. Most of the greatest political leaders have been profligate philanderers, from Lloyd George to Mao Tse-tung and John F. Kennedy, yet this reflected in no way on their reputations.

Social class is also an important facet of reputation. It is frequently implied in court cases that the higher the defendant's social class, the less likely he is to be a rapist and the more reliable is his word. Lower down the social strata, it is assumed that lack of previous criminal convictions denotes reliability.

The defendant's attitudes and behaviour towards women are therefore rarely questioned. Juries are instructed to attach enhanced credibility to a man who has no previous convictions. The woman's lack of convictions does not enhance her credibility. It is seen as irrelevant. Witness the following instructions Judge Smedley gave in a summing-up to the jury at the Old Bailey on 31 August 1993:

When you judge him as a witness, bear in mind that he has never been convicted and this affects his credibility.

Judge Davies, in another case heard in August 1993, argued:

The defendant gave evidence. He was twenty-four years old at the date concerned, and of good character. That is a matter you should give credit to the defendant for. It's relevant to his credibility. You may think it is also relevant to whether a man of twenty-four is less likely to commit the offence he is charged with.

The judge's direction in another case that August was even more explicit:

You have been told he is a man of good character with no previous convictions. What relevance does his good character have? It is relevant in two ways. Firstly, when you judge him as a witness, is he telling the truth? Bear in mind that he has never been convicted and this affects his credibility. Secondly, if he is a man of good character, what relevance does it have to whether or not he is likely to have behaved as the complainant suggests? Bear in mind when you assess what he has told you.

No mention was made of the lack of previous convictions of any of the complainants in these cases. The assumption surely must be that a woman's lack of convictions does not enhance her credibility and that previous sexual exploits do not detract from his.

A further anomaly arises where the man does have previous convictions. According to the Sexual Offences (Amendment) Act (1976), Section 114, whether or not the defendant gives evidence, his previous convictions or bad character can be referred to when he has attacked the reputation of the complainant. However, the case of Selvey set a precedent that, in sexual cases, previous convictions for sexual offences should not be admitted as they were too prejudicial (see Iller 1992; Selvey v. DPP).

In some of the trials monitored, leave was given to mention past offences of the defendant, but only non-sexual offences. Normally in non-sexual offences, if a defendant attacks the credibility of the complainant, then the prosecution has the right to cross-examine him as to his previous convictions and character, because he would have 'thrown away his shield' under Section 1 (f) (11) of the Criminal Evidence Act 1898. Presumably it is up to the discretion of the judge to allow cross-examining of the defendant as to his previous criminal record, but in practice permission to do this is rarely given.

Martin Iller of the College of Law criticized the anomaly for sexual offences, emphasizing that, 'it is unjust to allow an accused to make such a direct attack on a rape victim's character with total impunity when he dare not do this in respect of other offences' (1992). Where the sole issue in the rape trial is 'consent' and the offence attacks the character and credibility of the complainant, then it should surely be open to the prosecution to attack the character and credibility of the man, including the admission of the defendant's previous convictions, if any.[10]

There are many ways in which the defence attacks the woman's character, yet this is done with impunity. In none of the cases were the defendant's previous convictions for rape admitted. Furthermore, why should the defendant's shield be protected simply because he did not enter the witness box. This rule should be abolished. For example, in the case of Mulherne's alleged rape of Stephanie, previous convictions were not admitted because he did not give evidence. Yet Stephanie's criminal offence, although it had occurred after the alleged rape, was seen as relevant and was enormously prejudicial.

Conclusion

In this chapter I have shown how the rules of evidence are highly discriminatory. There seems to be no justification for the assumption that a man's reputation, as defined by his occupation, social class or previous convictions, has any bearing on his predisposition to rape. Conversely, the relevance of a woman's sexual character and past sexual history are rarely, if at all, relevant. The Scottish Office study of the use of sexual history and character evidence put forward a number of recommendations for change (see Brown et al. 1992), which apply equally to England and Wales: a change in the discretionary nature of the legislation regarding sexual history or character evidence; the inadmittance of evidence when relevance is slight; a more active prosecution role in countering irrelevant or deliberately confusing evidence led by the defence; and if the character of the complainant is attacked, then the prosecution should attack the accused. Moreover, the failure to provide a lawyer for the complainant, or the alternative of allowing her to prepare the case with the prosecution beforehand, results in a highly disinterested representation on the woman's behalf.

I have shown how difficult it is for women to resist such cross-examination. Women are not passive victims and often adopt

10. Barbara Hewson, QC, when interviewed, pointed out that sexual history evidence is allowed when relevant to the issue of consent, which is often seen as having a bearing on the complainant's character. Bad character evidence is relevant to credibility or the likelihood that the woman is lying. Therefore, by sleight of hand the fact that the woman consented before implies she is lying, that she did consent this time.

different strategies to resist the questions asked. Four forms of resistance were identified: questioning the relevance of the more outlandish questions; trying to subvert the questions by showing how absurd they were; responding with anger; and refusing to answer. Only a few complainants grasp that the purpose of the cross-examination is not to reveal the truth or put forward their point of view, but to undermine their credibility. Michelle, in the trial reported above, subverts this pretence when she responds to the defence counsel by attacking the relevance of his questions and saying, 'You are just trying to embarrass me.'

In terms of the content of legal statutes concerning criminal behaviour, most historians would argue that the trend has been towards the elimination of particularism and differences in favour of equal treatment for all citizens. As far as women are concerned, it is still the case that laws are made and implemented overwhelmingly by men and involve male concepts that are deeply discriminatory and sexist.

Chapter 6

Serial Acquaintance Rapists Set Free

Nobody can tell me that everyone who comes to court as a complainant about rape is telling a lie. It may be that some are, but the vast majority aren't, and since those people – since those defendants on your figures – are being acquitted, then plainly they are being wrongly acquitted (High Court Judge Matthewman).[1]

We know that very few rapists are convicted. Yet it is often assumed that men who are acquitted of rape are innocent. Since only 463 out of 4,600 cases of rape resulted in a conviction in 1993, does this mean that 4,000 men are innocent and that all these women are making false allegations? By identifying three defendants, all of whom have been accused numerous times of rape, whose cases came to court during the four months when we monitored trials, I shall show how the judicial system is allowing rapists to go free or to be acquitted of some of their crimes.

The devastating effect of acquitting guilty men is movingly portrayed by the victims of the assaults. The indignity of being disbelieved and of being held responsible for the man's violence is a searing indictment of our judicial system. We traced the past criminal records and previous acquittals of the defendants and interviewed the defence counsels about their approach. The failure to convict rapists is not an inevitable result of the difficulty of proving rape, but is due to inbuilt imbalances in the judicial system, where evidence supporting the complainant's position is disallowed and she is often the butt of clever manoeuvring by defence barristers. The jury hear little of her side of the story, of her reasons for not resisting if she had no injuries, of her description of the alleged assault or of her reactions to what happened. Such details are either discounted, disallowed as evidence or reduced to the minimum. These imbalances are examples of the

1.Interview for the *Dispatches* programme, shown on Channel 4 in February 1994.

ways the law presents a male perspective through the notion that it invokes pre-existing legal principles in an essentially neutral fashion (MacKinnon 1987). In fact, the legal principles, as I shall show, are far from neutral. In rape trials they are weighted in favour of the defendant, which explains why the acquittal rate is so high and rapists often go free.

Various measures introduced in the 1970, 1980s and 1990s have been ineffective at improving the conduct of trials. This is mainly because the implementation of the changes was left up to the discretion of judges, the very people who appear to be most resistant to change. In particular the victim's past sexual history and sexual character, use of which should have been curtailed by the 1976 Sexual Offences (Amendment) Act. It is doubtful whether the 1999 Youth Justice and Criminal Evidence Act will improve the situation (see Introduction), are still being introduced in many trials, sometimes with and sometimes without the discretion of the judge. Defence barristers sometimes slip such questions into their cross-examination without even asking the judge. Normally speaking in criminal cases, when a defendant attacks a complainant on the grounds of credibility in a criminal trial, this gives the complainant the right to retaliate by challenging his credibility. The only exception is sexual cases, where the defendant's past sexual offences are allowed only at the judge's discretion, which is rarely granted. If the defendant chooses not to give evidence, then his character is protected in all trials. Since the change in the 'right to silence' under the Criminal Justice and Public Order Act (1994), the defendant can, of course, still refuse to testify, but judges now have discretion to direct the jury to draw inferences from their silence. This may lead to more defendants testifying and open them up to cross-examination.

Sexism enters into the judicial process most starkly in relation to the different criteria used to judge male and female credibility. Apart from exceptions such as Donnellan (discussed in Chapter 3), cases normally go to trial only where there is some likelihood of conviction. As we shall see, the difficulty of gaining convictions is due to grave imbalances in the legal system which percolate down so that only very few cases reach curt. The small proportion of suspects that do stand trial are then usually acquitted where 'consent' is the issue, even, as I shall show, when they are serial rapists.[2] The percentage of cases not proceeded with has increased between 1985 and 1993.[3] In 1985 roughly one in three cases (31 per cent) recorded by the police proceeded to a crown court. By 1993[4] this had dropped to under one in five (19.4 per cent). This could very well be a cost-saving device.

In this chapter, I shall outline the cases of John Simpson and David Johnson (both defendants' and complainants' names have been changed), allegedly serial rapists who appeared at the Old Bailey for trial during our monitoring period. Both had some social contact with their victims before the assaults. They both had a history of violence towards women, although Johnson had never been convicted of an offence. They both appeared to have planned to isolate the women in order to rape them. They used charm to camouflage their intentions and may even have acted in the knowledge that having some social contact with the woman in advance would make it easier for them to get off. This shows how astute some seasoned defendants are at manipulating the jury and it is likely that after a few court appearances they learn how to play the system. It also indicates that piecemeal reform of the judicial system will be ineffective.

Simpson, who had two previous convictions for rape, was acquitted in October 1993 for the fifth time. The first of these convictions, in 1982, concerned a seventeen-year-old girl whom he had raped at knife-point. Johnson has never been convicted. He was reported to the police by seven women for rape. Four cases were prosecuted. He was acquitted for three of these, committed another offence while on bail awaiting a trial of the fourth case, and at the time of writing is still on the run. Finally, I discuss the case of another serial rapist, who was acquitted in the trial of one of the respondents to our questionnaire. Her case shows how acquitting dangerous men puts other women at risk. The tactics or *modus operandi* of these men are analysed and related to the problem of how men rape.

John Simpson

In the short four-month period of court monitoring at the Old Bailey, a convicted serial acquaintance rapist was listed for trial. John

2. The defence in stranger rapes is usually identification, which, with advances in forensic DNA analysis, has in recent years become more difficult to contest.

3. Out of 1,842 cases 'crimed' by the police, 569 appeared for trial at the crown court.

4. Out of 4,589 recorded, 892 appeared at the crown court.

Simpson was accused of rape by seven different women. He was acquitted for the fifth time. He had first been found guilty of rape in May 1982, when he was twenty-one, and was jailed for two and a half years, reduced to two on appeal. On that occasion, Mr Richard Latham, prosecuting counsel, said Simpson and the nineteen-year-old girl knew each other but had not had a sexual relationship. He explained:

During the course of the evening Simpson offered the girl a lift to the chip shop and then a lift home, which she accepted. They went to get some chips but then the girl asked Simpson for a lift back to the centre to collect her handbag. Instead of parking outside the centre, Simpson went to the nearby college car park. He put a cassette tape on and tried to kiss her, but she said no and after a brief struggle it stopped there.

Mr Latham said Simpson apologized to the girl and said he should take her home. He went on:

She believed he was sorry and was happy to stay in the car with him. But on the way he suddenly turned into a fairly deserted area and parked between two garages. He wedged over to her seat and as she felt for the door handle he put his right hand over her and pulled the seat reclining lever. With a bump she found herself on her back. He then climbed over her and tried to get her legs apart. Then in his right hand he produced quite a large knife, held it against her throat and said, 'I don't want to hurt you but I will if I have to.'

According to the prosecution, the girl continued to struggle but was overpowered and raped. Simpson initially denied any knowledge of the incident, but changed his story after a policeman who had picked him up for questioning heard him drop the knife in the gutter as he was getting into a Panda car. He claimed during questioning that the girl consented and added, 'I didn't think she meant it when she said "No".' The girl sobbed as she told the jury, 'I was lying there crying because there was nothing I could do. I couldn't believe it was happening to me', but Simpson told the court, 'She was perfectly willing. I asked her to move over and she did. We were kissing and cuddling and I was feeling her body. She was kissing me and I was touching her breasts.' When cross-examined, he claimed he believed the girl was willing to have sex and added that the knife had been on the back seat and he had picked it up only to move it out of the way. According to police evidence, he admitted having raped the complainant and made two statements under caution confessing rape. The jury found Simpson guilty. Passing sentence, Judge Peregrine Blomefield told him, 'It is my duty to protect girls so they can go about in cars without the risk of being raped.' Shortly after his release from prison, he was again charged with allegedly raping a nineteen-year-old girl in April 1984, but was acquitted.

In February 1985 he was accused of raping a seventeen-year-old girl who he apparently persuaded to watch an explicit sex film in his bedsit. While on bail, he was accused of committing yet another offence in central London. In this case, the victim, a shop manageress, was on her way home from work when Simpson approached her. They arranged to meet and the alleged rape at knife-point took place at his house in the early hours of 13 July. The two cases were heard together in February 1986. He was found guilty of raping the teenage girl but not the shop manageress and was sentenced to five years. He appealed against conviction on the grounds that the cases should not have been heard together. He served four and was released in 1989. Since then, he had been acquitted of rape five times, twice at the Old Bailey. He had got cleverer.

With great difficulty Dispatches managed to track down details of some of the cases where John Simpson had been acquitted. One case, in May 1989, involved two young women who had accepted a lift home from him. After dropping one of the women off, Simpson had told the other he wanted to 'build up' – make a joint. She told him to drop her off, but he drove straight on and stopped in a side street. He twisted her wrist, hurting her, and then allegedly raped her. There was no weapon involved. Afterwards he told her that he had been away for a long time. He said that he had been released from a five-year sentence only three weeks previously.

Sheri's Evidence

In September 1991 and December 1993 he was acquitted twice more. *Dispatches* traced one of the women, Sheri, a thirty-four-year-old nurse, a divorcee he had met on a plane coming back from the West Indies. She explained what happened. After chatting with her, Simpson had asked for her phone number and when she gave it to him, he had entered it into an electronic diary he carried. On their second date, after taking her to a nightclub, instead of taking her home, he drove her to a churchyard and parked by a tree.

Afterwards she realized he had parked very precisely, reversing in so that the passenger door was blocked by the tree. They started kissing but she did not want to continue. She described what happened next:

All of a sudden he pinned me down. I saw the look in his eyes. He had changed completely. He had his hands around my throat. He said, 'Don't think you can wind me up.' He just pulled his trousers down...I was struggling and begging him not to do it. I was trying to stall him by saying, 'We haven't got any condoms.' He told me, 'You'd better stop struggling.' When I realized that I wasn't going to stop him and that he was going to do it anyway, I just let him. I didn't want to get hurt. Afterwards he changed back and was normal again. He tried to make silly jokes and he dressed and drove me to my house. He was just acting as if he was OK. He gave me the impression that he didn't actually rape me. I don't know if he was doing this to make me feel that way too.

She told her flat-mate what had happened and decided to call the police. A year later the case came up at the Old Bailey. Sheri angrily denied that she consented: 'Do you think I'm going to put myself through this ordeal and waste all the time of the police and courts if it didn't happen?' she told the jury. In Spite of this, John Simpson was acquitted for the fourth time. Sheri cried when she heard the verdict. According to the news desk report, Simpson was dressed in a trendy suit and had a smart haircut. He smiled and clapped when the 'not guilty' verdict was announced and bowed to the jurors, saying, 'Thank you very much. Cheers.'

Mary's Evidence

In November 1993, during our monitoring period, John Simpson appeared yet again at the Old Bailey. After painstaking research involving ringing police stations and court offices in different parts of the country, we discovered that it was his seventh court appearance charged with rape. There is no country-wide data base of acquittals so it is difficult to collect such information, even where the police are aware of past appearances. If trials were fairer and more rapists were convicted, this kind of situation would not arise. At present there is an argument for recording acquittals of those who are known to be serial rapists, but only after they have been convicted and even then the civil liberties consequences should be carefully balanced against the need to protect women. (It is only recently that a country-wide data base of convictions has been set up.)

We obtained an official transcript of the trial and were able to analyse why Simpson was acquitted in spite of evidence that the victim, whom I shall call Mary, was a virgin and highly respectable. She was twenty-six years old and had a professional job. In Adler's research into rape trials (1987), she found that the complainant, in order to be believed and gain a conviction, needed at least some of the following: to be respectable, to be sexually inexperienced, not to have been raped by an acquaintance, to have fought and been hurt, and to have reported the case promptly. In this case three of these crucial elements were present, so there seemed a strong possibility that John Simpson would at last be convicted.

Simpson had met the complainant two weeks previously and spoken several times on the phone to her. Mary was young for her years, somewhat naïve, and still living with her parents. The alleged rape occurred on their first date. They went for a drink and then Simpson took her, believe it or not, to the very same churchyard where he had raped Sheri. Like her, Mary described how he suddenly changed and became very aggressive,' calling her a 'fucking bitch'. She had managed to get out of the car and ran towards the main road. She described what happened then:

He was behind me. He grabbed me, saying, 'You bitch, get back into the car. I know girls like you just want to run into the middle of the road and be a hero or something like that.' He was thumping me from behind. He forced me back into the car. He got angry and started saying, 'Did I like him?', that I was teasing him. I was telling myself, he's not going to do this to me and drop me off afterwards, he's going to kill me.

Afterwards he had changed back and 'become normal again' and said he would take her home. At her request he stopped at a petrol station and then at a chip shop, where, while he was talking on his mobile phone, Mary raised the alarm. She pretended to be waiting for some food and asked for someone to call the police. The police arrived and arrested Simpson. In spite of the surprise, Simpson was cool as a cucumber and gave nothing away to the police. He knew what was at stake. He argued that the complainant had consented and totally rejected the charge of rape.

Mary, on the other hand, was in a state of shock, and from the level of her heart rate, measured during her medical examination, was close to a heart attack. That this was due to the rape was, however, questioned by the defence counsel, who argued that it could have been caused by the stress of making a false allegation! Additionally, the defence cleverly cast doubt on whether or not she was a virgin as the police doctor had had difficulty examining her in such a state of high anxiety. He described how she was in great pain and having vaginal spasms which made a thorough examination impossible.

In giving evidence the doctor quite correctly argued that evidence shows 50 per cent of rape victims show no injury to their genital area and that while some skins bruise easily, others are more resilient. He added quite correctly that black skin does not show bruising as quickly or as easily as fair skin. He spent two hours with the complainant and found that her pulse and blood pressure were both 'so high that if the pulse rate went higher there would be some sort of heart failure'. The defence doctor refuted these arguments by emphasizing that you might expect a victim of sexual assault to have bruising or redness, especially if the victim was a virgin, and that the increase in the level of blood pressure and pulse rate could have been due to many other causes such as smoking cannabis or drinking (the complainant admitted to having two puffs of a spliff and one drink), running or consensual sexual intercourse. She argued that the very high blood pressure must have been 'pathological' and that the forensic doctor's examination had been inadequate. In further cross-examination by the prosecution, the defence doctor admitted that she was not suggesting that a fast pulse rate and high blood pressure could be faked but that there were other reasons than rape for their occurrence.

In spite of the evidence that the complainant had almost had a heart attack, the judge in his summing-up said that the medical evidence did not amount to corroboration. He pointed out that the defence doctor had had a great deal of experience of examining rape victims, and did not emphasize that some women are too terrified to resist and therefore show no physical signs of resistance. The judge repeated the defence counsel's argument that the pulse rate could just as easily be high as a result of the doctor's hands touching her legs as it could of rape.

At the trial the defence counsel cast doubt on whether or not she was a virgin,[5] calling their own medical witness to refute the findings of the forensic specialist who had undertaken the initial examination. John Simpson put up a brilliant performance in court, holding a Bible in one hand and taking a girlfriend who had had a child with him along. He was again acquitted.

It is impossible to know exactly why the jurors in this trial acquitted Simpson. The complainant was respectable, a woman of good reputation with a responsible job, living quietly with her parents, who reported the rape immediately, and had clearly been shattered by the experience. The reason suggested for her making a false allegation was that she was frightened of her parents' reaction should she return home late. There was no feasible reason for her to make up a false allegation against a man with a very dubious reputation. Yet he got off and was set free to rape again. The press were silent.

David Johnson Anna's Evidence

The second man who appears from the evidence we collected to be a serial rapist and whose trial came up during the monitoring period had never once been convicted. He has a history of burglary and theft offences. He was accused of rape by seven different women, and was acquitted of the three cases that came to trial, one after a retrial. He should have stood trial for the fourth time during our monitoring period on charges of rape, false imprisonment and indecent assault, but he disappeared.

Dispatches were unable to find out details of the first case but are led to believe that he was acquitted on charges of rape in 1988 or 1989. As already mentioned, the police do not know about previous acquittals unless they took place in the same area. The second rape case occurred in 1990, when a young single parent called Anna reported that Johnson had raped her. She told us she knew Johnson's family – his sisters, his aunt and his mother, and understood that he had a reputation for violence. She had met him

5. This was never really resolved, although there was no evidence that she was not a virgin The doctor who had examined her was criticized for not making a sufficiently thorough examination.

at a wedding, spoken briefly to him and a month or two later he had turned up at her door, although she had never given him her address. He started coming round to see her from time to time, sometimes bringing his younger brother to play with her children. Then one day he suggested they should have a sexual relationship. Anna refused and was relieved when he appeared to accept this and said 'Fine'. However, later in the day he returned uninvited. After drinking some lager and reading the children a bedtime story, he suddenly changed and began to abuse her, pulling her hair and holding her hands down. He kept saying, 'I want you, girl. Has any man made you cry like this before?' She described how, 'His eyes looked really evil, like he really was disturbed and he just wanted to hurt somebody. And he was hurting.' He threatened to force her in front of her children if she did not stop screaming. He held her down and raped her with her children sleeping in the adjoining room. As he was leaving, according to Anna, 'he took my hand and went down on his knees in the hallway. He asked me to see him again. He had tears in his eyes. I said he could do no such thing after what he had done to me. He said I'd forget about it by the morning.' When interviewed by the police, he said that she was 'completely willing' to have sex and that he believed she had changed her mind afterwards and made her rape allegation because she 'regretted it'.

At the trial in June 1990, Johnson did not enter the witness box and was acquitted. It appears that the jurors simply could not accept the contradiction between the image of a man reading children a bedtime story and the next minute raping their mother. They could not accept that Dr Jekyll could turn into Mr Hyde. Additionally, an ex-girlfriend of Johnson's reported that she had been raped by him, but she was not prepared to take the case further.

Birgitte's Evidence

The case we monitored involved Birgitte, a young Danish girl aged nineteen who had come over to England to learn English. She was staying in a hostel. Shortly after arriving, she met Johnson in a bar at Piccadilly Circus on 8 August 1992. She thought he was charming. He gave her his phone number and she phoned him the next day and arranged to meet. After a visit to his music studio, they went back to his house, where they had consensual sex. Throughout the following week the couple met on three or four occasions and each time they had consensual sex using a condom. Johnson gave her some earrings. Birgitte describes how she had then decided that she wanted to cool the relationship down. He had insisted that they 'remain friends' and meet occasionally for a drink.

On the night in question, Birgitte said she had met intending to end the relationship. As they sat in a wine bar, Johnson asked her if she had ever been sexually assaulted as a child. She replied that someone had tried to rape her in Spain but she did not want to talk about it. After buying a record and eating food, she said she was manipulated into catching a bus with him and, without her realizing it, they had ended up at Johnson's house, in an area of London she did not know. Birgitte described how the moment she entered the house, Johnson had suddenly changed and become violent. He had taken away her handbag and her watch and locked her in the house. She described how gradually he had become more and more dominating. Eventually:

He then pushed me on the chair. I got up and said I was leaving. He said he would not let me. He grabbed me by the shoulders and picked up scissors from the ironing board. I was afraid if I didn't cooperate he would use them. He cut my underwear. He was holding my leg. He said if I did not cooperate he would break my leg. I was afraid I would be killed. I had to well, I fought him but I had to cooperate, otherwise maybe I couldn't sit here today.[6]

Johnson had raped her twice as she struggled against him. She said she had cried all the time. While he was raping her, according to her, he said, 'Say you love me', to which she had replied, 'I don't', and he then stated, 'That's what you are doing right now.' I said, 'No I'm not.' She said he did not care what she said or did. She was too scared to escape and was terrified he would kill her. He made her have a shower and took her to a pub and a nightclub. She said she had no chance to escape. She said that if she did not do what he wanted, 'he would get mad, really mad'. For twenty-four hours he kept her a prisoner.

The following evening, it was only when he fell asleep on the sofa

6. Birgitte was interviewed by Jenny Cuffe.

that she felt it was safe to escape. She had to find her clothes. She left her purse, her shirt and her watch behind. She returned to her hostel, from where she called the police. According to her friend, she was in a state of great distress. She was examined by a police doctor and found to have a number of bruises.

When the police went to arrest Johnson, he had already moved to his aunt's house and was not detained until some weeks later. He had meanwhile washed the shirt Birgitte had left behind and returned it to the hostel where she was staying. He had also insisted Birgitte had a shower after the rape. The policeman involved in the case commented that this implied that Johnson was forensically aware. Birgitte noted that there were psychology books in his bedroom.

Birgitte discovered that she was pregnant and had an abortion. She was suicidal as a result and had some psychiatric help in Denmark. In the first trial the defence position was that she had made her allegation against Johnson because she was afraid to admit that she had become pregnant by somebody else before she had arrived in England. Police went to Denmark to get the foetus from the abortion to find out if it was Johnson's, but the results of the Home Office forensic analysis were inconclusive. (Why Birgitte should falsely attribute the pregnancy to Johnson would seem to be irrelevant and is a further example of how 'red herrings' can be introduced into court cases apparently to confuse a jury). According to the police officer there, Birgitte appeared to nervously 'giggle' in the witness box. This reaction could well be an indication of stress. The jury were out for four hours and were split nine to three. This is an example of where the judge should have insisted on the importance of their reaching a decision; they should have been given more time, even if this meant putting them up for the night.

At the retrial in May 1993, the police tried to bring in two other unconvicted cases to show evidence of 'similar fact' (that there was enough similarity between the cases for them to be heard together) but this was refused. Johnson put up a brilliant performance in court. He has had plenty of practice. He was described by the detective inspector involved in the case who has interviewed him on several occasions as an extremely articulate, well-read young man who 'does not present in any way the image of the stereotyped black rapist. He is witty, interested in the world around and thoroughly charming. Then suddenly he snaps.'[7] According to Birgitte, he appeared as 'a nice well-dressed young man who couldn't do anything wrong'. He wore John Lennon glasses in court although he does not need glasses. He said he had been deeply in love with her but the problem was that he did not mean anything to her, implying that she had led him on.

The tactics used by the woman defence counsel were similar to those used in the previous trial. She argued that the defendant could not be a rapist as he was good-looking and charming. When interviewed about her method,[8] she said, 'I find that a gentler approach is much more effective than a rude and unpleasant approach.' She made a great deal of the way Johnson had apparently appeared quite helpful and affectionate at times. He had given Birgitte earrings, washed the clothes she had left behind in her flight and cooked her a meal. When, for example, Birgitte had an asthma attack (probably brought on by the trauma), he opened the window for her so she could breathe more easily. This was interpreted by the defence in the following terms: 'That is a considerate action, the action of a lover, not the action of a brutal rapist.'

Birgitte's education was cleverly used against her. She planned to train as a social worker. The defence counsel implied that her superior education was one reason why Johnson was in love with her and she should have been aware of this. Birgitte described how humiliated she had felt because the defence asked her all kinds of questions and made her sound like a liar. Johnson's control and domination of her were presented as the result of his 'burning love for her'.

The grounds for excluding such evidence of distress as corroborative is that the victim is the source. A friend of the complainant, Pauline (not her real name), gave evidence that when Birgitte returned to the hostel she was in a terrible state. The Recorder of London, in summing up on 27 May 1993, directed the jury to discount this evidence as corroborative:

Pauline told you that when she saw Birgitte on 30 August, her friend was not only crying but was shaking all over. That evidence cannot be regarded as independent corroboration because in effect it derives from the

7. From telephone conversations on 22 and 23 November 1994.

8. By Jacqui Webster for *Dispatches*.

complainant herself and what she said to P comes directly from herself. You are invited to consider whether she exaggerated in suggesting that she was beaten up; that is not her evidence in the case, so is there some evidence of exaggeration in the account which she gave to her friend? Whether that throws doubt on her story is for you to say.

Despite forensic evidence of injuries, the fact that the rape had been reported immediately, the lack of a motive for Birgitte to make a false allegation of rape and his sudden disappearance, the jury only took two hours to acquit him on two counts of rape. One of the jurors apparently later said to a police officer, 'Well, of course it wasn't rape – she'd slept with him before.'

Throughout the year Birgitte had been writing letters to Victim Support. A few weeks after she had returned home the letters stopped arriving. Then Victim Support received a letter saying she had taken an overdose (she survived). The reason given was that she had not been believed. She explained how devastating it was to be raped by someone you knew and had trusted:

If you are raped by somebody you think you know you're totally shocked because you – you have an impression of this man, and you think you know him, and suddenly he shows a wild animal side of himself and you keep asking yourself, 'Was I blind? Did he show these signs before, early in our relationship? Didn't I want to see it, or has he suddenly changed?' It's harder to trust people. It's harder to trust your friends, because you knew this man and he was a friend and suddenly he shows this animal behaviour. Then you think, who are my friends? Who are my real friends? Where are they?

While on bail for Birgitte's rape, Johnson again appeared at magistrates court in May 1993 for raping a twenty-one-year-old woman, Helen, and yet again was bailed. According to an article in the Evening Standard (9 December 1993), this complainant had found out that there were eleven other allegations against her attacker, all of the same nature. Only three of the cases had reached court, all of which had resulted in acquittals. Giving Johnson bail exemplifies the lack of concern about the danger women face when serial rapists are allowed to walk free. Johnson's whereabouts are now unknown. However, in mid-1994 Birgitte ran into him at a Paris Metro station. On seeing her he beat a hasty retreat. She telephoned the British police but Interpol have not been able to locate him.

Reactions of the Victims to Their Attacker's Acquittal

Few jurors realize how devastating it can be for complainants when their assailant is acquitted and how terrified they often are that the defendant will retaliate for taking them to court. This is how Anna in the Johnson case described the experience of being disbelieved by the jury:

I think it made things worse if anything. I mean, 'cos you – you bring something to light, you're showing somebody what's been happening, and then all of a sudden it's – to them it's – nothing I went to court and I said what I had to say. I told them the truth, and he walked in the end. That was like a blow on top of a blow. The court was one of the hardest things about the whole incident.

You stand there, you're giving evidence and you're trying to tell these people what's been happening and you get manipulated by his defence counsel and questions are asked, silly questions. Like, where did I get my clothes from? How comes I look smart? Are my children getting money from their father? And as far as I'm concerned, that has got nothing to do with what we were in court for.

They didn't ask why I could not go out of the house. Why I didn't report it earlier. But basically I was asked, 'Was I having sex with the children's father? Was I seeing anybody at the time? How many partners had I had? And questions like that.

I was trying to get my views over and describe what was going on, but she [the defence counsel] was not having it. She did not seem to listen or even try to understand what I was trying to say to her. And in the court, I don't even remember seeing my prosecutor stand up or defend me in any way. I never spoke to her. I never had any communication with her.

There's not such a thing as justice. That's what I truly believe. And especially in this circumstance where it's a rape trial. I think they don't understand what needs to be done in a rape trial. They don't understand that the person sitting there is looking you in your face. You're standing up there and you're trying to put your questions and your feelings across to what's happening and they refuse to listen. I don't think they listened to anything I'd said to them. I can understand why a lot of women don't take rape to court, because it's a lot of stress. There are a lot of women out there who refuse to go to court.

The police are as helpful as they can be. They sat there with me for hours to do the statement, and they were very, very understanding people. The judge himself was insisting that I raise my voice and that was hard enough as it is. But the police know what it's like.

Because I was afraid of him coming back I moved. I moved to my mum's. I moved to another temporary accommodation. I moved altogether three times before I could really feel comfortable. I don't think I'll ever feel comfortable because I know he's out there. Every time I walk or go somewhere, I think I'm going to bump into him. It's like ever since it's happened. And there's no help, no help.

My life has been turned upside-down. He's still walking free, that's the most upsetting part. I went through tests and I had to go through clinics and get all sorts of tests taken.

They let a rapist walk free. He got away with it, and he thought he could do it again. I don't know how long it is going to go on for. I know he's going to do it again. I thought he was mad. He wasn't there, you know – that is, his eyes. I think it's like a game to him.

Alistair Winter (not his real name)

Even more typical than date rape, is the following acquaintance rape which led to an acquittal in court but received little press comment. In December 1984, Julie, who filled in one of the questionnaires we distributed, was twenty-five when she was raped. Her story is typical of many acquaintance rape cases in which the woman is persuaded to accompany the man to a location where he can assault her. Such complaints of rape are often doubted by jurors, who may believe it is the woman's fault for accepting an invitation to have a drink or for laying herself open to attack. They fail to take into account that it is almost impossible to prevent the kind of unforseen attack that Julie experienced.

Julie was living with her parents in Sussex and had a boyfriend at the time. On the evening in question, she was not out on a date but simply agreed to drop a man whom she met at a party home. She described what happened:

A man approached me at a party of a work colleague. He was very overbearing and loud, and offered to pour me a glass of wine. He talked at me, not to me. He asked if he and another man and woman could get a lift home after the party. Before this he had inquired which direction I lived and the fact that I had a car. Later when I dropped him off he asked me in for a Christmas drink, saying 'Come on, it's Christmas. Have a drink. I won't jump on you.' For some strange reason, this comment made me more relaxed.

She agreed to go to his flat and once there, the man's mood changed abruptly:

Once he had me in his flat, he became silent and took drugs. He stared at me without blinkin His eyes seemed black. He became forceful and I felt like prey. He tried to get me to smoke drugs but I refused. He physically stopped me from leaving, blocking the door and gripping my wrists, which hurt. The more frightened I became, the more it seemed to turn him on. He became more aggressive and threatened to break my arms and legs if I resisted. He continued to stare at me. I could feel the evil. It terrified me . . . He said, 'I'm going to have you. Don't struggle or I'll break your arms and legs. No one would hear.' I begged him to stop and pretended to have an asthma attack. I tried every emotion, but he raped me regardless. He called me a slut and told me I could scream as loud as I liked. Whilst raping me he held my arms. At one stage he gripped my throat. He was hurting me, but the fear numbed me a little. Once again I really felt I was prey to him. I was afraid he would pull out a knife at any time. I prayed for it to end. It seemed to go on for ever. After the rape, he said that he hadn't finished with me. At this point I pretended to like him to win his confidence. This had a very slight response.

Julie managed to convince him that she needed her Ventolin inhaler from her car as she was pretending to have serious problems breathing. Secreting her keys in her cleavage, she assured him that she would return if she left without her shoes and her bag. Winter accompanied her downstairs and, when they got to her car, she managed to leap in, locking the doors. She drove to the police station without her shoes, underwear or bag, with Winter chasing her, and managed to get away.

Terrified, she described how she had to use her strongest asset, her brain, 'to prevent being murdered or maimed':

He stopped after the rape, but kept repeating, 'I haven't finished with you.' I remember going through every emotion. My head was going 100 miles an hour. I knew I had to survive. I realized at this point what the survival instinct was. It was very strong. I tried anger but that made him worse. I tried hysteria, crying. That came naturally. I was terrified. I tried reasoning. None of it worked. I was running out of ideas. He called me an actress at one stage, but continued to make threats. I told him that my boyfriend would be looking for me. (Untrue, but it didn't work anyway.) Only pretending to fancy him had any effect.

My heart was racing. My brain was spinning. I felt I must escape. I was frantic for a sliver of a chance to get out. I saw a nail file out of the corner of my eye but I couldn't reach it. I would, I believe, have stabbed him in self-defence. I was so scared. I got my keys from my bag when he left the room for literally seconds and put them down my bra. I couldn't run for it then, as I knew he would have caught me. So I talked continually to him about anything, the weather, how I allegedly fancied him anyway. Anything to get a chance to escape. Eventually my break came. I knew I had one chance only. Luckily my acting got me out of there eventually.

The effect of the attack was devastating She had bruising and cuts. She discovered he had VD. She attempted suicide several times, slashed her wrists and went for psychiatric treatment. She described the effects:

I lost my job shortly afterwards. I lost my boyfriend. He once in an argument said I was 'soiled goods', which was cruel. We split up. I started reacting to stress by slashing my wrists. I took many overdoses, requiring immediate hospitalization and treatment. They placed me in a mental health institution twice. I have to this day become very anxious. I suffer panic attacks. I drink too much. I started smoking for the first time after the rape and I am asthmatic. I feel suicidal frequently. Intimacy is a problem. I relate to my female friends better and feel safer with them. The Health Service told me I needed two to three years' counselling but could only offer me three to six months. I had no back-up help at all. I was basically told to get on with my life and forget it . . . I have been left to rot by society and no one helped me.

What about Alistair Winter, what happened to him? Julie had arrived at the police station only half clad and without her bag or shoes. She had made a statement and was willing to testify in court. Winter was arrested and taken into custody. You might imagine this was a cast-iron case. At the magistrates court, to Julie's horror, he was given bail, even though the police had received a previous complaint of indecent assault. She was terrified she would be attacked again and kept seeing him in local pubs. It was over a year before the case came to the crown court for trial. Winter kept changing his plea from guilty back to not guilty. At the jury trial he pleaded not guilty and was acquitted. The judge most unusually made an order for him to pay his legal costs of £15,000.

Julie found the trial an appalling experience. She was subjected to demeaning questions about her lifestyle, about whom she shared a home with, whether she had had sex with anyone else, the way she was dressed at the time of the assault and when she had last menstruated. She could not remember and the defence counsel said, 'You're a woman of the world. Surely you know when your period was.' She was asked how short her skirt was and whether it was tight. She was asked whether she was wearing underwear. Her knickers were held up in court as an exhibit. One question she remembered vividly about the red shoes she was wearing: 'The defence counsel said, "You would admit these shoes are not leather. They are of the cheaper end of the market?"' If her shoes were cheap, then the implication was that she must be too.

Julie felt sure Winter had raped other women and would go on to rape again. A friend of his was quoted in the press, alleging that he used to have any girl he fancied and had probably raped many women and got away with it. After he was acquitted in 1986, he would apparently show a newspaper cutting to any girl who complained and tell her, 'You will have a hard time proving it. I've got away with it before.'

Investigations by Dispatches revealed that he had made a fortune out of a string of dating agencies, including a prostitutes racket, over the previous eighteen years. After the Official Receiver moved in, Winter fled abroad, but he slipped back into Britain under an assumed name and set up an escort agency in small back-street premises in the red-light district of a Midlands town.

In February 1993 Winter again appeared in court. On this occasion he was found guilty of rape, buggery and administering controlled drugs to have sex with a prospective female client. He had befriended the victim on the phone after receiving her application to the agency. Although he had asked her questions about her sex life the woman believed him to be a charming businessman. Julie also said that is how he had come across on first acquaintance. Eventually the woman agreed to meet him at her home after he had offered her a job in the business. The complainant, who was forty-five years old and a divorcee, told the court that Winter had spiked her drink shortly after arriving at her home for their first meeting. She fell unconscious but later became aware that he was having sex with her. He also buggered her. She said he was violent and she was frightened for her life. The police surgeon told the court the woman had suffered the worst anal injuries she had ever seen.

According to the complainant when interviewed, Winter was very relaxed in court, eating sweets and making eyes at the female jurors and even one of the female clerks. He was jailed for nine years. In summing up, the judge said:

You defiled that woman and put her to immense pain. You used your position in the dating agency, which you ran, to first get into contact with this woman. Then you came down to her home, prepared with drugs, so that if she was not cooperative you could have your own way – and your way you had. Your barrister says there is nothing he can advance in mitigation for this matter. This is an extraordinarily serious offence and the sentence I pass reflects this.

Had he been convicted of Julie's rape, he could not have gone on to rape again. There is little doubt that Winter was not only a serial rapist but an extremely dangerous man. In view of the degree of injuries, there were surely strong grounds for giving him a longer sentence, since parole can be granted after serving about half the sentence. Julie was extremely bitter that she was not believed. Winter's case is a mirror image of the cases described in the next chapter.

Conclusion

In all the above cases there was some consensual contact with the assailant. That serial rapists are often acquaintance rapists conflicts with the myth that 'real' rapists are strangers who leap in the dark. Jurors were not told that acquaintance rape is more common than stranger rape and has effects just as serious. The myth that it is only strangers who rape was shared by Shareen, who said:

I thought rape was something that strangers did. I thought rape was something that men jumped out at you and they did in secret. I didn't realize they'd do it openly. I didn't realize that a man could be so confident about it.

Lawyers encourage this myth and express surprise if rapists appear to be charming The Frankenstein model of the rapist is still all too prevalent. Yet men who rape appear to be perfectly normal. All the women were picked up shortly before the attack or persuaded to go on a date. This does not mean that the men were not cold-blooded rapists whose attacks were to some extent premeditated.

Even when men are convicted, date rape is not seen to be as serious as rape by strangers. For example, in the summer of 1993 Judge Michael Addison, sentencing a rapist who had attacked a woman after taking her out for a meal, to three and a half years' imprisonment, said, 'This is not in my view the more serious type of rape – that is, rape of a total stranger.' David Forrest, a cabinet-maker, aged thirty-six, attacked a twenty-four-year-old barmaid after taking her out for a meal. He invited her in for coffee, which he said he 'interpreted as an invitation to sex'. He grabbed her by the wrists and dragged her upstairs, then stripped and raped her. The terrified girl pleaded for him to stop. The judge said, 'I accept that you misread the signals.' The judge in this case, in spite of the guilty verdict reached by the jury, apparently failed to recognize the appalling impact of rape by an acquaintance – how it can shatter the victim's whole trust and judgement in others.

Judges take the view that acquaintance rape is less serious than stranger rape, but are neither clear about how exactly to define a stranger nor aware that rapists like John Simpson do not confine themselves to raping either strangers or acquaintances; they often rape both. Rapists such as Simpson and Johnson discussed here and Frederick West, charged in 1994 with raping, torturing and killing thirteen women (two were his own wife and daughter) were all acquainted with their victims. *The Times* leader of 30 April 1994 throws light on why there is a need for falsely distinguishing between rapes by strangers and rapes by acquaintances and intimates. When commenting on the very long sentence of twenty-eight years given to a serial rapist, Adrian Mole, after he was found guilty of ten charges of rape and attempted buggery of two girls, Judge Tucker described his assaults as 'disgusting depravity and unspeakable perversion'. '*The Times* took the opportunity to emphasize the distance between Mole's crimes and rapes by acquaintances. Yet Mole was no stranger to the women, now in their early twenties, who had been continually raped since early adolescence, one from the age of eleven. '*The Times* slid over this, emphasizing the difference between rapes by strangers and 'chosen companions'.

Is it really not worse to be held at knife-point by a deranged stranger, or repeatedly attacked by someone who threatens mutilation, than to be forced to have sex with someone who was, at least, a chosen companion? Rape is always criminal because it is an assault and a violation, but it is nonsense to pretend that some rapes are not worse than others, or that there are not real differences in degrees of guilt. There is no point either in denying that there are real conceptual problems for the courts in rape trials. Unlike other crimes, 'rape' is defined by the victim's experience of it.

Yet this false assumption can be very dangerous. As the cases discussed above show, it can lead to the acquittal of rapists on the grounds that if they have had any social contact with the complainants beforehand, then they cannot be rapists. The idea that a companion, if 'chosen', is any less dangerous is also misleading, as more women are killed by men they have had a sexual relationship with than by strangers.

Chapter 7

Problems of the Adversarial System

In this chapter, I discuss the limitations of the adversarial system of justice with particular reference to the case of William Mulherne, who stood trial on four counts of rape and one count of attempted rape during our monitoring of trials in 1993. This is a unique study,[1] as the television researchers and reporters were able to trace and interview all the victims (whose names have been changed) and some of the defence barristers involved in the cases. I shall show how rape trials such as Mulherne's, rather than the cases suggested by the press, are the real miscarriages of justice.

William Mulherne and 'Similar Fact'

In view of the number of different women who had reported being raped by Mulherne, and the DNA evidence which linked the cases, the prosecution applied for all five to be heard together, according to the 'similar fact' law, by which, if there is similarity between different allegations, all the cases can be heard together. This was rejected, despite the similarity between the allegations. As a result, each of the cases was heard separately and Mulherne was convicted only once of rape. We shall see how, by having each case heard separately, the defence counsel was able to undermine the cases of the complainants by the use of quite ruthless tactics, flying in the face of the constraints recommended by the Sexual Offences (Amendment) Act (1976). These young women, all mere teenagers, were rewarded for their bravery in giving evidence in these cases by being humiliated as all kinds of evidence against them was dredged up to undermine their credibility. For victims to then see their assailants walk free is an experience which leaves many women shell-shocked. Additionally, as a result of plea-bargaining the attempted rape,

1. Channel 4 *Dispatches* provided us with both the resources and access to police and barristers.

throughout which the victim had fought for her life and suffered severe injuries, was reduced to the lesser charge of indecent assault, apparently without anyone even informing her.[2]

If all the cases had been heard together, there is little doubt that Mulherne would have been convicted in all four cases which came to trial. It is also likely that the fifth charge would not have been reduced to indecent assault. By hearing the cases separately, he was acquitted of three and very nearly acquitted of the fourth case. In the latter, if he had not changed his plea half-way through and opted to enter the witness box, he might well have been acquitted altogether. Mulherne's case is important, as it shows that the judge's use of his discretion in not allowing the cases to be heard together led to a serious miscarriage of justice. Yet the complainants had absolutely no redress. It is difficult to estimate how common such cases are, but there is evidence that they do arise with some frequency. In 1989, when I sat in on trials at the Old Bailey, another defendant was tried for two offences separately, was found guilty of indecent assault in one case and acquitted altogether in the other. If the two cases had been heard together, there is little doubt that he would have been found guilty on both charges, in which case he would have received at least eight rather than two years' imprisonment.

William Mulherne faced four charges of raping women (and an added charge of buggery against one of them) between February 1991 and June 1992 and one charge of attempted rape. All the young women were well-adjusted sixteen–nineteen-year-olds, working class, comparatively hard-up and living in a radius of ten or so miles, off the M25. They were all single at the time, but one of them, Jessica, had a serious boyfriend. These women were in no way atypical of many young women of their age, and there is no reason to suspect any of them were lying about the rapes. Yet in court, as we shall see, all sorts of reasons were presented to throw doubt on their evidence and so undermine their credibility. All the rapes were connected by DNA evidence. Three other women also reported Mulherne to the police for rape but were unwilling to give evidence in court. In the face of the evidence, he appears to be a serial rapist, yet he was acquitted three times of rape and a further charge was

2. According to the victim, she was willing to give evidence for the charge of attempted rape and was not consulted.

reduced by plea-bargaining. Without the development in DNA analysis, these cases might never have been linked. But even when all five cases are reported by totally independent women and linked, not only by DNA evidence, but also by descriptions of very similar circumstances and tactics used by the accused, the cases were not heard together and the defendant was found guilty of rape only once. In each of the trials there were different factors that appeared to affect the jury's verdict. Among these were the introduction of the criminal offence committed by one of the complainants after the rape allegation, irrelevant reference to the women's past sexual history, distortion of the immediate effect of rape on the victim, inadequate explanation given for the absence of physical injuries and the failure to report the rape immediately (recent report) and, finally, the different weight given by the judge in his directions to the relevance of lying in judging the credibility of the complainant and defendant. If serial rapists are to be convicted, given the serious imbalances in trials, it is essential that cases should be heard together. Given the low level of reporting, such cases are likely to represent only a proportion of the number of women who have been raped. Leaving 'similar fact' evidence to the judge's discretion appears to seriously limit its effectiveness, as is the case with sexual history evidence. Moreover, judicial sabotage of this kind has an immobilizing effect on reform initiatives at earlier points in the criminal justice process.

The Law on 'Similar Fact'

In 1993 one of the main reasons why serial rapists were not convicted was the failure to allow allegations from quite independent women to be heard together. The general admissibility of evidence of previous convictions for similar offences threatened two central principles of the adversarial system: that the accused stands to be tried only in respect of the offence with which he is charged; and that the jury must be persuaded of the accused's guilt beyond all reasonable doubt.[3] To consider the latter principle, there is an air of mystery to the idea of 'beyond reasonable doubt', both conceptually and in terms of how jurors reach an agreement.

3. The Criminal Law Revision Committee (Eleventh Report, 1972) points out that such fears do not exist in France, where the defendant's criminal record is read out at the beginning of the trial.

According to Lord Justice Lawton, 'Judges would be well advised not to attempt any gloss upon what is meant by reasonable doubt.' Such comments are 'more likely to confuse than help'. He emphasized that 'if judges stopped trying to define that which is almost impossible to define, there would be fewer appeals'.[4] But a judge who is specifically asked for an explanation by the jury may be forced to attempt one if he or she feels the jury are in danger of thinking that they need to apply anything more than the common sense they use in matters of importance in their everyday lives. Lord Diplock recommends the approach of Judge Small, who clarified the concept to the jury as follows:

You remember that in dealing with matters of importance in your business affairs, you do not allow slight, whimsical doubts to deter you from going along; you brush them aside and go ahead. But surely, there comes a time when, dealing with matters of your own affairs, you stop to think and by reason of that doubt you decide what to do in your business of importance. Well, this is the quality and kind of doubt of which the law speaks when it speaks of reasonable doubt.

But is the meaning of reasonable doubt so obvious that elaboration is unnecessary? Studies in the United States have found that jurors are often confused if the concept is unexplained. In a recent decision by the US Supreme Court,[5] Justice Ginsberg approved the definition of reasonable doubt proposed by the Federal Judicial Center as a model instruction for judges. This states:

Proof beyond a reasonable doubt is proof that leaves you firmly convinced of the defendant's guilt. There are very few things in this world that we know with absolute certainty, and in criminal cases the law does not require proof that overcomes every possible doubt. If, based on your consideration of the evidence, you are firmly convinced that the defendant is guilty of the crime charged, you must find him guilty. If, on the other hand, you think there is a real possibility that he is not guilty, you must give him the benefit of the doubt and find him not guilty.

David Pannick, QC, (1995) argues that in Britain juries would also benefit from such an explanation.

4. See Pannick (1995).
5. See the case of Victor v. Nebraska, ibid.

Another factor that in rape trials should be debated is in what circumstances evidence should be heard in camera. The judge in criminal trials is expected to adjudicate on issues of law such as the admissibility of evidence and also on facts which affect admissibility. This must be done in the absence of the jury. The judge's decision may therefore deprive the jury of hearing certain items of evidence. Judges have a great deal of discretion in deciding what is and is not admissible. This was all too evident in the appeal case of R. v. Viola (1982) 75 Cr. App. R 125, where Lord Lane held that it was wrong to speak of discretion in the context of Section 2 of the Sexual Offences (Amendment) Act (1976) (banning evidence of a woman's previous sexual history – sex with a man other than the defendant). Lord Lane directed that the sole question here was relevance and if a matter was relevant, the judge had no discretion to exclude evidence. This was complete sabotage of the act, which aimed to restrict the circumstances in which defence lawyers could challenge the credibility of complainants in rape trials by introducing evidence concerning their past sexual history.

The judge has discretion on whether cases can be heard together. The law on 'similar fact' relies on the criterion of 'striking similarity' between offences. The basis for this decision is complicated and judges often disallow it. According to Richardson (1993: 1, 593), Lord Hailsham argued that cases could be dealt with together

as a matter of discretion...that a properly instructed jury, applying their minds to the facts, can come to the conclusion that they are satisfied so that they are sure that to treat the matter as pure coincidence by reason of the 'nexus', 'pattern', 'system', 'striking resemblances' or whatever phrase is used is 'an affront to common sense'...In this the ordinary rules of logic and common sense prevail...Attempts to codify the rules of common sense are to be restricted.

Further clarification was provided by the 1991 House of Lords direction, in which the Lord Chancellor stated that the essential feature of 'similar fact' is that its 'prohibitive force is sufficiently great to be just to admit it, notwithstanding that it is prejudicial to the accused as tending to show that he is guilty of another offence'.[6]

As we shall see from the Mulherne case, it appears that judges are

6. DPP v. P. (1991) 93 Cr App. R267.

still disallowing it, most likely because they are worried that the appeal court will criticize their interpretation and overturn convictions.

Anne Davies, Principal Scientific Officer with the Metropolitan Police, seconded to the British Home Office to research into serial rapists, confirmed[7] that when courts consider 'similar fact' where they have a series of rape cases involving the same defendant, they often consider only what is 'blindingly obvious'. They fail to understand that rapists, as in the above cases, go for picking up similar types of victim in similar situations, performing similar types of crime. She explained that she had detected strategies occurring time and time again in different rapes: for example, strategies for getting a woman to go with them, the type of victim chosen, the sexual acts, the way that some men compliment their victims. She explained what ought to be considered:

The sorts of similar facts I'd be looking for are the way he chooses to approach the victim m the first place, the 'con' approach or in surprise, the type of victim, whether he goes for a particularly high-risk vulnerable victim, or you get a man who likes particularly upmarket women, the sort of sexual acts he performs and the verbal strategies, the themes that are going through his mind, the things he talks about. It's not just the themes he may go in for boasting to the women or complimenting them – but it's also people's syntax and vocabulary that remain surprisingly similar over the years.

William Mulherne

Mulherne picked up his victims in discos, bars or clubs. He used at least five aliases. He was twenty-one years old, a well-off member of the traveller community, with a record of indecent assault and a string of other offences, including burglary and car theft. He was well dressed, drove expensive cars and lived in hotels. He came across as a 'charmer' and 'a womanizer'. Five women reported being raped by him between February 1991 and June 1992. In each case he used similar tactics (*modus operandi*). He would meet the woman in a social situation and chat them up. He would then use some pretext to get her into his car: he might offer her a lift home or to somewhere on her way. It is clear from the women's accounts that the rapes were

7. In an interview with Jenny Cuffe for *Dispatches* in autumn 1993.

strategic and premeditated. As soon as the woman got into the car, he would drive them off at great speed against their will to an isolated spot – a field, a lay-by or a car park. He would reject a location if it seemed there was any possibility of being observed. In each case Mulherne wound down the front passenger seat to a horizontal position, ripped the bottom part of the women's clothing off and raped them. In each case the woman commented how strong he was. All the women were terrified he would kill them. Mulherne would then apologize and offer the woman money. He would threaten them not to tell anyone. In two cases another man was present who also used a number of different aliases.

He evaded the police until November 1991, when he was stopped for driving a car without insurance. He fitted the description given by Stephanie, one of the young women involved, and she picked him out at an identification parade. His DNA profile was linked with two other rapes. He was charged with rape and first remanded in custody but later bailed. Two of the five reported rapes occurred when he was on bail and were matched with the other DNA evidence. He was arrested for the latter two rapes in August 1992 and another woman, Cora, picked him out of an identification parade in September. In one instance where he had originally been charged with attempted rape and indecent assault (oral sex), the CPS dropped these charges and Mulherne pleaded guilty to indecent assault. The attempted rape charge was left on file.

Five women, only one of whom had known him before the night in question, alleged rape. There is a strong argument that these cases should have been dealt with together. The defendant's identity was not an issue (except in Cora's case before he changed his plea from identification to consent). A number of women, quite independently and unknown to each other, had made similar allegations against him. In his statements to the police when arrested, he denied even knowing all of them, although later DNA evidence linked him to all the cases. The women's stories were all very similar. He appeared to have used very similar tactics and the attacks all took place within a period of months.

As we have seen, the prosecution applied to have the cases dealt with together, but the judge ruled against the application. If Mulherne's strategy had been examined more methodically, all sorts of similarities would have emerged. Several of the victims reported how he had used the same phrase, 'I swear on my mum's life, I'm not going to hurt you', before raping them.

Anne Davies (1992: 173) argues that a much more systematic approach should be taken to the investigation with a record of as much speech as can be recollected. Behaviour of rapists after the rape is also important to look at. As she explained:

They tend not to be quite so considerate before sex, but after sex they will offer to run somebody home or tell them not to leave their windows open again because somebody like him might come back and rape her again. You actually get this pseudo-consideration and kindness. I think it's possibly a strategy for getting away afterwards. It makes the offence look more normal and also facilitates his departure from the victim. After the rape the man is presented with a problem, he's got to get away, so some men will threaten the victim not to report the offence, tell her what he's going to come back and do to her. He may offer her money. One man who went on to murder ran one of his rape victims to Victoria station and from the money he'd stolen from her gave her some money back so she could catch a train.

Such 'consideration' is often presented in court as an argument that the man cared for the complainant and therefore could not have raped them. We saw this tactic used in the Johnson case (see pages 170 71). The fact that he had cooked the complainant a meal and washed the shirt she had left behind when she eventually escaped was presented as evidence that Johnson was concerned about her welfare, that this was not the behaviour of a typical rapist. Another very important factor which is overlooked by jurors is that rapists progress and learn from one offence to another, so their behaviour changes.[8]

In the Mulherne case, common sense dictates that there was a degree of similarity between the cases. However, judges seem to disagree as to how similar the cases should be. Lord Salmon, for example, argues:

8. One criminologist (Walker 1991) describes how little information is often given about the exact circumstances of attacks. He described how the clerk of the court in one case told the psychiatrist that the accused had 'taken a knife to frighten his wife'. In fact, he had stabbed her. The defendant was given day leave, went home and killed her.

It has, however, never been doubted that if the crime charged is committed in a uniquely or strikingly similar manner to other crimes committed by the accused, the manner in which the crimes were committed may be evidence on which a jury could reasonably conclude that the accused was guilty of the crime charged. The similarity would have to be so unique or striking that the common sense makes it inexplicable on the basis of coincidence (Richardson 1993: 1, 1594).

In practice, judges have tended to insist on behaviour being exactly replicated rather than very similar, so it is only in cases where a man has a very peculiar way of attacking women that 'similar fact' evidence is allowed. Leaving the admission of 'similar fact' evidence to the discretion of judges rather than codifying the grounds for admissibility exacerbates the injustice of rape trials and contributes to rapists walking free.

Jennifer McEwan, Reader in Law at Keele University, England, who specializes in criminal law and the law of evidence, argues (McEwan 1992) that in cases of 'similar fact' evidence, judges rely too much on the belief that cases must be uniquely and strikingly similar. The real test, she argues, is whether the evidence can be explained away as simply a coincidence. If a man is accused of rape by two different women, this should surely be seen as significant to the defendant's credibility. Three incidences would be more significant still. Yet we find that even previous rape convictions are treated as inadmissible unless the circumstances are strikingly similar. It goes beyond the realms of coincidence that a person previously accused of rapes (whether convicted of them or acquitted on a plea of consent) should be accused once again by a willing partner out of spite, bearing in mind that the argument is only for admitting the evidence, not for convicting the defendant. In practice, most judges routinely use their discretion to disallow 'similar fact' evidence on the grounds that it is irrelevant to the particular issue either credibility or guilt. McEwan argues that evidence relating to the defendant's disposition should be admitted as a matter of course. However, judges have considerable discretion on what evidence is admitted – that is, on the exceptions to exclusionary rules.

The police argue that they could secure more convictions if the law on 'similar fact' was liberalized. Ideally this would allow several cases reported by different complainants to be heard together and would also allow women who had been raped in the past to be witnesses in any new trial of a 'repeat' offender, if the circumstances of the rape were similar enough.[9] This is what was eventually allowed in the Nicholas Edwards case (see Introduction) and resulted in his conviction.

In the Kennedy Smith trial in the US, the prosecution tried to include testimony by other women (who claimed they had been raped by Smith) under what is called 'the common scheme or plan'.[10] This means that evidence can be heard if the other crimes appear to be 'substantially similar' to the crime for which the defendant is being tried. How similar is up to the judge's discretion. In the Kennedy Smith trial, as in the Mulherne trial, Judge Mary Lupo, the American judge, looked for 'virtual identity in method of commission', a more stringent interpretation than is often allowed in the US. This is why the public, but not the jury, heard about this evidence. Three women who had allegedly been raped in the same way by Kennedy Smith were not allowed to give evidence. According to one of these women, a medical student, Smith was notorious for picking up women in bars and holding orgies, and had pinned her down on a bed when she was drunk and raped her. Two other women, one a doctor and the other a law school student, also said he had brutally attacked them. All three women gave statements to the police. On appeal the US higher courts refer the trial judge's view only if there is 'a blatant abuse of judicial discretion' (see Boumil et al. 1992: 107). It is unlikely, therefore, that Judge Lupo's discretion would have been reversed on appeal. There is growing dissatisfaction with the greater emphasis placed on the need to protect the rights of criminal defendants as against the relative lack of emphasis placed on the rights of victims. The system seems to be out of balance in the US.

9. Channel 4 *Dispatches* wrote to the Lord Chancellor's Department on 5 November 1993 to ask for the views of judges on whether judicial reform was possible or desirable in regard to the question of the prosecution introducing 'similar fact' evidence – that is, getting more than one case tried together – asking, in other words, if the evidential rules for 'similar fact' evidence were too strict (see DPP v. P. (1991) 2AC 47). The Lord Chancellor's department declined to reply.

10. This is referred to in the US as the 'Williams Rule', a rule of evidence or rule of relevance which the disputed evidence must meet before the judge allows it to be presented to the jury (see Boumil et al. 1992: 105).

The Misuse of Sexual History Evidence

In England and Wales, according to the Sexual Offences (Amendment) Act (1976), questions regarding the past sexual history of the complainant were allowed at the discretion of the judge only where it was relevant to the case. One of the victims Mulherne raped (Jessica) had previously had consensual sex with him, so it was reasonable for the judge to allow questions regarding this. However, her cross-examination went far beyond her sexual relationship with him and should not have been allowed.

Jessica was the first to report Mulherne to the police in February 1991. At the time of the assault, she was seventeen, with a steady boyfriend. She was the only one of the victims to have had a sexual relationship with him beforehand. Out shopping with her friend, Mary, she ran into Mulherne in May 1990. He was with two other men, Henry, a second-hand car dealer, and Jimmy. Mulherne introduced himself as Mark. They chatted the girls up and persuaded them to accept an invitation to a club that evening. Jessica was impressed by their charm and apparent wealth. They drove a black BMW and wore gold chains.

The two young women went with them to a disco and Jessica had sex with him on that first night, which was not an unusual occurrence in the circles she mixed in. She did not meet him regularly and did not regard him as her boyfriend but just ran into him from time to time. She had a regular boyfriend, with whom she is now living. About two months after she had stopped meeting Mulherne, she saw him in the bank with a friend of his. She was furious when he boasted in public about having had sex with her. She told him to 'fuck off'. She already considered the relationship was over and did not see him again for several months. Then one day, when she was on her way to collect her six-year-old brother from school, he stopped the car and offered to give her a lift. She said she accepted because she was late and did not want her brother left unattended. Mulherne did not, however, take her to the school. Instead, he took her on a nightmare drive miles out into the country. She told us what happened:

When he went past the motorway bridge, I was scared. I didn't know where the hell he was taking me. I started to panic. I was just scared and when he said to me, 'If you don't do what I want you to do, I'll take you 500 miles away from here and you won't be doing anything', that sounded like that

I'd be dead and he would have killed me. I mean, when someone threatens you with that, you'll do anything, wouldn't you?"[11]

She said that Mulherne then raped her. She was terrified he would kill her. Before the trial Jessica alleges one of Mulherne's relatives came to her mother's house and offered her £500 to drop the charges. In court Jessica's version was not believed. The defence counsel argued that she had consented to sex on this occasion just as she had in the past. The jury found him not guilty. Jessica was branded a liar. Having sex with him the first night they met was fatal to her accusation of rape. The defence counsel implied that because she had had casual sex on one occasion, she must be generally promiscuous. This carried the implication that she was 'unrespectable' and could not therefore have been raped. The defence counsel asked her about having sex with Mulherne the first time she met him. In view of their previous sexual relationship, this fell within the provisions of the 1976 Sexual Offences (Amendment) Act and was allowed at the discretion of the judge. The defence counsel asked:

DEFENCE COUNSEL: And you were prepared when you first met to make love to a man who you had not met before in your life?

JESSICA: I didn't go out to do that. It was just that he used to keep asking all the time.

DC: You consented within minutes, did you not?

J: No, not within minutes. After persuasion, yeah, I did.

However, the defence counsel then went on to ask her a number of further questions which were not relevant and were exactly the type of question which the 1976 Sexual Offences (Amendment) Act was aimed at preventing. She was asked whether she had had sex or had given 'hand relief' to Mulherne's associates (she had not), about having sex the previous night with her boyfriend and finally about whether she had had an abortion when she was sixteen. Presumably the defence counsel had gained information about the abortion from Jessica's medical report. When asked why such questions about sex with her boyfriend and an abortion were allowed, the defence counsel, David Lederman, explained the

---

11. In an interview with Jenny Cuffe for *Dispatches*.

judge's use of discretion in allowing these questions in the following terms:

The judge in that case, because there had been consensual sexual intercourse, if you like, and further just 'off the cuff' sexual intercourse the following night, the judge felt the jury should know the girl's entire attitude towards casual sex when the whole defence was this was just casual sex...[12]

Clearly some lawyers view the sexual mores of lower-class women as entirely different to their own. Under cross-examination Lederman asked her whether she was wearing a red scarf, whether she had no bra and whether her fingernails were false. When interviewed after the trial, he commented:

We are here dealing with people who simply have no morality about sex at all. I mean, it's not for me to preach about it, but that is the actual position, that sex is a commodity. So you've got to start off on that basis and then decide whether or not, of course, she consented or not. That doesn't mean to say the crime of rape can't be committed, but that these two people looked upon sex simply as a casual commodity. It is relevant then to say that morality goes out of the window and you just look at whether or not this girl has consented to this commodity.'[3]

Previous Criminal History of the Defendant

In the same court, in the same month, another woman made an accusation of rape against Mulherne. Stephanie had an added ordeal. She alleged she was raped by Mulherne and also by Henry, his companion. She was a single parent, aged eighteen, when she first met him in March 1991 at a nightclub where she had gone with her friend Alison. On the way back to their seat from getting a drink at the bar, Mulherne deliberately bumped into them and pinched Alison's bottom, causing her to spill her drink. Stephanie kept out of the ensuing fracas where Mulherne told Alison he would like 'to get into her knickers'. The two girls called on the bouncers to deal with them and they did not see them again.

Stephanie ran into Mulherne again a month later. One night she

12. In an interview with Jenny Cuffe for *Dispatches*.
13. In an interview with Jenny Cuffe for *Dispatches*.

had dropped her baby at a minder and gone out for the evening. On her way back to collect him, Mulherne, who was with Henry, the same man as in Jessica's case, had drawn up beside her in his car. Mulherne apparently said, 'It's you from the Coliseum.' He was very charming and apologized for the 'fuss' at the Coliseum. He asked Stephanie if she wanted a lift home. It was freezing cold and Mulherne was being so nice, it did not occur to Stephanie that there was any risk, so she got into the car.

Stephanie explained to us what had happened. She said Mulherne introduced himself this time as Michael and Henry said he was Steve, both aliases. She started to panic when she realized that Mulherne was driving in the wrong direction and asked him where he was taking her. He said, 'We shan't be long.' She kept begging to be taken home. On the journey, Henry and Mulherne spoke in a kind of slang that she did not understand. She was driven hither and thither off the main roads through many country lanes on a terrifying drive. It was pitch dark. She remembers passing two houses with no lights on. She asked why he was taking her that way and he said 'to avoid the police'. Mulherne parked the car in a field beside a fence and some bushes. Henry got out of the car and said, 'My friend wants to talk to you. He wants a kiss.' Mulherne gave Henry the car keys, but seconds later he came running back saying, 'Quick, there's a woman walking her Alsatian dog.' Stephanie realized they were up to no good but hoped optimistically that they would take her home.

Mulherne drove on. After passing a field, Henry then said, 'Go in there. I was there the other day.' Stephanie was in the front of the car. Mulherne kept leaning over and saying, 'Where's my kiss?' She climbed into the back seat in an attempt to get out, but the door would not open. Mulherne stopped the car and climbed into the back and sat between her and the door that did open. He kept saying, 'I swear on my mother's life that I won't hurt you.' He pulled her legs up and pulled at her trousers. She screamed. He then just yanked them down in spite of Stephanie's struggling. She could not believe how strong he was. She described how she tried to resist:

The more I said no the more he... I don't know. He got like turned on by it. He got aggressive and I started screaming, telling him to get off me, and he raised his fist at me and told me to shut up.

She stopped screaming when he threatened her, telling her to 'fucking shut your mouth'. She was terrified that he would kill her. She said she had a period but that did not stop him. He penetrated her even though she was using a Tampax.

After the rape, Henry changed places with Mulherne and he raped her too. He also 'swore on his mother's life' that he would not hurt her while at the same time wrenching her trousers and forcing her legs up. He got on top of her and said, 'Wait till I come.' At around this time, Mulherne got back in the car and watched. He asked, 'Have you finished?' and laughed. Afterwards both of them said, 'See, we told you we weren't going to hurt you.'

Stephanie was appalled. They drove her back and nonchalantly Mulherne said, 'See you at the Coliseum.' They warned her not to tell anyone. She did not know what to do. She ran back to collect her child from the minder, told her she had been raped but not in any detail as the minder was not a close friend. In the morning she phoned Alison, who encouraged her to tell the police. She reported it that morning and was taken to a rape suite, where she made a lengthy statement.

A few days later, Stephanie was with Annette, her sister, and two other women. According to Stephanie, one of them assaulted and stole a woman's handbag in the street. The others ran off leaving her and Annette behind. Stephanie was the only one identified and it was she who was arrested. She had bleached blonde hair at the time. Although it was a first offence, she was given a six-month prison sentence for robbery and deception (the use of credit cards). Stephanie swears she was innocent.

The rape case did not come to court until over two years later, on 15 June 1993. Stephanie faced a horrendous ordeal. She had to give evidence on four separate occasions. At the first trial she gave half her evidence, but the case had to be stopped when Mulherne's family threatened the jury. At the second trial, after giving half her evidence, the case again had to be abandoned on discovering that one of the jury members could not understand English. The third trial was then interrupted when one of the jurors fell ill. This trial was held over until the next week with the same jury.

Stephanie was cross-examined for three and a half hours on the Mulherne charge alone and two further hours on the Henry case by a different barrister (see Chapter 5). Mulherne argued consent and Henry denied having had sex with her (in the Henry case there was no DNA evidence as he did not ejaculate). The defence argued that she could have got out of the car. She said they had no idea how impossible that would have been. It was pitch dark. It was isolated. Even if she had run, they would have caught up with her. She was made out to be a 'slut' and a liar. It was insinuated that she was drunk at the time, although there was no evidence for this. At one point in the trial Mulherne blew Stephanie a kiss.

Unnecessary Questioning of Complainant

Additionally, when the doctor who examined Stephanie after she reported the rape was cross-examined, she gave evidence that Stephanie had not been crying and had seemed very self-controlled. This was presented by the defence as evidence that she had not been raped. Stephanie, when interviewed, said she was a woman who only rarely cried. Women react differently to rape and, for some, an emotional reaction is delayed. Paradoxically, the only time Stephanie did break down was when Mulherne was acquitted. That was the final straw.

Stephanie was also shocked that her friend Alison was asked irrelevant and intimate questions about Stephanie, such as whether her boyfriend was the father of her child. It was implied that she could have avoided being raped by escaping, without any regard to the circumstances she was in. It was after one o'clock in the morning. She had no idea where they had taken her. They were two strong men and she was petrified. Yet the defence counsel implied she had stayed in the car because she had 'gone along with what Mulherne wanted' and was prepared to have sex. She was pressed as to why she did not run away and the following dialogue ensued:

STEPHANIE: He raised his fist at me. I wasn't risking getting beaten up or anything. I don't know what he was going to do.

DEFENCE COUNSEL: That's another fabrication, isn't it, that he raised his fist at you? He did nothing of the sort.

S: Yes, he did. He told me to shut up and he raised his fist at me.

Neither Mulherne nor Henry took the stand. Both were shown to have blatantly lied in their statements; neither of them gave evidence. Henry denied being in the car at all in his first statement to the police.

Very prejudicial to her case was the reference to her involvement in the robbery. Its relevance is highly debatable, particularly since it occurred *after* the rapes. More contentious still, although Mulherne had a string of offences (he had received six months' youth custody for indecent assault and ABH in 1987 and had served a further six months' imprisonment for burglary in 1989), no mention was made of his offences or their implication for his credibility. Mentioning Stephanie's conviction was enormously prejudicial to the case. Judge Bathurst Norman's warning to the jury in his summing-up must have had a very damaging effect on her case and shows starkly how unfair and unjust the trial process is:

When you deal with S's evidence you are entitled in deciding what weight you attach to her evidence to take into account the fact that she has a conviction for robbery. By the sounds of it, a very nasty robbery, for which she was sent to a young offender institution. It seems that fact in itself does not mean that she is lying to you about this matter. If it meant that, you would have wasted the last five days here, but you take it into account and weigh it on the scales in assessing her credibility to the extent that you think is right.

This points to one of the gravest imbalances in rape trials, which is that the defendant can attack the complainant's credibility and mention her past criminal record or her bad reputation, knowing that he does not run the risk of being cross-examined as to his previous convictions or bad character since this is up to the discretion of the judge, who rarely exercises the power.

Different Weight Given to Lies

The male standpoint, with its attendant bias, is often evident in the judge's summing-up. An example of this is the way the judge, following Court of Appeal directions,[14] advises the jury of the relevance of Stephanie's alleged 'lying' compared to the defendant's. Stephanie had initially said in her statement that when she was offered a lift by Mulherne and his accomplice, she had been 'bundled' into the car. On cross-examination she explained that she had been scared that her boyfriend (who had recently come out of prison) would be angry if he knew she had accepted a lift. This seems to be a perfectly reasonable explanation, but the judge, in summing-up, puts a quite different gloss on it and uses it to cast doubt on her general credibility. Added to this the slight variations

14. 98 Cr. App. R17.

in her account of what happened and her emotional control when she was medically examined were dissected and held against her.

This is an example of how the male point of view is taken for granted. In the light of the onus that is put on young women to avoid laying themselves open to risk, it is understandable that Stephanie should lie and, after a horrific experience, be afraid that she would be blamed and first attempt to cover up that she voluntarily got into the car. The fear Stephanie acknowledges of her boyfriend's anger is subtly used as a reason for her making a false allegation on the grounds that she wanted to cover up allegedly having sex with the defendants. It is also likely that a young woman trudging on foot, if offered a lift on a cold night by two young men, might well accept. The likelihood of her having consensual sex with both of them is surely pretty remote and, if she had, does not explain why she should make a false allegation. Yet Judge Bathurst Norman, in his summing-up, following Court of Appeal directions, suggested her so-called 'lies' cast doubt on her general credibility. According to Mays (14–22), 'The judge should not state his own views as to whether witnesses have told the truth or not, that is for the jury to decide.' (The jury are not aware, of course, that the defendant's past criminal record, for example, is protected in rape trials even when the credibility of the complainant is attacked.) This is how the judge summed up the case in regard to Stephanie's credibility:

It is perhaps right, at the outset, that I should set out the criticisms made on Stephanie's evidence so that you may have them in your mind when I come to review her evidence. The first criticism, of course, is a matter I have touched on already, namely that she is a person capable of dishonesty, because she has a conviction for robbery. However, more importantly15 the criticism relates to the lies that she told and told in graphic detail in her first statement to the police: about being bundled into the car – you will remember those graphic details; being struck across the back of the knees to make her legs bend and so on. That was not true. She says she told these lies through fear of her boyfriend but the defence say that they were not only told to the police, but they were also told to her best friend. To the

15. My italics: the point here is that some members of the jury were clearly very influenced by Stephanie's conviction (there was a gasp from one member of the jury when this was announced). To say her 'lies' are even more damaging is therefore very prejudicial.

doctors – something again not repeated to you – she claimed that one of the men had put his hands around her throat. To you the description was different, that he raised his hand as if to strike her and told her to shut up, so she kept quiet.

In regard to the two defendants' lies, although these involved denying ever having seen Stephanie and in Henry's case ever having been in the car with Mulherne, Judge Bathurst Norman takes a more sympathetic view. In his summing-up, he explained:

Lies in themselves are not evidence of guilt. There may be reasons farcing short of the fact that a person has committed an offence for why a defendant may lie. He may lie either out of panic, he may lie to himself because he does not think he will be believed if he tells the truth and he, therefore, seeks to bolster up what is a true defence. He may lie because he simply wants to conceal, perhaps disguise any worthy or unworthy contact falling far short of a criminal offence, but if you are sure at the end of the day that he did not lie for some such innocent reason but instead – this again applied in the case of each defendant considered separately – each lied because he knew he was guilty of the offence alleged and feared the truth coming out, then if you are satisfied that the.lie is deliberate and that it relates to a material issue [the defendant is guilty].

Stephanie's understandable 'lies' and her offence which happened after the alleged rape are presented as grounds for doubting her general credibility. On the other hand, all sorts of excuses are presented for the defendants' lying about having ever met the complainant. Obviously it is important that the jury should consider the complainant's credibility, but not in such a biased way so that the truth is distorted. This is exactly what happened in this case. After the judge's direction the jury predictably, after a short adjournment, returned 'not guilty' verdicts for both the defendants. Stephanie was shattered by the verdict. Remember, she waited two years for this trial to come up, said she had been raped not by one but by two men and had given evidence four times. Her emotional control, which had been held against her, cracked. When interviewed, she recalled how she had reacted: I cried, I burst into tears. After all that effort I put in in that court and still they don't believe me. They believe him. I think it was disgusting

Women who 'cry rape' have been blamed, silenced and disbelieved through the ages. In court, the processes through which such disbelief is nurtured are contrary to the tenets of equitable justice.

Mandy's Evidence

In the third case the defence counsel also concentrated on the fact that the victim, Mandy, who was only sixteen at the time when she first reported the case to the police, had denied she had been dancing close to Mulherne and repeated this when giving evidence at the trial. Before her friend was due to give evidence on another day, she rang her up and asked her not to contradict her evidence. The friend rang the police to ask their advice and they were obliged to pass this on to the defence. The fact that Mulherne's statement was full of holes, that she had injuries and had been buggered did not prevent the jury from acquitting him. He never took the stand.

Mulherne was charged with attempted rape and buggery of Mandy although she claimed she had been raped. She did not report the assault immediately, so forensic evidence was lacking She was living at home at the time of the assault. She too went to a nightclub in north-west London with her friends Sally and Jenny. They arrived about 10.30 p.m. Mandy had been drinking lager during the evening While dancing, Mulherne had grabbed her and kissed her. She kissed him back. When he put his hand on her inner thigh, she moved away. Mulherne said there was a rave party on and asked her and her friends to go with him. Mandy did not want to go but Sally, her friend, who by then was considerably drunk, got into Mulherne's car and refused to get out. Mandy and Jenny were forced to get in too. Mulherne drove them to the party some miles away in another part of London. As with Stephanie, he used the alias Michael.

When they got to the party, all the girls got out. Mulherne asked Mandy if he could have a word with her and so she got in the front seat of the car. Mulherne then drove off very fast and stopped the car between two houses near some kind of rugby/football pitch. Mandy thought Mulherne knew exactly where he was going. When interviewed,[16] she explained how Mulherne had put the passenger seat back and told her to relax. She said she did not want to relax. He tried to kiss her but she pushed him away. He held her down,

16. By Jenny Cuffe for *Dispatches*.

took her trousers off and pulled down her tights. She kept telling him to get off her. She was utterly terrified and thought he would kill her:

I scratched him once but then he just kept on pinning me down even more. So in the end I just started crying and screaming for my mum and dad... and for anyone mainly who I know. I even started screaming for God... like why is this happening to me? He inserted himself and when he did, I felt a very sharp pain. And it was – it was basically like if I was being ripped inside, like mainly – he may as well have got the carving knife and done it.

She realized that the sharp pain was Mulherne entering her anus. She pushed him off sobbing. She scratched his back. He then entered her again – she thought it was vaginally. He then warned her against reporting him and took her back to the party. When they arrived there were a number of police there for some other reason. She was too shaken to say anything to them. Mandy told Sally she wanted to go home and later told her about the rape. She did not feel able to tell her mother until the next morning. She begged them not to tell the police. The following day, she rang the Samaritans and a day later she reported the rape to the police. She was examined by a doctor. There were no injuries in her anal area, but she had a blue bruise on her inner right arm. There was semen on her knickers, which subsequently matched the DNA profile of Mulherne's blood. Mandy had been through hell after the assault and said she had contemplated suicide. She had received no counselling and found it impossible to talk to anyone about it.

Mulherne was interviewed on 19 August 1992 after being arrested in connection with another case. He made no comment. An identification parade was held and Sally, the friend who had insisted on getting into his car, identified him. Mandy was too nervous and upset to attend the parade. Mulherne was interviewed again and this time said Mandy had come across to him in the club, danced with him, put her arms around him and put her hand on his penis over his clothing. He had kissed her. He said she had consented to sex and had put up no resistance. He admitted anal intercourse, which he said was a mistake. He had intended to enter her vagina. The jury were unable to agree about the attempted rape but acquitted him of buggery, presumably accepting his version that he had meant to have sexual intercourse.

The Only Rape Conviction

Cora was the only contested trial which resulted in a conviction. It was the same story of abduction and rape. Mulherne first pleaded not guilty on the grounds that it was not him, but then changed his defence to consent. The change of mind was certainly an important factor in his subsequent conviction. It is likely that if he had used a 'consent' defence from the start, he would have been acquitted, in which case he would have been acquitted for all the rapes.

Cora came across as a nice, sensible girl. She was twenty, living with her younger brother at the time and met Mulherne in a pub where he was drinking with some other travellers. She was with her friend, Myra. Mulherne appeared to them to be a nice fellow and not bad-looking. Again he introduced himself with a pseudonym, 'Mark'. He did not speak much but asked her if she was local and said he'd like to talk to her later. She thought he seemed quite charming, 'not a creep'. He went into the other bar and the two girls followed later to have a game of pool. He asked them if they had boyfriends and both she and Myra laughed and said they were free and single. He asked if she would like to go out with him some time and she said, 'Maybe.' She did not have a relationship at the time. He suggested they went outside for a chat and she agreed. She left her jacket and handbag in the pub and, as it was a bit cold, he suggested they sat in his car, which was parked very close to the pub. As soon as she got into the car, he started it up and drove off, making out he was going to park it somewhere else, as in Mandy's case. She said he was driving very fast and erratically, but kept looking at her when he was driving He first drove several miles to a big car park in a secluded spot outside town, turned the engine off and turned a switch which sent the seat flying back. He did not say a word. She said, 'I was shouting and screaming at him to get off. All of a sudden he just got off and started saying he was sorry.'

He drove out of the car park and said he'd go back to the pub. They drove on, but suddenly he drew into a lay-by and just as she'd got the seat back to an upright position, she tried the door but found that it was locked. The seat had gone back again and he was on top of her. She was really shouting and screaming. She told him to get off her but he just smacked her across the face, saying that he was going to do bad things to her if she resisted. She was petrified. Then suddenly he got off her again and said he was sorry. She begged him to take her back to the pub and he agreed, but then again sped off in the opposite direction. Straight away she panicked. She begged him to take her back but he ignored her. She tried talking to him but he avoided answering questions about himself and was very vague about where he came from. This time h drove along country roads to a field, turned the engine off and made the seat shoot back again. Cora tried to sit up but he pushed her down. She was screaming and shouting. He smacked her across the face and said, 'I'm going to give it to you whether you like it or not', and raped her.

Cora describes how he suddenly changed. One minute he was so nice and then all of a sudden he was just totally different: 'He was trying to get all over me. I was telling him to get off. I was screaming and shouting.' She said he was 'an absolute monster. Sick. It's like a sick game for him.'

After he had raped her, he said he was sorry and that he shouldn't have done it. He offered her money to buy herself something nice. When she refused, he drove her back to the pub and offered to buy her a drink. She refused but had to go back into the pub to collect her jacket and bag which she had left there. Some of Mulherne's friends made some comments along the lines that they knew what he'd done. She said she was sure they had known all along what he'd planned to do and were colluding with him. They said, 'Do you want to come outside with me now?' She just wanted to get out and tried to act normally, picking up her jacket and then going straight home. She was terrified. She did not know what to do but could not face going to the police. She phoned a friend up that night who came and stayed with her. The next day she went to the police.

At the trial in June 1993 she was criticized for not reporting the assault immediately. Her lack of injuries was held against her. Cora's case was the first to come to court and she explained what happened:

They tried to make me look like I was some sort of tart, that I'd taken him to these places, that I'd said 'Yes' to sleeping with him. They tried to turn everything round. Because I hadn't had a boyfriend for a long time, they tried to say that I was dying to go to bed with someone. They asked questions about previous boyfriends.

Mulherne was found guilty, but only by the skin of his teeth.

Plea-bargaining

Shareen's attack occurred when Mulherne was on bail, awaiting trial for all the cases discussed above, and was the only case in which the defendant was apprehended immediately after the offence and where the woman had serious injuries. Yet the prosecution accepted the plea to a lesser charge of indecent assault and the attempted rape charge was dropped. This is an example of where plea-bargaining can allow men to get off lightly for very serious offences.

Shareen was twenty-two at the time of the assault. On 4 June she visited a nightclub in north-west London. She went there alone as she was going to video the club for the owner. She had had a couple of brandies and a few puffs on a joint. As she was leaving, Mulherne approached her and said something like, 'It's terrible to leave you waiting on a night like this.' She says she looked him in the eye and thought he looked trustworthy. She said, 'He looked like somebody who was saying to me, "There's people out there you shouldn't trust."' She was taken in by his apparent concern. She said, 'To me he looked like a very domestic person. He looked like somebody who lived with his mother and didn't really know a lot about life.' He was with another man (Henry again) who 'looked even more innocent'. He said his name was Steve. She got into the car and, instead of driving her home, they drove to various places, including the hotel where Mulherne and Henry were staying They said they had to drop into the hotel before taking her home. Shareen had a very heavy period, so she had to go into the hotel with them to use the lavatory. Afterwards Henry stayed in the hotel and Mulherne said he would drive her home. By this time it was in the early hours of the morning

Instead of taking her home, Mulherne drove to a nearby deserted spot and attacked her. Shareen was trapped in the car but she fought for her life. She was determined that she should die rather than be raped. She bravely told him, 'I'm the last girl you're going to fuck with.' She thought she was lucky to escape with her life. She said that Mulherne had had his hands round her throat and she had only escaped by agreeing to have oral sex with him and then by asking him for money, giving him the impression that she would not report him. She said:

After about five minutes of driving around, he pulled up by the side of the road. It was quite near big hotels. I thought then that he would kill me. Why let me live after what he had done? I knew it was important to get his trust. I wanted to get away. I thought the only way to get out was to act like a slag. I knew there was only one chance of getting away with my life, and that was to act like it was no big deal. I looked at him and it really came to me in a flash of inspiration. I looked at him and said, 'Give me money.' If he thought I was cheap anyway, he would let me go. The relief spread over his face. I could see that he was thinking that I was just a tart and nothing to worry about. He gave me £20. He was very pleased about it. I said to him, 'No, give me all your money.' I was determined to get his trust. He said, 'Show me your hands.' I held them out and he cleaned under my fingernails. I wasn't surprised. I knew what he was doing. He was looking at me. I couldn't show my discomfort or fear. My face was really mashed. I said something about my face, something like you would say, 'Oh, my lipstick is smudged.' I said it to absolve him of guilt. I got out of the car. I looked around and thought, 'He can't be falling for this.' He drove off. I ran along the road. I couldn't believe it was over. I was so scared. My God, I knew I had a chance. I was alive.

Shareen was sure he had done it before and knew exactly what he was doing:

I knew he had done it before because he was very patterned in his behaviour. He came out with patterned lines. He was practised. He was smooth. There was no fumbling. There was no 'maybe' about it. He'd done it before. He'd been successful at it before. I knew that. So I managed convincing him I was basically a prostitute, even though I'd fought with everything I had – my mind, my body, blackmail – everything. I had blood everywhere, black eyes, split lip, I looked like the Elephant man.

She said he smashed her face so badly that she couldn't go out even to sign on for two months:

It took time for the bruises to come up. They take two or three days, then they go from yellow to purple, and then the teethmarks take a longer time to heal and the scratches, then the scratch scars, because after the scab peels off you've got a scar, bloodshot in your eye can take a long time to go away. Your whole features change because you're so beaten.[17]

She remembered biting his penis, which she said was the only good thing she ever did. When she escaped from Mulherne,

17. In an interview by Jenny Cuffe for *Dispatches*.

Shareen ran to a nearby hotel, from where she phoned the police. She identified the hotel where Mulherne had taken her and he was arrested immediately. It was because of Shareen that he was caught for all the other rapes. She said she was questioned by the police for sixteen hours and was told to be ready to give evidence on a certain date, but she says the police never contacted her. She said she was not consulted over the case of attempted rape being reduced to indecent assault. This illustrates the lack of rights of the complainant even in cases as serious as this.

The Sentence

Mulherne was sentenced in July 1993. He was given five years for Cora's rape and was sentenced to three years for indecent assault of Shareen. The maximum sentence for indecent assault is ten years but the judge, in spite of all the aggravating features, gave him just three. Had Mulherne been found guilty of two rapes his status as a 'serial' rapist would have resulted in a much longer sentence than the eight years he served, or even longer if he had also been found guilty of the pair rape. Since the judge had discretion, there were strong grounds for awarding a longer sentence for Shareen's truly horrific attack. She had 'fought for her life', so a more appropriate charge might have been attempted murder.

Judge Bathurst Norman had heard five cases against Mulherne and had himself described Mulherne as a 'very dangerous man'. Through plea-bargaining, a serious case of attempted rape had been reduced to indecent assault. It is difficult to imagine a worse case of indecent assault than Shareen's, since it involved several aggravating features. First, it was a very serious case of attempted rape, where she had fought off her attacker for two hours; second, she was forced to have oral sex; third, she had been abducted and threatened with her life; fourth, she had been imprisoned in a car at dead of night; and fifth, she had sustained substantial injuries. According to the Billam guidelines which apply to rape cases, these factors are 'second-order factors' and should have led to a substantial sentence.

Reducing the charge from attempted rape to indecent assault and not hearing all the cases together also resulted in Mulherne's not being seen as a 'serial' rapist. The judge's summing-up conflicted with the sentence Mulherne received in view of the gravity of his crimes. He said:

You are a very dangerous man. The rape of Ms P was an appalling crime. In the case of Shareen you pleaded guilty, but you were on bail when you committed this offence. You offered the girl a lift. The amount of violence you showed to that girl was far greater in this instance. It was a truly horrific attack. These offences were of a violent and sexual nature. I am giving you a custodial sentence. If you behave in this horrifying way you will be in prison for a very long time. To young women you are a very dangerous man. You do not believe that they have the right to say no.

The most ludicrous aspect of these trials, and the main barrier to obtaining convictions for reports of rape by separate women over a comparatively short period of time, is that the cases were all heard by separate juries. There is no justification for not hearing the cases together when, as here, there is such similarity between them. The defence was delighted that Mulherne had got off so lightly. Mulherne is appealing against his single rape sentence on the grounds that the judge acted as his own expert witness. He instructed the jury that lack of physical injury did not mean that Cora had not been raped, although she was not a virgin before the assault.

Reaction of the Complainants

All the women were appalled by the acquittals, including Cora, whose case resulted in Mulherne's only rape conviction. She was upset that he was not found guilty in the three other cases. Jurors are given a very one-sided account in rape cases. They often appear to have no idea what taking a case to court involves or what effect acquitting guilty men has. They are not told of the long delays, the intimidation or fears of retaliation, the lengthy investigations, the horror of identification parades when confronted with your rapist and the trauma of the aftermath of rape. They do not realize the defendant has a lawyer to present his case but the complainant is not even allowed to speak to the prosecution counsel beforehand and is allowed little chance to describe what she has been through.

Jessica could not understand how the jury could not believe her. It left her feeling upset and angry: 'When I stand there and think about it, I'd like to just lash out at all of them, the jury. I'm angry at them as well, for not believing me. I hate them actually.' Mandy had a nasty gut feeling that it was all a set-up: 'Knowing that he's got one up on me and that he's most probably laughing at this moment at me, you know. You just . . . You're not meant to win, that's the whole thing.' The odds are so stacked against the complainant that it is impossible not to conclude that the trial is a charade, a mockery of justice. Asked in August 1993 what she thought about Mulherne's sentence, Shareen replied:

I think he actually managed a lot more than indecent assault. I'm convinced he'll never stop. The man has no sense. He doesn't have any interest in any kind of seduction or romance. He only has interest in rape, in forcing somebody who does not want to do it. I don't think he's very excited the minute somebody does want to do it. He threatened me, saying if I didn't stay still he would bury me in the field – on his mother's life he would do it. From looking at him and from the amount of evidence against him, in a way that was the only way he could escape, was by killing me because there was so much proof otherwise. He'd bitten my hands, because I'd been fighting him, and he'd bitten my face, he'd bitten my body, he'd bitten my breast. I had teethmarks in my body. He had his hands round my neck. I couldn't stand him putting anything into any part of my body. So I was pushing his face away from me and he was biting my hand and it didn't even hurt. I didn't even notice the pain. But he left a whole set of teethmarks in a perfect semicircle across my hand. And I scratched him and I knew I had like his blood in my nails and even bits of skin in my nails and when I got out of the car he was completely relaxed because I'd asked him for money. He knew the police. He knew the methods they were using. So did I. He scraped under my fingernails to get the skin and the blood out. I managed to convince him that I didn't look upon it as rape, even though I'd struggled completely for two hours. I knew my only chance was to make it come across like it didn't hurt me. So I managed to do that. I really thought he'd come back and run me over.[18]

In two of the cases there was another man present – William James Henry – alias Gary Stevens, Steve and Tony. Henry was a codefendant in the case of Stephanie and a witness in the Shareen case. Henry was acquitted of raping Stephanie and is presently a free man.

There is strong evidence that these were not the only women

8. In an interview by Jenny Cuffe for *Dispatches*.

whom Mulherne raped. Apart from the five women who reported
him to the police, three other women later reported that he had
raped or attempted to rape them. One woman did report Mulherne
to the police for rape, but later dropped the charges against him.
Dispatches traced another woman who, when she was only sixteen,
had been driven off into the country by Mulherne, who had
attempted to rape her. Finally, after the Dispatches programme,
Stephanie was walking down the high street when a woman
recognized her from the programme and told her that she and three
of her friends had also been raped by Mulherne but had not
reported it. It is more than likely that other women have been raped
by him, as only a few women report rape to the police. Seeing what
happens in court makes one understand why.

Conclusion

In this chapter I have shown how difficult it is to gain a conviction
in rape trials, even when the defendant is charged with multiple
rapes. Our conception of the serial rapist must change, and the
grave imbalances in rape trials be addressed. In spite of a strong
body of research, knowledge about rape is kept well out of the
courtroom. Expert witnesses are rarely called. Judges appear to be
unconcerned that they are allowing guilty men to go free. The result
of their ignorance, blinkered vision or collusion is that serial rapists
are set free to rape again and women are discredited and disbelieved
in court. In particular, 'similar fact' evidence should be applied as in
the Nicholas Edwards case, so that cases are dealt with together. In
the next chapter I shall discuss what we know about rapists and
whether this can help us detain them.

Chapter 8

Challenging the Stereotypes of Rapists

My mother couldn't believe how normal he looked and I said, 'Well, what do you expect, a werewolf or something? Of course he's a normal-looking bloke.'

In this chapter, with reference to the research conducted with *Dispatches* into how women saw their attackers and to research into convicted rapists, I shall investigate what characterizes men who rape and the tactics commonly used (*modus operandi*). I show how inaccurate stereotypes of rapists distort jurors' judgements and lead them to acquit dangerous men. Rapists are depicted in the press as fiends, psychopaths or disturbed isolates with overbearing mothers. Research is still dominated by psychological approaches which assume that there is a typical rapist 'profile' if only it can be uncovered. Some indicates that rapists are more likely to be black and lower class. In this chapter I shall refute both these assumptions. Empirical research has repeatedly failed to find a consistent pattern of personality type or character disorder that reliably distinguishes rapists from other groups of men (see Bart and Moran 1993: 27). Nor can any connection with class and race be upheld. What is relevant to an explanation of the prevalence of rape are the characteristics of a particular type of hegemonic masculinity and the way the legal system fails to condemn it. I shall show how men's sexual violence is sustained and supported through the ruling norms of society,[1] with reference to the cases in my survey and those of Mulherne, Simpson and Johnson described in the last chapters.

It is now recognized that there is a connection between sexuality, aggression and violence as the primary components of masculinity. Normative masculine behaviour involves practices using dominance,

1. In her recent survey of men's attitudes to violence in north London, Jayne Mooney (1993) found that only 37 per cent of men did not see violence as an option to be used against their partners.

control and independence, and men are encouraged to engage in or approve a degree of sexual violence – or at least are not discouraged from doing so. Additionally, characteristics of masculinity embrace such values as rigidity, insensitivity, assertiveness, competitiveness and superiority, the very characteristics which promote rape. Yet the association with normative masculinity and coercive sexual behaviour whereby men are 'socialized' to view women as the appropriate objects of violence is not widely recognized. Instead the victims are blamed and seen as provoking assaults. Men are encouraged to behave in a sexually coercive manner and to boast about their sexual exploits, so that rape can be seen as one end of a continuum of abusive male sexuality, ranging from milder forms such as sexual harassment, flashing and wolf-whistling to, at the extreme, rape and sexual assault and sex murders (see Kelly 1988). This is not to take the view that rape is a biological inevitability but rather that, in a male-dominated society, abusive behaviour can be rewarding to men as it maintains their position of dominance and in some contexts enhances their social status. Attributes of masculinity are not biologically determined but vary from group to group, from society to society, from one context to another, and from one historical period to another.

British studies of adolescent boys show how violence is a crucial component within their lives, becoming encoded within their behaviour and shaping the contours of adult masculinity. Moreover, the emergence of particular masculine forms develops out of complex social and psychological processes of negotiation and confrontation, so that not all men accept the same form of masculinity within a society. Madeleine Arnot (1984) sees the development of the dominant (or hegemonic) 'macho' form of masculinity as a dual process of men distancing women and femininity from themselves and maintaining the hierarchy and social superiority of masculinity by devaluing all that is feminine or associated with femininity, such as gentleness, empathy and sensitivity. Sexism also appears to be an important feature of male bonding, where denigration of women is a crucial ingredient of male camaraderie. Learning to be masculine invariably entails learning to be sexist; being a bit of a lad and being contemptuous of women go 'naturally' together. Boys are not taught to be responsible for their sexual antics. On the contrary, their status in more 'macho' groups depends on 'having' as many girls as they can and they brag about their sexual exploits to their friends. Sex affirms their masculinity, so they are encouraged to be assertive or even aggressive with women. Risk taking and daring rather than responsibility are the main bulwarks of male reputation. Women, on the other hand, until recently had to keep quiet about sex, as any suspicion of 'promiscuity' was fatal to their reputation. Yet if they keep men at a distance, they can be accused of being cold and unfeminine. Even today, a woman may risk not only pregnancy and HIV but her reputation, which rests not on conquests but on a degree of abstinence.

For women rape carries not only the stigma that is attached to consensual sex but also the even more damaging stigma of being a victim. The effect of this double standard on women's speaking out about male violence is the reason why women often keep quiet and do not report rape. As we have already seen, for a woman to give evidence in open court about intimate sexual activities is an appalling ordeal when her knickers are handed round as exhibits and her injuries presented as 'what she really wanted'.

Seen within this context, it is hardly surprising that studies of adolescent sexuality present a generally unromantic picture of the quality of relations between young men and women whereby men sometimes pressure women into sex, regardless of their wishes (see Halson 1991; Thomson and Scott 1991). Some degree of coercion in dating relationships is taken for granted. Power differences are also implicit in who initiates the date, who pays or who drives. If the man is driving, the woman is faced with the difficulty of getting home by other means if she is not happy about how he is behaving. Often the woman is in a weaker position, yet it is she who is held responsible for setting limits to sexual activities for contraception and for keeping control of her and the man's emotions. From start to finish, the relationship is unequal (see Muehlenhard and Linton 1991: 19).

In the same way that there are different kinds of femininity which are in flux, masculinity also takes a variety of forms in different social classes, in different cultures or racial groups and in different historical periods (see Connell et. al. 1987: 6). Bob Connell, the Australian sociologist, suggests there are 'multiplicities of masculinities' (not all of which embody aggressiveness and a predisposition to rape) that are hierarchically ordered. Traditional masculine ideals, what Connell (1987) refers to as 'hegemonic' masculinity, frequently involve acts of violence and aggression and comprise, in his view, the dominant form of masculinity in Western society. Closely parallel is the type of masculinity that is adopted by academically successful white youths, where a 'calculative attitude is taken towards one's own life' and the crucial themes are 'rationality and responsibility rather than pride and aggressiveness', combined with a high degree of competitiveness (Connell 1989: 296–7). Connell's approach avoids treating men as a homogeneous sex which stands always to benefit from the law and never to lose. Yet both these forms of 'hegemonic' masculinity are oppressive, being founded on and enforcing the subordination of women. Such constructions of masculinity do, however, carry rewards for men and such attributes as competitiveness and violence are functional for maintaining their position of dominance. As we shall see, men who embrace or aspire to this form appear to be most prone to rape or to justifying it.

It is in adolescent gangs or male institutions such as the army, or in male groups involved in competitive sport or university fraternities, that this type of 'macho' masculinity is most prevalent. An elitist, hierarchical, competitive, combative, aggressive, arrogant, patriarchal authoritarian form of masculinity is, of course, reflected in the adversarial system of justice.

Rape, unlike sex, is not about pleasure and connection but about predatory conquest and anger. The difficulty with this kind of generalization, though undoubtedly true, is that seduction can also be more about conquest and anger than intimacy. The problem with coercive sexuality is deciding where seduction ends and rape begins. Men rape for all sorts of reasons, sometimes with a greater sexual motivation than at other times, but this does not mean it is biological. One important way rape is encouraged is through myths that male sexual urges are uncontrollable once aroused. There is nothing natural about rape, and nothing uncontrollable about men's sexuality. The line between rape and what is regarded as 'normal' aggressive sexuality is clouded in our culture, where male identity is enhanced by this macho form of sexuality.

An examination of the typical tactics rapists use could help jurors not to be misled by inaccurate stereotypes. In court, rape is still seen as the act of a stranger who pounces in the night but not as the act of an ordinary-looking 'macho' man who may 'chat up' his victim and behave quite normally before the rape. This distorted picture drawn of rapists leads some jurors to fail to convict on the spurious grounds, as one juror put it to me, that 'the defendant did not look like a rapist'. The media depiction of rapists as fiends distorts their appearance of normality.

Yet not even homicidal rapists fit the stereotype of the 'fiend'. John Duffy, convicted of multiple murder and rape, had been married. He was sometimes accompanied by a friend who raped the victim on more than one occasion. This friend testified against him when he was tried for murder and was not charged with the rapes (see Chapter 2). John Cannan, convicted of murder and rape, appeared to be a womanizer and charmer. Alan Conner committed suicide on 15 August 1994, after admitting to the murder and rape of a twenty-two-year-old woman, Sandra Parkinson. Her murder was later linked to six other murders, twenty-two rapes and five other serious sex offences. Yet Conner was described by a neighbour who knew him as an adolescent as 'a quiet shy lad – but one of a group, not a loner. He had a regular girlfriend.'[2] In fact, she was going out with him when he was first arrested for raping a sixteen-year-old girl in 1984, who 'was found bound, gagged and naked from the waist down and screaming with pain'.[3] He was believed to have fathered seven children in different parts of the country and to have used a number of different aliases. One of Conner's neighbours said, 'He was a good bloke and we used to have a bit of a laugh together. I knew him when I was eighteen. All his family were great. He just liked a few drinks with the lads. I can't believe it was him.'

Misleading Stereotypes

Social Class and Race

It is difficult to assess whether rapists share particular characteristics when so few rapists are convicted. Convicted rapists represent only the tip of the iceberg, as so few women report rape to the police for the reasons we have seen – unwillingness to go to court, embarrassment

2. Martin Wainwright, 'Suicide Killer Linked to Six Other Murders', *Guardian* 16 August 1994.

3. Rob Fairburn, 'We Wanted Him Alive So He Could Be Executed', *Daily Record*, 16 August 1984. Aged twenty-four, he got six years for rape and three for robbing her, but was let out un 1990 after serving only four years for this horrendous crime. Yet no one appears to have linked his fingerprints with the other murders and rapes, although the police must have had his DNA details.

about talking about such personal questions, intimidation from the assailant, or lack of confidence in the police and judicial system. While British and American studies all report a significant increase in reported rapes, and a higher proportion of 'acquaintance' rapes are now coming to light, it is difficult to estimate the level of under-reporting.[4]

A number of recent population surveys have thrown some light on the 'dark figure' of unreported rapes. The largest random survey of women was carried out in the US by Diana Russell in 1984. Nine hundred and thirty women, randomly selected in San Francisco, were asked about their experiences of all forms of sexual violence. Forty-one per cent had been raped at some time in their lives. Only 9.5 per cent of the non-marital or attempted rape cases were reported to the police. Overall she found the higher the rate of rape, the higher the social class. Nearly half the women whose fathers had upper-middle-class occupations had been victims of rape or attempted rape at some time in their lives. This compares with a third of women whose fathers had middle-class occupations and those who had lower-class occupations. In a student union survey at Cambridge University, England, it was found that one in five of 1,500 students surveyed had been victims of rape or attempted rape and one in nine had been raped. Only one in fifty had told the police.[5] Many of these rapes were by intimates: fathers, husbands, friends and lovers. Another student union survey of 2,000 women at Oxford Brookes University showed that 90 per cent of women who had never been the victim of sexual assault or rape thought they would report it to the police, yet only 6 per cent of those who had been raped had reported it. When asked why they did not report, women said they feared an unsympathetic response from the police and had little faith in the judicial system.[6]

Studies of convicted rapists in the US indicate that race and class are certainly important variables in differentiating rapists. The lower the social class, the greater is the likelihood that the offender

4. Studies by Hall (1985: 106) and Godenzi (1994) suggest only one in ten report rape.

5. According to BBC 2's *Public Eye* documentary 'Hidden from View, Hidden from Justice', February 1992.

6. Monique Faizy, 'Let Down by the Law', *Guardian*, 20 August 1994.

will be reported and convicted. Stranger rapes, where the assailant is more often of a lower social class, are the most likely to be reported. The problem is that convicted rapists may not be at all typical of the average rapist. Amir (1971) found in his study of convicted rapists, carried out in a predominantly black neighbourhood of Philadelphia, that around 80 per cent of both assailants and victims were black and were within the same racial group. At first sight Amir's study appeared to show that most rapists were black and from a lower social class. Yet his research was conducted in a predominately black neighbourhood so the high proportion of black defendants was only a reflection of the population studied.

In Britain Lynne Segal, a British feminist, argues that 'rapists are most certainly not all poor black or from specific ethnic minorities. Yet these are the men most likely to commit the most common form of non-marital rape' (Segal 1990: 245). Yet studies of the incidence of rape across different social class and ethnic groups are by no means consistent and it is too early to draw such conclusions. Some researchers argue that in understanding violence against women the concept of class is simply not a significant factor in identifying the victim or the offender (see Hanmer and Maynard 1987: 11; Stordeur and Stille 1989: 35).

Research on rape in marriage indicates that class differences appear to be related to the prevalence of reporting rather than to the actual incidence of rape. There appear to be differences in tolerance levels within social class groups. In the study by Painter (1991), the higher the social class, the less likely women were to define the experience of coercive sex as rape. Mooney (1993), in her study of domestic violence, found that women from a higher economic social class were the least likely to report domestic violence to outside agencies, which contributed to the myth that domestic violence was largely a problem for the lower socio-economic groups.[7]

The relation of race and rape is extremely sensitive and complex in view of the history of lynching. Paradoxically, most lynchings did not involve the accusation of sexual assault, but the racist cry of rape became a popular explanation to justify mob attacks on black

7. An Australian study of 127 spouse assault cases, which often involved rape, by Scutt (1990: 106) found more wife beaters in the professional/managerial and sales/skilled categories than among the unskilled.

men. The myth of the 'black rapist' is still prevalent and feeds off racist ideology (see Davis 1981: 199). Lower-class and black men are much more likely to be reported and arrested. Of reported rapes, very few result in conviction, as I have indicated. American researcher LaFree (1980, 1989) points out that-as one moves further away from the commission of the crime towards the point at which a conviction is secured, it is paradoxically often the less frequent types of assaults that result in conviction. An example of this is interracial sexual crimes (those in which the complainants and suspects are in different racial groups), particularly involving black males and white females. Such offences are rarer than intraracial crimes (those within the same racial group) but are more likely to be reported and appear in the figures with increasing frequency as other cases drop out. In other words, due to racism interracial crimes where the victim is white are taken more seriously by the police and are more likely to reach court and result in a conviction.

The 1984 American National Crime Survey also found the level of reporting was race-related, with predictably more white victims reporting rapes by black males (23 per cent) than black victims reporting rapes by white males (8 per cent) (see Bourque I989). Over the past twenty years, for example, the rate of black on white rape in studies of unreported rapes has significantly exceeded the rate of white on black rape (LaFree I982, 1989). This preponderance of white women victims is likely to be connected to the segregated nature of many black ghettos, where whites would be unlikely to be a target for burglary or other offences (see Scully 1990). In Britain too, white women are more likely to *report* rape by a black than a white man (L. Smith 1989).

American black feminist bell hooks (1992) challenges the whole idea that black men rape in order to assert their masculinity; rather she sees rape representing a form of domination that is the very essence of white patriarchy. Lower class and/or black men are more likely to be seen by the court as the sort of men likely to have committed rape and therefore they are more likely to be convicted and labelled 'rapists'. The relationship between masculinity and patriarchy is also developed by bell hooks. She challenges the argument that the prevalence of sexual assault is a result of economic deprivation, whereby men are encouraged to enhance their masculinity through sexual prowess (cf. Staples 1982). Her arguments are important as she refutes many of the taken-for-granted myths about rape: that more black men are rapists; that black men are more prone to rape white rather than black women; and that black men rape in reaction to failure to assert their masculinity in other ways through work, for example. She also raises the core issue of the relation of sexual domination to patriarchal domination. She strongly repudiates the view that men would not rape if they could achieve 'satisfactory manhood' according to the patriarchal ideal, or if they could dominate women more effectively through economic means (again cf. Staples 1982). It is safe to assume, she observes, that the 'satisfying manhood carries with it the right of men to dominate women, however benevolently'. She points out:

In every segregated black community in the US there are adult black men living in households where they do not assert patriarchal domination and yet live fulfilled lives, where they are not sitting around worrying about castration (1992: 93).

She outlines how black lifestyles that opposed the status quo were to be found in black culture and how white men, seeking alternatives to a patriarchal masculinity, turned to black men – man as outsider and rebel. The ultimate travelling man is the man who takes risks and is a free man. Any critique of black male sexism that does not acknowledge the actions of black men who subvert and challenge the status quo cannot be an effective critical intervention, she concludes. It is only then that the possibility for change and for resistance is affirmed.

Evidence that race is relevant to the incidence of rape is contradictory and unconvincing. American research indicates that most sexual crimes are intraracial. However, as one moves further away from the commission of the crime towards the point at which a conviction is secured, the processes of attrition operate in such a way that some of the patterns occurring less frequently are the ones which gain ascendancy. Interracial crimes appear in the figures with increasing frequency, particularly sexual encounters involving black males and white females. These findings have to be treated with extreme caution, as they tell us more about the willingness of women to report crimes, and their expectations as to how they will be received if they do report, than about the actual patterns of crime. The complexity of reasons deterring black women who are the victims of violence within their own community from reporting the crimes has been described with sensitivity and clarity by Amina Mama (1989).

To sum up, the lower-class or black representation among convicted rapists should not lead to the assumption that rape is necessarily class- or race-related. This is supported by Canadian researchers, who also concluded that neither the types of rape for which men are imprisoned nor the sociocultural background of imprisoned rapists was a reasonable basis for making any generalization about rapists or their victims (Clark and Lewis 1977: 99–100).

Personality

On 14 June 1994 the former heavyweight champion Mike Tyson, aged twenty-two, appealed against his six-year sentence for raping Desiree Washington, a contestant in a beauty competition, in an Indianapolis hotel room in July 1990[8] In the original court case, Tyson denied doing any harm because he did not blacken the raped woman's eye or break her ribs (see Bart and Moran 1993: xi, 4). He had served twenty-seven months of his sentence. He was unrepentant, saying, 'I am in prison because of bad judgement in picking up Desiree. I have committed no crime. I'm going to stick to that to the grave. I never violated anyone's chastity.' Under intense questioning by state prosecutors, Tyson flatly refused to admit rape. He finally agreed that his conduct had been 'ungentlemanly' and said he was 'sorry for the entire incident', but when offered the opportunity to make an apology to Ms Washington he refused. Superior Court Judge Patricia Gifford, who presided at the first trial, said she had hoped to hear more self-criticism. 'Your conduct, while not admitting guilt, was inexcusable.' His appeal was dismissed and he was sent back to jail for refusing to admit rape until his release date in 1995. Tyson's attitude, in failing to admit guilt, is typical of that of most convicted rapists, but no convicted man would ever be asked such a question in a British court.

8. Ben Macintyre, 'Tyson Sent Back to Jail After Refusing to Admit Hotel Rape', *New York Times*, 14 June 1994. Tyson's lawyers emphasized how he had begun reading widely, in history, biography, politics, poetry and fiction. However, his favourite book is said to be *To Kill a Mocking Bird*, Harper Lee's classic novel about a black man unfairly convicted of rape.

No personality differences have been found between rapists and non-rapists, but men who rape are more likely to hold sexist views (such as blaming victims for causing their own rapes by their way of dress or actions, denying the extent of injuries). Diana Scully interviewed 114 convicted rapists in the US who had been sentenced to between ten and thirty years, and compared them with a control group of seventy-five other felons.[9] The vast majority were young (between nineteen and thirty-five) and had previous offences, mainly for non-sexual offences, and were working class. Slightly more than half were black. Rapists could not be differentiated from other offenders of similar social and racial background in regard to any previous offences, family background or personality character-istic. In regard to the level and variety of sexual encounters, for example, they appeared to be quite similar. There was no evidence that the rapists were sexually frustrated at the time of the rapes; nor did they lack consensual sexual opportunities, as almost half were married or cohabiting (Scully 1990: 90). Other studies of convicted rapists also concluded that rapists did not differ in personality characteristics from other offenders (Scully and Marolla 1985; Grubin and Gunn 1990). Both rapists and the other felons were, however, more conformist to the traditional male role epitomized by toughness, preoccupation with athletic physique, defiance of authority and seeing women as conquests.

Scully (1990) suggested that there was a crucial difference between offenders who were 'admitters' and those who were 'deniers' of the act. The admitters often wanted revenge and acted out their anger. They often saw the victim as the reason for their act and blamed her, but did not condone sexually violent behaviour. The deniers, on the other hand, did not see anything wrong in their action and disputed their violence, arguing that it was 'normal interaction'. They identified with a strong form of masculinity which legitimated toughness in handling women.

Scully argues that rather than looking for the cause of rape in

9. She asked them detailed questions about their childhood, sexual experience, relationships with other women and attitudes to women. Eighty-five per cent had previous convictions, 23 per cent had previous convictions for sexual offences, 39 per cent had convictions for burglary and robbery, 29 per cent for sodomy and 11 per cent for second-degree murder. Previous studies had explained rape as irresistible impulse, disease or victim precipitation. Her results contested these assumptions.

disturbed personalities, it is far more likely to be found in 'compulsive masculinity', which can be viewed as a form of normal deviance acquired through socialization in a culture that places tremendous importance on masculinity and male traits. What rapists have to tell us about how men learn to justify and excuse their violent degradation of women is of relevance here. The rapists she interviewed did not experience guilt or shame, nor did they experience any feelings for their victims. This reflects the extent to which culture has enabled them to objectify women. They were more likely to have strong beliefs in the double standard, to believe in rape stereotypes, and to be strongly identified with the traditional male role. They were not less liberal in their attitudes to women but put 'women on a pedestal'. They were more likely to subscribe to the idea that women need male protection and they should be more virtuous than men, and should not tell dirty jokes, drink or pay their share of a date. More recent research has confirmed this. Rapists are not psychotic or psychologically disturbed, but perfectly normal men who are at the more sexist end of the spectrum of sexist attitudes. Scully concluded that in a patriarchal society where women's views are unrepresented, men are able to ignore sexual violence, especially where the culture provides them with all sorts of justification. She concludes:

This leads men who rape to ignore or misinterpret how they appear to their victims, who are to them only objects, and consequently their behaviour provides none of the emotions to regulate their sexually violent acts.

British researchers Grubin and Gunn (1990), who interviewed 100 British convicted rapists, also found that on the whole sexual offenders failed to confront their guilt. Almost half (42 per cent) considered themselves innocent and only 32 per cent believed their victims had been harmed. In other words, many of these men saw themselves as lovers. The lack of treatment for sexual offenders to help them confront their responsibility is of paramount importance but is clearly not regarded as a priority. Instead, Ray Wyre's Gracewell clinic, an innovative group treatment programme for sexual offenders, has been tragically closed down (see Wyre 1995). We need to know more about unconvicted rapists, since the proportion convicted is so small and therefore likely to be unrepresentative. There are, however, obvious problems in locating men who admit rape as so many deny it even when convicted. Two researchers have managed to reach small groups of unconvicted rapists. Daniel Smitheyman (1979) in the US advertised for men who had committed rape (defined as non-consensual penetration of the vagina, anus or mouth) to volunteer for confidential interviews. Fifty men living in Los Angeles in 1976 were interviewed. The majority had degrees and 84 per cent had completed high school, as compared to only 2 per cent of convicted rapists. Smitheyman concluded that rapists appeared to be evenly spread throughout the population, although there might be discernible differences in the types of rape committed by men in different social strata.10 It is likely that rape takes different forms in different social classes. Reported stranger rapes appear to be far more common among the working class, whereas marital rape is likely to be just as common in the middle class as the working class. This may be due to the greater access middle-class men have to women as a result of economic advantages.

Fifteen years later a Swiss researcher, Godenzi (1994), by using a broad media appeal, managed to contact a small group of unconvicted rapists and compared them with thirteen convicted rapists. His research is revealing as it throws light on why and how unconvicted rapists, compared to the convicted, rationalize their behaviour, and the contradictions between being a 'real man' and able to 'pull' women and 'rape' or forcing a woman to have sex, which, according to the unwritten law, means he isn't a real man. For men to admit they are guilty of rape and responsible for it is tantamount to admitting that they are not 'real' men, unless, of course, the rape is a weapon to enforce dominance or is rationalized as due to the woman's provocation.

Godenzi and his colleagues invited adolescent sexual offenders to document verbally their violent actions, promising anonymity and confidentiality. Thirty-five of the reports received were sufficiently detailed to be analysed; 70 per cent were from middle-class men.

Unlike the convicted rapists, they placed great emphasis on sexual motive, saying they acted out of sexual need (they could not restrain

10. Stordeur and Stille (1989: 35) see the causes of male violence in the home as rooted in the norms of our culture that 'permeate the attitudes of all males in a pathological manner and set dysfunctional standards for all heterosexual relationships'. They also do not see class as in any way causal, since the dominant culture determines the culture of the whole society.

themselves), rejecting the portrayal of rapists as violent offenders. They rarely saw any reason to feel guilty but instead saw their violence as provoked by the woman's behaviour, above all by her appearance. The fact that there were no consequences guaranteed their assumption of 'innocence'.

The convicted rapists, on the other hand, did not see their actions as sexual but as violent. Godenzi argues that imprisoned men attached importance to not being seen as sexual offenders, as they did not want to appear as men who have to resort to violence in order to have access to sex with women. This would render them 'not real men', which is why sexual offenders (nonces) are at the bottom of the prison hierarchy and are often segregated in order to protect them from assaults from other prisoners. When they admit the crime, it is only in relation to the violence, and, like the unconvicted group, they attribute it to the woman's provocation.

The two groups do share similarities. Both had misogynist attitudes to women and both differentiated themselves from 'real' rapists, whom they saw as 'the scum to be punished', 'castrated' and 'isolated'. Thereby their own violent behaviour becomes innocent, or legitimated as a sign of their continuing status as 'real men'. This study is interesting as it indicates that rape is legitimated both by the convicted and by the unconvicted, whether seen as a violent or a sexual act, and the responsibility is subtly shifted on to the victim. It also indicates that rapists come from all social classes.

What are Rapists Really Like?

In order to find out more about rapists, I adopted a different approach from psychological profiling or interviewing convicted rapists in the Channel 4 *Dispatches* survey. Instead, as we have already seen, women were given lengthy questionnaires to fill in about the men who raped them (see pages 5–36).

The first major finding was that certain myths about rapists need to be challenged. The typical rapist is not a stranger who pounces in the street or breaks into houses at dead of night, but some kind of acquaintance. Respondents reported that of acquaintance rapes, their assailants came from all walks of life, with the highest proportions among skilled manual workers, reflecting the proportion of that group in the community. They included a doctor, police officer, head of a university department, shop manager, engineer, insurance salesman, estate agent, teacher, nursing attendant, employer and bank manager. Respondents were asked to describe how they thought the men would come across to others. The replies reflected the apparent normality of the men: 'a normal working-class young man', 'not distinguishable in any way', 'nice person, from good background, no reputation for violence', 'hippie, into peace', 'nice, calm, friendly, well dressed', 'comes across as a nice family man', 'verbally articulate, quick thinker, fast talker, quite attractive', 'he came across as very nice, well mannered, the perfect gentleman', 'he was polite, so I think people would see him as a young man to envy and admire', 'smartly dressed, affable – really not a person you'd think of as violent – with a sort of boyish charm', 'he was knowledgeable and friendly, viewed as a family man, a leader in our little village', 'a respectable doctor nearing retirement', 'rather conceited and confident', 'an ex-public school boy, vaguely handsome, challenging man, arrogant', 'very polite and gently spoken, very smartly dressed, soft Irish accent, a real charmer', 'my parents really liked him', 'flash, Jack the lad, earned his money dealing drugs, flash car, suits'.

Predictably less was known about the social class, status, age, occupation, residence and marital status of the stranger group, so comparisons are not valid. With regard to the men the victims knew well or fairly well, first contact with the victim was most likely to be made in the woman's home (30.2 per cent), an inside public place (17 per cent) and least likely to be made on a date (3.8 per cent). Strangers predictably were more likely to approach the women in a public place, with 14 per cent breaking into the woman's home or posing as a salesman. Age was a relevant characteristic. Fifty per cent were estimated by victims as being between the ages of fourteen and twenty-one years and another 22 per cent were between twenty-two and twenty-five. Therefore almost three-quarters were estimated to be under twenty-five years old. Our sample included only a few women who had been raped by husbands or cohabitees, but this may be partly a function of the preponderance of unmarried respondents (78 per cent were single at the time of the assault). However, a feature of convicted rapists is that a high proportion are under twenty-five years old.

The second major finding was that respondents described the behaviour of both strangers and acquaintances during the assault in a remarkably similar way. Comparisons were made with regard to the tactics these different groups of men used and their behaviour during and after the assaults. The three most common attitudes identified by respondents were confidence, indifference and anger. In roughly half the cases, strangers and acquaintances were seen as uncaring, angry and confident (with more acquaintances seventy-two per cent – described as confident). A higher proportion of the acquaintances (42.9 per cent as against 29.4 per cent) insulted or ridiculed the victim. A significant proportion of both groups (35.3 per cent and 32.7 per cent) used obscene language and laughed and joked during the assault. More of the acquaintance group gave the impression that they believed the respondent was willing to have sex (42.6 per cent as against 26 per cent). More of the strangers demanded that the women say that she was enjoying herself (34.8 per cent as against 16.4 per cent). After the assault the most common response was for the men to be indifferent or unconcerned (57.9 per cent and 54 per cent respectively), with the next most common reaction being triumphant or pleased (32 per cent of both groups). One man expected the woman to be grateful. Anger had largely subsided. Very similar proportions of both groups were described as apologetic, frightened or upset. Intimate acquaintances were the most likely to be apologetic or sorry afterwards (47 per cent as against 17 per cent of general acquaintances).

The third major finding was that the use of violence was similar and substantial in both the stranger and acquaintance groups (69.6 per cent and 63.9 per cent respectively). A higher proportion of strangers threatened to kill their victims (39 per cent as against 14 per cent) and more of the women raped by strangers believed their life was in danger (81.1 per cent as against 42 per cent). These figures indicate how terrifying many women find rape. The most common form of violence used by all rapists is to forcibly hold down their victims. A large proportion also slapped, pushed or handled their victims roughly (70–80 per cent). The levels of beating, punching and kicking which would leave marks on the woman's body was much lower. A breakdown of the different types of acquaintance rapist shows that intimates are more than twice as likely to use a weapon than strangers or any other types of acquaintance (16 per cent as against 8 per cent of strangers). The following threats were made to respondents: to kill, to use a knife or gun, to stick scissors in her, to break her fingers, to punch through her skull, to knock her 'bloody head off', to pour boiling water over her. More of the acquaintance group choked or strangled their victims (23 per cent as against 15 per cent).[11]

Some of the things men asked respondents to say during the assault were astonishing: that she understood and forgave him, that his penis was big, what a beautiful body he had, that she was enjoying it, that she loved him, that she'd go back to him and not end the relationship, to compliment him on his performance, to beg him to do it, to 'talk dirty', to tell him that she fancied him, to moan with pleasure.

Others were abusive. Another survivor said:

He was calling me a bitch, slut, etc. and telling me I deserved what I was going to get. When I tensed myself, he was shouting more 'you bitch' and that kind of thing.

And another:

He was bending my fingers and told me if I screamed no one would hear me. He then climbed on top of me, saying he would have the last laugh. Then he told me to wiggle and enjoy it. His penis was very large and he was hurting me.

Two rapists urinated on the women; another insisted she pose for pornographic photographs before and during the assault. The respondents described what the man had said during the rape. These included such comments as 'I'm not going to hurt you', 'keep still I want to fuck you, not to fight you, you silly bitch', 'I bet you've never done that before'; with a knife at the woman's throat, 'fuck me'; a stranger who broke in said, 'Man, I'm going to make love to you. I'm going to come back every day until you show that you are enjoying yourself', while he lay on top of the woman, running a knife up and down her leg; 'Don't you think I'm big? I'm not hurting you too much, am I?'; 'I'll fucking kill you, you queer' (to a woman who was a lesbian).

Injuries and physical effects suffered by the victims in both groups were remarkably similar. About half of both groups suffered minor bruises, scratches and soreness and over a quarter of both groups

11. Strangulation is important, as this is such a common cause of death among murder victims.

suffered severe bruising, and 2 per cent serious cuts and wounds. One woman raped by a stranger had a fractured jaw, another raped by an acquaintance a fractured rib.

After the rape men usually instructed women to keep quiet. Some, however, seemed to fail to acknowledge that the rape had even taken place: they went to sleep or watched TV. One man threatened to kill himself if the woman told anyone of the assault. Eleven per cent (similar proportion of strangers and intimates) threatened to kill the woman if she told and a further 9 per cent to harm those close to her. Others insisted what had happened was normal and that no one would believe they were raped. One man forced a pregnant colleague who had come to deliver some documents for work into his flat, where he repeatedly raped her and forced her to have anal and oral sex. When he finally let her go, he said he would be in 'touch for another date'. He turned up at her flat several weeks later. She barricaded herself in. He apparently maintained that they had had a 'great night of passion' and seemed genuinely confused. They were both campaigning for an antiracist cause. In spite of this horrific attack, she did not report the assaults because she was afraid of a racist response from the police.

Serial rapists appear to be perfectly normal-looking men who may be amusing, entertaining and well turned out. Many of them are married or have girlfriends and are not 'psychopathological loners'. We do not, of course, know how many serial rapists there are. However, the chance that any rapist rapes only once is low. In her seminal study, Susan Brownmiller concluded that the typical rapist was

no weirdo, psychoschizophrenic, beset by timidity, sexual deprivation, and a domineering wife or mother. Although the psycho rapist, whatever his family background, certainly does exist, just as the psycho murderer certainly does exist, he is the exception and not the rule. The typical American perpetrator of forcible rape is little more than an aggressive, hostile youth who chooses to do violence to women (1978:176).

The typical British (non-marital) rapist, according to our respondents, does not even necessarily appear to be an aggressive, hostile youth. He is, however, typically a youth or in his early twenties, but is of any social class, is often smartly dressed, good-looking and charming (76 per cent described the assailant using the three previous adjectives) and is indistinguishable in any way from other male friends they have. It is this that makes the experience of rape by an acquaintance so unnerving. Only 14 per cent were described as having a reputation for violence, or a previous record; the same proportion were described as articulate, well-educated professionals.

It appears from this study that a rapist can be of any race or class and have any character. They do appear to display similar patterns of behaviour, which are difficult to distinguish from normal male courting behaviour both before and after the rape, but are quite distinctive during the rape. From women's accounts it does appear that rapists know exactly what they are doing and gain sexual satisfaction from the power and domination they exercise over their victims. This interpretation is never in my experience mentioned in court. Instead such 'normal' behaviour before and afterwards is presented as evidence that the man is not really a rapist and the actual rape is presented as sexual rather than violent. This is why some legal definition of consent is needed if men are not to camouflage their rapes as seduction.

Modus Operandi

Insufficient emphasis is placed by the CPS and by prosecution counsels on the common *modus operandi* or tactics that many rapists use. Jurors should be told that rapes are often planned or premeditated. The defendant should be cross-examined about his sexual habits and experience. If he decides not to give evidence, to opt for the 'right to silence', the prosecution could still propose some interpretation of his police statement. The failure of the prosecution to question the conduct and the attitude of the defendant is a major shortcoming of trials.

It is often argued that differentiating between tactics of seduction and of rape is impossible. This is partly because it is insufficiently recognized that right up to the time of the assault the man's behaviour may appear to be perfectly normal. The first moves can be confused with picking up a girl with the aim of possibly seducing her. The rapist may talk to her at a party or at work, give her his telephone number and suggest they have a date. Or he may approach her in a bar or nightclub and persuade her on some pretext to have a lift. At this stage the man is charming and appears in no way a threat. Jessica described Mulherne in the following terms:

He had fairish brown hair, and blue eyes, and he did have a very innocent face when he looked at you with his eyes. That would draw you. He looked as though butter wouldn't melt in his mouth. He was very innocent looking.

Cora, as we have seen, described how Mulherne seemed quite charming, 'a nice fellow, not bad-looking. He wasn't a creep. Well, he didn't look a creep. He seemed very charming and polite.' Women themselves are misled or fooled by the traditional stereotype of a rapist.

The 'professional' serial acquaintance rapist gives away very little about himself, often uses a pseudonym and tries to get his victim talking. What the victim tells him about herself will be valuable as a defence if he is arrested for rape. Ironically, Mulherne used the ploy of 'women being at risk' as an argument to encourage women to take a lift with him. On another occasion, the first thing he said to Jessica was, 'I don't want to get into your knickers or anything.' Shareen, whom Mulherne tried to rape, described how:

He came up to me when I was outside the door and asked me who I was waiting for, where they were. I felt that he had a good basis for making that judgement, even though I knew I wasn't waiting for anybody. He seemed very innocent and inexperienced. He seemed very, naïve. I felt I would be protected by him. He spread his hands, opened his palms and said 'no strings' and I said 'no strings'. He looked me right in the eye. And I looked him in the eye. I was convinced that he meant what he said. As far as I was concerned at that point, the only strings there were involved was that he wanted more than a lift, he wanted to get to know me. That was the catch. Because he had somebody with him I didn't feel that I owed him anything. It was a cold night. It was dangerous out there, and I felt these two young men were kind enough to offer me a lift because there was danger there.

After reassuring his victim, the serial rapist's next task is to isolate or confine her in some way. Mulherne confined all his victims in his car. In each case, Mulherne drove off at high speed and then stopped in a deserted spot where he sent the seat flying back. En route, he would talk in a reassuring way to his victims, promising that they would come to no harm.

When the woman is isolated, it is then that the violent behaviour of the rapist can often clearly be seen. Yet in court this change of behaviour is played down and the defence, by emphasizing the 'normality' of the previous behaviour, implies that the subsequent assault is no more than seduction. In almost all cases of acquaintance rape, the behaviour of the men suddenly changed dramatically from being charming and chatty to being verbally abusive (calling the woman a bitch, whore or slag) or ordering the victim (to take off her clothes or cooperate in some way). In the Johnson case, the victim described how the defendant suddenly changed and smacked her across the face. She said:

I was petrified. It was the way he kept changing He'd be so nice. Then all of a sudden he'd be totally different. He said, 'I'm going to rape you if you like it or not.'

The woman is humiliated by verbal abuse, physical coercion or violence. Jessica described how Mulherne's behaviour changed in a flash once he stopped the car. He called her a 'bitch' and threatened to drive her 500 miles away where 'she would not be doing anything'. Jessica assumed this was a threat to kill her. In the Simpson case, the woman he assaulted, Mary, (see page 164), said that when she had tried to run away, he had caught hold of her and said, 'You bitch, get back into the car. I know girls like you just want to run into the middle of the road and be a hero or something like that.' In the case of Johnson, according to Birgitte, the Danish social worker, he threatened to cut off her underwear with scissors and said that if she did not do what he wanted, he would break her legs. She was terrified he would throw her out of the window. Any resistance is usually met with heightened violence or threats (sometimes threats to kill). In Shareen's case Mulherne threatened to 'put me in a field', which she understood as a death threat.

Often the rapist behaves in a quite bizarre way by telling the victim that 'he loves her' or, after ordering her to take her clothes off, he insists she says that she loves him or is enjoying herself. If she complies through fear, such behaviour is then used against her in court, or if she refuses, as happened in the Johnson trial, it is used to suggest that the rapist was 'in love' and the victim had 'led him on'.

Similarly, the behaviour after ejaculation can confuse jurors, as the attacker often returns to his previous demeanour and may appear as normal as before the rape. He sometimes apologizes, asks for forgiveness, offers to buy the woman something to eat, give her money or drop her home. Often he asks her to meet him again. It appears that this is some attempt to normalize the situation.

Mulherne usually offered to drive his victims home after he had assaulted them. In Stephanie's case, he dropped her at the school where she was to pick up her brother and gave her money for her bus fare. in Cora's case, he dropped her back at the pub. Only in Shareen's case did he leave her in the middle of nowhere, perhaps because he had lost his cool in view of her resistance.

Anna, in the Johnson case, could not understand how her attacker could act as though nothing had happened. She described how, after raping her, he changed back again to the man she knew, went down on his knees and with tears in his eyes begged her to continue to meet him. She could not comprehend how he could suggest this after what he had done. When asked whether she thought Johnson had convinced himself that she wanted sex, she disagreed. He just did not care about her feelings. She explained:

I didn't believe it. I think he must be crazy or he's very, very clever. I didn't know what to believe, because if you'd committed a crime you wouldn't ever go back. If you robbed a bank, you wouldn't ever go to the bank to put your money in, you'd stay away. But he came back. It could be that he was very clever and he could say, 'Yes, I went to her house afterwards. I never thought anything was wrong.' Yes, I think he was very clever.

Sometimes the woman is told with threats to keep quiet. The rapist may threaten to return and rape her again; this had happened in two cases I heard in court. He may threaten to kill her if she reports the attack, and in several cases has indeed returned and killed. In one case I monitored, after the rape the man kept saying, 'You are going to see me again.' As we have seen, with such threats, many women fail even to report rape.

Jurors would be better able to differentiate between rape and seduction if they were given more information about the way rapists operate. Wyre and Swift (1990), in their British research on convicted rapists, offered insight into how the rapists planned their attacks, drawing on prevalent myths about women to justify what they did, and the effect the tactics had on victims. They categorized rapists into types, such as sexual, angry, sociopathic and sadistic, and saw these as associated with different motivations. They described rape as 'essentially an attempt by a person or group to subject another individual to their control' and conceptualized it not as a single event but as a process made up of several phases. Their conclusions were pessimistic, for they found that men who rape are likely to rape again and be encouraged every time they get away with it.

Our questionnaire analysis confirmed this concept of rape as a process involving different phases which are usually carefully planned. In regard to the assaults almost half (48.5 per cent) described the man's behaviour as undergoing a sudden change, from affection to violence. One survivor described an assault in June 1992 by a bank manager who initially appeared to be very nice and polite:

He gave me a kiss and seemed affectionate but became very nasty when I backed off. Then he said, 'Come on. What's the matter?' He grabbed my hand and pushed it on to his erect penis, which was still inside his trousers. I pulled it away and he grabbed my dress and pulled it down. He was smiling but his voice turned very nasty and he said, 'I'd love to fuck you. You're not a lesbian, are you?' Then with one hand he tore my dress off one shoulder, pulled it down to uncover my breast and bit my breast hard.

Other survivors described similar experiences:

He changed from being friendly, treating me like a confidante, to hatred and treating me like an object. He had a hold of me, telling me how I wanted him and if I didn't I would never get back to my friends.

He suddenly became verbally and physically violent – using demeaning language. He pushed and hit out, jabbed my throat. He was enjoying controlling me and the fact I was unable to leave.

Another young woman was raped by the father of the children she was babysitting for. She wrote:

I went to his house to babysit. I asked to go to the toilet. He followed me unknowingly and shouted at me to remove my clothes.

We have already seen how several women were asleep when raped.

Tactics After the Rape
Women described their assailants as displaying behaviour following the rape which astounded them. A few apologized, others expressed affection or tried to arrange to see them again. Others threatened them. A few actually asked if they had enjoyed themselves or looked smug and exultant. Generally there appeared to be an attempt to 'normalize' the situation, or behave as though nothing had

happened, by asking victims to have a drink or by offering to drive them somewhere. As one survivor described:

He became cold towards me, didn't say anything and pinned me to the ground. He raped me and then walked me home as if nothing had happened.

Various tactics were used to normalize the situation. They included offering to buy the woman something to eat, to give her money, to meet again.

He offered to waive his fee [accommodation bureau agent] but I insisted on paying. He gave me a lift to the tube station. On the way he again asked me for a kiss and I reiterated that my boyfriend was jealous and might be violent (a lie).

I wanted to leave but he wanted me to drink some orange juice. I did so and he allowed me to leave. I tried with great difficulty to cross the main road and get home. Passers-by shouted at me. I acted as if I was drunk. This must have been shock.

When he ejaculated he got in the car and told me he'd take me home to the road end. He knew I'd not say anything. I was afraid. I told nobody until much later – I told my boyfriend [now husband].

Sometimes the normalizing tactic seems to have worked and the victim ended up blaming herself.

I can't explain the shock and shame I was feeling. I was so confused and disgusted. He appeared so normal that I started to wonder if I had led him on, if I was to blame. I stayed to clean my teeth. I even borrowed his toothbrush. I wanted to be 'normal'. It was only six months later that I accepted it as my being forced into having sex. I couldn't believe it.

Some rapists threatened their victims or incongruously suggested making another date.

As soon as he had ejaculated he got off of me, put himself straight, told me not to phone the police, because I wouldn't be believed, and he also asked if he could phone me and take me out the next day.

Women who had sustained injuries were most likely to be threatened. One woman who had met an Australian in a pub allowed him to stay at her house, which she shared with several others, because he said he had nowhere else to go. She described what the man did afterwards:

He was telling me how it was pointless to tell anyone because they'd say I'd

asked for it by staying in the restaurant with him after everyone had left and that I'd invited him back to the house.

A number of women who were raped described how the assailant apologized afterwards. Women found apologies incomprehensible and were dumbfounded by them.

I dressed myself and wanted to leave. Only then he started to apologize, offered me a ride. I didn't say one single word and left. I was shaking, couldn't talk, went home, took a shower, spent the next two days in my room. I didn't talk to anyone.

Some of the most sickening reports describe how the men asked whether the women had enjoyed themselves. This seems to be an extension of the way some rapists insist that the woman pretends to enjoy the assault.

He demanded that I made happy, sexy noises while this went on and I did because I wasn't sure what would happen if I didn't. He wanted to be complimented on his performance and wanted me to purr and moan sexily.

Another woman, who woke up to find a man she had met the previous night at a party had broken into her house and was raping her, described how smug her assailant had looked:

After the assault, when he had finished, he rolled off and let me see his face for the first time. I will always remember the way he was grinning. It wasn't natural. I became annoyed for the first time. I had been scared and confused to that point. I hit him in his face to stop him grinning at me. We both jumped up together. He got to the door before me. He didn't let me leave the house.

One woman, raped by her ex-boyfriend, who had physically assaulted her and had a court order out against him, described how arrogant her assailant had been:

He said, 'Do you feel like you have been raped?' When he got off me he fixed himself. He just sat in a chair and said not to tell anyone because he had enough problems. I couldn't stop crying I told him I was going for my lunch. He followed me, so I went into the nearest public house. The landlady saw I was very upset, so took me into the living quarters of the pub and I stayed there until I was able to go home, which was some hours later.

A young girl of fifteen who was babysitting did not understand what was happening:

I stayed with him watching TV. I did not understand it was wrong. I thought that was the way it was. My mother was always raped, my father made pornography in our home. I saw it many times. I thought it was normal. If a man wants you, you let him have you. I did not react, I was too scared. I let him do it as I felt it was easiest to let him have what he wanted. I did not fully understand what was happening I believed if I let him do it then he'd leave me alone. He won't hurt me any more. He drove me home as if nothing had happened, so I thought it was my fault that I'd done wrong, even though I didn't want it.

It is difficult to know whether rapists really see themselves as lovers, and are living in a fantasy world, or use such arguments as a cover. It is possible that some may have accepted the fantasy, so often promulgated in pornography and even voiced by the occasional judge, that women really want sex regardless of any denials.

Conclusion

Neither the type of rape for which a man is imprisoned nor the sociocultural background of imprisoned rapists is a reasonable basis for making generalizations about either the distribution of various types of rape or the types of men who commit them. The pattern of rapists' behaviour is often difficult to untangle from the apparent normality of their behaviour. Most rapists do not break into women's homes or pounce in the street. The majority are perfectly normal men, married and unmarried, with and without girlfriends. All men do not, of course, rape, but we have seen that there are important cultural supports for rape and other forms of aggressive male behaviour. A us&l analogy could be made with theft. Not all men thieve, but in a capitalist society making money by dishonest means is prevalent. We do not assume that thieves or burglars are psychologically sick. However, it would be useful, as Hirshi (1969: 34) suggests in regard to delinquency, not to ask, 'Why do they do it?' but instead to ask 'Why don't men do it?'

The characteristics of convicted rapists described by Scully (1990) reflect a certain masculine type reminiscent of the authoritarian personality of supporters of Fascism as depicted in Adorno et al.'s (1950) research, one of the first contributions to the development of a historically constructed range of masculinities. Rather than seeking psychodynamic origins, this form of hegemonic masculinity can be viewed as normal deviance acquired through socialization in a culture that places tremendous importance on masculinity and male traits. Although there are no clear-cut personality characteristics which differentiate rapists from men who do not rape, rapists do share strong misogynist attitudes. It is such attitudes which are at present supported and reinforced by the judiciary and the media.

Chapter 9

Reforming the Police and the Judiciary

We must seize the legal system and turn it upside down to shake out the fear, cowardice and hypocrisy (Johnson 1986:177)

In spite of the alarming attrition rate, the picture emanating from the judiciary conveys the belief that all is well with the judicial treatment of rape and that the main problem is to protect men from false allegations. This illusion of justice is compounded by the deeply rooted complacency emanating from the press whose reporting of the 'date rape' cases discussed in Chapter 3 are a striking example of this trend.[1]

The Police

If the judges seem impervious to criticism, a chink has appeared in the armour of the criminal justice system, at a point more responsive to pressure from women than the judiciary (see Gregory and Lees 1996). The police service, in adopting new policies and practices in its treatment of women reporting domestic violence, rape and sexual assault, broke ranks with the complacency of the judiciary and opened up the possibility of change. Since the notorious 1982 documentary (see BBC television series *Police*, 1982) which showed Thames Valley police officers bullying a woman who had reported rape, progress has undoubtedly been made. Temkin (1997b) conducted an in-depth study of the experience of women reporting rape in Sussex in 1995. Although two thirds of her sample were wholly, mainly or partly positive about the way the police had treated them, a third were wholly, mainly or partly negative about their experiences. While some officers went to endless trouble and

1. The Donnellan case, as we have seen, made headline news in most of the press for several days, whereas serial rapists were being set free to rape again and rarely received any publicity whatsoever.

treated victims with great understanding and sympathy, other women seem to have been treated disgracefully. The attitudes of some police officers to rape were still highly sceptical.

In some areas, the police are improving their response, providing more resources, and multi-agency co-ordination is being developed. However, training is still inadequate in many areas. Temkin (1997b) interviewed sixteen police officers in her research. Only one had received any training about the effects of rape on victims. Five of the sixteen felt that the training they had received was completely inadequate and a further five who had been on the detectives' training course felt that the training neglected victims and concentrated on investigatory techniques. Moreover, she found that myths about rape were still widespread. Half of the sixteen officers considered that a quarter of all rapes reported to the police were false. Victims who knew the assailant, reported late and had no injury were still regarded as objects of suspicion. She argues strongly that training should involve challenging the myths of rape and the stereotypes of victims and offenders.

Moreover, in the metropolitan police area, since their procedures were overhauled in the early 1980s, the number of rapes reported has increased so dramatically that it is not clear that existing systems can cope without further funding. Occasionally, resources are forthcoming, albeit only after offenders have been undetected for years. An example of this is the following massive operation set up to catch the serial rapist, Clive Barwell. This involved 180 officers and the largest computer inquiry in British policing history and led to his eventual and long overdue arrest.

The Barwell Case

Clive Barwell was first reported for rape in 1982, but it took until 1998 before he was finally arrested. During the intervening years he committed a catalogue of horrendous rapes, abductions and attempted murders.

It appears that police and prison authority blunders may have compounded the situation.[2] Barwell carried out two attacks while serving a sentence for armed robbery in an open prison; a third followed within weeks of his release. A murder now suspected to

2. According to a telephone conversation with Nick Davies, *Guardian* journalist who investigated the case in 1999.

have been committed by him, where the victim was found in a lake with hands and feet bound, was believed to be suicide by the pathologist and recorded by the coroner as an open verdict. An attempted rape was recorded as attempted burglary. On 6 October 1999 he was convicted for rape and sentenced to 20 years in prison. The unit deserves congratulation for finally catching, him, but the case raises serious questions about the policing of sex crimes (see Lees 1999b).

It is significant that Barwell was caught only after five police forces combined to set up a specialist squad in 1997. Such squads do not normally exist. There are several squads that handle property offences, including one for 'Arts and Antiques' but there are only three squads dealing with paedophiles, and not one devoted to sex crimes against women. Detectives who do specialize in these areas say they have to justify themselves and the resources committed to sex crimes are comparatively low. It appears that the law is more concerned with protecting property than people.

This lack of resources to locate rapists even when they have been identified is duplicated at the police service level where, if cases are not solved early on, they tend to get shelved. In one of the cases I monitored in 1993, a serial rapist who failed to appear was no longer on the wanted list two years later when the detective involved was promoted and moved to another area. Whereas police treatment of rape complainants has undoubtedly improved since, not uncommon police policy was to let a woman 'make her statement and then drive a coach and horses through it' (BBC *Police* series 1982), the investigation of offences is still far from adequate.

Equal Opportunity Policies and the Police

Additionally, the problems posed by the sexism endemic in police culture need to be addressed. Research shows that certain features of organizations can significantly increase gender stereotyping, sexual harassment and other forms of sexism. These features include women comprising less than 20 per cent of the organization and the availability of sexually explicit material, both of which are present in the police force (Brown et al. 1995; Gregory and Lees 1999). Women officers are not immune to sexual harassment and several have made allegations of rape against their colleagues.

Police forces have now introduced equal opportunity policies and are beginning to address such issues. However, the danger that officers may themselves be involved in harassment of victims needs to be addressed. This was said to have occurred in Barwell's case apparently one officer even tried to visit a victim at her home and have sex with her (see Lees 1999). Greater monitoring and accountability is clearly called for.

The occupational culture of organizations such as the police and the military, which are overwhelmingly white male preserves, is characteristically sexist and racist. The reasons for this are rarely addressed. Racism and sexism function both to create and enhance solidarity in the organization. If this solidarity is questioned, when, for example, women enter the police, thereby encroaching on the male domain, the level of sexism often increases. Addressing sexism, like racism, is no easy task as it is embedded in both the internal processes and the service delivery of the police. In other words it is institutional (see Lea 1986, 2000). Any attempt to contest such attitudes is likely to meet with a backlash aimed at preserving the status quo. Those who hold sexist and racist attitudes, therefore, rather than being deviants as the 'bad apple' theory implies, are the conformists.

In the same way that there is a link between the way black officers are treated in the force and the way members of the black community are treated, so too is the treatment of black and white women police officers connected to the way sexual assault is responded to. If women police officers are referred to by their colleagues as 'whores, bitches and slags', as Kay Kellaway alleged in her successful sex discrimination case against Thames Valley Police in 1997, a sympathetic reception for rape complainants is hardly likely.

Attempts have been made to address discrimination within the force. In 1986 a formal equal opportunities policy was produced by the Metropolitan Police. Equal opportunities guidelines for police managers were distributed to all officers and provided the basis for the Home Office Circular 87/1989 issued to police forces in England and Wales. By March 1992 all forces had published equal opportunities policies and associated grievance procedures.

Despite these developments, there has been a failure to change the composition of the force to reflect the community. Women still only represent 14 per cent of the force, concentrated at the bottom of the hierarchy. This not only reflects recruitment strategy but the failure to create a positive working environment for women. Her Majesty's Inspectorate of Constabulary (1992) found that policewomen were suffering from persistent low level harassment unchecked by supervisors. A second report was no less critical finding 'scepticism, tokenism and indifference' to sexual harassment (HMIC 1995:9).

Paradoxically, the police have become among the most vociferous groups in favour of reform of the judicial system, as they are increasingly frustrated by the failure of the system to convict suspected rapists. In September 1997 they took the unprecedented step of calling for change. At the Police Superintendents' Annual Conference in Bristol, the motion 'Are rape victims on trial?' was unanimously supported; the conference called for urgent reform of the criminal justice system. In October 2000 they held a global conference in London on domestic violence entitled 'Enough is Enough' with representatives attending from police forces all over the world. This change in police culture and attitude is to be commended.

We now have a contradictory situation where the police are expressing increasing frustration at the inadequacies of the court process and the waste of their efforts in referring dangerous men to the CPS, only to see their cases dropped or, if the case goes to trial, to see them freed by the courts. Commander Tom Williamson of the Metropolitan Police expressed this view in no uncertain terms in a barrister's seminar chaired by Lord Justice Butler-Sloss in October 1995 when he said:

Any progress that the police have made over the last decade is negated by the adversarial ordeal which victims have to face. Just because a victim is giving evidence about a rape, it should not entitle a barrister to metaphorically rape them a second time *(Guardian,* 25 October 1995).

The Judiciary

In commenting on political correctness Judge Graham Boal QC told the criminal bar association annual dinner in 1999 that an ideal candidate for promotion would have 'the breasts of a lesbian, the backside of a homosexual and a large black penis'.[3]

One of the unique features of the English judiciary is its highly unrepresentative character as a social group. It remains an upper-

3 Gary Younge, 'The Badness of Words', *Guardian,* 14 February 2000.

class white male élite and it is difficult to find any other branch of the ruling élite, including senior civil servants and military officers, which conforms so closely to the model of a small, exclusive, self-perpetuating club. These characteristics extend from the judiciary itself into the senior echelons of the legal profession, barristers in particular, from which it recruits and perpetuates itself.

The judiciary is overwhelmingly male. In 1995 there were no women Law Lords among the ten in the House of Lords, only one in the Court of Appeal, only six among ninety-five High Court judges and twenty-nine among 514 circuit judges (Gibb 1995). Only forty (5 per cent) of Queen's Counsel (QCs) were female in 1992 (Nacro 1992). Moreover, a survey showed that 84 per cent of the twenty-seven judges appointed to the Lords, the Court of Appeal and the High Court of Appeal between 1989 and 1991 had been to public school, and 77 per cent to Oxford or Cambridge.[4] Most high court judges are appointed between the ages of fifty and sixty. The judiciary, therefore, are largely comprised of a group of upper middle-class, predominantly white, elderly, highly paid men,[5] many of whom have been educated in single-sex male public schools. It is exactly such institutions that tend to foster extreme forms of masculinity.

It is no surprise, therefore, that by 1999 women were still very much in the minority throughout the criminal justice system. Seventy-one per cent of solicitors on the Law Society's roll were male as were 78 per cent of barristers and 94 per cent of Queen's Counsellors (QCs). Among the judiciary, the absence of women was even more marked. Those women who were employed as judges were working mainly as assistant recorders, district judges, deputy district judges or stipendiary magistrates; even in these categories they were overwhelmingly outnumbered by men. At the top of the profession, the 12 House of Lords (Law Lords) were all men; there was still only one woman Appeal Court judge out of 36 and 7 among the 97 High Court judges (*Independent*, 29 June 1999).[6] Ethnic minority judges have even lower levels of representations. According to the Labour Research Survey (1999), fewer than one

4. See Andrew Billen, 'The inJudiciary' *Observer Supplement*, 13 December 1992.

5. See 'Crown barristers earn up to £500,000 a year at Old Bailey', *The Times*, 26 June 1995: the top five defence barrister earn over £1 million.

6. 96 in 1997 according to EOC 1997. In 2001 Lady Justice Hale and Lady Justice Arden were appointed to join Dame Butler-Sloss in the Appeal Court (see Clare Oyer, 'All-woman court to make history', *Guardian*, 2 February 2001).

per cent of the judges come from ethnic minorities and all of them sit in junior court, as circuit judges.

The immediate instrument of perpetuation of this state of affairs is the process whereby judges are recruited. In England and Wales judges are appointed by the Queen on the advice of the Lord Chancellor. The current system of appointments to the judiciary seems far removed from modern principles of equal opportunities. Appointments are made by 'a system of secretive patronage' which involves 'merit' (something left undefined), proof of competence and ability according to standards elicited entirely from the norms and standards of existing judges, and taking 'soundings' from other judges and lawyers as to the worth of potential candidates, overwhelmingly senior male QCs.

In such an informal process the views and attitudes of existing judges are paramount, and candidates from non-traditional groups are unlikely to share their social interests and background. Kate Malleson (2000: 121) notes Sir Robert Megarry describing the effect of judges and barristers sharing lunch at the Inns of Court:

The atmosphere is one of ease and friendliness: and informal though it is, it has a constitutional importance. It is in these regular contacts that we find so much of value rubbing off on each other (Megarry, 1973: 103).

This secretive process, combined with the virtual absence of any rigorous training system with the capacity to weed out those with inadequate competence at the actual tasks for which they are being appointed, ensures that the suitable candidates are approximately carbon copies of the present judiciary which is thereby enabled to clone itself over and over again. As previously mentioned, most High Court judges are appointed between the ages of 50 and 60, by which time they will have been well integrated into the conservatism of the Bar.

Conversely, it is very difficult to get rid of judges who demonstrate a manifest incompetence. Dismissal is a complex process involving both Houses of Parliament. Fear of compromising judicial independence has inhibited criticism of individual judges. Even when suspected of criminal offences, judges are not necessarily dismissed. Judge Richard Gee who was a circuit judge at Middlesex Crown Court pleaded not guilty in 1998 to charges of conspiracy to defraud banks and building societies to the sum of £1m by falsified mortgage deals and obtaining services by deception. The jury failed to agree on a verdict after a 76-day trial. He escaped a retrial by producing medical evidence from psychiatrists that he was a suicide risk. Since November 1995 when he was arrested he had been suspended on full pay rising in 1998 to £92,810 a year. In October 1998, the attorney general caused an outcry when he stopped any further prosecution. Only after the police announced that Gee was under investigation for possible falsified claims of legal aid did the Lord Chancellor announce the judge's impending resignation (see Dyer 1998b).

The most obvious consequence of the domination of a self-perpetuating patriarchal clique is the social isolation of the judiciary, an isolation described by David Pannick in the following terms:

English judges have the vices of priestcraft. They have their own language and dress, which isolates them from laymen who find it difficult to understand the workings of the legal system. They carry out their important duties in the absence of the camera and the microphone, their existence known to the public primarily through the often misleading and sensational newspaper reports and idiosyncrasies of judicial mavericks... They are treated as symbols of an all powerful but incomprehensible force which is not susceptible to the standards of rational analysis applied to all other public institutions. (Pannick 1987: 14).

The result, according to the survey by Labour Research (1997:14) is that

today's judges are even less in touch with the life experience of those on whom they deliver judgements than a decade ago. Mr Justice Jeremiah Harman, the High Court judge who had never heard of Bruce Springsteen or Gazza, is not alone.

Judges have little contact with the lifestyle or experiences of their clientele and hold themselves ostentatiously aloof from everyday life. Their courts are presented as neutral islands of rationality, sealed off from an imperfect society. But the very concepts of 'neutrality' and 'rationality' to which the courts adhere are, as we have seen, infused by male ideologies. Judges respond to criticisms in two contradictory ways: by outright denial of their unrepresentativeness and social isolation, or by portraying it as a virtue.

Judicial Views of Equal Opportunities

The refusal of the judiciary to accept their socially unrepresentative nature is exemplified by Lord Taylor who, as Lord Chief Justice, argued in his 1992 Dimbleby lecture that things had changed:

I believe that the judges today are drawn from an increasingly broad spectrum of society. They are younger, better trained, more in tune with current social problems and needs than ever before but they could be even more closely in touch without prejudicing judicial independence, and there are certainly no grounds for complacency (Lord Taylor, Dimbleby Lecture 1992).

He was prepared to admit that problems remained, such as, '... the present imbalance between male and female, white and black in the judiciary', but that their solution was a matter of time and he had 'no doubt that the balance will be redressed in the next few years ... Within five years I would expect to see a substantial number of appointments from both these groups.' Lord Taylor was reluctant to condone any measures, such as positive discrimination in favour of women or ethnic minorities, which might hasten the arrival of such a state of affairs. Such measures would

... breach the principle of appointing the best candidates and be demeaning and unfair to those selected on merit. It would be said that X was appointed only because she was a woman or Y only because he was black.

Nevertheless, the unrepresentative nature of the judiciary has not gone unchallenged from within the legal profession and among politicians. In 1991 Geoffrey Bindman, a leading solicitor, suggested that the appointments process for judges might amount to a breach of the Race Relations Act 1976 and the Sex Discrimination Act 1975 which both prohibit indirect discrimination. He argued that the process of 'soundings', referred to above, whereby suitable candidates for judicial appointment emerge, could be indirectly discriminatory and therefore illegal. Lord Mackay, the Lord Chancellor at the time, after seeking legal advice, claimed that this argument was 'wrong in law and fact'.

The second incident, which revealed the utter complacency of senior members of the judiciary, involved an exchange between Sir Thomas Legg, Permanent Secretary at the Lord Chancellor's Department between 1989 and 1998, and Chris Mullin MP concerning the appointment of a female judge, then called Lord Justice Butler-Sloss. The exchange took place during the taking of

7. Quoted in Malleson 2000: 119.

evidence by the House of Commons Home Affairs Select Committee in 1996:[7]

Chris Mullin: I am sure that Lord Justice Butler-Sloss is a very capable judge who would have got to where she is on her merits, but she is also the sister of a Lord Chancellor and the daughter of a previous High Court judge is she not?
Sir Thomas Legg: Yes.
Chris Mullin: Does it not strike you as remarkable that the only woman who has ever reached these rarefied circles, at the moment, appears to be extremely well-connected?
Sir Thomas Legg: It does not strike me as particularly remarkable. It is a complete coincidence in her case.
Chris Mullin: So a woman who was perhaps not the daughter of a High Court judge or a sister of a Lord Chancellor would have an equal chance of reaching the upper levels of the judiciary?
Sir Thomas Legg: Absolutely.
Chris Mullin: Has anyone ever done so?
Sir Thomas Legg: Not yet.
Chris Mullin: Thank you.

In a later exchange, before the same committee, Lord Taylor claimed a woman without Lord Butler-Sloss's connections could equally have made it to the senior bench, and went on to promise that there would be many more senior women judges, and not all of them would be the sister of a Lord Chancellor (Malleson 1999: 120).

It is the unscrutinized and private system of appointment which explains why so few women judges have been appointed. As Helena Kennedy argues, if women represented 30 per cent of the judiciary, tokenism would cease to function and a real difference would be felt. In order for such a radical transformation to be accomplished, far-reaching changes in the methods of recruitment and training for the profession would be needed and this in itself would ensure greater diversity within the judiciary and necessitate a cultural shift. Some of the more archaic practices associated with trials would be abandoned and the court would become a less intimidating place for witnesses.

A variation on the theme of denial of unrepresentativeness is the claim that, quite irrespective of social origins, the very work of judges and the years of experience of senior barristers from whose ranks they emerge guarantees their acute understanding of society, or at least those sections of it that come into contact with the criminal justice system. The West End play *Murmuring Judges*, by David Hare, features a judge replying to criticism that he was out of touch by claiming that judges are very familiar with common folk since they see them in court every day! Lord Taylor argued along exactly these lines when, in a BBC radio interview on 26 February 1995, he claimed:

The judge who has been to Oxbridge, take myself, who spends twenty-five years interviewing and appearing for criminals and people accused of crime, or prosecuting them, sees more of what goes on and is more in touch, I should have thought, than any other source of judicial candidates that you could find (*On the Record*: Lord Chief Justice Interview, 26 February 1995).

He had announced the same theme in his 1992 lecture:

In the course of 26 years' practice at the Bar, I visited the cells more frequently than the oldest lag to see clients, hear their stories, their excuses, their lies and their genuine problems . . . What better experience could there be for appointment to the Bench or for being in touch with litigants' problems? (Dimbleby Lecture 1992).

In contrast to these attempts to neutralize the socially unrepresentative character of the judiciary one sometimes encounters the contrary argument that such unrepresentativeness is indeed a virtue: a way of guaranteeing judicial independence. This argument, of course, blurs the distinction between being free from improper interference and being plainly ill-informed concerning current standards of morality, what people regard as right and wrong conduct and indeed the working of ordinary processes of everyday life. Some judges appear to belong to a different world. When I was serving on a jury involving computer fraud, the judge began by asking counsel if he could explain to him what a monitor was. The prosecution pointed to one in front of him!

Such humorous incidents aside, the consequences of the socially unrepresentative and cliquish nature of the English judiciary are substantial. They illustrate the need for reform not only on the important grounds of equal opportunities and representativeness of the increasing social diversity of British society but also on the grounds of effectiveness. Even within the relatively closed world of the legal profession, the nature of judicial selection privileges certain types of legal expertise at the expense of others. Thus there is a tendency for Law Lords, the most prestigious and senior judges in the system, to be selected from the ranks of commercial lawyers to the detriment of criminal lawyers. It is hardly surprising that commercial law is the most prestigious and well-paid work of trial advocates in a capitalist society! In a similar way, as Helena Kennedy remarks, 'Not many human rights lawyers appear on the secret list which circulates among the judicial fraternity for their comment,' (Kennedy 1992: 268).

Yet the role of Law Lords has changed fundamentally with the implementation of the 1998 Human Rights Act in 2000. The Law Lords become far more influential precisely in the field of human rights. They have taken on a role similar to the United States Supreme Court. In the United States, candidates are cross-examined publicly about their views. Yet in the United Kingdom, twelve judges have been appointed to the Court of Human Rights without any advertisement, interview or selection panel, but only through secret soundings (Dyer 1998a). These twelve – all male – are the defenders of our newly won human rights through European legislation now incorporated into United Kingdom Law.

The cliquish nature and social isolation of the judiciary potentially facilitates its penetration by such apparently secretive organizations as freemasonry, an organization which many believe flourishes in parts of the criminal justice system. Membership of the freemasons came to light during the investigation of the West Midland Serious Crime Squad who were involved in a number of miscarriages of justice. Criticism of the secret membership of such organizations by senior members of both the police and the judiciary has led the Home Secretary to demand that the names of members working in the criminal justice system should be made public. This is in spite of intense opposition from the Lord Chancellor, Lord Irvine, who has fought to protect senior judges from this exposure (*Guardian*, 18 February 1998).

In May 1999 the Commons Home Affairs Committee demanded the publication of the names of thousands of magistrates and judges who had failed to disclose whether or not they were masons. The MPs were critical of the failure of attempts to set up voluntary registers of masons within the criminal justice system, pointing out that of the 2,097 members of the Crown Prosecution Service 48 per cent had refused to disclose whether or not they were masons. The Committee report concluded:

There is a great deal of unjustified paranoia about freemasonry, but there is widespread belief that improper Masonic influence does play a part in public life. The solution is a simple one ... It merely requires public servants who are members of a secret society to disclose their membership.

They concluded that a firm timetable for the establishment of registers in every police force and other parts of the judicial system should be drawn up and, if necessary, legislation should be passed to compel full public access (Travis 1999).

But the most serious consequence of the character of the judiciary is an apparent lack of number of convictions in the criminal courts considered, on later investigation, to be unsafe. What is remarkable, however, is the fact that major revelations of unsafe evidence, including high-profile terrorist cases of the 1970s such as the Birmingham Six and Judith Ward, led to a cynical response from the judiciary. As Helena Kennedy commented:

Far from being humbled by these recent experiences, there are still members of the judiciary who are resentful and angry that they have come under scrutiny at all ... They claim that it was the system that failed, not the personnel and ... point the finger at others in the dock, blaming anyone but themselves: overzealous policing or, at worst, police corruption in the face of crimes with a high emotional charge; inadequate protection for vulnerable defendants of low intelligence or with psychological problems who therefore made undetectably false confessions; scientists lacking in rigour (Kennedy 1992: 2).

She argued that the main problem was profound resistance by senior judges to a changing order and above all a lack of commitment to the meaning of liberty, a lack reinforced by recent restrictions on the right to silence and curtailment of trial by jury. These changes, introduced by government, reinforce the self-satisfaction and lack of self-criticism by the judiciary. This sense of self-satisfaction contributes to a growing legitimation crisis of the criminal justice system, not simply among the countless women documented in this book who have suffered the process of rape trials, but also among wider sections of the public for whom the judiciary are considered out of touch with modern life.[8] In the 1991 national census a majority expressed their lack of confidence in the

8. According to the National Centre for Social Research survey carried out in

criminal justice system. In 1999 the largest study ever undertaken into people's attitudes to the judicial system found that two thirds of those asked agreed with the statement that 'most judges were out of touch with ordinary people's lives'. Helen Genn, who conducted the study, *Paths to Justice*, concluded that:

'there were virtually no significant differences in the response to this question depending on age, education, employment status, problem type, previous experience of legal advice, or involvement in legal proceedings. This is important because many of those most likely to have had experience of judicial behaviour expressed the same negative attitudes as those who had not' (Genn 1999: 239).

Tinkering with the System

Partly as a response to the growing sense of public dissatisfaction the last decade has seen a growing profile of reforming activity. The Royal Commission on Criminal Justice, reporting in 1993, together with other initiatives, set off a wave of reforms which might have been expected to break down the exclusivity and isolation and create a modern, socially aware judiciary. Changes have been initiated in several areas.

Recruitment and selection An overhaul of recruitment and selection of women and ethnic minorities for the Bar and judiciary was recommended in 1992. A full-scale study of discrimination within the profession revealed problems at all levels: in obtaining training places (pupillages), and permanent jobs (tenancies), in the allocation of work by clerks, in earnings and in the selection process for promotion.[9] The most important reforms have, unsurprisingly, been concentrated at the bottom of the hierarchy with the introduction in 1994 of open competition for the most junior (circuit) judges aimed at opening up the judiciary to a wider field of candidates. At the level of senior appointments since 1994 the completely private and 'smoke-filled room' methods of selection have been modified, with candidates becoming subject to interview by a panel consisting of a judge, a member of the Lord Chancellor's department and a lay person appointed by the Advisory committee of magistrates. In

9. 'Sex Prejudice Findings Prompt Demand For Overhaul Of Bar', *The Times*, 25 November 1992.

1997 the role of the interview panel was expanded to include the selection of candidates for interview. But the results of the interview are only one source that is taken into account by the Lord Chancellor. As argued by Gareth Williams, a former Chairman of the Bar and Labour peer, the changes reflect no more than 'cosmetic tinkering' since final decisions regarding appointments are still personally made by the Lord Chancellor, with the result that the 'old system of secret reports and comments will continue'.[10]

At the level of senior appointments there was talk of introducing into the UK the US and Canadian model of Judicial Appointment Commissions whereby panels made up of socially representative lay persons have an input into decisions regarding senior appointments. A number of countries already use commissions including Canada, the US, Ireland, South Africa, Israel and many European jurisdictions. They range from five to twenty-three members drawn from judges, lawyers, members of the legislature, the executive, lay members and academics. In most cases the final decision still rests with the minister who makes the selection from a list provided by the commission. Many commissions also fulfil a disciplinary function. Laziness, rudeness and insensitivity make up a significant portion of complaints received. The sexist remarks quoted above made by Old Bailey judge Graham Boal could have been dealt with.

In the UK the idea of such a statutory commission was first put forward by the legal pressure group Justice First in 1972 and the call was repeated in 1999. But despite the general atmosphere of change such reform, which could substantially alter the whole character of the judiciary, was rejected. In the run-up to the 1997 general election the Labour Party had thrown its weight behind the idea of a commission which would take the process of appointments out of the hands of the Lord Chancellor. *The Labour Party Policy Handbook* for election candidates stated:

Labour will replace the current system of secretive patronage with a judicial appointments and training commission, independent of the Lord Chancellor's Department, to advise on all aspects of judicial appointments and training. It will oversee the advertisements of all judicial posts and selection procedures, will be responsible for judicial performance appraisal

10. 'A New Tune for Old Tricks', *Guardian*, 24 May 1994.

and will ensure that complaints about judges' behaviour are taken seriously (see Travis 1998).

But on this, as on other matters, the acquisition of high office caused a rapid evaporation of the zeal for modernization. The new Lord Chancellor, Derry Irvine, rejected the idea on the grounds that it would introduce the 'horrific' prospect of a repeat of the political battles by US senators over who should be confirmed as members of the Supreme Court.

In rejecting such proposals Lord Irvine was fully in accord with the sentiments of senior judges. Lord Taylor, then the Lord Chief Justice, and widely considered a 'liberal' had already rejected the idea in his 1992 Dimbleby Lecture on the grounds that 'the lay members would have little direct knowledge of the candidates and interview by such a commission would be a poor and perfunctory substitute for the present system of screening and selection'. Taylor, interviewed on BBC radio in 1995 (Radio 4 *Today* Programme, 26 February), reinforced his earlier fears and made a powerful plea for the status quo on the grounds that candidates for judicial office 'have all had many many years of practice in open court' such that their abilities are well known to those presently responsible for appointments. He therefore doubted '...whether, however nice it might be for appearances, an appointments commission, drawn from people who won't have had that experience of seeing the candidates is going to be able to make any more sensible decision than is made already'. This includes the issues of privilege, power politics, nepotism and social exclusiveness which many feel characterize the present appointments system. In any case, once Labour came to office, Taylor's fears were proved groundless and the status quo was confirmed.

Others were capable of even greater feats of intellectual gymnastics in justifying the status quo. Sir Thomas Legg, in a public lecture,[11] argued both

that the modern system for appointing judges had been consciously developed with the aim of professionalizing the process and securing a judiciary appointed on merit alone

11. Judges for the Twenty-first Century: A Permanent Secretary's View', Harry Street Memorial Lecture, Manchester University, 16 November 2000.

and that this state of affairs was actually a consequence of the existing system whose

essential nature was appointment by a specialised minister, the Lord Chancellor, without corporate involvement of the rest of the executive, but with intensive involvement of the judiciary.

Irvine also stood his ground against any more radical proposals for changing the composition of the judiciary such as the introduction of positive discrimination into the appointment procedure. In 1997 Lord Irvine, in evidence to the Home Affairs Select Committee, demonstrated the strength of feeling against such mechanisms for changes:

We cannot have affirmative action, we cannot have positive discrimination, and appointments must continue to be made on merit. You cannot have the judiciary as some kind of social experiment and you cannot run risks with the administration of justice for us all simply to correct gender or other imbalance on the bench (Home Affairs Select Committee: The Work of the Lord Chancellor's Department, Minutes of Evidence, and 13 October 1997, para. 69).

Reforms which were part of the Labour Party manifesto have therefore not been implemented and the only changes that have occurred have been token and insignificant (such as the introduction of advertising posts for judges in February 1998, but where applicants must have served as barristers for ten years or circuit judges for two and are still appointed by the Lord Chancellor). However, the incorporation of European Human Rights legislation into British law, in giving judges a much wider political role, is likely to create pressure for a more politically balanced system of appointments. But at present there is no sign that changes will be anything more than cosmetic.

Training Unlike the rest of Europe, in England, Scotland and Wales judges are not specially trained, but are chosen from barristers in practice. The assumption that the way the judge views the world embodies some incontestable 'common sense' and 'rationality' underlies this aversion to training. In his autobiography, Sir Neville Faulks explained how, after a successful libel practice at the Bar, he was appointed a judge of the probate, divorce and admiralty division of the High Court in 1963. The only training he had was to spend his Christmas vacation 'reading very carefully the leading textbook on divorce law' (see Pannick 1992).

There have been some advances since then. The Judicial Studies Board was established in 1979 to develop training but it is regarded 'with a degree of indifference verging on contempt' by some. It is argued that training would render judges more like assessors or expert witnesses than judges of fact and law (see Pannick 1992), but, as we have seen, 'fact' and 'law' are not the impartial, objective and neutral body of knowledge and practice they are assumed to be. Another argument presented by Lord Devlin in 1979 was that judicial training would involve too great a risk of an 'official' view being imposed on an independent judiciary. In the case of rape it is difficult to know what an 'official' view would be.

Some lawyers and judges appear to be woefully ignorant and prejudiced about rape and sexual assault. They receive virtually no training about the effects of rape, the characteristics of rapists, the effects of rape on victims, and the imbalances in trials (or the relevance of sexual history evidence). Many appear to mistakenly believe that women commonly make false allegations although there is no evidence that such allegations are higher for rape than for other offences (see Temkin 2000).[12]

In May 1990 a training programme to prepare judges for handling cases under the Children Act (1989) was introduced. The programme aimed to provide a specialist corps of 'children's judges'. In July 1994, following a training programme in racial awareness, the board has set up a working group under Mr Justice Potter, a High Court judge, to see how such training might be broadened in an attempt to stop the kind of comments made by judges in rape and other sexual offence cases which imply that the woman was to blame or 'got what she deserved'.

The idea was at first to tackle 'gender awareness' but was extended to all groups who are or perceive themselves to be disadvantaged. A number of judges apparently did not consider they needed such training but 'most accepted that it might help to eradicate the occasional but unacceptable blunder which can cause disproportionate but lasting damage to the image of the bench'.[13]

12. *Dispatches* interview with Barbara Hewson, QC, September 1993.

13. Frances Gibb, 'Insulting Judges Go To Charm School: Judicial Studies Board', *The Times*, 29 July 1994.

This is a far cry from erasing the double standard that permeates the rules of evidence and other measures as outlined in the Introduction and previous chapters and the need for judges to know about research on rapists as outlined in Chapter 8.

Lord Justice Sedley, however, now a Court of Appeal judge, has castigated the gladiatorial style of many rape trials and argues that all judges should undergo training for rape trials. He also called on judges to submit formal reports on aggressive barristers. He said that some judges still took the view – inherited from when they were at the Bar – that 'you let the parties take off their gloves and see who is dead on the floor at the end of the trial'.[14]

Performance Appraisal The Royal Commission on Criminal Justice in 1993 took the unprecedented step of arguing that judges should be subjected to a performance appraisal system. Judges, the commission suggested, should be assessed on the job by other judges who would sit in on trials. The proposals, needless to say, were met with the usual opposition to change.[15] Lord Taylor, the Lord Chief Justice, was dismissive of the commission's proposal for monitoring, arguing that there was already an informal system of performance appraisal at work:

The presiding judges on each of the six circuits and resident judges receive information as to the conduct and capacity of the judges in their areas. Each judge is also subject to adverse comment where necessary from the Court of Appeal, as well as, in extreme cases, from the Lord Chancellor. This is quite apart from the criticism of the media (Gibb 1993).

Some lawyers favour performance appraisal. David Cocks QC, for example, said that barristers have to endure judges who 'flounder outside their competence...' and others who are '...case hardened through sitting continually alone and who have become appalling judges on the fact'.[16] Lord Justice Farquharson, chairman of the Judicial Studies Board, said in 1993 that 'obviously some

14. See Francis Gibb, 'Judge Attacks Trial By Combat in Rape Cases', *The Times*, 17 May 1999.

15. Judge Derek Holden, 'Time to Judge the Judiciary', *The Times*, 9 November 1993, who argued in favour of appraisal. See also Frances Gibb, 'Time to Judge the Judges', *The Times*, 10 August 1993.

16. F. Gibb, 'Time To Judge the Judges', *The Times*, 10 August 1993.

judges are less competent than others and that 'there are judges who should not be sitting'. He did not rule out judicial appraisal but considered that the problem was how to do it.

Many judges believe they are above criticism. They sometimes attribute their lack of popularity to unfair press attention. Lord Woolf, Master of the Rolls, who spoke at the launch of the survey *Paths To Justice*, blamed 'irresponsible media reporting' for the negative image of judges. He remarked: 'It behoves the media to learn from this and recognise the dangers posed to confidence in the judicial system' (Genn 1999). In other words, the press should keep quiet.

To criticize judges from inside the profession is widely felt to be suicide for one's chances of promotion and those who are promoted are perceived as being unlikely to encourage change. Lady Justice Butler-Sloss[17] refused to be president of the Association of Women Barristers. She explained that she could not accept the role because it would be too political and she felt it necessary to advise women not to rock the professional boat too strenuously. Robert Hazell put his finger on the issue when he wrote:

There is one other way in which the conventions and traditions of the Bar affect the development of the law and its institutions, and that's by ensuring that barristers who challenge the conventions do not reach positions of importance in which they can influence matters. Lord Justice Butler-Sloss was right in realizing the dangers of 'rocking the boat' by leading such a threatening organization as the Organization of Women Barristers. Such an organization might call for more women to be appointed!' (quoted in Kennedy 1992: 61).

In order to fit into the system, therefore, many women appear to adopt the status quo uncritically and identify with the men. The idea that the institution should change is not considered. In a 1991 TV programme, *Judge for Yourselves*, Mrs Justice Bracewell dismissed the idea of taking positive steps to promote women, as it would reduce the quality of judges, and it was very hard to combine a family with a career at the Bar. Appointing more women in the context of the culture of the Bar is not likely to change very much (see Temkin 2000).

Sexual Harassment This may well mean keeping quiet about sexual harassment. When the Lord Chief Justice enquired whether sexual

17. She later took the title of Lady.

harassment was a problem at the Bar, he came close to being booed (Hewson 1998). Since the Bar issued its equality code of conduct in 1993 several reports have indicated that there is widespread harassment. The code set out in detail how discrimination can occur, and recommends good working practices (including complaints procedures) to avoid or minimize discrimination and victimization. Sexual harassment by male judges and barristers of their colleagues is beginning to come to light. In March 1998, the first judge was found guilty of sexual harassment of a pupil by a Bar disciplinary tribunal, and resigned (Dyer 1998).

A questionnaire was issued by the Bar to all 805 barristers who had finished their pupillages in 1994, and received a 50 per cent response rate. The results indicated that various kinds of harassment were commonplace. The report denounced certain graphic and disturbing accounts as 'disgraceful' and noted; that the pupil/master relationship was one in which pupils were particularly vulnerable. However, Hewson reports that anti-harassment policies and procedures are regarded as unnecessary. Heads of Chambers tend to react to complainants by putting pressure on the women concerned to drop the complaint or leave Chambers. One woman barrister I spoke to described how she had been beaten up by a colleague with whom she was having an affair. When she had wanted to cool the relationship, he had become increasingly possessive. She had received no help from her women colleagues who had distanced themselves in order to avoid trouble for themselves.

Accountability and Monitoring The judiciary has traditionally resisted any proposals for accountability and external monitoring on the grounds that such measures would undermine judicial independence. The issue of accountability of judges for sexist or other comments potentially prejudicial to trial outcomes is by no means trivial.

As regards the behaviour of trial advocates, the Bar has a Code of Conduct which states that a practising barrister 'must not make statements or ask questions which are merely scandalous or intended only to vilify, insult or annoy a witness'. Yet, as we have seen in this book, it is not uncommon in in rape trials for this code to be breached by defence counsel, and prosecutors do not always intervene to protect the complainant. Judges, however, are not even governed by such a haphazardly enforced code. Calls have been made for a code of conduct which would render judges more accountable, particularly with regard to inappropriate comments from the bench which arouse public reaction. Part of the problem is that research into judicial practices is almost non-existent in this country.[18]

The long-standing rule that a judge cannot be sued has been questioned by a High Court judge. Mr Stephen Sedley asked why judges should not be accountable like others if they do unjustifiable harm to people who have come or been brought before them for justice. The judge, a leading left-wing QC before his appointment to the bench, commented in 1995:

Of course, there are good reasons for not allowing every disappointed litigant to have a go at the judge, but there are few good reasons for shielding from ordinary civil liability a judge who has deliberately or recklessly abused his or her office and done harm to an individual.[19]

He concluded that any sane society wants its judges to be independent but independence need not require immunity from being sued. 'Judges have no authority to act maliciously or corruptly. It would be rational to hold that such acts take them outside their jurisdiction and so do not attract judicial immunity. Either a special court with a majority of lay members or a judicial ombudsman could judge the judge. He argued:

Neither institution is unthinkable. If there is little work for it, all to the good. But would its very existence, the very possibility of challenge to judicial competence, which it would bring, compromise the independence of the judiciary? Long-standing legal doctrine says Yes, but if there is a topic on which it is Parliament and not the judges who ought to lay down the law, surely this is it.

Others regard the Lord Chancellor's disciplinary powers over judges as quite sufficient. It is argued that judges can be dismissed for misconduct, but such powers are rarely exercised and only

18. I have made several attempts to obtain research funding with minimal success. The early research reported here was carried out in my own time and the court monitoring and questionnaire study was financed by Channel 4 *Dispatches*.

19. In Justice Stephen Sedley's review of *Suing Judges: A Study of Judicial Immunity* by Abimbola Olowofoyeku, *London Review of Books*, Vol 16, No 7, 7 April 1994.

where judges have been convicted of offences. Supreme Court judges can only be dismissed on the motion of both Houses of Parliament.[20]

Plus ça change . . . The conclusion is that over the past decade, despite the impetus to reform initiated by the Royal Commission in 1993 and the election of a New Labour in 1997 on a programme of 'modernization' of many aspects of British public life and institutions, very little has, in fact, changed. A noteworthy feature of the New Labour regime has been the way in which reforms which were part of the Labour Party manifesto prior to election in 1997 have been ignored.

In 1999 the independent organization Labour Research analysed the composition of the judiciary 'to see whether Labour in office had made any difference to the "old boys' club". Its investigations revealed that the senior judiciary had not changed in the two years since Labour came to power. Of the eighty-five judges appointed or promoted to the circuit bench, High Court, and Court of Appeal since 1997, only seven were women, and only one of those had made it to the High Court bench.[21] The proportion of women in the judiciary remained at 6 per cent – the same as 1997. Labour has appointed no female judge to the House of Lords, which has never had a woman member.

Meanwhile the most common route to becoming a judge remained public school, followed by Oxbridge. Over 80 per cent of senior judges were educated at public schools, and 86 per cent had attended Oxbridge. This is actually considerably higher than in 1992 (see page 242). The average age of circuit judges had also gone up from 59 in 1997 to 60 in 1999. One in five High Court judges are over 65. The average age of Law Lords was 66.

Judges' conduct of trials

So how much power do judges have over the conduct of trials? Trial judges in British courts have considerable influence on what evidence is presented, the way in which it is presented, and the way in which it is considered. They can question witnesses at any stage and cross-examine the accused if he gives evidence, as long as such questions do not indicate that he is guilty. After the prosecution and the defence have summed up the evidence, the judge, in his final

20. Frederick Lawton, 'When Judges Should be Judged Fit To Judge', *The Times*, 1 November 1994.

21. By 2002 two more women had been appointed to the High Court.

comments, directs the jury on how to evaluate it in order to reach a verdict. Fear of excessive judicial influence has led many US states to restrict the summing up to an explanation of the law, leaving the jury to untangle the facts for themselves. In the UK judges sum up the facts as well as the law, which gives them considerable scope for influence (see McEwan 1992).

In criminal trials the defence may submit, at the close of the presentation of the evidence for the prosecution, that there is no case to answer. If successful, trial judges can direct an acquittal if they consider the prosecution case is not sufficiently strong. Although they can direct an acquittal, they must not usurp the jury's function by directing a conviction.

In their summing up, judges instruct jurors to judge one person's word against another and then go on to advise them how to do this. They are entitled to express themselves strongly on the facts in the case, and the relevance and significance of the evidence in its bearing on the facts. Judges are, therefore, free to tell juries that they may find the witness's account 'incredible' or 'almost beyond belief' as long as they are careful to remind the jury that ultimately it is for them to decide whether to believe it or not. This occurs after the prosecution and the defence barristers have presented the evidence, just before the jury withdraw to decide the verdict. Most trials last over a week so the evidence of the complainant, which is taken on the first day, is often not uppermost in juries' minds. How the judge sums up is of great importance.

It is the judge's role to summarize all the evidence including the summing up of the prosecution and the defence in rape trials. The prosecution is often very much less skilled than the defence, is paid lower rates and suffers from not being allowed to meet with the complainant. The defence, on the other hand, can meet and prepare his case with the defendant. The judge can intervene and ask questions if he regards the prosecution as failing to ask a crucial question, but part of the inadequacy of the summing up could be attributable to the inadequacy of the prosecution. The judge can also intervene if he[21] considers the defence is not asking appropriate questions. However, when I monitored trials, judges very rarely intervened and when they did so, it was often in an insufficiently firm way.

21. Judges have been referred to as 'he' as the vast majority are male.

Reforming the Rules of Evidence

How the character of the defendant and the complainant are described is crucial to determining credibility, in a trial where the jury has to decide who is speaking the truth and where there is often little corroboration. It is here that sexism is inserted into the trial process for the criteria on which the jury are directed to judge the respective reputations of men and women are different. In court, a woman's reputation is judged on the basis of her assumed sexual character (the implication being that a woman of good reputation is chaste). For a man, his occupation and lack of previous criminal record are the two main factors deemed to be relevant. Quite apart from the personal bias of individual judges, sexist assumptions are already built into the way the rules of evidence on character and credibility are interpreted and applied in court.

The way a judge sums up the trial and the character of the defendant and complainant is often crucial to the issue of credibility. For example, in one case that I examined during the *Dispatches* monitoring of trials during February 2000, a sixteen-year-old woman was seduced by a pizza delivery man who was in his late 30s, over 20 years older than her. She said she had moved in with him and immediately he had become very controlling and prevented her from seeing her mother. Three months later she left him and returned home because, she said, 'I couldn't take it any more and I lost contact with my mum.' She described how her partner began to threaten her by saying that there was someone after her mum and her sister. The prosecution alleged that her father had died in suspicious circumstances although details of his death were not given to the court. After these threats she said she had returned to live with the defendant because she was frightened of what he might do to her mother and sister and not because she really wanted to. However, he became increasingly controlling, as she described:

It was like if I went out I went with him or like if he was going to work or the shops I wasn't allowed to go down to the local shops on my own and I wasn't allowed to use the phone unless I was ringing up about something but I wasn't allowed to ring my mum (Court Transcript, February 2000, Old Bailey).

She had managed to escape, but alleged she had been raped at knifepoint when she returned to collect her cat and some money she was owed.

The judge at Shrewsbury Crown Court directed the jury with regard to the credibility of the complainant in the following terms:

This is not an easy case, is it ladies and gentleman? What should your approach be? *You have a young, silly, misguided, naïve, immature, mixed-up girl* [my italics]. In the background is her mother from whom she was estranged for significant periods, particularly when she was living with the defendant. You have a significantly older man with whom she was, at least for periods, clearly infatuated, a man who, though he denies it, is said to be a control freak who dominated her, against whom, the defence say, she has made up and persisted in as serious an allegation as a girl can make against a man.

The judge's summing up of her character as 'silly, misguided, immature and mixed up' is surely only one view of her character. To say that she was estranged from her mother is also misleading. She could just as well have been described as a young woman trying to survive in difficult circumstances, who had become involved with a highly controlling man twenty years older than her, and who desperately wanted to retain contact with her family but was being threatened. The jury could usefully have been told that rape commonly occurred in just these circumstances, at the break-up of a relationship with a controlling man.

Judges' rules lay down that the credibility of the defendant does not rest on his lifestyle, or his previous or present sexual partners. Instead, the judge directs the jury to consider whether or not he is a man of 'good character'. That depends, so the judge emphasizes, on whether or not he has committed any criminal offences. If he has not, the judge directs that this should be taken into account in two ways. First, it supports his credibility, and second, he is less likely than otherwise to have committed the offence. As one judge said, 'He is entitled to say' "I should be believed".'

Previous Record

In all trials apart from those involving sexual offences, if the defence has attacked the credibility of the witness (which is invariably the case in rape trials), then the defence would automatically have to reveal past criminal offences. In rape trials, however, this is left up to the judge's discretion. In some cases, of course, criminal acts emerge in the evidence, where, for example, as in the Crown v. G, the defendant had illegal drugs on the premises which he had given to the complainant. Here the judge directed that 'this should not be held against him'.

Even where the defendant has a very violent record, and judges decide that this should be revealed to the jury, the rules of evidence lay down that the jury should be directed along the following lines as one of the judges summed up in the *Dispatches* monitoring of trials:

The one thing you cannot do is say, 'Well clearly he is a man of bad character. He has been before the courts for offences of violence. He's been to detention in a young offender's institution. He's a man of violent disposition. Therefore, he is likely to have raped her because he's that sort of man.' That, members of the jury, would be quite wrong, and I direct you, as a matter of law not to do it. All right?

Do not for a moment think that just because he has a number of convictions, he has been lying to you. That would be quite wrong. Some things you simply take into account in assessing his credibility. In fact, in the circumstances of this case, it may be best if you dismiss such convictions from your mind, and judge the case on the facts. All right? It might be wisest (Court Transcript, February 2000, Old Bailey).

Very different views are taken if the complainant has a previous criminal record. It is also unfair that whereas judges are required to emphasize the fact that the defendant is a man of previous good character if he has no previous convictions, they have no duty to say the same of the complainant. The implication to the jury of omitting reference to the woman's good character is that she is not a woman of good character and is therefore likely to be unreliable. It is unrealistic to expect juries to understand the minutiae of the rules of evidence and, therefore, they are likely to draw their own conclusions if reference to the woman's good character is omitted at the point where the defendant's is mentioned. Clearly the new decision on sexual history evidence would exacerbate the situation for them.

Character Witnesses

Additionally, there is an argument that the complainant as well as the defendant should be allowed to have character witnesses in rape trials where the credibility of the witness is so crucial. Where the defendant has no previous convictions, he is now allowed to have character witnesses to give evidence in regard to his credibility. Yet no one is allowed to give evidence in support of the complainant where she has no previous convictions. In trials where so much rests on the credibility of the defendant and complainant, this is unfair. There is also a strong case that the complainant should be allowed character witnesses even when the defendant has previous convictions and is, therefore, not allowed any. This is a way of supporting the woman's credibility without revealing to the jury the defendant's past criminal career, and thereby not undermining a cornerstone of British law – that everyone is innocent until proved guilty so previous convictions should not be revealed to the jury. The reason why the witness is not allowed character witnesses is due to the fundamental principle of British law that the witness should be judged on his or her demeanour alone. This makes sense in most trials but I would argue that an exception should be made in rape trials.

Court of Appeal Decisions

The repeated refusal of the Court of Appeal to overturn patently unsafe convictions contrasts sharply with their willingness to overturn rape convictions, a quite staggering tendency in view of the very low conviction rate for rapists.[22] We have seen how the implementation of reforms is hampered by the lack of any monitoring of the judicial decisions and that most of the reforms have been left to the judges' discretion. How judges use their discretion should be seen in the context of decisions made by the Court of Appeal. No comprehensive study has been carried out of all the rape cases which have gone to appeal, and I was unable to find out what proportion of convicted men appeal. My impression is that many do, since preliminary evidence indicates that a significant number of sentences are quashed or reduced and therefore defendants find it worthwhile. Studies have, however, been carried out on appeals concerned with the issue of credibility. Such appeals are concerned with the judges' summing up, where it is argued that reference to the sexual history and sexual character of the complainant should have been allowed or that insufficient emphasis was placed on the 'good character' of the defendant(s).

22. As James Garvie (1993) perceptively argued, it is possible to develop a radical position with regard to the role of the prosecution and the needs of the victim, without attacking the civil liberties of the defendant.

First, research into the effectiveness of the Sexual Offences (Amendment) Act of 1976 carried out by Adler (1987) indicated that this legislation had been largely ineffective. She found that the few judges who did attempt to implement the new rules were soon stopped in their tracks by the Court of Appeal, who proceeded to quash a number of convictions on the grounds that defence lawyers had not been allowed by the trial judge to introduce 'relevant' sexual history evidence (see, for example, R. v. Viola (1982) 75 Cr. App. R (125).This and other cases with disturbing implications for case law are discussed by Jennifer Temkin, Professor of Law at the University of Sussex, in her analysis of judgements made by the Court of Appeal. She points out that in the case of R. v. Bogie (1992 CLR 301: No. 91/2831)[23] the Court of Appeal made it clear that, in assessing whether or not to exclude sexual history evidence, 'the only material question is whether it would be unfair to the defendant to exclude it'. Temkin argues that this overlooks how the introduction of such evidence can be unfair to the complainant, can mislead and confuse the jury, can be time wasting and how its evidential value can be materially outweighed by the substantial danger of undue prejudice (Temkin 1993: 11). Although since 1976 some trial judges have disallowed sexual history evidence, the willingness of the Court of Appeal to see a wide range of evidence as of relevance to consent means that trial judges who disallow it do so at considerable risk of a quashed conviction on appeal (Temkin 1993:17).[24] The Law Lords' decision in regard to the Youth Justice and Criminal Evidence Act (see Introduction) is likely to mean that sexual history evidence will continue to be allowed, albeit somewhat curtailed.

The other important ground for successful appeals concerns the 'good character' of the defendant. In 1986, for example, the group of paratroopers we considered in Chapter 2 had their sentences drastically reduced on the grounds that they were 'fine men and good soldiers who had thrown away their careers for activity, albeit

23. This was one of three cases from the Islington sample of 109 which resulted in a conviction where the complainant had had some social contact before the attack. The other two convictions involved a defendant who attacked a fifty-year-old woman and two boys who raped a girl in a children's home.

24. An anomaly in rape trials where consent is the issue is, as we have seen, that where the cross-examination of the complainant regarding her sexual behaviour is allowed, this does not allow the accused's record of bad character to be heard except at the discretion of the judge.

disgusting, that lasted for only minutes'. The victim was described by Lord Justice Watkins as 'dissolute and depraved' (Temkin 1987:20). In 1990 the conviction of PC Peter Anderson,[25] sentenced to seven years for raping a nineteen-year-old girl in his patrol car, was reversed on appeal on the ground that Judge Jowitt at his trial had failed to direct the jury properly on his previous good character and it was not enough for the jury to know that he was a police officer.[26] The same three Court of Appeal judges who overturned the conviction blocked an attempt by the prosecution to have the conviction reinstated by the House of Lords on 31 July 1990. They refused a request by the Director of Public Prosecutions to certify that the case raised a point of law of public importance meriting a prosecution appeal to the Law Lords (*The Times*, 31 July 1990). It seems extraordinary that the appeal judges involved in the initial decision should also decide whether the appeal should go to the House of Lords.

Inevitably judicial decisions of this kind have an immobilizing effect on reform initiatives at earlier points in the criminal justice process. They affect the way rape cases are treated from the time a case is reported to the police, as only cases which are likely to result in a conviction are taken seriously and the police and the CPS know that most cases are dismissed in the present court system.

Estrich (1987: 80) noted similar attitudes to rape reflected in recent appeal decisions in the US. She found that 'judges in the 1980s continued to think about women and rape in the same way as the law-review writers of the 1950s and 1960s or even the judges of the 1940s' and that in spite of rape law reform being enacted in all the states,[27] little had changed in the legal system. Bohmer (1991:36) also concluded that 'many of the reforms have had limited effect on the experience of the victim or the likelihood that there will be a conviction'.

25. P. Wynne Davies and H. Mills, 'Judges Free Policeman in Rape Case', *Independent*, 3 July 1990.

26. see *Eve was Framed* (Kennedy 1992: 170–1) for a report of the racist undertones of the case.

27. In spite of most states enacting 'rape shield' laws that preclude questions about sexual history evidence.

Recommendations for Reform
Reform of the Court of Appeal

- The Court of Appeal is in need of radical reform in its composition, training and accountability. More women need to be appointed, and special training is required with regard to the effects of rape, reforms in other countries and research on rapists.
- The grounds for appeal should be stringently defined and monitored. The Court of Appeal should look carefully at the grounds of recent appeals and stop reversing the tiny number of convictions unless there has been a real miscarriage of justice.
- Although it is important that the judiciary should have some independence, some accountability to an independent democratically elected body is needed. At the very least a Royal Commission with representatives from women's groups working with survivors, academics and others should be appointed to oversee the decisions of the Court of Appeal and the crown courts.

Reform of the Trial Process

- Special judges more representative of the community in terms of class, race and gender should be appointed for sexual assault trials.
- A more extensive training programme on rape should be introduced at the Judicial College which all judges and Lord Justices of Appeal should have to attend where they should come face-to-face with the survivors and experts in the field.
- Judges' discretion in relation to the introduction of sexual character and sexual history evidence by the defence should be curtailed. Circumstances under which such evidence should be allowed should be codified. Where the woman's credibility is attacked by disclosing her past criminal offences or sexual history, the defendant's past record or sexual history should also be disclosed as is the case in other trials (where he gives evidence). In all trials bar rape if the complainant's reputation is attacked then this means the defendant has 'thrown down his shield' (Section 1 (f) (11) (Criminal Evidence Act 1898) and his reputation can be attacked.
- The corroboration warning should be abolished. According to the Criminal Justice and Public Order Act 1994 Section 32 it is now discretionary. Court of Appeal guidelines on the court's discretion state that no special warning is necessary but that where the witness had been shown to be unreliable or if the witness had been

shown to have lied, to have made previous complaints, or to bear the defendant some grudge, the warning would be appropriate. Their lordships stressed that they would be slow to interfere with the exercise of discretion by a trial judge who had the advantage of assessing the manner of a witness's evidence.[28] In Australia when this was left up to the judges' discretion, judges continued to use it. It has now been abolished altogether.

- Regarding recent complaint, or where the complainant has not told anyone immediately about the rape, it should be compulsory for the judge to warn the jury that absence of complaint does not imply falsehood on the part of the complainant and that there may be good reasons why she did not complain as is the case in New South Wales, Australia.

- Judges' direction to the jury regarding finding defendants guilty 'beyond reasonable doubt' should be clarified. The English Court of Appeal, following the example of the US Supreme Court, should qualify the meaning with the proviso along the lines 'There are few things in this world that we know with absolute certainty and in criminal cases the law does not require proof that overcomes every possible doubt. Jurors should therefore find the defendant guilty where they are "firmly convinced that the defendant is guilty of the crime charged". If, on the other hand, they think there is a real possibility that he is not guilty then they should give him the benefit of the doubt.' Judges should emphasize to jurors the importance of coming to a verdict and be less inclined to dismiss them after a few hours as commonly occurs.

- Victim impact evidence should be given by expert witnesses regarding the victim's state both at the time of the offence and when giving evidence. It is often difficult for people to understand that emotionless control can be a way of distancing oneself from very painful feelings. The victim lobby supports this recommendation and in the US such evidence is mandatory.

- There should be provision for all women complainants to give evidence in court by screening or video link, without having to face their alleged attackers.

28. See criticisms made by James Richardson, leading criminal barrister and editor of *Archbold* (regaded as the 'bible' of criminal lawyers and judges) in 'Appeal Judges Throw Law into Confusion', *Guardian*, 3 February, 1995.

- All kinds of coercion – physical, financial and emotional – should be recognized, and where women do not physically resist, it should be pointed out that male victims of assault do not often fight back any more than female victims.
- An effective complaints procedure, with powers to strongly penalize barristers, should be set up where complainants can seek redress for inappropriate cross-examination.
- The rules of evidence should be reformed. Similar criteria should be used to judge the credibility of the complainant and the defendant. Where the complainant has no previous convictions, juries should be directed that this should be taken into account in assessing their credibility.

Controversies around the Definition of Rape

One of the main disputes about rape has centred on how to define rape. Many feminists have argued that rape should be seen as an act of violence and humiliation rather than, as it is defined in Britain, as sexual coercion. Zsuzsanna Adler, a British criminologist, who carried out the only previous study of English rape trials in the early 1980s suggested that 'so long as rape is seen as an act of sexuality rather than aggression and hostility, it will continue to be interpreted as predominantly pleasurable to both parties rather than harmful to the victim' (Adler 1987: 11). The refusal, by feminists, to link the crime to sex can be seen as a reaction to claims that rape was the inevitable result of innate male aggression coupled with an uncontrollable sexual need. Research does not support this assumption. Groth, an American psychologist who ran a treatment programme for convicted rapists, concluded that rape should be considered as a pseudosexual act, a pattern of sexual behaviour that is concerned more with status, hostility, control and dominance than with the sensual pleasure of sexual satisfaction. He concluded that men did not rape because they were sexually frustrated. The offender always had other alternatives or outlets for his sexual desires (see Groth 1979). In a series of articles in the *Guardian* written in 1995,[29] Germaine Greer attempted to resolve the question of how to define rape by partitioning off the violence from

29. 'The Refusal to be Bowed by Brutality, *Guardian*, 20 March 1995: 'A Phallo-centric View of Sexual Violence', *Guardian*, 3 April 1995; and 'Call Rape by Another Name', *Guardian*, 6 May 1995. The quote here is taken from the first article.

the sex and prioritizing the violence. Drawing on her own experience of being raped, she went as far as to say, 'I was more afraid of the rapist's fists and his vicious mind . . . In a sense the penis came to my rescue'. In her view, there was no reason why penetration of the vagina by the penis should be regarded as any more serious than forced oral sex, coercive male buggery[30] or penetration of other orifices by other objects, a position that has been argued for by others such as the National Council for Civil Liberties. Adler (1987: 159) says that the important issue is not whether the definition should be altered but that such offences should be treated with similar gravity. Greer, on the other hand, argues for the abolition of the crime of rape altogether and its replacement by assault.

Greer's argument raises the question of whether it is important to see rape as a particularly serious crime at all. She takes the controversial view that in a society such as ours where sexual interaction 'is more frequent and often without intense emotional significance', a woman 'may be outraged and humiliated but cannot be damaged in any essential way by the simple fact of the presence of an unwelcome penis in the vagina'. While rape may involve less stigma than in the past, this view misrepresents what is involved in rape. Rape has nothing to do with the availability of consensual sex and everything to do with power and misogyny. Sex cannot be divorced from rape any more than violence can. Greer's position fails to address the question of why men rape and what function rape plays in women's subordination. To talk about rape as the presence of an unwelcome penis is to belittle its effect totally and to misunderstand the way that, in rape, violence and sex are inextricably bound together.

Lessons can be learned from the experience of other countries. As we have seen, calling rape by a different name, as Greer suggested, became part of Canadian law in 1981. The crime of rape was abolished and replaced by three levels of sexual assault, from simple assault to sexual assault involving wounding or endangering life. The reforms were introduced on the grounds that since consent was difficult to prove women would obtain justice only

30. Greer fails to acknowledge that the definition of rape has already been broadened to include coercive male buggery (see the Criminal Justice and Public Order Act 1994).

if the crime of rape was defined as assault rather than as a sexual crime. The impact of the changed Canadian law has been minimal, since sexual imposition is not considered to be of much consequence unless it is accompanied by violence (see Temkin 1993: 18).

A major drawback, therefore, in seeing rape as violence is that in law, if there is violence done to the person, the law presumes there will be some physical damage. Thus GBH and ABH are linked to perceived physical injury and, where there is no injury, this is perceived as common assault. As Carol Smart, Professor of Criminology at Leeds University, points out:

Consent is a defence against the accusation of common assault just as it is in rape. So, for example, if one boarded a crowded bus and another passenger stood painfully on your foot, he/she would have the defence that in entering such a situation you knowingly took the risk of some harm. In many rape cases the fear of greater injury is enough to make many women submit and, as is well documented, she may have little in the way of bruises or cuts. Thus to call rape a simple assault, or even actual or grievous bodily harm, would do little for women who are already particularly vulnerable in rape trials because they do not have visible physical injuries (Smart 1995: 111).

Calling rape violence fails to address the coercive nature of some male sexual behaviour when this is exactly what rape and rape trials are all about. If rape is to be seen as a sexual crime, this does not mean that it is an expression of sexual desire.

Catherine MacKinnon (1987) agrees that in defining rape as a crime of violence, the sexual aspect can be overlooked. Her analysis not only keeps sexuality central but she opposes ideas that reduce rape, sexual harassment and pornography to a single category of 'violence against women'. In her view we should see them as forms of sexuality which are inherently abusive. It is the prevalence of such abusive forms of sexuality that makes them so difficult to confront and contest in court and it is such abusive forms of sexuality which need to be challenged if women are to obtain justice in the courts.

The Adoption of a Communicative Model of Sexuality

It can be seen that academics recently, in insisting on the importance of viewing rape as both sexual and violent, have highlighted the coercive quality of many heterosexual relationships in the culture as a whole and the way sexual conquest is still seen as the hallmark of masculinity. One of the most disturbing aspects of sitting in on rape trials was my growing awareness that for all the 'apparent' rationality of the proceedings, the ambivalence of male attitudes towards rape colours everything. Outside the courts, in the listings office at the Old Bailey, I looked at the notice board which contains details of cases coming up. Someone had written in pencil under the charge ATTEMPTED RAPE the word SHAME – shame, that is, that he had not succeeded.

Ngaire Naffine (1994) of the Faculty of Law, the University of Adelaide, identifies the main barrier to gaining justice in rape trials in jurisdictions such as Australia, where, as we have seen, the conviction rate is far higher than in Britain, a dated and sexist view of heterosexual relations. She illustrates how the assertion of the sexual autonomy of men is still defined by lawyers as appropriation and possession of the woman and the consequent denial and erasure of women's sexuality. She argues that we need to address the specific realities of possessive heterosexual relations in the wider culture and the violence such relations do to women. She suggests:

We should observe that rape is a crime whose setting is a society where women are expected to repress their desires, where they are expected to want what a man wants, where women's sexual wishes are actively (though never completely) suppressed or rendered mysterious or incredible whenever they cease to fit the possessive form.

Within this context it is very difficult for women to assert that they have been raped and have not wanted what the man was demanding. Judges and jurors need to recognize the effects of this form of coercive sexuality, so movingly expressed by the survivors of assault throughout this book. They need to not discount but listen to women's evidence in trials. Naffine insightfully reasons that the meaning of consent is subject to judicial interpretation, and it is judges who have decided that it should be consistent with the application of so much pressure, with the absence of any positive desire on the part of the woman. It is judges too who have used their discretion to equate a woman's credibility with her 'sexual reputation or relationships'.

The main reason why the rape law is so unsatisfactory in all advanced countries is due to the failure of judges to adopt a modern communicative model of sexuality which implies that there must be some positive responses by both parties. This concept of sexuality is very similar to ideas expressed by Giddens (1992) who argues that recent changes have led to a *transformation of intimacy* where marriage is less important and where relationships are entered into more freely and on a much more equal basis. This new form of sexuality, according to Giddens, is mutually negotiated, on an equal footing and seeks mutual sexual satisfaction.

What Giddens does not appreciate is that women are still far from equal and not often in a position to negotiate sex on equal terms. As Naffine proposes, judges should be aware that women who do not actively resist or say nothing do not necessarily want to have sex but may acquiesce because they see no alternative. This has already become law in Australia, where in 1992 the Victoria Parliament passed an amendment to its Crimes Act which requires a judge, in relevant circumstances, to direct the jury that 'the fact that a person did not say or do anything to indicate free agreement to a sexual act is normally enough to show that the act took place without the person's free agreement'. The South Australian Supreme Court has endorsed a similar model of communicative sexuality by indicating that where a man has received signals of non-consent, he can no longer assume that the woman is consenting. He must enquire. For such reforms to become acceptable here requires dramatic changes in the attitudes and composition of the judiciary in England and Wales.

Stephen Schulhofer, Professor of Law at Harvard University, in his book *Unwanted Sex: The Culture of Intimidation and the Failure of Law*, published in 1998, calls for a radical reconstruction of such laws. His starting point is the failure of the law to combat exploitation, sexual harassment and rape. He leaves no stone unturned in addressing the question of how to create a law which will take sexual autonomy seriously – the right to choose freely whether and when to be sexually intimate with another person. He argues that, unlike laws that provide for comprehensive protection for property rights, labour and other important interests, laws on sexual autonomy have failed – from the excessive degree of force needed for an action to be defined as rape, to the grey areas in which coercion and exploitation can be used to elicit a false legally valid 'consent' between, for example, professionals, such as doctors, lecturers, lawyers and even therapists and their clients/students.

He does not shirk difficult questions – he draws on research which found that a third of women in the US do not always mean 'no' when they say 'no'. He nevertheless disagrees with such feminists as Naomi Wolf, who has insisted that women have the responsibility to be clear about their sexual boundaries, and Katie Roiphe, who has argued that rules to protect women who don't make their unwillingness explicit amount to a 'denial of female sexual agency' and that rape law treats women as if they were not adults or free agents. She says that the woman who is uninterested should just dump a glass of milk on the jerk's head (Roiphe: 1993). Instead Schulhofer concurs with radical feminists who have argued that there is a need to change society's view of what 'no' means and that power relations must be taken into account. He suggests, for example, that in a liaison between a supervisor and a subordinate, teacher and student, or doctor and patient, the less powerful participant may consent out of fear rather than genuine desire. Such liaisons, he persuasively argues, when initiated by the more powerful, should be prohibited, and he puts forward ways in which this could be achieved.

The most controversial question Schulhofer addresses concerns what evidence should be required to prove 'consent', which he argues should shift from physical evidence to evidence of autonomous choice. The significance of equivocal behaviour would therefore be reversed as such behaviour would reinforce prosecution claims that consent was absent. Thus silence, ambiguous behaviour and absence of clearly expressed unwillingness should be treated as evidence that affirmative consent was absent. Rejecting the more extreme proposal that nothing less than verbal permission and explicit 'yes' should count as consent on the grounds that it would destroy spontaneity, he supports the view that the legal standard must move away from proof of resistance to *affirmative indications* that the complainant chose to participate. This is a far cry from the passivity and silence which most courts now accept as consent, and would pose problems in the adversarial system where the defendant is innocent until proved guilty, and should not have to prove anything.

It is not only the judiciary who are prone to adopt a dated view of heterosexual relations Press reporting of rape, by depicting the complainant as the culprit, endorses rather than contests the injustice of trials. Helen Benedict, an American researcher, in her description of how the press reported US sex crimes, pointed to the complete absence of any recognition or reference to misogyny in press reports and to the tendency of the press to prefer individual to cultural explanations of rape. She concludes that there is still a complete absence of recognition of the deeply misogynist thinking behind rape myths and no understanding of rape as a gender-based crime. She concludes:

These reporters and editors were willing to go to sociologists, psychologists, and community leaders to talk about class and race hatred but not about the hatred of women which revealed the extent to which they considered racism a subject of news stories, but saw sexism as fit only for columns and editorials. It also revealed that . . . these reporters and editors seemed more able to admit to racism than their sexism – they were apparently more comfortable talking about the sick socialisation of blacks in urban ghettos than the sick socialisation everyone gets at schools, fraternities, and in society at large (1992: 246).

Similarly, in Britain, one of the most shocking aspects of this study is the biased and distorted nature of press reporting. Rarely is criticism made of the judicial system or of reasons for the falling conviction rate in rape cases. Instead, the press mirrors the trial process, by attacking the complainant, often on the basis of unfounded allegations.

In court, as we have also seen, the defence counsel uses all his wits to destroy the complainant's credibility. That is his task, a task, I suggest, that is not all that difficult. He has her medical history, culled from the police medical examination, which will often give details of any past abortions, pregnancies, infections or sexual experience.[31] He will have access to her statement to the police, often made when she is most vulnerable, shortly after the assault. She will often have been asked all sorts of questions about her sexual history, her lifestyle, and her relationships. She will have had to describe in intricate detail exactly what sexual acts ensued. Above all he will have at his fingertips a history of misogynist thinking to draw on about women's mendacity, untrustworthiness, spitefulness, impurity, provocation, wildness, unpredictability, irrationality and general unreliability, and perhaps most relevant of all to rape trials, where consent is the issue of contention, the idea

31. There is evidence that complainants' statements are circulated in prison as pornography (see Radford 1989).

that all women are 'whores' who cannot really be raped as they want it anyway.[32]

The complainant's voice, her experience, her account of what happened is from the start constricted and curtailed. Instead of hearing about the assault and the effect it has had on her life, the ground rules are laid by the defence barrister, whose task is to use every trick available to discredit the complainant. That is his explicit role in the adversarial process of justice. The whole process is conducted from the male perspective, from the criteria used to establish credibility and the way rape is defined to the presentation in defence evidence of all the age-old myths about mendacious and promiscuous women who make false allegations.

Conclusion

The instrumentality of the law in condoning rape is the most shocking conclusion of this study. I have documented how the English adversarial system appears to be entrenched in protecting the *status quo*, a status quo where men and women are not equal and where the law acts as an effective tool to maintain that inequality. The iniquity of rape trials is defended on the grounds that proving rape presents unique problems since it occurs in private and involves one person's word against another's. Although this is the case, it is not unique to rape trials. In most trials the jury have the task of deciding whom to believe. Moreover, in rape trials there is often some degree of corroboration for one person's testimony. But the reasons for the difficulty of proving rape have far more to do with the way that at every turn the complainant's evidence is either disallowed, discounted or demolished by unfair attacks on her credibility.

Perhaps the most significant change that has occurred in the past five years is the extension of similar fact evidence. Changes recommended by the Sex Offences Review are in the pipeline, but, as outlined in the Introduction and this chapter, without a radical reform of the rules of evidence and of the culture of the Bar, little will change.

For a legal system to be fair it is, of course, vital that the rights of the defendant for a fair trial are protected, but they should also be balanced against the rights of the complainant to obtain justice.

---

32. In Paul Willis's research Spike, one of the boys he interviewed, said of girls, 'After they've had it, they want it all the time, no matter who it's with' (Willis 1974: 56).

Women should be enabled to obtain justice without jeopardizing the rights of the accused. At present, as we have seen, men guilty of rape are going free and go on to rape over and over again. This is unnecessary and is a reflection of a judicial system that not only fails to protect women from violence but also puts their credibility on trial, a process which many women describe as a 'second rape'.

Rape Conviction Rates 1985-2000

	Total no. of cases recorded by police	Total found guilty	%
1985	1,842	450	24.4
1986	2,288	415	18.1
1987	2,471	453	18.3
1988	2,855	540	18.9
1989	3,305	613	18.5
1990	3,391	561	16.5
1991	4,045	559	13.9
1992	4,142	485	11.7
1993	4,589	455	9.9
1994	5,039	425	8.4
1995	4,986	578	11.6
1996	5,759	573	9.9
1997	6,281	599	9.5
1998	7,139	656	9.2
1999	7,809	631	8.1
2000	7,929	594	7.5

Source: Home Office Statistics

Summary of Four Research Projects

1. Investigation into the Process of Attrition by Examination of Police Record Forms

Police record forms of all cases of sexual assault reported between September 1988 and September 1990 at two London police stations were analysed. The research was funded by the Department of the Environment through the Islington Crime Prevention Unit and included interviews with twenty-eight women who reported rape to the police, and agencies such as Victim Support, Rape Crisis and child protection teams, as well as the Crown Prosecution Service.[1] Our research plan was developed on the basis of three major objectives: first, to investigate the impact of the innovations in police practices on women reporting sexual offences, to see whether they were satisfied with the way their complaints had been handled; second, to take a new look at the rates of attrition (the process by which cases are dropped), to see whether these had declined as a result of the new policies; and third, to assess the role of the CPS in terms of its impact on service delivery and attrition rates.

2. Monitoring of Rape Trials 1989–1993

The second research project involved an investigation into why juries acquit defendants in so many rape cases. In 1989 I sat in on ten trials at the Old Bailey, the Central Criminal Court, and took verbatim transcripts. I also wrote some articles, which led to a meeting with Lynn Ferguson, an independent TV producer. Three years later she managed to get a programme commissioned by Channel 4 *Dispatches* into the deficiencies of the legal system. We were given funding for a year's background research for this programme and monitored the results of all rape trials at the Old Bailey over a four-month period in 1993. Researchers also attended and took verbatim transcripts of a sample of ten trials at the Old

Bailey. Additionally, official court transcripts were obtained of another eleven trials – five at the Old Bailey and six at other high courts in Britain between June and November 1993. Altogether thirty-one trials were analysed.

3. Survey of Survivors of Rape and Attempted Rape 1993

This involved an investigation of rapists through the eyes of women survivors: who their assailants were and how they behaved before, during and after the rape. This comprised a unique survey of over 100 women who had been raped and sixteen women who had been victims of attempted rape.[2] We aimed not merely to break through the silence and shame the topic of rape is shrouded in, but also to investigate, for the first time, survivors' reports of the tactics men used when assaulting women. Asking women to reveal their experiences in such detail was undertaken only on the understanding that the results would be used to try to bring about improvements in the present situation whereby women are disbelieved and humiliated by the judicial system. The results were analysed by the University of London Child Abuse Studies Unit.[3]

4. Monitoring of all Rape Trials Throughout the Country in 2000.

Dispatches took transcripts of the cross-examinations and summing up of 15 of the 30 trials heard throughout England and Wales between 24 January and 4 February 2000. I analysed these transcripts and was the consultant for the programme. Only 10 out of the 30 cases heard during this two-week period resulted in a guilty verdict. This is a low proportion taking into account that 80 per cent of reported cases do not reach court at all. The cases that tended to result in a conviction were those involving defendants who had met the complainant within twenty-four hours before the rape: two serial rapists, a member of a gang, a virgin with injuries, three cases where there was a wide age gap between the two. Of the seven

---

1. The research was undertaken with Jeanne Gregory, Professor of Gender Studies at Middlesex University.

2. Attempted rapes usually involve serious attacks where the woman has resisted.

3. The programme was screened in February 1994 and articles appeared in all the quality national newspapers – *The Times, Guardian, Independent* – on 16 February 1994.

cases where there had been a sexual relationship, only two cases resulted in a conviction. One of these involved a woman whose ex-husband had broken into her parents' house and stabbed her in the stomach; and in the other, in which the jury took eight hours reaching a verdict, there was a 20-year age gap between the two. In four of the five remaining cases there was evidence of severe domestic violence – in two cases lasting years. In eight out of fifteen of the transcripts I examined the woman was asked about her sexual history: about, for example, her past boyfriends, who had nothing to do with the rape, or with her alleged sexual practices.

Additionally a survey of 120 women from all over the country who said they had been raped in the past five years was carried out. Only a quarter of these cases had gone to trial.

Appendix 3

Changes to the Law 1956–2001

Date	Change	Implications/impact
1956 Sexual Offences Act: Section 1(1)	States a defendant can only be found guilty of rape if he knows the other person was not consenting to sexual intercourse or was reckless. Known as 'the mistaken belief in consent' defence.	Rape allegations dismissed on the ground that men believed the woman was consenting even though she was not.
1976 Sexual Offences (Amendment) Act	Restricted evidence of sexual history to where judges considered it to be 'relevant'. Known as the 'rape shield law'.	Most cases considered 'relevant' and sexual history of woman still raised in court.
1998 Human Rights Act (came into force 2 October 2000)	Incorporates the European Convention on Human Rights into UK law (e.g. the right to a fair trial).	Judges have to consider the Human Rights Act in rape trials.
1999 Youth Justice and Criminal Evidence Act (relevant section 41 implemented December 2000)	Restricted evidence of sexual history with the accused and/ or with other people. Maintained 'mistaken belief in consent' defence.	Potentially limits the raising of a woman's sexual history in rape trials.
2001 (March) Court of Appeal	Section 41 of the Youth Justice and Criminal Evidence Act (see above) challenged on the grounds that it breaches the Human Rights Act (the right to a fair trial).	Two areas of law are argued to be conflictual so case referred to Lords.
2001 (June) House of Lords	Law Lords revise Section 41 of the YJCE Act and allow sexual history evidence where it is considered to enable a fair trial (see Human Rights Act above). They also confirm 'the mistaken belief in consent' defence.	Does this bring the law back to the status quo? Is women's sexual history with the alleged perpetrator and with others likely to be raised in future trials as was the case with previous legislation? Since this is up to the judges' discretion, it appears little has changed.

Bibliography

Adler, Z. 1987. *Rape on Trial*. London, Routledge

Adorno, T. Frenkel-Brunswick, E., Levinson, D. J. and Sanford, R. N. 1950. *The Authoritarian Personality*. London, Harper & Row

Allen, J. 1990. *Sex and Secrets: Crimes Involving Australian Women since 1980*. Oxford, Oxford University Press

Allison, J. and Wrightsman, L. 1993. *Rape: The Misunderstood Crime*. London, Sage Publications

Amir, M. 1971. *Patterns of Forcible Rape*. Chicago, University of Chicago Press

Amnesty International. 1991. *Rape and Sexual Abuse: Torture and Ill-treatment of Women in Detention*. London, Amnesty International Secretariat

Arkinson, J. 1990. Violence in Aboriginal Australian Colonization and Its Impact on Gender. *Refractory Girl*, No. 36, pp. 21–4

Arnot, M. 1984. How Shall We Educate Our Sons? In *Co-education Reconsidered*, ed. R. Deem. Milton Keynes, Open University Press

Ashiagbor, D. 1995. Sexual Harassment and the Law. *Rights of Women Bulletin* (Summer)

Baker, K. 1997. Once a Rapist? Motivational Evidence and Relevancy in Rape Law. *Harvard Law Review*, Vol. 110, No. 3, (January)

Barak, G. 1994. *Media Process and Social Construction of Crime*, Current Issues in Criminal Justice, Vol. 10, New York, Garland

Bart, P. 1978. Rape as a Paradigm of Sexism in Society – Victimization and Its Discontents. *Women's Studies International Quarterly*, Vol. 2

Bart, P. and Moran, E. G. (eds.) 1993. *Violence Against Women*. London, Sage

BBC. 1982. Documentary series, *Police*

Beauvoir, S. de. 1949. *The Second Sex*, trans. 1972 by H. M. Parshley. Harmondsworth, Penguin Books

Benedict, H. 1985. *How to Survive Sexual Assault for Women, Men, Teenagers, and Their Friends and Families*. New York, Doubleday

———1992. *Virgin or Vamp: How the Press Covers Sex Crimes*. New York, Oxford University Press

Bennett, C. 1993. 'Ordinary Madness', *Guardian*, 20 January

Bienen, L. B. 1981. Rape 111: National Developments in Rape Reform Legislation. *Women's Rights Law Reporter*, Vol. 6, pp. 171–213

Blair, I. 1985. *Investigating Rape*. London, Croom Helm

Bohmer, C. 1991. Acquaintance Rape and the Law. In *Acquaintance Rape: The Hidden Crime*, ed. A. Parrot and L. Bechhofer, pp. 317–33. New York John Wiley

Bottomley, A. and Coleman, C. 1981. *Understanding Crime Rates*. London, Saxon House

Boumil, M., Friedman, J. and Taylor, B. 1992. *Date Rape: The Secret Epidemic*. Florida, Health Communication

Bourque, L. 1989. *Defining Rape*. Durham and London, Duke University Press

Bowley, M. 2001. 'Action, Please, on Sexual Offences Law', *Guardian* Letters, 17 July

Brandes, S. 1981. Male Sexual Ideology in an Andalusian Town. In *Sexual Meanings*, ed. S. Ortner and H. Whitehead. Cambridge, Cambridge University Press

Bremner, C. 1989. '"Wolfpack" Rape in Central Park Sparks an Outcry Across US', *The Times*, 3 May

Brown, B., Burman, M, and Jamieson, L. 1992. *Sexual History and Sexual Character Evidence in Scottish Sexual Offence Trials*. Edinburgh, Scottish Office, Central Research Unit Papers

——1993. *Sex Crimes on Trial: The Use of Sexual Evidence in Scottish Courts*. Edinburgh, Edinburgh University Press

Brown, J., Campbell, E. A. and Fife-Schaw, C. 1995. Adverse Impact Experienced between Police Officers Following Exposure to Sex Discrimination and Sexual Harassment. *Stress Medicine*, Vol. 11, pp. 221–8

Brownmiller, S. 1978. *Against Our Will*. Harmondsworth, Penguin Books

Buchwald, E., Fletcher, P. and Roth, M. 1993. *Transforming a Rape Culture*. Minneapolis, Milkweed

Carmody, M. 1992. Uniting all Women. In *Crimes of Violence*, eds. J. Breckenbridge and M. Carmody. Sydney, Allen & Unwin

Chambers, G. and Millar, A. 1983. *Investigating Sexual Assault*. Edinburgh, Scottish Office Central Research Unit Study, HMSO

——1986. Prosecuting Sexual Assault. Edinburgh, Scottish Office Central Research Unit Study, HMSO

——1987. Proving Sexual Assault: Prosecuting the Offender or Persecuting the Victim? In *Gender Crime and Justice*, eds. P. Carlen and A. Worrall. Milton Keynes, Open University Press

Clark, A. 1987. *Men's Violence, Women's Silence*. London, Pandora

Clark, L. and Lewis, D. 1977. *Rape: The Price of Coercive Sexuality*. Toronto, Women's Press

Cohn, C. 1987. Sex and Death in the Rational World of Defence Intellectuals. *Signs*, Vol. 12, No. 4, pp. 687–714

Coles, J. 1990. 'Standing on a Point of Principle', *Guardian*, 16 March

Connell, R. 1987. *Gender and Power*. London, Polity Press

——1989. Cool Guys, Swots and Wimps: The Interplay of Masculinity and Education. *Oxford Review of Education*, Vol. 15, No. 3, pp. 291–303

——1990. The State, Gender, and Sexual Politics: Theory and Appraisal. *and Society*, Vol. 19, No. 5 (October), pp. 507–44

Radican, N. and Martin, P. 1987. *The Changing Faces of Masculinity*. Macquarie University

Cooper, S. 1992. *Blackstone's Annual Update*. London, Blackstone Press

Davies, A. 1992. Rapists' Behaviour: A Three Aspect Model as a Basis for Analysis and the Identification of Serial Crime. *Forensic Science International*, Vol. 55, pp. 173–94. Elsevier Scientific Publications Ireland Ltd

Davis, A. 1981, *Women, Race and Class*. New York, Random House

Department of Health. 1991. *Health of the Nation*. London, HMSO

Dispatches 1994. *Getting Away with Rape*, First Frame, Channel 4, February 6

Dispatches 2000. *Still Getting Away with Rape*, First Frame, Channel 4, March 16

Dobash, R. E. and Dobash, R. 1980. *Violence Against Wives*. London, Open Books

——1992. *Women, Violence and Social Change*. London, Routledge

Douglas, M. 1966. *Purity in Danger: An Analysis of Concepts of Pollution and Taboo*. London, Routledge & Kegan Paul

Dyer, C. 1998a. 'Analysis Law Lords', *Guardian*, 5 August

Dyer, C. 1998b. 'Judge Quits Among New Allegations', *Guardian*, 18 December

Dyer, C. 2000a. 'Test for Ban on Questioning of Rape Accusers Tested', *Guardian*, 12 December

Dyer, C. 2000c. 'A Shield for Some', *Guardian*, 26 June

Dyer, C. 2001a. 'Lords Rule Rape Shield Law Unfair', *Guardian*, 18 May

Dyer, C. 2001b. 'Should We Be Shielded from the Past?', *Guardian* features pages, 20 March p. 16

Edinburgh Rape Crisis Centre. 1993. *Third Report*. PO Box 120, Edinburgh

Edwards, S. 1981. *Female Sexuality and the Law*. Oxford, Robertson

Enloe, C. 1988. *Does Khaki Become You: The Militarization of Women's Lives*. London, Pandora

Estrich, S. 1987. *Real Rape*. Cambridge, Harvard University Press

Ettorre, E. 1992. *Women and Substance Use*. London, Macmillan

European Community Commission. 1993. *Final Report of EC Investigative Mission into the Treatment of Muslim Women in the Former Yugoslavia*. Brussels, 2 February

Faludi, S. 1991. *Backlash*. London, Chatto & Windus

Family Studies Centre. 1994. *Lone Parenthood and the Family*. London

Foley, M. 1994. Professionalizing the Response to Rape. In *Working with Violence*, ed. C. Lupton and T. Gillespie. London, Macmillan

Frohmann, L. 1991. Discrediting Victims: Allegations of Sexual Assault – Prosecutorial Accounts of Case Rejections. *Social Problems*, Vol. 38, No. 2 (May)

Garvie, J. 1993. 'In Defence of the Prosecution', *Guardian*, 31 August

Genn, H. 1999. *Paths to Justice*. Oxford, Hart Publishing

Gerrard, N. and Dyer, C. 2000. 'The Price of Crying Rape', *Guardian*, 9 February

Gibb, F. 1995a. 'Time to Judge the Judges', *The Times*, 10 August

Gibb, F. 1995b. 'Raped Women May Face Sex Life Scrutiny in Court', *The Times*, 18 May

Gibb, F. 1995c. 'How Does One Apply to Become A Judge?', *The Times*, 8 August

Giddens, A. 1992. *The Transformation of Intimacy*. London, Polity Press

Gidycz, C. and Koss, M. 1990. A Comparison on Group and Individual Sexual Assault Victims. *Psychology of Women Quarterly*, Vol. 14, pp.325–42

Godenzi, A. 1994. What's the Big Deal? We are Men and They are Women. In *Just Boys Doing Business? Men, Masculinities and Crime*, ed. T. Newburn and E. Stanko. London, Routledge

Gostin, L., Lazzarini, Z., Alexander, D., Brandt, A., Maye, K. and Silverman, D. 1994. HIV Testing, Counselling, and Prophylaxis After Sexual Assault. *Journal of the American Medical Association*, Vol. 271, No. 18 (11 May), pp. 1436–44

Grace, S., Lloyd, C. and Smith, L. 1992. *Rape: From Recording to Conviction*. London, Home Office Research Unit

Gregory, J. and Lees, S. 1994. In Search of Gender Justice: Sexual Assault and the Criminal Justice System. *Feminist Review*, No. 48 (Autumn)

——1996. Attrition in Rape and Sexual Assault Cases. *British Journal of Criminology*, Vol. 36, No. 1 (January)

Gregory, J. and Lees, S. 1999. *Policing Sexual Assault*. London, Routledge

Griffiths, J. 1993. *Judicial Politics Since 1920*. Oxford, Blackwell

Groneman, C. 1994. Nymphomania: The Historical Construction of Female Sexuality. *Signs*, Vol. 19, No. 2 (Winter)

Groth, A. N. 1979. *Men Who Rape*. New York, Plenum

Groth, A. N and Mcfadin, J. 1982. Undetected Recidivism among Rapists and Child Molesters. *Crime & Delinquency*, Vol. 28, No. 32, pp. 450–58

Grubin, D. and Gunn, J. 1990. *The Imprisoned Rapist and Rape*. London, Home Office Research Unit

Hall, R. 1985. *Ask Any Women*. London, Falling Wall Press

Hall, S. 2000. 'Drug Rapists Often Act in Pairs, Police Warn', *Guardian*, 22 June

Halson, J. 1991. Young Women, Sexual Harassment and Heterosexuality: Violence, Power Relations and Mixed Sex Schooling. In *Gender, Power and Sexuality*, ed. P. Abbott and C. Wallace. London, Macmillan

Hane, M. 1982. *Peasants, Rebels and Outcasts: The Underside of Modern Japan*. New York, Pantheon

Hanmer, J. and Maynard, M. 1987. *Women, Violence and Social Control*. London, Macmillan

Hanmer, J. and Saunders, S. 1984. *Well-founded Fear: A Community Study of Violence to Women*. London, Hutchinson

Harding, S. (ed.) 1986. *The Science Question in Feminism*. Milton Keynes, Open University Press

Harris, J. and Grace, S. 1999. *A Question of Evidence? Investigating and Prosecuting Rape in the 1990s*. London, Home Office

Heilbron Committee. 1975. *Report on the Advisory Group on the Law on Rape*. Cmnd 6352, London, HMSO

Hewson, B. 1998. Sexual harassment at the Bar. A Recent Problem? *Counsel of the Bar*, p. 625

Hirshi, T. 1969. *Causes of Delinquency*. Berkeley, University of California Press

HMIC (Her Majesty's Inspectorate of Constabulary) 1992. *Equal Opportunities in the Police Service*. London, Home Office

HMIC (Her Majesty's Inspectorate of Constabulary) 1995. *Developing Diversity in the Police Service*. London, Home Office

Holmstrom, L. and Burgess, A. 1978. *The Victim of Rape: Institutional Reactions*. New York, John Wiley and Sons

Home Office 1998. *Speaking Up for Justice. Report of the Interdepartmental Working Group on the Treatment of Vulnerable or Intimidated Witnesses in the Criminal Justice System*. London, Home Office

Home Office Communications Directorate 2000. *Setting the Boundaries. Reforming the Law on Sex Offences*, Vol. 1, London, Home Office

Home Office Criminal Statistics, 1995–2001. London, Home Office

Home Office Bulletin. 1989. *Statistics on Offences of Rape 1977–1987*. London, Home Office (England) 4/89

Home Office Statistics. 1993. Available from Home Office Research and Statistics Department

hooks, b. 1989. *Talking Back*. London, Sheba Feminist Publishers

——1992. *Black Looks, Race and Representation*. London, Turnaround

Iller, M. 1992. A Fair Trial for Rape Victims. *The Law Society's Gazette*, No. 9 (4 March)

Jamieson, L. 1994. The Social Construction of Consent Revisited. Paper given at the British Sociological Association Annual Conference, Preston

Johnson, R. 1986. Alice through the Fence: Greenham Women and the Law. In *Nuclear Weapons, the Peace Movement and the Law*, ed. J. Dewar *et al*. London, Macmillan

Jones, T., Maclean, B. and Young, J. 1986. *The Islington Crime Survey*. London, Gower

Jordan, J. 1992. Requiem for the Champ. In *Technical Difficulties: Selected Political Essays*, ed. J. Jordan. London, Virago

Katz, J. 1984. *No Fairy Godmothers, No Magic Wands: The Healing Process After Rape*. California, R & E P

Kelly, L. 1988. *Surviving Sexual Violence*. London, Polity Press

Kelly, L. and Humphreys, C. 2000. 'Stalking and Paedophilia: Ironies and Contradictions in the Politics of Naming and Legal Reform'. In *Women, Violence and Strategies for Action*, eds J. Radford, M. Freidberg and L. Harne. Buckingham, Open University Press

Kennedy, H. 1992. *Eve was Framed*. London, Chatto & Windus

Kinsey, A. 1948. *Sexual Behaviour in the Human Male*. Philadelphia, Saunders

Klein, R. and Steinberg, D. 1989. *Radical Voices: Women's Studies International Forum*. London, Pergamon

Koss, M. 1988. Stranger and Acquaintance Rape. *Psychology of Women Quarterly*, Vol. 12, pp. 1–24

Koss, M. and Harvey, M. 1991. *The Rape Victim: Clinical and Community Interventions*. London, Sage

Koss, M., Gidycz, A. and Wisniewski, N. 1987. The Scope of Rape: Incidence and Prevalence of Sexual Aggression and Victimization in a National Sample of Higher Education Students. *Journal of Consulting and Clinical Psychology*, Vol. 55, pp. 162–70

Labour Research, 1997. 'Judging from On High', *Labour Research Bulletin*, Vol. 86, No. 7, pp. 13–15

Labour Research, 1999. 'Judging Labour on the Judges', *Labour Research Bulletin*, Vol. 88, No. 6, pp. 13–14

Lacey, N. 2001. 'Beset by Boundaries: The Home Office Review of Sexual Offences'. *Criminal Law Review*, January, pp. 1–14

LaFree, G. 1980. The Effect of Sexual Stratification by Race on Official Reactions to Rape. *American Sociological Review*, Vol. 45, No. 5, pp. 842–52

——1982. Male Power and Female Victimization: Towards a Theory of Interracial Crime. *American Journal of Sociology*, Vol. 88, pp. 311–28

——1989. *Rape and Criminal Justice*. Wadsworth, Belmont California

Lea, J. 1986. Police Racism: Some Theories and Their Policy Implication. In *Confronting Crime*, ed. R. Matthews and J. Young. London, Sage Publications

Lea, J. 2000. The Macpherson Report and Questions of Institutional Rascism. *The Howard Journal of Criminal Justice*, Vol. 39, No. 3, pp. 219–33

Lees, S. 1986. *Losing Out*. London, Unwin

——1989. 'Blaming the Victim' and 'Trial by Rape', *New Statesman*, 24 November and 1 December

——1993. *Sugar and Spice: Sexualiy and Adolescent Girls*. Harmondsworth, Penguin Books

Lees, S. 1999a. 'Women: When in Rome ...' *Guardian*, G2, 16 February

Lees, S. 1999b. 'Sex Crime: Institutional Misogyny in the Police,' *Guardian*, 7 October

Lees, S. and Gregory, J. 1993. *Rape and Sexual Assault: A Study of Attrition – Multi-agency Investigation into the Problem of Rape and Sexual Assault in the Borough of Islington*. London, Islington Council

Lloyd, C. and Walmsley, R. 1989. *Changes in Rape Offences and Sentencing*. Home Office Research Study, No. 105. London, HMSO

London Rape Crisis Centre. 1984. *Sexual Violence: The Reality for Women*. London, Women's Press

——1989. *Annual Report*. London, Rape Crisis Centre

Lorde, A. 1984. *Sister Outsider*. New York, Crossing Press

Lupton, C. and Gillespie, T. 1994. *Working with Violence*. London, Macmillan

MacKinnon, C. 1987. *Feminism Unmodified: Discourses on Life and Law*. London, Harvard University Press

——1989. *Toward a Feminist Theory of the State*. Boston, Harvard University Press

——1993. Rape, Genocide and Women's Human Rights. In *Mass Rape: The War against Women in Boznia-Herzegovina*, ed. A. Stiglmayer. Lincoln and London, University of Nebraska Press

McEwan, J. 1992. *Evidence and the Adversarial Process*. Oxford, Blackwell

McMullen, R. 1990. *Male Rape*. London, Gay Men's Press

McNeill, S. 2001. 'House of Lords Case'. In *Working to End Rape: Newsletter of the Rape Crisis Federation Wales and England*, Spring 2001. Nottingham, Rape Crisis Federation

McVeigh, K. 2001. Law Lords Decision on Women in Rape Cases. *Scotsman*, 21 March

Malleson, K. 2000. *The New Judiciary: The Effects of Expansion and Activism*. Aldershot, Ashgate

Mama, A. 1989. *The Hidden Struggle*. London, Runnymede Trust

Matoesian, G. 1993. *Reproducing Rape: Domination through Talk in the Courtroom*. London, Polity Press

Miller, J. Baker. 1976. *Towards a New Psychology of Women*. Harmondsworth, Penguin Books

Millett, K. 1972. *Sexual Politics*. London, Abacus

Mooney, J. 1993. *The Hidden Figure: Domestic Violence in North London*. London, Islington Council

Moran, R. A. 1994. Personal Responsibility without Personal Control. Paper given at the British Sociological Association Annual Conference, Preston

Morrison, T. 1987. *Beloved*. London, Chatto & Windus

Moxon, D. 1988. *Sentencing Practice in the Crown Court*. Home Office Research Study, No. 103. London, HMSO

Muehlenhard, C. and Linton, M. 1991. Nonviolent Sexual Coercion. In *Acquaintance Rape: The Hidden Crime*, eds. A. Parrot and I. Bechhofer. New York, John Wiley

Nacro Briefing. 1992. *Statistics on Women Working in the Criminal Justice System*. London

Naffine, N. 1994. Possession: Erotic Love in the Law of Rape. *Modern Law Review*, January

Nardi, P. M. 1992. *Men's Friendships*. London, Sage

O'Sullivan, C. 1993. Fraternities and the Rape Culture. In *Transforming a Rape Culture*, eds. E. Buchwald et al. Minneapolis, Milkweed

Painter, K. 1991. *Wife Rape, Marriage and the Law*. Faculty of Economic and Social Studies, University of Manchester

Pannick, D. 1992. 'Why Judges are Better Trained', *Law Times*, 28 January

——1995. 'Jurors Who are in Reasonable Doubt', *The Times*, 17 January

Patullo, P. 1983. *Judging Women*. London, NCCL

Phillips, M. 2001. 'The Judges Quietly Play Politics with the Rape Law', *Sunday Times*, 20 May

Pitch, T. 1995. *Limited Responsibilities: Social Movement and Criminal Justice*. London, Routledge

Polk, K. 1985. A Comparative Analysis of Attrition of Rape Cases. *British Journal of Criminology*, Vol. 25, No. 2 (July)

Radford, J. 1987. Policing Male Violence: Policing Women. In *Women, Violence and Social Control*, eds. J. Hanmer and M. Maynard. London, Macmillan

——1989. When Legal Statements Become Pornography: A New Cause for

Concern in the Treatment of Rape in the Legal Process. *Rights of Women Bulletin*, Autumn

Ranke-Heinemann, U. 1991. *Eunuchs for the Kingdom of Heaven: The Catholic Church and Sexuality*. Harmondsworth, Penguin Books

Richardson, P. J. 1993. *Archbold: Criminal Pleading – Evidence and Practice*. London, Sweet & Maxwell

Roberts, C. 1989. *Women and Rape*. London, Harvester Wheatsheaf

Robertshaw, P. 1994. Sentencing Rapists: First Tier Courts in 1991–92. *Criminal Law Review*, Summer

Rodkin, L., Hunt, E. and Cowan, S. 1982. A Man's Support Group for Significant Others of Rape Victims. *Journal of Marital & Family Therapy*, Vol. 8, pp. 91–7

Roiphe, K. 1993. *The Morning After: Sex, Fear and Feminism on Campus*. New York, Little, Brown

Rotundo, E. 1989. Romantic Friendships. *Journal of Social History*, Vol. 23, pp. 1–25

Rowland, J. 1986. *Rape: The Ultimate Violation*. London, Pluto

Rozee-Koker, P. and Polk, C. 1986. The Social Psychology of Group Rape. *Sexual Coercion Assault*, Vol. 1, No. 2, pp. 57–65

Rubin, L. 1983. *Intimate Strangers*. New York, Harper & Row

Russell, D. 1984. *Sexual Exploitation*. Beverly Hills, Sage

Sanday, P. R. 1981. *Female Power and Male Domination*. New York, Cambridge University Press

——1990. *Fraternity Gang Rape: Sex Brotherhood and Privilege on Campus*. New York, New York University Press

Saward, J. 1990. *Rape: My Story*. London, Bloomsbury

Schulhofer, S. 1998. *Unwanted Sex: The Culture of Intimidation and the Failure of Law*. London, Harvard University Press

Scott, S. and Dickens, A. 1989. Police and the Professionalization of Rape. In *The Boys in Blue*, ed. C. Dunhill. London, Virago

Scully, D. 1990. *Understanding Male Violence*. London, Unwin

Scully, D. 1990. *Understanding Sexual Violence: A Study of Convicted Rapists*. London, Unwin Hyman

Scully, D. and Marolla, J. 1985. Riding the Bull at Gilley's: Convicted Rapists Describe the Rewards of Rape. *Social Problems*, Vol. 32, No. 3, pp. 251–63

——1986. Attitudes Toward Women, Violence and Rape: A Comparison of Convicted Rapists and Other Felons. *Deviant Behaviour*, Vol. 7

Scutt, J. 1977. Consent Versus Submission: Threats and the Element of Fear in Rape. *University of West Australian Law Review*, Vol. 13, No. 1, pp. 52–76

——1990. *Even in the Best of Homes*. McCulloch Publishing, North Carlton, Victoria

Seabrook, J. 1990. 'Power Lust', *New Statesman & Society*, 27 April

Segal, L. 1990. *Slow Motion*. London, Virago

Seifert, R. 1993. War and Rape: A Preliminary Analysis. In *Mass Rape: The War against Women in Bosnia-Herzegovina*, ed. A. Stiglmayer. Lincoln and London, University of Nebraska Press

Sentencing Advisory Panel 2001a. *Sentencing Guidelines on Rape*, Section 7, 12 September, p. 4

Sentencing Advisory Panel 2001b. *Sentencing Guidelines on Rape*, Section 32, 12 September, p. 10

Skeggs, B. 1994. Refusing to be Civilized. In *The Dynamics of 'Race' and Gender*, ed. H. Afshar and M. Maynard. London, Taylor & Francis

Smart, C. 1989. *Feminism and the Power of Law*. London, Routledge

——1990. Feminist Approaches to Criminology or Postmodern Woman Meets Atavistic Man. In *Feminist Perspectives in Criminology*, eds. L. Gelsthorpe and A. Morris, pp. 70–85. Buckingham, Open University Press

——1995. Law, Feminism and Sexuality: From Essence to Ethics. In *Law, Crime and Sexuality: Essays in Feminism*, pp. 100–123. London, Routledge

Smith, J. 1989. *Misogynies*. London, Faber and Faber

Smith, L. 1989. *Concerns About Rape*. Home Office Research Study, No. 106. London, HMSO

Smitheyman, D. 1979. Characteristics of 'Undetected' Rapists. In *Perspectives on Victimology*, ed. W. H. Parsonage, pp. 99–120. Beverly Hills, Sage

Soothill, K. 1991. The Changing Face of Rape? *British Journal of Criminology*, Vol. 31, No. 4

Soothill, K. and Soothill, D. 1993. Prosecuting the Victim. *Howard Journal*, Vol. 32, No. 1

Soothill K. and Walby, S. 1991. *Sex Crime in the News*. London, Routledge

Soothill, K., Walby, S. and Bagguley, P. 1990. Judges, the Media and Rape. *Journal of Law and Society*, Vol. 17

Soothill K. et al. 1999. 'Homicide in Britain: A Comparative Study of Rates in Scotland and England and Wales', *Crime and Criminal Justice Research Findings*. No. 36

Special Report 2001. 'Human Rights in the UK: Ban on Sex History in Rape Cases Challenged in Lords' (Press Association), *Guardian*, 27 March

Spencer, J. 1989. *Jackson's Machinery of Justice*. Cambridge, Cambridge University Press

Stanko, E. 1990. *Everyday Violence: How Women and Men Experience Physical and Sexual Danger*. London, Pandora

Staples, R. 1982. *Black Masculinity: The Black Male's Role in American Society*. San Francisco, Black Scholar Press

Stark, E. and Flitcraft, A. 1996. *Women at Risk*. London, Sage

Steketee, G. and Austen, A. 1989. Rape Victims and the Justice System: Utilization and Impact. *Social Service Review*, Vol. 63, No. 2

Stevenson, M. 2001. 'Absence of Women in Highest Court', *The Times*, 23 March

Stiglmayer, A. 1993. The Rapes in Bosnia-Herzegovina. In *Mass Rape: The War against Women in Bosnia-Herzegovina*, Lincoln and London, University of Nebraska Press

Stordeur, R. and Stille, R. 1989. *Ending Men's Violence against Their Partners*. London, Sage

Sturman, P. 2000. *Drug Assisted Sexual Assault*, Drug Rape Trust, Essex

Temkin, J. 1987. *Rape and the Legal Process*. London, Sweet & Maxwell

——1993. Sexual History Evidence: The Ravishment of Section 2. *Criminal Law Review*, Vol. 1

Temkin, J. 1997a. 'A Singular Victory', *Guardian*, 11 September

Temkin, J. 1997b. 'Plus Ca Change: Reporting Rape in the 1990s', *British Journal of Criminology*, Vol. 37, pp. 507–27

Temkin, J. 2000a. 'Evidence of Prior Acquittals is Admissable', *The Times*, Law Report, 23 June

Temkin, J. 2000b. 'prosecuting and Defending Rape', *Journal of Law and Society*, Vol. 27, No. 2, p. 219

Thomson, R. and Scott, S. 1991. *Learning About Sex: Young Women and the Construction of Sexual Identity*. London, Tufnell Press

Travis, A. 1998. 'Analysis: How to be a Judge', *Guardian*, 25 February

Travis, A. 1999. 'Article T/C', *Guardian*, ???Date

Tweedie, J. 2001. 'Abernethy Sets Rape Rights Back Decades', *Scotswoman*, Worldwoman.net, 13 June

United Nations Commission. 1992. Appendix 2 of the Third Situation Report to Investigate the Human Rights Situation in the Former Yugoslavia, published in Geneva, 12 February, p. 72 (quoted in Stiglmayer 1993: 167)

Vickers, J. 1993. *Women and War*. London, Zed Books

Walker, N. 1991. Dangerous Mistakes. *British Journal of Psychiatry*, Vol. 158, pp. 752–7

Walklate, S. 1989. *Victimology: The Victim and the Criminal Justice Process*. London, Unwin Hyman

Ward, L. 1999. 'Ministers to Tackle Out of Date Rape Law', *Guardian*, 1 July

Warshaw, R. 1988. *I Never Called It Rape*. New York, Harper & Row

Weiner, R. 1983. Shifting the Communication Burden: A Meaningful Consent Standard in Rape. *Harvard Women's Law Journal*, Vol. 6, pp. 143–61

Wells, C. 1990. Corroboration of Evidence in Criminal Trials. *New Law Journal*, 20 July

Willis, P. 1977, *Learning to Labour: How Working Class kids get Working Class Jobs*, Farnborough, Saxon House

Wilson, M., Daly, M. and Wright, C. 1993. Uxoricide in Canada: Demographic Risk Patterns. *Violence and Victims*, Vol. 8, No. 1, pp. 3–60

Wolf, N. 1991. 'Fair Play for the Fair Sex', *Guardian*, 10 December

Wolf, N. 1994, *Fire with Fire*. New York, Fawcett Columbine

Women against Rape and Legal Action for Women. 1995. *Dossier: The Crown Prosecution Service and the Crime of Rape*. London, Crossroads

Women's National Commission. 1985. *Violence against Women*. Report of an Ad Hoc Working Group, London, Cabinet Office

Wright, R. 1984. A Note on Attrition of Rape Cases. *British Journal of Criminology*, Vol. 24, No. 4, pp. 399–400

Wyre, R. 1995. *The Murder of Childhood*. Harmondsworth, Penguin Books

Wyre, R. and Swift, A. 1990. *Women, Men and Rape*. London, Hodder & Stoughton.

Index